GERMAN EPIC POETRY

The German Library: Volume 1
Volkmar Sander, General Editor

GERMAN EPIC POETRY

Edited by Francis G. Gentry
and James K. Walter

Series Foreword by Volkmar Sander

CONTINUUM • NEW YORK

1995

The Continuum Publishing Company
370 Lexington Avenue, New York, NY 10017

The German Library
is published in cooperation with Deutsches Haus,
New York University.
This volume has been supported by Inter Nationes,
and by a grant from Stifterverband für die Deutsche Wissenschaft.

Library of Congress Cataloging-in-Publication Data

German epic poetry / edited by Francis G. Gentry and James K. Walter ;
foreword by Volkmar Sander.
    p.   cm. — (The German library ; v. 1)
    Contents: the older lay of Hildebrand — The Nibelungenlied — The
younger lay of Hildebrand — The battle of Ravenna — Biterolf and
Dietleib — the rose garden (Version A).
    ISBN 0-8264-0742-0 (alk. paper). — ISBN 0-8264-0743-9 (pbk. : alk.
paper)
    1. Epic poetry, German—Translation into English. I. Gentry, Francis
G. II. Walter, James K. III. Series.
PT1414.E5G46   1995
831'.03208—dc20   95-8461
                                                            CIP

Contents

*Foreword to The German Library, with Some Thoughts on Canon
Revision*: Volkmar Sander   vii

Introduction: Francis G. Gentry   xx

THE OLDER LAY OF HILDEBRAND   1
Translated by James K. Walter

THE NIBELUNGENLIED   9
Translated by Frank G. Ryder

THE YOUNGER LAY OF HILDEBRAND   295
Translated by James K. Walter

THE BATTLE OF RAVENNA   303
Translated by James K. Walter

BITEROLF AND DIETLEIB   319
Translated by James K. Walter

THE ROSE GARDEN (Version A)   332
Translated by James K. Walter

Foreword to
The German Library

WITH SOME THOUGHTS ON
CANON REVISION

The German Library—begun in 1982, conceived eventually to encompass one hundred volumes, and at this writing about two-thirds finished—comes at a critical period. It seems both unique and overdue, and yet at the same time culturally dubious in its narrow national focus.

It is unique in the sense that nothing of this scope has ever been attempted in English for a foreign culture. There are no comparable series of French, Spanish, Russian, or Italian literature in translation. Nor is the series restricted to literature, but is designed to include a representative selection of German thought as well, such as philosophy, psychology, history, sociology, music, politics, and criticism. The claim of The German Library is thus to convey a representative survey of an entire culture, from its beginnings around 800 A.D. up to the present day.

The German Library has been overdue for several reasons. For one, German studies, like most foreign language studies, has been in decline in the United States for some time, with little prospect of being revived soon. This trend, combined with the diminishing influence of the once strong German immigrant generation of the Hitler years, has led to the expulsion of many whole areas of German thought from the consciousness of the American public. Since the number of German-reading people here is also steadily declining, it is imperative at this time, if one is still interested in participating in an intelligent conversation with the past, to make a wide variety of texts available in English.

This, of course, has not always been the case. German literature—both in the original and in translation—was long popular in the United States, and was freely reprinted and published until the introduction of the U.S. copyright law in 1896. Translators of classical German texts during the nineteenth century included, among many others, such luminaries as John Quincy Adams, Thomas Carlyle, Samuel Taylor Coleridge, George Eliot, and Henry Wadsworth Longfellow. But German literature was also read in the original:

fully one-fourth of the population was able to read books in German, and many did. The leading texts did not have to be translated then; authors such as Goethe, Schiller, E. T. A. Hoffmann, and Heinrich Heine each had up to forty editions of individual works printed in German in this country alone. The last great contribution to the influence of German literature in America was made by Kuno Francke, first recipient of the chair for German Culture and Civilization at Harvard University and a prime mover in the Busch-Reisinger Foundation's efforts to found a German museum in Cambridge. The publication of Francke's German Classics Series (1909–13, 20 volumes) was the first and last attempt to present German literature to the English-speaking public in a comprehensive form. Despite the fact that this series has been out of print for over thirty years, it remained, until recently, the basic source for German literature in many libraries and universities. Attempts to introduce German literature in the English-speaking world after World War II were sporadic and limited to a few American publishers. Even when individual works were translated, they usually appeared in small editions, and were out of print within a year or two. With the exception of a few authors who have been commercially successful, such as Thomas Mann, Böll, Freud, and Kafka, this is also true of the translations of German literature since 1945. As a rule, books published in America are out of print within three years.

This ever faster pace of publishing—the shorter "shelf-life" of books, the quick disappearance of publications with little mass appeal from publishers' backlists—is another compelling reason for providing not only individual books but a library series. Anyone who has ever taught a course on foreign literature in translation and tries to repeat it after even a short time knows the frustration when he or she finds that most, if not all, texts are no longer available, and hence the course can no longer be taught. What seems needed, above all, is not only to *make* certain texts available in translation but to *keep* them available for a sensible length of time. The series format best promises to guarantee that.

Fifty years ago there were at least a dozen German bookstores in Manhattan, all prospering. Now there is only one. For anyone interested in German texts, both traditional and contemporary, and without access to a well-stocked research library, there is little recourse other than the cumbersome and time-consuming process of ordering books by mail. As far as books are concerned, it seems that our "multicultural" society has fallen on hard times. In that respect, this country is now on par with others where, except for isolated locations in major capitals, it was always difficult to obtain foreign language books in the original. The difference is that due to its large German immigration during the last century, and the smaller but powerfully influential influx of refugees from Nazism during this century, this country was spoiled for so long by having more than its share of German texts available, and is only now beginning to see that input drop to normal levels. This gives all the more reason to provide these texts in translation as part of an intellectual tradition of this country as well; not just as a canon of surviving texts, but also as a storehouse of information and a source for discovery and reference.

Deutsches Haus at New York University, under whose auspices The German Library is published, was founded in 1977. In contrast to the regular Department of Germanic Languages and Literatures, whose primary tasks are research and teaching, the purpose of this German–American cultural center has been to reach out beyond the student body and the university community to the general public. Like the university, this cross-cultural meeting place is situated in the historic Washington Square district of Greenwich Village, housed in a small landmark building that in itself is a tourist attraction. Since its inception almost twenty years ago, Deutsches Haus has hosted close to two thousand events—on an average about one hundred per year—with special focus on contemporary authors from the German-speaking countries and cross-literary influences between the continents. The regular lectures, readings, and conferences were facilitated by the establishment of a writer-in-residence program that brings two German authors to Manhattan every year. They have been augmented by the sponsorship over the years of fourteen doctoral dissertations, written across the street in the NYU German department and dealing with the ups and downs of the reception of German literature in this country. During an annual German Book Week, conducted since 1981 and sponsored by the Börsenverein des Deutschen Buchhandels, there have been meetings of German publishers and editors with their American counterparts on how the presence and visibility of German book publishing in translation might be improved. One result of these discussions was the decision in 1980 to embark on The German Library.

Apart from the formidable task of financing such a series (of which more later), the first question was that of selection: what to

include and what to exclude. An editorial committee of ten prominent American scholars of German was formed; during the next
two years and after long debates, they drew up a tentative program. Although later refined (and still being revised occasionally
even now), we have stuck to the first fundamental position: "The
Major Works of German Literature and Thought from Medieval
Times to the Present," as the subtitle of the series has been from
the outset. The literary discourse, as important as it is or can be, is
but one aspect of a country's culture, and despite Goethe, Heine,
Thomas Mann, and Kafka, one need only look at other names like
Bach, Beethoven, Kant, Hegel, Marx, Nietzsche, Freud, and Einstein to realize that there are many impulses from fields other than
literature that have helped to shape our collective Western consciousness in important ways.

Although in some areas the choices seemed obvious, it was
almost impossible to reach consensus in others. Philosophy was
relatively easy: Kant, the school of German idealism, Hegel,
Schopenhauer, Feuerbach–Marx–Engels, Nietzsche, Heidegger,
and the Frankfurt School were to have their own volumes, respec-
tively. In addition, there should be one volume on German mysti-
cism (Hildegard von Bingen, Mechthild von Magdeburg, Meister
Eckhart, et al.) and at least one on twentieth-century philosophers
such as Wittgenstein, Simmel, Gadamer, and Bloch. But what
about Walter Benjamin and Jürgen Habermas, clearly both seminal
writers with a still growing international impact? The editorial
board was divided.

Another area of major importance—one that can easily tran-
scend national and linguistic boundaries even more than philosophy and where the German contribution is hard to overlook—is
music. Its ephemeral nature makes it difficult to document, of
course, but clearly the series would be incomplete without at least
attempting to represent a sector that looms so large in the collective
culture and has had such lasting influences. Eventually it was
decided to include five volumes. The most obvious choice (vol. 42)
collects texts of German lieder, both in the original German, as they
are usually sung in recitals, and with facing translations, including
works by Mozart, Schubert, Hugo Wolf, and Richard Strauss. The
second (vol. 43) features essays on music, written by a variety of
authors beginning with those of the eighteenth century and continuing to Theodor Adorno in this century, and ranging from aesthetic
criticism to the emergence of musicology as an academic discipline.

The third music volume (vol. 51) gathers writings by forty-four composers over the past 250 years from Händel, Bach, Mozart, Beethoven, Schumann, and Wagner to Hindemith, Mahler, and Schönberg. The fourth (vol. 52) is devoted to libretti of German operas, and the fifth (vol. 53) to folk songs, political songs, Christmas carols, and hymns. Many of these have been adopted in this country, and adapted in one form or another, from Martin Luther's "A Mighty Fortress Is Our God" to "O Haupt voll Blut und Wunden" from Bach's *St. Matthew's Passion*, from "Silent Night, Holy Night" to the popular "Mack the Knife" by Brecht–Weill.

Next to music, we decided to include at least one volume on art (vol. 79). Our primary concern here was not so much with the writings of visual artists as with the theoretical contributions by German authors such as Winckelmann, Lessing, and Goethe in the eighteenth century, and Warburg and Panofsky in the twentieth. Of course, there have always been authors theorizing on art, from Plato to John Ruskin, but they were philosophers, free-lance critics, or, like Jakob Burckhardt, professors of history. As in musicology, the German predilection for theory led to the establishment of art history as an academic discipline toward the end of the nineteenth century. The first chairs were established in Basel, Vienna, and Berlin; many of the chairs in this country were created to accommodate refugees from Hitler—something we felt should be documented as part of the historic record.

Two other relatively new academic disciplines, psychology and sociology, were also deemed necessary for inclusion, since German contributions played an important role in their early development. Hence there are two volumes on psychology, one dedicated to Freud alone, the other to C. G. Jung, Adler, Reich, and others. Of the two volumes on sociology, the first gives an overview of writings by Max Weber, and the second provides excerpts from K. Mannheim, members of the Frankfurt School, and Habermas.

Definitely not a new discipline, but one in which Germany has always been strong, is theology. In a volume entitled *German Essays on Religion* (vol. 54), we tried to give at least a glimpse of the wealth of material from Luther to Martin Buber, Albert Schweitzer, Karl Barth, Karl Rahner, and others. Other single volumes covering whole fields, if only in seminal excerpts, are anthologies of criticism of film (vol. 81), *German Essays on Theater* (vol. 83), *German Essays on Socialism in the Nineteenth Century* (vol. 41), and *German Essays on History* (vol. 49).

Another field, usually left out of lists of "Great Books," but one that we feel to be crucial when trying to present German culture, is that of the natural sciences. After all, it was the flowering of mathematics, physics, chemistry, and medicine at universities like Heidelberg, Goettingen, and Berlin during the last century on which much of their fame rests, and that made them models. (The University of London was founded as an urban university in 1828 after the pattern of Wilhelm von Humboldt's University of Berlin of 1810, closely followed by New York University in 1831. The Johns Hopkins University was founded in 1876, also on the German model, and introduced the concept of graduate school to this country.) It was this preeminence of science in Germany more than anything else—until Hitler put a stop to it—that shored up study of German in American schools, and until the early 1970s made the language a requirement for graduation at most colleges. How to deal with this—with so many scientific fields, so many names—within the confines of our series?

The eventual and still somewhat unsatisfactory outcome was to arrange essays in chronological order and to have two volumes, one dealing with the nineteenth century, one with the twentieth century. The first volume could accommodate A. v. Humboldt (naturalist), J. v. Liebig (chemistry), K. F. Gauss (mathematics), H. v. Helmholtz, R. Virchow, and P. Ehrlich (medicine). The second has a preponderance of modern physicists: E. Mach, Albert Einstein, Erwin Schroedinger, Lise Meitner, Otto Hahn, Werner Heisenberg, and Max Planck, as well as K. Gödel (logic), Konrad Lorenz (behavioral sciences), Robert Bosch (inventor), and others. This list, impressive as it might seem, leaves out an equally impressive range of fields and names who also had a lasting impact such as Clausewitz (military strategy), Pestalozzi (pedagogics), Bachofen and Savigny (law), and Euler (mathematics). Others that had to be accommodated included the pioneering engineers, inventors, and founders of industrial empires like Daimler (automobile), Siemens (electric motor), Diesel (engine), Oberth (rockets) who were instrumental in profoundly changing our world. Also for reasons of space—and with great reluctance—we decided not to include other areas, such as international law, to name but one. The case has been made that the writings on constitutional law by men like Grotius and Pufendorf, via their British counterparts, had a great influence on Jefferson and the Founding Fathers of the United States. Later developments on the continent in "Staats-" and "Rechtsphilosophie"

(Liszt, Savigny, Kelsen, Radbruch) are indispensable for understanding the fundamentally different concept of state the Europeans have, which underlies the very fabric of society, especially their view of government and its role. Eventually, the idea was abandoned as too specialized for a general audience. As it was, we had already committed about one third of all planned volumes to primarily nonliterary subjects.

Having made these difficult decisions, the editorial board turned to literature proper, its more defined field of expertise. In itself, this did not make discussions any easier. An undertaking of this scope always implies an attempt at canon revision, with all its inherent dangers. But the eighty years since the publication of Francke's German Classics had left traces in scholarship and fostered new insights that could not be ignored. Feminist theory has opened our eyes to how one-sided our perception of traditional literary history had been and has created a whole new field of literary criticism. Sociology of literature and reception studies have made us aware of nonaesthetic extraliterary conditions that can influence rather decisively the production, dissemination (or suppression) of—and public reaction to—literary works. More fields, different authors, shifting accents of taste and interest resulted in a very different selection of authors and their relative importance.

Rather than concentrate only on the past 150 years, we would try to give a larger overview of the more than eight hundred years of German literature from its beginnings to the present. Without at least excerpts from the great medieval epics of *Parzival*, *Tristan und Isolde*, and *Nibelungenlied*; one volume each on other medieval tales, humanism and the Reformation; and at least one volume each of prose, theater, and poetry before 1750, The German Library would be incomplete. But that decision alone encompassed nine volumes and made other cuts necessary later on.

The next section deals with the areas of the Enlightenment, Sturm und Drang, and classicism. Here a new problem arose. Fiscal prudence and the desire for a series format imposed certain restrictions. If at all possible, each book should be about 320 pages in length. With poetry, short prose, or criticism this presented no problem. Even plays could be accommodated uncut as a rule. To print excerpts from large epics seemed at least defensible. But now we were reaching the age of the novel. Relatively short ones, like Goethe's *Werther* or Fontane's *Delusions, Confusions*, easily fit the format, but many—and among them some of the greatest—did not.

Keller's *Green Henry*, Thomas Mann's *Buddenbrooks* or *The Magic Mountain*, Döblin's *Berlin Alexanderplatz* or Grass's *The Tin Drum*, for instance, would have required two volumes each. To cut them and reprint only abbreviated versions seemed unwise. So the decision, reluctantly arrived at, was to forgo them altogether and thereby to open up space for other seminal texts. Of course, this does not mean that these authors are not represented in the series: in the Thomas Mann volume there are *Tonio Kröger*, *Death in Venice*, and other novellas no less popular than his monumental novels; the Günter Grass volume includes *Cat and Mouse* and *The Meeting at Telgte*, as well as some essays and political speeches.

The third section comprises volumes 21 through 50. A comparison with traditional histories of literatures and anthologies shows the shift away from some authors (less of Friedrich Hebbel, Conrad Ferdinand Meyer, Theodor Storm) and more emphasis on others (Heinrich Heine, Georg Büchner, more women authors). Included for the first time, to the best of my knowledge, are two volumes of fairy tales and one of satirical writings. Fairy tales were an obvious choice; the collection by the Brothers Grimm is by far the most popular one of stories in and outside of Germany. They are reprinted regularly to this day and there are new translations, singly or collectively, every year. What is perhaps less known is that their popularity has inspired almost every German author of note since the Romantic period, from Goethe to Kafka and Hermann Hesse, to try his or her hand at such tales. In German they are called *Kunstmärchen*, as opposed to Grimms' *Volksmärchen*, and are considered a genre of their own. The best known example in this country perhaps is E. T. A. Hoffmann's *Nutcracker and Mouse King* of 1816, on which Tchaikovsky later based his famous ballet. So we included a volume on *Literary Fairy Tales* (vol. 30). The volume on satirical writings, on the other hand, concentrates largely on the *Bildergeschichten* of Wilhelm Busch, which were not only hugely popular in Germany, but also widely read (and imitated) in this country. His picture-story of *Max and Moritz* greatly influenced the Katzenjammer Kids and thus became the father of the American comic strip. As such, this form is the last in the ubiquitous triumvirate, together with Santa Claus and the Christmas tree, bequeathed by late nineteenth-century Germany to popular American culture.

That brings us to the last section in my editorial report, the twentieth century. Whereas to most people the most interesting, it is also the most controversial (and—because of reprint rights—the most expensive). As of this writing, the series is virtually complete up to the time of World War I. Several volumes for the Weimar period, World War II, and the half-century since have been published; a larger number have been commissioned and are now in preparation, but quite a few are still being discussed. It is a truism that the closer we are in time to something, the more difficult it is to assess with assurance what will last and what will not. Rather than try to explain individual choices or justify omissions, I should like to leave the evaluation of our efforts in this respect to readers and future critics. Suffice it to say that the editorial committee has tried its best to represent at least some trends, and has done so acknowledging its limited vantage over a landscape on which the dust has not yet fully settled. In the case of Germany, this task is more complicated than it would be for any other place. During the first half of the century, Germany was twice at the center of—and the cause for—the most bloody conflicts the world has seen so far. During the latter half of this same century, it remained at the center of the cold war, with one leg of the divided country in each superpower camp. Even after unification in 1989, the country has not come to rest. Various kinds of indoctrination at various times have left their marks: the necessity of examining history and somehow coming to terms with the national past; questions of guilt and responsibility, of what constitutes loyalty and what treason; and finally the problem of national identity—whether it is even necessary and how Germany will fit into the new Europe—all are problems that were and continue to be widely debated. All of these issues have found their way into literature—and not only into *The Tin Drum* or the novels of authors from the German Democratic Republic. Whether we have presented an adequate mirror of this bewildering disarray must indeed be left to other critics to decide.

There is, however, one other aspect to The German Library, a serious one that was touched upon earlier, but one that is bound to loom large over the whole enterprise: that of canon formation and canon revision. Like political and social history, so also the history of literature is not static and fixed for all time. Literary history not only is history, but by constantly reflecting backwards upon itself, it also *makes* history. Making history in that sense is seen as a cultural remembering which, like all remembering, involves actively reconstructing the past. By definition there is a connection between "making history" and constructing canons.

"Canon," when not used in the restricted religious sense, is usually understood as a body of texts by which a particular culture defines itself. To look at a canon is therefore to look at a self-portrait of a culture, to see the traditions it wants to uphold and the picture it wants to present, first to its own community and secondly to the outside world. This, indeed, is also the express intention of The German Library. In a modest way, it *is* a canon, it is revised when compared to previous efforts, although not very radically, and it *is* restricted to a national culture, although a long and powerfully influential one. In an age of internationalism, it thus becomes in a sense obsolete even before it is completed.

It might be instructive to follow the current debate that started as an intrafaculty curriculum discussion at Stanford University but quickly caught the attention of a wider audience after the publication of the University of Chicago's Allan Bloom's *The Closing of the American Mind* in 1987. That book, with a preface by Nobel Laureate Saul Bellow and a hearty endorsement by William Bennett, then-President Reagan's secretary of education, became a best-seller, had a huge impact, and set the tone for the ensuing debate. It was followed by many others, most importantly *The Western Canon* by Harold Bloom of Yale and New York University in 1994, which catapulted what had been an "academic" issue to national attention and hence to a fiercely ideological and ultimately political controversy. For once, literary critics were speaking not only to themselves.

Although not the only cause by any means, the debate probably provided some of the theoretical underpinnings that resulted in the recent Republican comeback. To the best of my knowledge, it was the first such major debate in America to originate at least partially from academia and the cultural sector, rather than the political or economic one; after the Vietnam trauma and the widespread sense of moral insecurity thereby engendered, it was a debate that had been long in the making. Similar canon debates in Germany, given its violent history in this century, occurred with great regularity with Weimar, the Nazi takeover, American "reeducation" policies after 1945, the establishment of democratic rule first in the West, then finally in the East. Each time that which was to be taught in schools and universities—the canon—was modified if not changed radically. Several generations of Germans now have learned that revisions are the rule, and in the process have become cynical but also accustomed to challenging ideological agendas.

It was in fact just that skepticism of the Hitler generation refugees and their teaching here that Allan Bloom made largely responsible for the current malaise in his *Closing of the American Mind*. In this scathing critique of American higher education, he discerns an erosion of respect for traditional Western thought, culminating in "cultural relativism." On closer inspection, he finds "the overpowering visions of German philosophers" at the root of the dilemma, philosophers who, although "thinkers of the very highest order," nonetheless "are preparing the tyranny of the future." Those visions, according to Bloom, have erected a "new language of good and evil," with vocabulary which includes *values, beliefs, culture*, and *the Self*. Over and over he quotes Marx, Nietzsche, Weber, Freud, and their teaching to show how corrosive, in his opinion, their ideas have been. The argument of relativism to the point of obliteration of all value statements is taken one step further by Harold Bloom in *The Western Canon*. His main thesis is that a group of critics, which he calls "the school of resentment," tries to put the arts, and literature in particular, in the service of social change. He passionately argues against "the astonishing garbage called 'cultural criticism,'" the overdeterminations of race, class, and gender, and calls for restoring aesthetic values as the only criteria of what and whom to read. Critics on the other side of the issue, arguing for a forward-looking, plural, and multicultural education, want to stop teaching the old canon altogether. Terry Eagleton of Oxford University referred to the traditional canon of European literature as "increasingly an ancient monument, a cultural Stonehenge" and mocked that "we might as well hand over responsibility for its preservation to the National Trust right now."

Both Blooms, by the way, writing half a century after C. P. Snow, for all their pleas for Great Books, pay scant attention to any of the natural sciences. Even more importantly, however, is the short shrift given by the whole debate to what seems to me to be the disconcerting basis of it all. The deep shock that lay at the foundation particularly of the German side of the debate was the profound doubt in the *humanizing* effect of the humanities. Already in 1965, George Steiner pointed out in *Language and Silence* that the worst atrocities of this century occurred "not in the Gobi desert or the rainforest of the Amazon" but in a country that had prided itself on its cultural achievements, where there were more theaters, libraries, and concert halls than almost anywhere else and whose educational system had been the envy of the world. And as Hannah Arendt wrote, coining the concept of "banality of evil," it appeared to be quite possible for an Eichmann to enjoy reading Rilke while listening to Schubert at night, and yet continue his horrible job the next morning. German history and Auschwitz are of course no counterarguments to liberal education, but they are a caveat to the kind of rational and moral optimism that underlie the current debate. Our experiences with the horrors of Nazism has fundamentally shaken our beliefs. It seems as if our former link between literature and civilized values has been radically and permanently altered.

Preservation seems to me to be the key to the entire debate, and to preserve either actively through teaching or by research and storing for future reference surely cannot be a bad thing. German culture, for better or worse, has played a large role in the formation of Western culture, and has thus become part of our collective roots. If we want to achieve a greater degree of clarity about the way we look at the world, we have no choice but to start with looking at our own past. Surely the argument is not that the study of ourselves should replace studying other cultures, merely that it is the necessary precondition for doing so.

This also answers the other objection mentioned earlier, that of providing a nationally confined *German* library at a time of increasing globalization and openness to alternatives more or less close at hand. How much sense does it make to collect essays on art history, or any other field, on heterogeneous topics in one volume, the only unifying principle being that their authors came from one particular culture? Seen from the perspective of contents, there is none. A reader's interest is in the topic, and whether or not the information provided is new and of value to him or her; it is not the nationality of the author or the language the information was written in originally. The justification of our anthologies lies less in their individual contributions, although only seminal essays of demonstrable impact on later scholars were included, in their role of being part of a larger whole. By the same argument, The German Library is meant both as a depository and a quarry from which individual stones can be taken and rearranged by topic, period, or genre.

One last observation of a rather speculative nature. I had mentioned at the beginning that the series comes at a critical period. It seems the height of folly, in the age of information explosion that is now upon us, to embark upon such an old-fashioned book venture. We may indeed have no great hope for a place in the sun—most books today do not enjoy one—but we do at least hope for a permanent place in the shade. CD-ROM and technologies of the future may make it possible. The sheer wealth of data they provide, the possibility of cross-referencing and searching topics in the blink of an eye are something of a scholar's dream. In a way, it is old-fashioned nineteenth-century philology reasserting itself. That, too, was a quarry that produced great wealth.

As for publishing the series, one good reason why nobody has tried doing it before is its almost prohibitive cost. What should motivate American publishers to do for a foreign literature what they found themselves unable to do for their own? When Random House eventually published The Library of America, it did so only after being guaranteed subsidies of several million dollars from Washington.

Our series, too, has enjoyed the support from the beginning of Inter Nationes, the German government organization set up to help with costs of translations and foreign copyrights. But additional funds had to be raised for each volume from private sources and industry. In this we were greatly aided by the Stifterverband für die Deutsche Wissenschaft, which under the guidance of Dr. Horst Niemeyer acts as a form of clearing house for German corporate giving. Their seal of approval was, and continues to be, crucial in our fundraising efforts.

This editorial report would be incomplete without mention of two names: Werner Mark Linz of The Continuum Publishing Company and Dr. Walther Casper. Mr. Linz, the publisher, was instrumental in organizing the meetings of German and American editors mentioned earlier, and eventually and idealistically committed himself and his publishing house to our venture. The late Dr. Casper, German industrialist, first director of the German Peace Corps, and lifelong champion of German–American relations, was chairman of the executive council of Deutsches Haus. Without his active encouragement, I would never have committed Deutsches Haus to this daunting experiment, which everybody warned us against and which we believe has turned out so well. Having come this far, we are confident in soon seeing its completion.

New York City
June 1995

VOLKMAR SANDER
Erich Maria Remarque Professor
of German at New York University,
Director, Deutsches Haus

Introduction

Heroic poetry is found among all peoples, cultures, and eras, continuing up to the recent present, as the research of Milman Parry and Albert S. Lord, among others, has demonstrated. In heroic poetry the exceptional hero is portrayed. He (since heroes in epic poetry are predominantly male) is usually a representative of a tribe or a people and performs deeds on their behalf, undertakes difficult tasks, or is confronted with fateful situations that far exceed the normal demands placed on the individual, thus evoking admiration and amazement in the listener or reader. The purpose of such poetry is not to glorify the individual hero, but rather to present him *in loco nationis*. In heroic poetry the myths (i.e., history) of a group are played out time and time again. By the retelling of these tales, the group reinforces its own sense of identity as well as the perception of cohesion among generations. This awareness will continue as long as poetry remains in oral form and its apprehension occurs within the group.

What are the events that should be commemorated and, thus, remembered? More importantly: what are the timeless lessons for the group contained in these episodes? Focusing on the underlying themes in the tales (honor, loyalty, revenge, and so forth) also serves to move away from "mere" historical recitation of events in chronological order and glorification of heroic models. Indeed historical events and personalities are often telescoped in heroic literature because what is important is not so much "who," "what," "when," or "where," but rather "why." For that reason, incidents like the annihilation of the Burgundians by the Huns under the command of the Roman Aetius (ca. 436), and personalities like Attila (died 453) and Theodorich the Great (died 526) can appear as contemporaries, e.g., in the Middle High German *Nibelungenlied.*

Because heroic poetry is founded in the oral tradition and is transmitted orally from one singer to another, it is difficult, if not impossible, to replicate the original text of a heroic piece. As modern scholarship has shown, the composition is altered each time it is retold, sometimes with significant changes in the text. Only with the recording of the text in writing does the work become "historical." In other words, from that point on it is transmitted in one specific form and with a definite, more or less fixed content, even though the mode of presentation remains primarily an oral one as it did until the late Middle Ages.

German heroic poetry had its origin among the Goths (although all Germanic tribes, especially the Burgundians and Franks, created significant heroic poetry) at the time of Germanic migrations commencing roughly in 375 after the defeat of the Ostrogoths by the Huns and ending sometime in the sixth century—an assumption that is corroborated by the sixth-century Gothic historian, Jordanes. In his history of the Goths (commonly known as the *Getica*, Jordanes reports that even from earliest times, the Goths sang of the deeds of their ancestors to the accompaniment of a musical instrument. In turn, this statement supports the observation of the first-century Roman historian Tacitus in his *Germania* that the Germanic tribes composed heroic songs in honor of their great heroes. As is to be expected, nothing survives of these early songs, although it is reasonable to assume that heroic literature maintained an enduring vitality throughout the centuries. This assumption is borne out by chapter 29 of the *Vita Caroli Magni* (ca.830), in which Einhard (ca. 770–840) reports on Charlemagne's order to collect the ancient "barbaric" (vernacular) songs about the exploits and wars of bygone kings. According to tradition, this collection was later destroyed by Charlemagne's son Louis the Pious (778–840), who was no friend of secular poetry. Of course, whether the collection of the songs and their subsequent destruction ever happened is a matter of dispute. And while attempts have been made to "reconstruct" the contents of Charlemagne's "book" of heroic songs, the unfortunate reality is that only one fragmentary example from that period has survived, the *Hildebrandslied* (ca. 800), which is included in the present volume. Aside from the Old High German Hildebrandslied, the only other tales that permit some insight into the original content of heroic poetry are to be found in the Old Icelandic collection, the *Edda Saemundar* (after 1220).

This volume offers examples from the broad spectrum of German heroic literature beginning with the *Hildebrandslied* to the massive and magnificent *Nibelungenlied* (ca. 1205) and culminating in several examples of the later medieval development of the genre with the *Jüngere Hildebrandslied* (late thirteenth century), the *Battle of Ravenna* (ca. 1280), *Biterolf and Dietleib* (ca. 1250), and the *Rose Garden* (ca. 1300). Although the three last-mentioned works, taken from the cycle on Dietrich von Bern (Theodorich), appear in long excerpts, the *Hildebrandslied,* the *Jüngere Hildebrandslied,* and the *Nibelungenlied* are presented in their entirety. The specific introduction to each work will appear directly preceding the text and the notes immediately following.

Note

James K. Walter is responsible for the introduction, translation, and notes to the *Hildebrandslied,* the *Jüngere Hildebrandslied,* the *Battle of Ravenna, Biterolf and Dietleib,* and the *Rose Garden.* Francis G. Gentry is responsible for the general introduction, and the introduction and notes to the *Nibelungenlied.*

F. G. G.

The Older Lay of Hildebrand

The *Lay of Hildebrand* was copied out by scribes in the monastery at Fulda a decade or two prior to 850, and is therefore easily the oldest work presented in this volume. Even older than the copied down version of the *Lay* found in the Fulda manuscript are the historical events reflected in this work, events that took place several centuries earlier far to the south, during the reigns of the rival Germanic rulers Theodorich and Odoaker in fifth-century Italy. The general consensus of scholars has been that songs about the battle between Hildebrand and his son originated in the Lombard kingdom of Northern Italy a century or so after Theodorich's reign, and were composed in the Germanic language of that kingdom. This material, then, was carried north through the Bavarian dialect area and finally to Central Germany, where it was "translated," albeit very imperfectly, into the Low German language of that region. In the later Middle Ages, this tale of father–son combat spread widely and was even represented in several Old Norse works. The *Lay of Hildebrand* survives in an odd mixture of Old High German and Old Saxon forms, and contains a number of words not found elsewhere in Old Germanic literature, which many have presumed to stem from a Southern, Lombardic origin. Along with the language employed, the poetic structure, too, has suffered in transmission, but where best preserved is identical to the alliterative half-line verse found elsewhere in Old High German, in the Old Saxon *Heliand*, and in Old English literature such as *Beowulf*. That this verse form is preserved here as well, maintained perhaps from original Lombardic workings of the material, is evidence for the antiquity and universality of the alliterative half-line in oral-formulaic poetry through the ancient Germanic world.

Also surviving a rough transmission is the dramatic tone of the *Lay of Hildebrand*, and the forcefulness and vigor of brief sixty-eight-line work can still be felt. The tale of tragic irony, in which a father is forced to fight a son who will not be convinced of that father's very existence, carries with it a sense of deadly seriousness that is kept at the forefront of the poem. The tersely worded exchanges between father and son sidestep any kind of easy sentimentality, and the characters' motivations are derived from a code of conduct long vanished from the Western world. This code is part of an ethical system upheld by a warrior caste, a code that never allows a man of arms to refuse a challenge or shirk his duty to fight, which demands unflinching bravery and firmest resolve in the face of adversity. That some means of societal advancement and even personal enrichment (by winning a fallen adversary's battle gear) is entailed in this ethic is also by no means unlikely. Hildebrand's view of the restrictions placed on him by adherence to this code of conduct is clear: in his estimation, only the lowest of men would attempt to extricate themselves from this challenge, no matter how tragic the outcome of the combat. Despite these cultural differences between the *Lay of Hildebrand* and its modern readers, it nonetheless appeals to our sensibilities, from outrage at the unfairness of this twist of fate, to sympathy for the father's shock and grief when he realizes what the outcome of this now unavoidable fight must be.

Because it is nearly impossible, in a prose translation, to do justice to the restrained, yet deeply expressive style inherent in old Germanic alliterative verse, the *Lay of Hildebrand* is presented here in a verse translation which retains, along with the original's half-line structure, as much of the alliteration and metric schemes as modern English usage and faithfulness to the meaning of the original will allow.

1–6   I've heard tell[1]
          that champions met   man against man:
          Hildebrand and Hadubrand   between two hosts,[2]
          a son and his father.   Having fastened their armor,
          readied their battle-dress,   belted their swords on
          over their ring mail,   the men rode to the fight.
7–13   Hildebrand Herebrand's son   made a speech:
          older and wiser from life,   he started to ask
          (few were his words)   who the other's father might be

in that troop of fighters,   "or from which family are you?
If you name me one,   the others I'll know.
All this realm's nations   are known to me, boy."[3]

14–29   Hadubrand Hildebrand's son   then responded:
"Certain ones of our people,   old and wise,[4]
alive at that time,   have told me
that my father's name is Hildebrand;   Hadubrand is
    mine.
Long ago he headed east,   fled Odoaker's hatred,[5]
went away with Theodorich   and many of his thanes.[6]
Back home he left   a little boy sitting
in the chambers for women,[7]   a child not of age,
without an inheritance.   From here he rode east.[8]
Of that man thereafter   Theodorich had need
of my father, that is,   for that was a friendless man.[9]
He was utterly hostile   toward Odoaker,
for Theodorich   a most welcome thane.[10]
Always in the front lines,   always loved fighting so,
among fearless men   he was famous.
I no longer believe   that he is alive."

30–35   Hildebrand said:
"Almighty God[11]   from up in heaven
I name as my witness   that you've nonetheless never
entered a contest   against such a close kin."
Then he unwrapped from his arm   spiral-shaped rings,
made from imperial coins[12]   given him by the king,
the lord of the Huns:[13]   "These I now hand you in
    friendship."[14]

36–44   Hadubrand Hildebrand's son   then responded:
"With a spear one should take up a gift,   tip to tip.[15]
You are, old Hun,   so utterly cunning!
You draw me in with your words,   your wish is to
    spear me.
You've gotten so old   by always playing such games.
Sailors from west on the Wendel Sea told me[16]
that battle consumed him;   Hildebrand Herebrand's
    son is no more."

45–62   Hildebrand Herebrand's son   made a speech:
"I see well   by your weapons
that at home you enjoy   a generous lord,
that you've not yet known exile   under this ruler."[17]

Hildebrand said:
"Alas, O Great God,   a grievous fate's falling![18]
Sixty summers and winters   I've wandered from home,
where they always assigned me   to spear-throwers' ranks.[19]
While no one could slay me   at any stronghold,[20]
now by the sword   my own son must kill me,
strike me down with his blade,   or I be his slayer.[21]
—Now you can,[22]   if your courage avails,
easily wrest armor   from such an old man,
lay hold of the prize   if you have any rights there.
The most useless only   of men from the east
would refuse you a fight now,   since you so firmly desire
to take up this strife.   Let us see who can do it,
which one will give up   his gear on this day,
or be in possession   of both of these byrnies!"[23]

63–68   At first they let   their ash lances fly[24]
in sharp showers   that stuck in their shields.
Then they closed on each other;   battle-swords clanged.[25]
Grimly they hacked   at the gleaming white shields
till their linden wood boards   grew rather little,
beaten by blades . . . .[26]

Translated by James K. Walter

Notes

The line numbers given in the margin reflect the numbering used in the Braune/Ebbinghaus edition.

1. **"I've heard tell"**: With this formula, the author assures his audience of the veracity of his tale. In the *Lay of Hildebrand*, the verb "sagên"/"seggian" is used to testify to the truth of past events; compare lines 15 and 42, where first the "old and wise" people of Hadubrand's clan and then the sailors from the west "tell" him about his father. This formula reflects a preliterate era of oral formulaic poetry in contrast to the later Middle Ages when authors insist on the veracity of their tales by referring to what they have read in books. (See the *Battle of Ravenna*, strophe 154.)

2. **"between two hosts"**: If the situation here, joined *in medias res*, reflects the series of events narrated in the *Dietrich* epics, then one army is led by Theodorich (Dietrich), who has returned to Italy in order to regain his kingdom, and the other by Odoaker. The *Lay* itself offers us no such information. Also uncertain is why the two men have accepted this challenge to combat. Later in the poem Hildebrand offers a gift of peace to Hadubrand,

and so there is reason to assume that the younger man has challenged the older man. (Such is the situation in the younger *Lay of Hildebrand*.) In the poem, however, there is some emphasis on a judgment; the winner will gain the loser's armor (ll. 55–57), and Hildebrand in line 32 calls this fight a "dinc," a term in older Germanic languages replete with connotations of a regularized juridical proceeding, in this case, that of trial by combat. A victory in such combat is proof of one's right ("reht") in the matter. (See line 57: "if you have any rights there.") Herein lies the tragedy of the situation for Hildebrand: he cannot be proven right by winning this fight, for a victory means the death of his son and the end of his family name. A loss, of course, means his own death. Little wonder he bemoans the "grievous fate" ("wewurt") that has brought him to this combat.

3. We are told (line 8) that Hildebrand is "frot," "wise," or "experienced" and thus knows the histories of the famous families and their descendants. He wishes to know from which family the younger warrior comes in order to evaluate the worthiness of his opponent.

4. "old and wise": Hadubrand falls back on his own "experts," the older people of his clan who, being "frot" as well, know as much about the past as does Hildebrand.

5. Odoaker: deposed the last Western Roman emperor in 476 and named himself ruler of Italy. Upon Theodorich's arrival in Italy, a shared rule was arranged, which ended when Theodorich murdered his rival in 493. Subsequent legend treats Theodorich well, for the *Lay of Hildebrand* and the *Dietrich* epics are premised around a different set of events: Odoaker forces Theodorich/Dietrich into exile by treacherous usurpation of Dietrich's kingdom. Hildebrand, Dietrich's loyal teacher and vassal, accompanies his master to the east, where Theodorich, finds assistance from the Huns in his bid to regain Italy.

6. "Thanes": warriors loyal to a particular lord.

7. "in the chambers for women": manuscript "prut in bure"; thus the author does not tell us explicitly that Hildebrand abandoned a wife as well. I take this line (emended slightly to "pruti . . .") to contain a construction parallel to ones found in "fireo in folche" (line 10) and "folches at ente" (line 27), that is, a noun in the genitive case separated from its antecedent by a preposition, thus "in the chambers of women," "in the troop of men," "at the front end of the troop." All the emphasis in this section of the *Lay* is on the young boy who has been left behind by his father. Mention of a young wife ("prut") is out of place in Hadubrand's depiction of his childhood, which is not meant to be sentimental but is instead centered around the fact that Hildebrand left his son without the inheritance that would normally ease a young man's entry into the desired position of warrior, the vassal of a king or other ruler.

8. "east": to the Huns' kingdom. Hildebrand's ties to the Huns are clearly stated in the poem; his arm-rings are made of gold given him by the

Huns' lord. Hadubrand makes this connection as well, deriding the older man as an "old Hun." These references to the Huns reflect the situation clearly depicted in the later *Dietrich* epics, where the Italian king flees to Attila, king of the Huns, in order to find first refuge and then military support in a bid to recapture his lost lands.

9. **"a friendless man"**: Theodorich. He needs friends (loyal warriors) in order to survive exile to regain his lands.

10. In the manuscript this line ends in "darba gistontun," which differs only slightly from previous line 23. Most editors have seen in these words a scribal copying error, and so omit them and read "miti Theotricche" ("with Theodorich") for the manuscript's "unti Theotricche" ("as long as Theodorich . . ."). If the line is left as it stands in the manuscript it could read ". . . as long as Theodorich needed."

11. **"Almighty God"** ("irmingot"): Compare "irmindeot" (Old English "eormentheod":"mighty nation") in line 13. From this form as well as a number of Old English forms such as "eormencynn" ("mankind") and the Old Saxon *Heliand's* "allaro irminmanno" ("of all the entire nation"), it is clear the "irmin-" is a prefix used in compounds to mean "mighty" or "all." Thus "irmingot" is "mighty God" or "God of all." Whether this mighty god is the Christian god or a Germanic deity has long been a point of controversy. Two points seem to favor a Christian concept of God: the following "from above in heaven" probably reflects the Christian "pater qui es in cœlis." Later in the *Lay of Hildebrand* (line 49), this deity is referred to as "waldand got," very reminiscent of the *Heliand's* frequent use of "uualdand" to describe God or Christ.

12. **"imperial coins"**: that is, coins which bear the likeness of a Roman emperor.

13. **"lord of the Huns"**: in the framework of the Dietrich epic, a reference to Attila, who, however, died in 453 and cannot be connected in any way to the historical Odoaker or Theodorich.

14. **"in friendship"**: Hildebrand makes an attempt at peace; he is now certain of Hadubrand's identity and must find an honorable way to avoid the contest. Hadubrand's refusal to accept this gift and continued insistence on a fight leave Hildebrand no choice: he cannot refuse combat without suffering a loss of honor (line 58). He will not allow himself to be seen as "useless" ("arg": "cowardly," "despicable") by not fighting a willing opponent and challenger. It is just this code of behavior which places Hildebrand in this tragic no-win situation and imparts real force to the "grievous fate" about which he complains.

15. Normally one would extend such a gift on the end of a spear, and would therefore be unable to use that spear as a weapon. This is what Hadubrand expects. But Hildebrand apparently offers the rings to his son with one hand while maintaining a hold on his spear in the other. Hadubrand is thus rightly suspicious of the older man's gift.

16. **"the Wendel Sea"**: the Mediterranean. The seamen came to Italy westward over the Adriatic Sea from the Huns' kingdom, where Hildebrand had gone into exile with Theodorich.

17. Many scholars prefer to emend the text so that lines 46–48 follow line 57. Deleting line 45 on the grounds that it is a copyist's error, or emending it to read "Hadubrand Hildebrand's son made a speech," so that it is Hadubrand who takes note of Hildebrand's armor. In this way Hadubrand would further refute the older man's claim to be Hildebrand by pointing out that he does not appear to have been in exile with Theodorich. Hildebrand's response in lines 49–52 can then be understood as an attempt to refute his son's accusation. In addition Hadubrand's praise of Hildebrand's armor would be quite in line with the view that it is he who has challenged the older man to a duel in order to win that armor. In the *Younger Lay of Hildebrand*, it is also the younger man who makes remarks about his father's armor. The translation here, however, follows the order of lines as they are found in the manuscript.

18. **"a grievous fate's falling"** ("wewurt skihit"): This fate is an element of pre-Christian Germanic thought, the concept of an unpredictable chain of events beyond the bounds of human understanding or influence.

19. **"spear-throwers"**: These fighters stood the farthest forward in the ranks (line 27: "folches at ente"), a most dangerous position from which they launched their spears in order to provide cover for other troops. Because Hildebrand "loved fighting so" (same line), he was naturally assigned to a position which promised him a good deal of action in battle.

20. **"at any stronghold"**: Hildebrand has survived the siege of many fortresses, where as spear-thrower he has had to provide cover for those who would storm the walls.

21. In these lines Hildebrand clearly expresses the nature of the predicament in which he finds himself. Bound by his warrior's ethic and the expectations that go with it, he has no way out. He must either die or kill his own son.

22. **"Now you can . . ."**: Hildebrand turns from a lament addressed to God to speak to his challenger. In so doing he adopts the confrontational tone expected in such a situation, one which does not reveal the inner turmoil he has just expressed.

23. **"byrnies"**: suits of chain-mail.

24. **"then first . . ."**: The combat opens with the throwing of spears ("ash lances": spears made from the hard wood of the ash tree), and follows with close combat with swords.

25. **"battle swords"** ("staim bort"): The meaning of these words remains a puzzle. Most translators have understood the words to signify the men's shields, but Willy Krogmann (*Hildebrandslied*, 1959) gave a sound argument for seeing a reference to their swords here. The Middle High German word "steim"/"stîm" must derive from an Old High German word

very much like "staim," and is found in connection with battle to mean "a rush, throng." While "bort," meaning most simply "board," often refers to shields, it can also refer to a board in the sense of a sword. The meaning "battle sword" here fits the context very well; since lines 66–68 refer to the hacking of the shields, one would expect a previous line containing a reference to those swords with which the hacking is done. If "staim bort" means the shields here, then shields would be the topic of four consecutive lines.

27. "**battered by blades**": The poem breaks off after this half-line. The *Lay of Hildebrand* was written in its extant form on the outer first page of a manuscript book (page 1 recto) and continued on the outer back page of the volume (page 76 verso). While the scribes could have continued to write on the inside of the back cover, it is also quite possible that they had no intention of copying out a complete version of the poem, and may have simply used the text for practice. See R. D'Alquen and H.-G. Frevers "The Lay of Hildebrand, a Case for a Low German Written Original" in *Amsterdamer Beiträge* 22, 1984, pp. 11–72, for an explanation of the scribes' work as well as a different view of the origin of the written version of the poem. In any case it cannot be ascertained how much of the poem is missing. As for the outcome of the battle joined by Hildebrand and Hadubrand, an Old Norse parallel, the *Asmundrsaga Kappabana*, ends with the death of Hadubrand at the hands of his father. This ending best satisfies the tragic demands of the poem, for only Hildebrand, who knows the identity of his opponent—Hadubrand does not—truly understands and thus suffers at the nature of the fate that has overcome father and son.

The Nibelungenlied

The *Nibelungenlied* (ca. 1205) is one of the major literary accomplishments of medieval German literature—indeed of world literature. Few works have exercised such a hold on later generations as this epic narrative of the deeds of bold warriors and lovely ladies, of high-spirited festivals and solemn ceremonies, of great battles, and, foremost, of revenge.

But the epic has been enjoying great popularity not only in modern times; even during the Middle Ages it was considered to have been a sort of "best-seller." The work exists in thirty-four complete and partial manuscripts, stemming primarily from the southern German area, which date from the first half of the thirteenth century to the beginning of the sixteenth. In turn, the manuscripts can be divided into two major groups, the *–nôt* group (represented by the complete manuscripts *A* and *B; B* is the basis of the present translation) and the *–liet* group (represented by the complete manuscript *C*), so named because of the last lines in each group, e.g., "daz ist der Nibelunge nôt" ("that is the sorrow of the Nibelungs") and "daz ist der Nibelunge liet" ("that is the song of the Nibelungs"). Although both versions represent the one *Nibelungenlied,* there are subtle differences in the characterization of the beautiful Kriemhild and her nemesis Hagen. If in manuscript *B,* for example, Kriemhild is painted in progressively more negative tones while Hagen comes to be portrayed very positively, manuscript *C* contains little criticism of Kriemhild for her part in the final tragedy. On the contrary, her actions, while lamentable, are by and large excused because of the great offenses committed against her by Hagen, who, in turn, is reviled persistently throughout the *C*-version. Also the central thematic complex of the *B*-version—how loyalty becomes disloyalty and what constitutes vassal fealty—does not play a dominant role in the *C*-version. Instead the conflict is personalized and viewed solely in terms of a legal dispute. A possible reason for this difference could be that the C-redactor was a priest/monk, who had little contact with reality of feudal life and custom. We also know nothing definite about the B-poet, although there has been no lack of attempts to discover his identity. All that we can surmise with any degree of certainty is that he was a cleric, an educated, administrative official at a court, somewhere in the Bavarian language area, probably from around the Passau region. The poet of the B-manuscript (ca. 1205) was not the original poet, but rather the last in a probable series of compilers. Since anonymity is in the nature of the heroic genre itself, it is not unusual that the poets remain unidentified. We are not certain, for example, that any individual named Homer actually did compose the *Iliad* and *Odyssey*. We also do not know the name of the *Beowulf* poet. Thus it should come as no surprise that the Nibelungen poet chose not to identify himself. What is interesting, however, is that, in view of the apparent "popularity" of the work, the poet is not identified by contemporaries, or if he is, then not as the poet of the *Nibelungenlied*. Given the present state of available information, this is a problem that will remain unsolved.

Although written down, the *Nibelungenlied* was intended for and admirably suited to a dramatic oral presentation. The structural basis of the epic is the so-called Nibelungen strophe, which consists of four long lines, each with a caesura. The first three lines contain a total of seven stresses each, four in the first half-line and three in the second. The fourth line has eight stresses, four and four. The fourth line of the strophe tends to contain the most important information of the strophe, e.g., proper names, epic foreshadowing, etc. (see Notes). For that reason, the strophic translation by Frank G. Ryder was chosen for this edition. In addition to its being extremely well-done, Ryder's translation has maintained the strophic quality and integrity of the original, so much so that reading it aloud can convey to a modern recipient the actual impression of a medieval performance.

The *Nibelungenlied* is a tragic epic, one with a very human face. Because of the actions of individuals and the misunderstanding on their part of their responsibility to others, a whole society is destroyed. In the past two centuries the epic has been used to promote the nationalistic striving first of imperial and later of fascist Germany. This was a misuse of the work, for a close and attentive reading will demonstrate that rigidity and obsession are not being praised. Rather the poet is stressing that human beings, regardless of established systems of authority, must be able to think and act for themselves and must recognize their obligation to fellow human beings. As such, the *Nibelungenlied* is always a timely work and one worthy of recommendation to a new circle of readers.

FIRST ADVENTURE

1 Wondrous things are told in ancient tales
Of famous men and bold, of great travails,
Of joy and festive life, of woe and tears,
Of warriors met in strife—the wonder shall fill your ears!

2 There grew a royal child in Burgundy—
In all the world none lovelier than she.
Her name Kriemhild. Great her beauty when,
In womanhood, she cost the lives of many men.

3 Love was fitting tribute where she reigned—
Desired by valiant men, by none disdained.
Her charms exceeded praise; she was refined
And virtuous enough to grace all womankind.

4 Three lofty kings were guardians of her ways:
Gunther and Gernot, warriors high in praise,
And a knight preeminent, young Giselher.
This lady was their sister, and she was the princes' care.

5 Those lords were generous men, and well descended,
Unmatched in strength and valor, in station splendid.
Their country bore the name of Burgundy.
Attila's land would witness their feats of bravery.

6 At Worms on Rhine they dwelt in all their power,
Served by their proud knights—until the hour
Of their death—in high and honored state.
They ended wretchedly, from two women's hate.

7 Their mother's name was Uta, mighty queen;
Their father, Dankrat—he whose youth had been
So full of glory, whose courageous name
Was greatly honored still. From him their heritage came.

8 The three kings were, as I have said before,
Men of highest valor. What is more,
They had as subjects knights whom men accounted
Best in strength and brave, in bitter war undaunted.

9   Hagen of Trony was one of them, another
Was Ortwin of Metz; also Hagen's brother,
Able Dankwart; Counts Gere and Eckewart;
And Folker of Alzei, armored with a stalwart heart.

10   Rumold the Kitchener managed household things
With Sindold and Hunold—men of the three kings,
Paying courtly form their full attention.
Other lords they had, more than I can mention.

11   Dankwart was the marshal; Royal Steward,
His nephew Ortwin, Sindold (he was no coward)
Served as the King's Lord Butler; as Chamberlain,
Sir Hunold. Masters of courtly taste were all these men.

12   The story of this vast court, their dignity
And great extent of power, of Chivalry,
Which all their days they cherished as their goal—
Truly, no one has the gift to tell it all.

13   Surrounded by this glory, Kriemhild dreamed
She raised a fair, wild falcon, which it seemed
Two eagles clawed to death while she looked on.
No sorrow could be worse than this, that it was gone.

14   She told the dream to Uta, who could see
One meaning only: "In life this bird must be
A noble lord. Unless God's hand is strong
In his defense, I fear he'll not be yours for long."

15   "Sweet mother, do not speak of that again;
I mean to live without the love of men,
And I will keep the beauty given me,
Till death, and no man's love shall bring me misery."

16   Her mother said, "Oh, make no vow so bold!
Whatever happiness this world may hold
Comes from a man's love. If God provide
A noble lord for you, you'll be a lovely bride."

17   "An end to our debate, my Lady dear!
In many women's fate this much is clear:
Pain is the price of pleasure when all is done.
But I am safe from danger, for I'll have neither one."

18   From love the lady turned her thoughts away,
And thus she lived for many a happy day,

Knowing no man by whom her heart was stirred.
And yet one day, in state, she wed a gallant lord.

19   He was the falcon of her dream, the one
Foretold by Uta—by her own kin undone,
On whom she took most awful vengeance then.
And one man's dying brought the death of many men.

SECOND ADVENTURE
Sigfrid

20   In Netherland lived the son of a royal house,
Child of King Sigmund and Siglind, his spouse.
They dwelt in a mighty city, wide in fame,
Set on the lower Rhine—Xanten was its name.

21   This was Sigfrid, of all bold men the best,
Strong in will, he put whole lands to test,
And many, in strength of limb, he rode to see.
Ah, what courageous knights he found in Burgundy!

22   They tell great things of Sigfrid in his prime,
His days of youth, and how he grew in time
To be a man of high renown and handsome—
How he was loved by many women, fair and winsome.

23   His education there was duly nourished,
While in his heart courtly virtues flourished.
His ever noble bearing people found
A splendid thing by which his father's land was crowned.

24   And soon he was of age to go to court,
Where he found welcome. It would please the heart
Of many maids and ladies if he desired
Soon to return. He knew that he was much admired.

25   They seldom sent him riding unescorted.
His parents dressed him well, and he consorted
With masters of chivalry, who lent their hands
To teach him ways of knighthood, winning of men and lands.

26   Now his strength was such that he could look
To bearing arms—he had the stuff it took;
And taste enough with lovely ladies to broach
His suit with them. Loving him was no reproach.

27   The king now had his vassals summoned in,
Announcing a tourney for all his kith and kin.
To other sovereigns' lands they bore the tiding.
He gave to stranger and friend good clothes and steeds for riding.

28   Whatever noble youths his heralds met
Who were by age and background fit to get
The promise of accolade, these they invited
To the feast, there to be with Sigfrid knighted.

29   What stories one could tell of the tournament!
Sigmund and Siglind gained, for the wealth they spent,
Increasing honor. They gave with a generous hand,
Bringing a host of strangers riding to their land.

30   Four hundred squires were robed at his accolades,
And out of love for Sigfrid beautiful maids
Busied their hands, working each precious stone
Into the cloth of gold, for in this way alone

31   Could all the clothes be made for lords so proud.
Their host gave out command that for the crowd
Of stalwart men seating be provided,
For the summer-solstice feast at which his son was knighted.

32   Many the lord and squire who went to service
At minster. Master there attended novice—
The custom, once accorded him as boy.
This they did in pleasure and thought of future joy.

33   Men sang mass to God. Through the crowd,
A mighty motion surged, as squires vowed—
New made knights, in knighthood's regimen,
With splendor such as the world will hardly see again.

34   They hurried where the saddled horses waited.
Melee and noise continued unabated,
Till Sigmund's palace rang, and the halls around.
Gay and haughty knights raised a mighty sound.

35   And you could hear from knight and novice blows
So numerous the shatter of lances rose
To the sky—and see the splinters whirl and fall
From the eager hands of men, all the way to the hall.

36   The host cried halt, the horses were led away.
Bosses were broken, and many jewels lay,

Precious stones from rims of the bright shield tossed
Upon the grass—and all of this from the crash of the joust.

37 The guest were given seats. Excellent food
In plenty put an end to their weary mood—
And the best of wines, served with a generous hand—
Paying to stranger and friend the honors of the land.

38 They turned their time to pleasure all the day,
While many minstrels gave up sleep to play
And sing for rich reward their songs and lays.
And through them all the lands of Sigmund shone in praise.

39 In grant of fief the king now asked his son
To give out lands and towns as he had done.
Richly Sigfrid gave to his friends who took
The sword with him. How sweet it made their journey look!

40 The celebration lasted one whole week.
The wealthy Lady Siglind, to bespeak
The love she had for her son, gave of her gold,
Repaying the people's love for him, as they did of old.

41 There wasn't a minstrel poor in all the land.
Horses and clothes ran from their hands like sand,
As if they hadn't another day to live.
I doubt if ever court has had such wealth to give.

42 The tourney now dispersed, with splendid rites.
Soon this wish was heard from powerful knights:
Might not the young prince now be king alone?
But their desire did not accord with Sigfrid's own.

43 With both Sigmund and Siglind hale and sound,
Their son had no ambition to be crowned.
He wished instead to gain the upper hand
Of that which worried him: injustice in the land.

THIRD ADVENTURE

How Sigfrid Came to Worms on the Rhine

44 The prince's heart was rarely sorrow-laden!
Once he heard there lived the fairest maiden
In Burgundy, the model of loveliness—
Later cause of his many joys, and deep distress.

45   Word of her beauty traveled far and wide,
Nor did she make a secret of her pride
From the countless heroes who, as strangers, came
to royal Gunther's land, attracted by her fame.

46   However many came to press their case,
Kriemhild in her heart would never face
The thought of yielding to any lover's will.
The man she later wed—he was a stranger still.

47   Now courtly love took hold on Sigfrid's mind.
Others' wooing was a sigh of wind
Compared to his! Well he knew the way
To court a beauty, and Kriemhild would be his one day.

48   All of Sigfrid's courtiers and his kin
Advised him now that he should try to win
A lady worthy of him, since he was filled
With visions of courtly love. "Then I will have Kriemhild,

49   Princess of Burgundy, for none is fairer,"
Sigfrid said. "In this I make no error:
The greatest emperor, if he would marry,
Could give this princess his love—never would he be sorry."

50   Sigmund heard this tale, told around
Among his vassals. Thus it was he found
His son's intent—and with misgiving viewed
The choice of the brilliant lady for whose hand he sued.

51   Siglind, too, found out, and worry grew
In her mind, for the sake of her son. Well she knew
King Gunther and his men. With common voice
They joined in showing him the folly of his choice.

52   Sigfrid made reply, "I always planned,
My dear father, to live without the hand
Of any lady, unless I were disposed
By heart and love to court. In this my mind is closed—

53   Let people talk as they will." Replied the king:
"If you will not give in—well, everything
You wish is fine with me; I'll help you out
As best I can, but Gunther has proud men about.

54   Hagen alone would be sufficient trouble—
Such a proud and overbearing noble,

That we may well regret it, I'm afraid,
If we should set our minds on courting your fair maid."

55 Sigfrid said, "How is that to hold us back?
What can't be got from them on a friendly tack
I'll take with the strength of my hand—valor's course;
I think I can seize their country, men and all, by force."

56 "These," said the king, "are words I must deplore.
Let news like that be heard by the Rhenish shore
And you will never ride to Gunther's land!
He and Gernot are men I know and understand."

57 "Force will never win the princess's love,"
Spoke Sigmund, "that much I am certain of.
But if you must approach their land in force,
We'll summon whatever friends we have, from every source."

58 Sigfrid replied, "I have no wish to see
Warriors off to the Rhine, following me—
Or any kind of expedition sent
To help me conquer my love. That's not what I meant.

59 This hand alone can win her. I shall go
As one of twelve to Gunther's land, and so,
My father, help me in this!" (He gave away
To Sigfrid's men clothes of fur, vair and gray.)

60 His mother Siglind also heard the news.
She mourned for the child she loved and feared to lose
To Gunther's men. In her anxiety
The noble queen commenced to weep most bitterly.

61 Lord Sigfrid saw his mother, in compassion
Went to her, and said in kindly fashion:
"You must not cry for me, my lady dear.
Let any warrior face me, I shall have no fear.

62 Support my trip to Burgundy! Provide
For my knights and me the kind of clothes with pride
And honor worn by men of lofty mood—
For that I pledge to you my trust and gratitude."

63 She spoke, "Since you will not be reconciled,
I'll help you with your trip, my only child,
Making clothes for you and your men, of stuff
The best that knights have worn. You'll take with you enough."

64   At this young Sigfrid bowed and said to her,
"Twelve knights will go with me, for I prefer
To take no more. Let clothes for them be planned.
I mean to find Kriemhild and see how matters stand."

65   Night and day lovely women stayed
At work—no rest for them until they made
Sigfrid's clothes. The trip was on his mind,
And he refused to hear advice of any kind.

66   At Sigmund's word, they adorned with lavish hand
The clothes in which he left his father's land.
His vassals readied arms to take along:
Bright byrnies, sturdy helmets, shields broad and strong.

67   The day of their trip to Burgundy drew near.
In hearts of men and women grew the fear
That they might not return, once they were gone,
But they had ordered clothes and weapons loaded on.

68   Their steeds were handsome, their harness red with gold.
How could there live a man so overbold
As to rank himself with Sigfrid's company?
And now for the royal leave to go to Burgundy:

69   They granted it in sadness, queen and king.
He spoke in loving kindness, comforting,
And said, "Never weep, for sake of me.
My life is safe, you need have no anxiety."

70   Knights were sad and many maidens cried.
I think the heart within had prophesied
How vast a death of friends would now ensue.
Oh, they did well to mourn—they had good reason to.

71   The seventh morning, the heroes reached the shore
Of the Rhine at Worms. All the clothes they wore
Were red with gold, their harness skillfully wrought,
Smooth the gait of the steeds that Sigfrid's men had brought.

72   The shields they had were new and broad and bright,
Their helmets proud, as now the valiant knight
Lord Sigfrid rode to Gunther's land and castle.
Such splendid gear was never seen on lord or vassal.

73   The tips of their pointed swords hung to the spur,
Sharp were the spears these perfect warriors bore.

Sigfrid's measured two hands broad in the blade,
And what a fearful cut its double edges made!

74   In hand they carried golden colored reins,
The horses' martingales were silken chains.
Thus they came to the land. Everywhere
The crowds of common people stopped to stare.

75   Many of Gunther's men, knights and squires
Proud in bearing, ran (as form requires)
To welcome them—guests to their master's land.
Here they took their steeds and all their shields in hand.

76   About to lead the horses to food and stall,
They heard Lord Sigfrid loud and boldly call:
"Leave our mounts alone—my men's and mine.
We shall soon be leaving. This is my firm design.

77   Speak up, if you know—do not conceal it.
Where do I find the king? Come now, tell it.
Mighty Gunther, I mean, of Burgundy."
Someone told him (well he knew where the king
    would be):

78   "If it's the king you want, he's easily found.
I saw him there in the hall. All around,
His knights were standing. Go where I told you to,
You'll find he has some worthy men in his retinue!"

79   By now the king himself had heard report
How lusty-looking men had come to his court
In splendid clothes and gleaming coats of mail.
But none in Burgundy knew them or knew whence they
    might hail.

80   On this the king was greatly curious, too—
About these elegant knights whose garments' hue
Was shining bright, whose shields were new and wide.
His question went unanswered, the king was not satisfied.

81   Then it was that Ortwin of Metz spoke out
(A powerful man and brave, beyond a doubt):
"Since none of us can say, have someone go
And get my uncle Hagen; show him these men below.

82   He knows our realms and foreign lands as well.
Let him see them—if he knows he'll tell."

The king now sent for Hagen and his men—
A splendid sight they were, as they came to court again.

83   Hagen asked his king's desire. "My hall,"
He answered, "is host to strangers. If you recall
(As none here can) seeing them anywhere,
I want you to tell me, Hagen, the truth of this affair."

84   Hagen walked to the window. "That I'll do."
He turned his gaze to the strangers, whose aspect drew
His pleased attention, in garb and general grace.
But never in Burgundy had he seen a single face.

85   "These riders to the Rhine, wherever be
Their home, are princes or prince's embassy.
Their steeds are handsome, the cut of their clothing grand.
These are men of spirit, whatever be their land."

86   And then he spoke: "It would come as no surprise—
Although I never saw him with my own eyes—
If that were Sigfrid walking so proudly along.
This at least is my opinion, right or wrong.

87   His coming means great news within our land.
The sons of mighty Nibelung died by his hand:
Shilbung and Nibelung, each a valiant prince.
And his amazing strength has worked more marvels since.

88   Once as he rode along, without escort,
By a mountainside—I have it on good report—
He found some stalwart men by the treasure-store
Of the Nibelungs, men he had never seen before.

89   They had brought the cache from the hollow mountainside—
Nibelung's men, preparing to divide
The Nibelung hoard. (This is the strange account.)
When Sigfrid saw them there, his wonder began to mount.

90   He came so close he could see the men and they,
In turn, had noticed him. One rose to say,
'Here comes Sigfrid, Netherland's champion.'
(Among the Nibelung men there would be strange things done!)

91   The two young princes made him welcome there,
In common council asked that he set the share
That each of them should get of all this treasure.
They urged and pled, till he agreed to do their pleasure.

92   A hundred carts, they say, could hardly hold
        The precious stones he saw, and more red gold
        From the land of Nibelung. All this they planned
        Should be divided out for them by Sigfrid's hand.

93   By gift of the sword of Nibelung they bought
        His services, and ill return they got
        In the job he did for them, Sigfrid the fair.
        The task was never done, there was anger in the air.*

C94   He had to leave the treasure undivided.
        The two kings' men commenced a fight and sided
        Both against him. With Balmung, their father's sword,
        He wrested from them their lands and all the Nibelung hoard.

94   Beside them twelve courageous vassals stood,
        Giants all—it did them little good!
        The angry hand of Sigfrid cut them down,
        And seized the seven hundred knights of the Nibelung crown.

96   The two great kings as well he struck and slew,
        And out of this his trouble with Alberich grew,
        Who hoped to avenge his lords that very hour,
        Until he learned the true extent of Sigfrid's power.

97   In battle, the fearsome dwarf could not prevail.
        Like savage lions they raced the mountain trail,
        Where the Magic Cloak fell prize to the dreaded lord,
        And with it Sigfrid's title to the treasure-hoard.

98   Those who had dared to fight lay slain and dead.
        The rest should haul and carry the gold, he said,
        To where the Nibelungs had it previously.
        He left it there in mighty Alberich's custody.

99   The dwarf was forced to swear an oath of service,
        And willingly has done his every office."
        Thus said Hagen. "All this he has done.
        Greater power never fell to anyone.

100   And I recall one other thing I knew:
        Once there was a dragon Sigfrid slew

---

* This sequence of stanzas in MS *B* gives a confusing picture of
the scene. The next stanza is interpolated from *C*, and one of *B*'s succeed-
ing quatrains is omitted.

And bathed himself in his blood. His skin was turned
To horn no blade will cut, as many men have learned.

101   We'll make the warmth of our welcome that much stronger
Lest somehow we incur the young man's anger.
So bold a knight, whose past has thus disclosed
So many marvels done—let's keep him well-disposed!"

102   The mighty king replied, "You may be right.
See how like a battle-eager knight
He stands with all his men. It seems but fair
That we go down the stairs and meet this warrior there."

103   "No loss of face," said Hagen, "if this be done.
He comes from a noble line, a great king's son—
God knows he looks the part. And I dare say
No trivial thing would bring him riding here this way."

104   The king of the land now spoke, "Then let him be
Our welcome guest. Your words have pictured me
A bold and noble man; he shall be rated
High in Burgundy." Gunther went where Sigfrid waited.

105   The host and his men received their guest so well
That not the slightest flaw could Sigfrid tell
In their demeanor. He felt well inclined,
Their way of greeting him had been so very kind.

106   "Tell me," said the king without delay,
"From where, oh noble Sigfrid, you come our way,
Or what you hope to do, here at Worms."
His guest replied, "That I shall, in the plainest terms.

107   I heard reports of you our country over,
The truth of which I wanted to discover:
You have the bravest men, so people claim,
That ever served a king. And that is why I came.

108   I also hear that you yourself enjoy
A name for courage. Never king could toy
With danger, all the people say, like you.
I'll not give up until I see if this is true.

109   I also am a knight, crown and throne
Will soon be mine. I want all men to own
That I have gained my whole domain by merit.
I offer pledge for that: by honor and life I swear it!

110   Since you are brave—this is the word I've got—
I don't much care if anyone likes or not,
I mean to conquer what you have—your castles,
All your lands. And all your people shall be my vassals."

111   The king was much amazed at what he heard,
As were his men, to find that it occurred
To him to seize their lands. Anger broke
Upon them all as they listened to him. Gunther spoke:

112   "And do I merit this? To let another
Take by show of power what my father
Long in honor cherished—that would be
A sorry show of how we practice chivalry."

113   Undaunted, Sigfrid answered, "This is my stand,
From which I will not yield. Unless your land
Gain its peace by your power, I'll have it all—
And mine besides, which if you win, to you shall fall.

114   Thus it shall be: my heritage and yours
Alike at stake. Whichever one secures
The victory, all is his: people, town,
And country." Hagen and Gernot tired to talk him down:

115   "We have no intention," Gernot said,
"Of seizing any place, when men lie dead,
At heroes' feet, as price of it. Our lands
Are rich and rightly ours. They rest in proper hands."

116   In angry mood his friends were standing by,
Among them Ortwin of Metz. "I loathe this try
At soft appeasement," Ortwin answered back,
"When Sigfrid threatens you with unprovoked attack.

117   If you and your brothers had no armed defense
And if he brought with him a force immense
As any king's, I still am confident
That I could give him cause to be less arrogant."

118   The hero Sigfrid cried, his anger fanned:
"Not against me shall you dare lift your hand!
I am a mighty king, and what are you?
A vassal! This is more than twelve of you could do."

119   Ortwin called for swords, with a mighty shout.
He was Hagen's kin, beyond a doubt!

(The king was vexed by Hagen's lengthy silence.)
Gernot, the bold and merry, stepped in, forestalling violence—

120 Crying out to Ortwin, "Stop the fuss!
Sigfrid has done nothing so bad to us
That we cannot secure some peaceful end,
With honor, and more to our credit, gain him as a friend."

121 Said mighty Hagen, "All of us may rue
His riding here—the love of strife that drew
This man to the Rhine! He never should have come.
What hostile act of my lords has he ever suffered from?"

122 Mighty Sigfrid answered him this way:
"Does it bother you, Hagen, to hear what I say?
Then I will give you, instead, a chance to see
What power my hands will wield, here in Burgundy!"

123 "I'll see to that myself," Gernot cried,
Forbidding his men to speak a word in pride,
By which he might be angered. It happened too
That Sigfrid began to think of the woman he came to woo.

124 "What cause have we to fight you?" Gernot said.
"Think of all the heroes lying dead—
Small glory to us, and little good to you."
Sigfrid, son of Sigmund, cried, when he was through:

125 "What's Hagen waiting for? Why not rush in—
Ortwin too—and fight, with his friends and kin,
Of whom the land of Burgundy is full?"
They dared not say a word, for this was Gernot's will.

126 "You all are welcome," answered Uta's son,
"You and your companions, every one.
My kin and I will gladly do our best
To serve you." Gunther's wine was poured for every guest.

127 "All we have is yours," the king declared.
"So long as you take it in honor, be it shared
Equally with you, our men and the wealth we own."
(Sigfrid's mood took on a somewhat gentler tone.)

128 They had their garments brought and stored away,
And found for Sigfrid's men a place to stay,
The best they could, to make them feel at home.
Their guest became a welcome sight, in time to come.

129 Men came to pay him homage, many a day,
A thousand times more often than I can say.
His valor earned it, on this believe my word.
In no one's heart who saw him was any rancor stirred.

130 With kings and men at play, whatever test
They turned their hand to, he proved himself the best.
So great his strength that none of them came near,
Whenever they hurled the heavy stone or cast the spear.

131 And if the merry knights made love their sport,
For sake of chivalry, and paid their court
To the ladies, Netherland's lord was welcome there.
Chivalric love had now become his constant care.

132 In all of their pursuits he gladly joined,
The fairest maid envisioned in his mind—
And he in the mind of one he'd never seen,
Who secretly often spoke of him with kind esteem.

133 And when the younger knights and men would fill
The courtyard with their games, from the windowsill
The gracious princess Kriemhild now would gaze—
And wanted no more pleasant way to pass her days.

134 What lasting joy for him, if he had known
That she whom he loved was watching! Her sight alone,
Of this I'm certain, would have been so sweet
That all this world could hold no pleasure more complete.

135 When he stood with heroes at court, as still is done
By men for their pleasure now, Siglind's son
Looked so handsome that he greatly swayed,
For heart's love of him, many a highborn maid.

136 And many times he thought, "How may it be
That ever with these eyes of mine I see
The princess I have loved so long and well,
For she and I are strangers still, sad to tell."

137 Whenever the kings would visit their domain
The knights were called upon to join the train,
And Sigfrid too, for which his lady grieved.
For love of her, what blows of fortune he received!

138 And so he dwelt in the land of Gunther here,
Among the noble lords, for one whole year.

No glimpse in all this time did he ever gain
Of the beauty who was to bring him pleasure, yes, and pain.

FOURTH ADVENTURE
How He Fought the Saxons

139   At this time now there came a strange report
Sent by distant heralds to Gunther's court,
Of unknown knights whose anger they'd incurred.
Truly, it made their spirits sad to hear this word.

140   I'll tell you who they were: from Saxony
Lord Liudeger—a powerful prince was he;
And Liudegast, monarch in Denmark reigning.
They brought a splendid host for their campaigning.

141   His foes had sent out men to make their entry,
Coming as heralds, into Gunther's country.
They summoned the strangers to royal audience,
Asking them to tell the purport of these events.

142   "Welcome," cried the king, with a friendly word.
"Who may have sent you here I have not heard.
And this is what I'd have you tell me," he said.
The thought of Gunther's fierceness gave them much to dread.

143   "Grant us your permission to reveal
The news we bring and we shall not conceal
But name the lords who sent us: Liudeger
And Liudegast together—they come here bent on war.

144   You have roused their wrath. The story goes
That both regard themselves as your bitter foes.
Worms on Rhine is the goal of their campaign,
And many knights are with them—the truth I tell is plain.

145   Within twelve weeks they march. If you have friends
Good enough to help in your defense
Of lands and castles, let that be soon revealed,
For they will shatter here many a helm and shield.

146   Or if you'd rather sue for peace, then send
The message to them and they will not descend
In all their great and hostile force on you,
With havoc and pain and the death of knights that must ensue."

147   Answered the king, "Wait for a moment or so,
That I may think it over and let you know,
If I have loyal friends, I must not turn
This serious news from them but tell them my concern."

148   Mighty Gunther felt in full the smart
Of the secret pain he bore within his heart.
He summoned Hagen and many another vassal,
And sent men out to find Lord Gernot at the castle.

149   They came, the greatest lords of high position.
"Powerful forces plan an expedition
Against out land. Take this to heart," he cried.
To which Lord Gernot, champion gay and bold, replied:

150   "Well then, our swords must see to that," he said.
"Only the doomed will die, let them lie dead.
For this I can't forget my own good name.
Welcome these foes of ours, let us be glad they came."

151   "That seems to me unwise," Lord Hagen cried.
"Liudegast is a man of violent pride,
And Liudeger. We cannot recruit so fast,
In so few days. Why not tell Sigfrid what has passed?"

152   They had the heralds lodged within the town.
Foes or not, the king would have them shown
The best of care (and this was right to do),
Till he could learn what friends of his would see him through.

153   Still the king was saddened by his care.
A certain lord, who could not be aware
Of what had happened, saw him deep in worry
And bade King Gunther tell him what might be the story.

154   Sigfrid spoke, "It greatly surprises me
How you have put an end to the gaiety
Which up to now was your accustomed way
Of treating us." Handsome Gunther turned to say:

155   "Not to everyone can I impart
The secret fear that occupies my heart.
True friends alone can share our deep concerns."
Noble Sigfrid's face grew pale and flushed by turns.

156   He said to the king, "There's nothing I've denied you.
I'll help to see that future ills avoid you.

If you are looking for friends, let me be one.
That I can promise, with honor, till my days are done."

157   "God reward you Sir, your words are pleasant!
Your valor may never help me, and though it doesn't,
I still am glad to hear of your loyalty.
If I should live, you'll be repaid, and suitably.

158   I'll tell you why I stand thus deep in worry.
Heralds of my foes bring me this story,
Saying they have planned a great invasion—
More than knights have dared on any past occasion."

159   Sigfrid answered, "Set your mind at rest.
Never worry, do as I suggest.
Let me secure your interest and your honor.
And ask that they too help who serve beneath your banner.

160   Though your mighty foes had thanes to assist them
As many as thirty thousand, I'd resist them
With only a thousand men. Count on me."
Said the king, "For that I promise constant fealty."

161   "Give me a thousand of your men on loan,
Since I have brought with me of all my own
Barely a dozen, and I'll defend your land.
You shall have loyal service always from Sigfrid's hand.

162   Hagen shall give us help, Ortwin too,
Dankwart and Sindold, lords of your retinue.
Another who shall ride: Folker the Brave,
As standard-bearer—there's no one I should rather have.

163   Send the heralds home to their masters' land.
They'll see us first—make sure they understand.
This is the way to protect our towns and castles."
Gunther the king sent word to summon kin and vassals.

164   Back to Gunther's court went Liudeger's men,
Happy to be going home again.
He offered them rich gifts and guaranteed
Safe conduct through his lands. Proudly they agreed.

165   "Now," said Gunther, "tell my powerful foes
They'd best stay home, as far as this war goes.
But if they mean to encroach on my domains,
Unless my friends desert me, they'll suffer for their pains."

166   They handed Liudegast's men expensive things
       Which Gunther could give in number like few kings.
       To this the heralds did not dare say no.
       They left rejoicing as soon as they had leave to go.

167   When the messengers arrived at the Danish court
       And gave King Liudegast their full report
       Of how they left the Rhine, he was irritated,
       Through and through, at the tale of arrogance they related.

168   They told him Burgundy had brave men to spare,
       And they had seen a knight among them there,
       A hero of Netherland, Sigfrid he was called.
       When Liudegast heard this, his heart was greatly galled.

169   And when the Danes found out, they called their kin
       And friends in haste, bringing more troops in,
       Until Sir Liudegast had managed to gain
       Twenty thousand men to join his campaign.

170   The King of Saxony also armed for war,
       Until they counted forty thousand or more
       Ready to ride with them to Burgundy.
       At home King Gunther too recruited a company

171   Of kinsmen and his brothers' men to lead
       Into combat now that war was decreed—
       Together with Hagen's troops—the only path
       Now open to them and one on which brave men faced death.

172   They hurried preparations. Leaving there,
       Folker took the standard (his to bear).
       As soon as they had quitted Worms and planned
       To cross the river Rhine, Hagen took command.

173   With them Sindold and Hunold rode away,
       Well equipped to merit Gunther's pay;
       Dankwart, Hagen's brother; Ortwin too,
       An honor and credit to this warlike retinue.

174   Said Sigfrid, "Stay at home, your Majesty,
       Since all your knights will come along with me.
       Remain with the ladies, proudly, nothing loath!
       I surely can guard for you honor and property both.

175   Those who thought to hurl their full attack
       At Worms on Rhine—I'll see that they stay back,

Close to home. We'll strike their country yet,
So hard that we shall turn their pride to sad regret."

176   From the Rhine they rode through Hessia with their lords
Toward Saxony. There was fighting afterwards!
They burned and pillaged, laying the country waste,
Till both the kings knew well the bitter fear they faced.

177   They reached the border, there the squires withdrew.
Mighty Sigfrid asked, "Our retinue
Of service troops—who'll stay and be their chief?"
(No one ever rode to the Saxons' greater grief.)

178   They said, "En route let Dankwart guard the pages—
A stalwart man, bold when the battle rages—
Liudeger's men will hurt us all the less.
Ortwin and he can watch the rear with all success."

179   "I shall take the van," Lord Sigfrid chose,
"Riding on the lookout for our foes
Till I discover where their men may be."
They armed fair Siglind's son and did it speedily.

180   He gave command of the knights in their main body
To Hagen and to Gernot, brave and sturdy.
Alone to Saxony he rode away.
Many helmet straps he cut in two that day!

181   Soon he saw a mighty host deployed
Across the field, outweighing his, but void
Of true distinction—forty thousand or more.
This was a happy sight, causing his pride to soar.

182   There too a knight had taken up his post,
Well armed for war to watch for the enemy host.
Sigfrid saw this man, and he saw him.
They followed one another, their gazes fierce and grim.

183   I'll tell you now by whom the watch was manned.
A shining shield of gold was in his hand;
King Liudegast it was, guarding his force.
The noble stranger, stately and proud, spurred on his horse.

184   Liudegast also had his foeman spied.
Each one put the spurs to his horse's side
And, aim on shield, lowered his mighty lance—
For all the king's great power, a threatening circumstance!

185   Their lances crashed. The horses bore them past,
One prince crossing before the other so fast
They seemed like wind. Reining, these gallant lords
Wheeled and savagely took up the fight with swords.

186   Sigfrid struck so hard the whole field crashed
With the echoing blow and fiery red sparks flashed
From the helmet stroke like flames that fan
From some great conflagration. Each had found his man.

187   And fierce the strength that Liudegast revealed
In the blows he hit him. Heavy on each man's shield
Lay the other's valor. Thirty came on the run
To cover the king—before they reached him Sigfrid won,

188   Wounding the king three times, striking through
To pierce his excellent mail. The sword blade drew,
Where the edges cut, blood from the wounds it made—
By which the royal Liudegast was much dismayed.

189   He begged for his life, pledging his domains,
And said he was Liudegast. All his thanes
Came running up, for they had seen full well
What both were doing at their post, and what befell.

190   About to lead him off, Sigfrid faced attack
By thirty of Liudegast's men. He fought them back,
Guarding his mighty hostage with savage blows.
The gallant knight would cause more losses for his foes!

191   All thirty he was strong enough to slay,
Except for one, who promptly rode away
And gave the rest report of what occurred.
The red on his helmet vouched to them for the truth of his word.

192   Told the king was a prisoner, every Dane
Was struck with wrath at the news and filled with pain.
They told his brother, who began to storm
In a great and towering rage, for this was grievous harm.

193   And so he led away King Liudegast then—
Sigfrid in all his power—to Gunther's men.
He gave him over to Hagen, in his safekeeping.
Hearing it was the king, they felt no need for weeping.

194   They bade the Burgundians fasten their pennants on.
"Forward!" Sigfrid cried. "More's to be done

Before the day is through. If I keep my life,
We'll leave in care and sorrow many a Saxon wife.

195 Warriors of the Rhine, listen to me.
I'll guide you to Liudegast's army. Then you'll see
Helmets hewn to bits by heroes here.
Before we head back home, they'll learn the taste of fear."

196 Gernot and his men leaped to their horses.
A mighty minstrel rode at the head of their forces,
Noble Folker, taking in hand their banner.
Their troops were ready for war, armed in the fines manner.

197 They had a thousand men—only those
And Sigfrid's twelve. Clouds of dust soon rose
Along the roads. They rode across the fields,
And you could see before them the glitter of splendid shields.

198 Now there came the army of Saxony,
With sharpened swords—so it was told to me—
Swords that could really cut, in the warriors' hands,
To push the strangers back and defend their towns and lands.

199 The king's commanders moved the army ahead.
Sigfrid also came with the knights he led
In company with him from Netherland.
That day's fighting left many a bloodstained hand.

200 In battle Sindold and Hunold and Gernot slew
More than one before he even knew
The measure of their valiant bravery—
A cause of grief for women of noble ancestry.

201 Folker and Hagen and Ortwin in the fight
Put out with flowing blood the flashing light
Of numerous helmets—heroes in battle heat!
And Dankwart too performed many a marvelous feat.

202 Men of Denmark also tried their mettle.
The sound was loud of shields in the crash of battle,
And of sharp swords, swinging constantly.
Damage enough they caused, bold fighters of Saxony!

203 When Burgundy's men rushed into battle there,
They plied their swords, and many wounds lay bare.
Over the saddles streams of blood ran down.
Thus did valiant warriors seek to gain renown.

204 The sound of sharpened blade in hero's hand
Resounded loud when the men of Netherland
Followed their lord, to join the mighty throng.
Models of knighthood, they and Sigfrid rode along.

205 Where Sigfrid went no Rhenish knight would go,
But one could see a bloody river flow
Through rows of shining helmets—the work of his hand—
Till he found Liudeger at the head of his warrior band.

206 Through his foes for the third time he rode,
To the end and back, when out Lord Hagen strode,
To help him sate his spirit in the fray.
Many warriors had to die at their hands that day.

207 When Liudeger saw Lord Sigfrid riding by,
And saw that in his hand he held on high
Balmung the mighty sword and that he killed
So many men, with savage anger his heart was filled.

208 Now with a mighty surge and noise of swords
The armies approached each other, both the lords
The more intent to find which one was stronger.
The others now withdrew. The air was full of anger.

209 By now they had informed the Saxon chief
Of his brother's capture, a cause of pain and grief.
Not knowing yet that it was Siglind's son,
They blamed Lord Gernot. He found out soon by whom it
  was done!

210 Such was the power Liudeger revealed
That at his blows Lord Sigfrid's charger reeled
Beneath his saddle. Gaining control of his horse,
Sigfrid renewed the fight with savage and cruel force.

211 Hagen and Gernot helped him, Dankwart too,
And Folker the minstrel—many men they slew.
Sindold and Hunold and Ortwin there in the heat
Of warfare struck them down in numbers dead at their feet.

212 Fighting they kept each other close in view,
These splendid princes. Over helmets flew
Spears from heroes' hands to strike their way
Through shining shields on which the color of blood
  now lay.

213 In storm of battle many a fighting man
   Dismounted from his horse. Two heroes ran
   At one another, Sigfrid and Liudeger.
   Lances and sharpened spears went flying through the air.

214 Sigfrid cut the straps that held his shield.
   He thought that he would make the Saxons yield,
   Brave though they were, with their many casualties.
   Dankwart cut through shining rings of mail with ease.

215 Then Liudeger saw a shield with crown all painted
   In front of Sigfrid's hand. Well acquainted
   Now with its owner—a valiant man, he knew—
   The king called out aloud to all his retinue:

216 "Men of mine, stop now, the fight is done.
   The man that I see here is Sigmund's son,
   Sigfrid the strong—I know that it is he.
   The cursed devil himself has sent him to Saxony."

217 In the midst of battle he had them lower the standard,
   And sued for peace—in which he was not hindered,
   But had to go as hostage to Gunther's land—
   Tribute forced from him by the power of Sigfrid's hand.

218 In common council they set an end to war.
   Punctured helms and the massive shields they bore
   Were not put down—and not a one was free
   Of marks the color of blood, from the hands of Burgundy.

219 They took as hostage (having given no quarter)
   Whomever they chose. By Gernot and Hagen's order
   The wounded were put on stretchers. They carried off
   Five hundred captives to the Rhine—all brave enough.

220 The Danes rode home deprived of victory,
   Nor had the Saxons fought so gloriously
   That one could praise them for it—much to the pain
   Of proper heroes. Friends and kinsmen mourned the slain.

221 They packed their arms and armor home again
   By horse to the Rhine. Sigfrid and his men
   Had proved their merit—his was a noble deed.
   This the men of Gunther would readily concede.

222 The king sent Gernot back to Worms to tell
   His friends and kin at home, and say how well

He'd fared himself, and all his retinue:
Brave men were they, honor was their guide and due.

223 The pages came running, and passed the message on.
Faces were bright with joy, all sorrow gone,
At such auspicious word as now was passed.
Noble women's questions soon came thick and fast:

224 How, they asked, had the great king's warriors done?
To Kriemhild went a messenger alone—
A secret others could not be witness of,
For one among those warriors was her heart's true love.

225 When she saw the herald coming to her place
The lovely lady spoke with kindly grace:
"My gold is yours if you have good news to repeat.
I'll always owe you thanks if you do it without deceit.

226 How did my brother Gernot leave the field—
And my other kin? Did we lose many killed?
And who gained most distinction, tell me this."
Quickly the herald replied, "No one showed cowardice.

227 But in real combat no one rode so well,
My noble queen (since I have this to tell)
As did our highborn guest from Netherland.
Amazing was the work of valiant Sigfrid's hand!

228 However well our heroes fought the fight—
Dankwart or Hagen or any other knight
Of our great king—however they fought for glory,
What Sigfrid did alone was quite another story.

229 In battle they accounted for many slain.
And yet I doubt if anyone could explain
The wonders Sigfrid did when he rode in.
He fashioned women's grief from what he did to their kin.

230 Many sweethearts fell and never rose.
So loud upon their helmets were his blows
That they brought forth from wounds the flowing blood.
He excels in every point—a gallant man and good.

231 Much as Ortwin of Metz accomplished there
(For if his sword could reach them it was rare
To find them whole—and mostly they were dead!)
Still your brother Gernot gave them more to dread—

232   The worst that could befall in battle-hue.
One must give these excellent men their due:
Such the work of our proud Burgundian nation
That not a hint of shame could touch their reputation!

233   Men of the Rhineland emptied saddles bare
Before their hands, as swords flashed in the air
And the field resounded. So hard they rode and fought
That what their foes had started it were better they had not.

234   Men of Trony inflicted bitter losses
When the armies met (and both supporting forces).
Brave Hagen himself accounted for many killed—
Feats with which reports to Burgundy are filled.

235   Sindold, Hunold, Gernot's warriors there,
And Rumold, fought so well that Liudeger
Had something to be forever sorry for:
His message to your kinsmen here, declaring war.

236   The noblest fight that anywhere has been
Or, first and last, ever men have seen—
This was the willing work of Sigfrid's hand.
And he brings mighty hostages to Gunther's land,

237   Conquered in valor by this handsome knight—
For Liudegast the king a bitter plight,
And for his Saxon brother Liudeger.
Now hear, most noble, gracious queen, the news I bear.

238   Sigfrid captured them both! Never before
Have so many come as hostages of war
To Burgundy as by his work at present
Approach the Rhine." For her, no news could be more pleasant.

239   "We bring five hundred men or more, my lady,
All unhurt. Of the badly wounded eighty
Who come on blood-red stretchers to our land,
Most of them struck down by valiant Sigfrid's hand.

240   Those who sent to the Rhine their arrogant call
To battle now must be in Gunther's thrall,
And carried back to this land, a joy to their foes."
The tidings made her bright skin blossom like a rose,

241   Her lovely face all red with blushing to hear
That out of combat in good health and cheer

Gallant Sigfrid had come, her fine young knight.
She also rejoiced for her kinsmen—which was only right.

242 Fair Kriemhild said, "You've brought good news to me,
And you shall have rich clothes as herald's fee
And ten marks of gold I'll have them get."
(How nice when good news puts a lady in your debt!)

243 They gave him his reward, his gold and clothes.
To the windows many lovely maidens rose,
To watch the road below—there to see
Riding in all their pride the knights of Burgundy.

244 Sound of limb or wounded, on they came,
To hear their kinsmen's welcome—joy without shame.
The king rode out to them with a cheerful face,
His trouble and pain had ended and joy was in their place.

245 He greeted his foreign knights like his own force—
For a mighty king no other fitting course
Than generous thanks for those who came to his aid,
For the victory they had won and the merit they displayed.

246 Gunther asked for news of kin and friend:
Who in this campaign had met his end.
Their losses were only sixty. An end of sorrow
Had to come for these, as still with the death of a hero.

247 Uninjured men brought back their shields, all shattered,
To Gunther's land, and helmets badly battered.
Before the royal hall the troops dismounted,
And there the cheerful noise of welcoming resounded.

248 They took the knights to town and found them quarters—
Good treatment for his guests, by the king's orders,
And for the wounded shelter, care, and rest.
In the treatment of his foes his merit was manifest.

249 "I offer you welcome," he said to Liudegast.
"Much that through your doing I have lost
Will now be repaid if my good luck holds through.
For all my friends' support may God give them their due."

250 "You give them thanks," said Liudeger. "Well you may!
More noble hostages never fell to the sway
Of any king. For honorable custody
We'll pay you well—and mercy to your enemy."

251   "On your parole I'll let you both go free
Provided that my foes stay here with me,
And not without permission leave my land;
On this I want some pledge." And Liudeger gave his hand.

252   They found them all a comfortable place to rest
And good beds for the wounded. Meanwhile they pressed
On those who were well excellent wine and mead,
Until they were a joyous gathering indeed.

253   They stored away their shields, all hacked in battle,
And ordered hidden many a bloody saddle—
No lack of these!—that women might not weep.
Good knights arrived from that campaign in need of sleep.

254   What full and generous service the king bestowed
On all his guests! His country overflowed
With friends and strangers. He ordered the finest care
For the badly wounded. All their pride was vanished in air.

255   Physicians there were given rewards untold:
Silver without a scale, and shining gold,
To heal the heroes after battle stress.
The king gave proof to all his guests of his largess.

256   Those who had a journey home in mind
They begged, as one does friends, to stay behind.
The king took counsel now on how to pay
The men who had done his will in such a glorious way.

257   And Gernot said, "We ought to let them ride.
In six weeks' time—so have them notified—
They shall return again for a festival.
Many who now lie wounded will then be healed and well."

258   Then Sigfrid too requested leave to go.
When Gunther heard that he'd decided so,
He asked that he remain, most courteously.
(Except for his sister's sake, this would never be.)

259   Too high in wealth and power to take reward,
He well deserved the king's most fond regard—
Shared by all his kin who had been witness
To what occurred in battle through his strength and fitness.

260   For his fair lady's sake he thought to stay,
On chance of seeing her—which he would one day.

(He met the maiden, as he had hoped and planned;
And afterward rode happily to Sigmund's land.)

261   The king arranged full tests of chivalry,
Which youthful knights pursued most willingly.
Meanwhile he ordered seats upon the strand
For those who were to come to Worms in Burgundy land.

262   At this same time, when all the guests were due,
The news had come to lovely Kriemhild too
That for his friends the king had planned a fete,
And lovely women now were busy early and late,

263   Preparing the clothes and headdress they would wear.
Great Uta also heard the tidings there
Of the warriors soon to come—men proud and bold.
Lavish clothes were taken from the garment fold.

264   For sake of her children Uta ordered made
Clothes in which they all would be arrayed—
Ladies, maids, and knights of Burgundy—
And fashioned for the strangers elegant livery.

FIFTH ADVENTURE
How Sigfrid First Saw Kriemhild

265   To the Rhine they rode, guests on their eager way
To the tourney—you could see them every day.
Out of love for the king they gathered there.
Many were given steeds, and splendid things to wear.

266   Seats were all set up in preparation
For the high and the mighty who came to the celebration—
No less than thirty-two princes, they say. Meanwhile,
Fair ladies planned ahead—a rivalry of style.

267   Young Giselher had no lack of things to do,
He and Gernot (with each his retinue),
Greeting all the guests, strangers and friends—
The sort of generous welcome chivalry extends.

268   Saddles the red of gold, shields ornate,
And clothes of splendor they brought with them to the fete,
These guests who came to the land along the Rhine.
Many among the injured soon were looking fine!

269   And those who lay in bed and those who bore
The pain of wounds forgot how close was the door
Of bitter death. People soon had ceased
To pity the injured and ill—for joy at the coming feast.

270   They thought of times they'd have as guest or host.
Delight was boundless, joy was uppermost
In all their hearts, overflowing on every hand.
Great was the happiness that came on Gunther's land.

271   The morning of Pentecost, from every door
They poured, in elegant dress, five thousand or more—
Stalwart warriors bound for the festive scene.
Each vied to show the other what sport and pleasure mean.

272   The host was not a fool. He long had known
How fond of his sister Netherland's lord had grown,
Though he had never seen the fair princess,
Whose beauty, they said, excelled all other loveliness.

273   His vassal Ortwin spoke to the king. He cried,
"If you would earn in full the honor and pride
That go with this feast, let the beautiful girls appear,
Who to our greater glory live in Burgundy here.

274   What is a man's delight, to still his care,
If not a pretty girl or a lady fair?
So let your sister come before your guests."
For heroes' hearts he spoke. "Agreed as he suggests!"

275   Thus the king replied, "So be it done."
The news they heard delighted everyone.
To Uta, and her comely daughter too,
Went word to come to court, with maids of her retinue.

276   They chose from wardrobes clothes of the finest kind,
All the noble garments they could find;
Bracelets, too, with silk-and-golden chains,
And all the maidens dressed and primped with endless pains.

277   Every novice knight was out to make
A fine impression for the ladies' sake—
He wouldn't take a kingdom for his chances.
Women he'd never met he watched with eager glances.

278   As escort for his sister Gunther sent
A hundred men or more. On service bound they went,

Kin of his and hers, sword in hand.
They were the vassal lords in liege of Burgundian land.

279   Uta also came, Her Majesty.
In many lovely ladies' company,
All richly dressed—perhaps a hundred or more.
Charming maidens followed, her daughter walked before.

280   From ladies' chambers people saw them go.
Among the heroes moved a surge and flow,
A pressing forward in the hope, meanwhile,
If luck was kind to them, they'd see their princess smile.

281   She came in loveliness, as does the dawn
From somber clouds. His many cares were gone,
Who bore her in his heart (as long he'd done).
She stood before him now, his fair and radiant one.

282   Bright from her garments shone the precious stones,
And sweet the cast of her flesh, its rose-red tones.
No man who lived, however prone to error,
Could say that in all this world he had seen a woman fairer.

283   As the clear moon stands alone in starry skies,
Its image bright on clouds, in similar wise
She stood before these comely women then,
To lift with pleasure the hearts of many handsome men.

284   Chamberlains, resplendent, walked in advance,
But dashing knights would not give up their chance
Of pushing out in front where they might gain
A glimpse of the charming princess—Sigfrid's pleasure and pain.

285   He thought to himself, "What ever made it seem
That I could hope to love you? A childish dream!
But if I should give you up, I'd rather be dead."
Reflecting thus, he swiftly paled and then blushed red.

286   The handsome son of Sigmund, standing there,
Was like a portrait done with artful care
By a master, on a parchment page,
The fairest knight, they say, of this or any age.

287   The lords in escort bade a path be made
For the ladies. Falling back, the knights obeyed,
Their eager hearts the cause of much delight.
What lovely women they saw! How gracious, how polite!

288   Lord Gernot spoke, "He who kindly made
Offer of service now should be repaid,
Dear brother, in equal fashion, before the eyes
Of all these knights. This I'm not ashamed to advise.

289   Have Sigfrid come before my sister in state
That she may greet him—our profit will be great.
Let her who has never greeted knight extend
Her welcome to him, and we have won our handsome
    friend."

290   Kin of the royal host went out to bring
The news to Sigfrid. "As honor from the king,"
They said, "you shall come to court and there receive
Your welcome from his sister, by the royal leave."

291   His heart was lifted up, his soul was stirred
With pleasure free of pain, as now he heard
That he should see the princess, Uta's child,
She welcomed him—with tact and sweetness
    reconciled.

292   The proud knight stood before her. Color broke
Like flame upon his face. The maiden spoke,
"Sir Sigfrid, here be welcome, noble knight!"
Her greeting left his spirits high; his heart was bright.

293   Attentively he bowed; she clasped his hand.
How charmingly the young lord took his stand
Beside the lovely lady. Tenderly
They glanced at one another—they meant no one to see.

294   Whether lovingly, in heart's devotion,
White hand was pressed, I have no notion,
But I cannot believe it otherwise:
She never tried to hide her love from Sigfrid's eyes.

295   These were the days of May, the time of summer.
His heart would never hold a feeling warmer
Than the joy he felt as now he walked
With her he hoped to win, their two hands interlocked.

296   And many a warrior thought, "That I could stand—
His sort of luck—to wander hand in hand
With her the way he does, as I have seen—
Or sleep with her." (No knight has better served a queen.)

297 Whatever land the guests might call their own,
Their eyes were fixed on this one pair alone.
They gave her leave to kiss the handsome knight,
And all this world had never brought him such delight.

298 The King of Denmark cried on seeing this:
"Men have paid with life and limb for that kiss,
As well I know, for Sigfrid's hand is clever.
God keep him out of my domains henceforth forever."

299 And now on every side they cleared the road
For her to the church. Respectfully they strode,
The knights who walked as escort on the way.
But here her gallant lord was forced to turn away.

300 She went to the minster then, in company
Of many women, adorned in such degree
That many high-flown hopes were left forlorn.
To many a knight she seemed for his eyes' own pleasure
born.

301 Sigfrid could hardly wait till mass was through.
He owed eternal thanks that she was true
In her affection for him—she whose image
Filled his heart—to whom in turn he rendered homage.

302 When, like him, she left the minster door,
They summoned the valiant lord to come before
The lovely princess again. She spoke her thanks
For the splendid way he fought at the head of her brothers'
ranks.

303 "Sir Sigfrid, God reward you. You have earned
The loyal trust of your men, as I have learned
From their ungrudging words." With this he cast
A tender glance at her, and so replied at last:

304 "I mean to serve them always, nor even sleep
At evening, Lady Kriemhild, unless I keep
My deeds to their desire, and never waver
All my life. This I do in hope of your favor."

305 The space of twelve whole days, from start to end,
They saw the gracious maid with her warrior friend,
Whenever before the eyes of all her kin
She went to court—all for the love she held him in.

306   And all this time the joys and robust sounds,
The great delight of jousting filled the grounds
And palace of Gunther. Valiant men were there,
But Ortwin and Hagen performed feats beyond compare.

307   What anyone would do, they were ready for.
In generous measure, too, these men of war.
They made themselves well-known on every hand
Among the many guests—to the glory of Gunther's land.

308   Wounded men were seen to rise and start
Off to the games, eager to take their part,
To feel the shock on their shields and shoot the spear.
No lack of those to help them—a mighty throng was here.

309   On the festive day, the host decreed
His guests be royally fed, for he had freed
His name of all reproach that strikes a king.
A friend among his guests he walked, in welcoming.

310   He spoke, "O noble knights, before you leave,
Accept the gifts I offer. I would grieve
If you should turn them down, for I am true
In this my purpose: to share my worldly goods with you."

311   The men of Denmark answered, "Sir, once more
Before we journey home, we all implore
A lasting peace, our need for which is plain:
Your men have cost us many friends—our battle-slain."

312   The Saxon chief and Liudegast were healed
From all the wounds they suffered in the field,
But not a few were dead, and left behind.
Now Gunther went to Sigfrid and bade him speak his mind:

313   He asked, "Advise me what you think is best.
Our foes would leave tomorrow. They request
A guarantee of lasting peace from me.
Sigfrid, what do you think the wisest course would be?

314   I'll tell you now the terms they swear to keep.
They'll give me all the gold that they can heap
On five hundred horses, if I accede
To letting them go in peace." "A most unworthy deed,"

315   His stalwart guest replied. "Let them rather
Go from here at once, with no more bother,

And take the two kings' pledge that never again
Will hostile warriors dare encroach on your domain."

316   "I'll do as you advise." So the foe was told,
After their talk: "No one wants your gold."
And now at home families longed once more
To see their men, and they who fought were tired of war.

317   Shields were brought and in them gold was laid.
He gave in plenty to his friends, unweighed.
Five hundred marks or so—to many, more.
(Gunther had the counsel of Gernot on this score.)

318   As they desired, so now they took their leave.
They went to Lady Kriemhild to receive
Her word of parting, or to Uta the queen.
Finer granting of leave the world has never seen.

319   Lodgings were empty as they rode away
But many noble men were still to stay:
King and kin, of perfect breeding all,
Who daily came to Kriemhild to pay her formal call.

320   Sigfrid, too, was ready to depart—
Renouncing the hopeful wishes of his heart.
But now the king found out how matters lay,
And youthful Giselher persuaded him to stay:

321   "Where are you riding, Sigfrid, proud as ever?
Stay with our warriors here—do me this favor.
Stay with Gunther the king and his retinue.
There are beautiful women here, as we'll gladly prove to you."

322   Then Sigfrid said, "Leave our mounts behind!
I was about to ride—I've changed my mind.
Take back our shields, though we were homeward bound,
Giselher, with his loyal heart, has won me around."

323   So he remained by friends' affection there.
Not in all the world, not anywhere,
Would life be sweeter. And here the reason lay:
That he could see the lovely princess every day.

324   In pleasure he passed the time with them, detained
By her great beauty there, and never pained
But by his love, through which he was sadly tried—
And for which later, wretchedly, the brave man died.

SIXTH ADVENTURE
How Gunther Went to Iceland in Quest of Brunhild

325   Along the Rhine was heard a new report
     Of lovely maidens, filling Gunther's heart
     With hope of wooing one to be his bride,
     And lifting up his knightly mind with joy and pride.

326   They said there was a queen beyond the sea.
     Her like was never known, of such degree
     Her beauty was, her strength without a peer.
     She challenged every suitor to contest with the spear.

327   In two more tests she threw the heavy stone
     And made a great leap after. Not one alone
     Had he to win, but all; and if instead
     The suitor failed a single trial, he lost his head.

328   (Precisely this had many times occurred.)
     Such is the news our handsome knight had heard.
     He turned his thoughts to winning her as bride,
     And all for this, in time, many a warrior died.

329   The lord of the Rhineland spoke, "Down to the sea
     To Brunhild I will go, whatever the cost may be,
     And for her love I will risk my very life.
     Rather dead than never to have her as my wife."

330   "I advise against it," Sigfrid warned.
     "This queen is a thing of terror. Many have mourned
     The price they paid to sue for her love and hand.
     So you might well give up this journey you have planned."

331   "I'll tell you what to do," Lord Hagen spoke.
     "Ask that Sigfrid share with you the yoke
     Of this great burden. I think you'll find it pays,
     Since he seems to know so much of Brunhild's ways."

332   Then Gunther spoke, "My Lord, will you then aid
     My wooing of her? If so, and if the maid
     I love becomes my lover, I will stake
     My honor and my life for noble Sigfrid's sake."

333   In answer Sigfrid, Sigmund's son, replied,
     "Give me your sister then, to be my bride,

And I will do it. The princess, gracious and noble—
She is the sole reward I want for all my trouble."

334   "I give you my word and hand," Gunther swore,
"If beautiful Brunhild comes to the Rhenish shore,
Then I will give my sister to be your wife,
And you may live with her for the whole of your happy life."

335   On that the noble warriors took their oath.
Far more trouble lay ahead for both
Before they brought the lady back to the Rhine—
Men of highest valor, plagued by fate's design.

336   Sigfrid had to take the Magic Cloak,
The same that he had gained when once he broke
The power of Alberich the dwarf in fearful battle.
(They all prepared for the journey, men of proven mettle.)

337   When Sigfrid had the magic mantle on
His power was great enough! The cape alone
Brought the strength of twelve to his renewing.
And thus he set his subtle skill to the great queen's wooing.

338   This cloak was also made in such a fashion
That any man, secure from mortal vision
Could in it do whatever things he chose.
And thus he won Brunhild—and a multitude of woes!

339   "Now tell me, Sigfrid, sir, before we start,
Should we take knights to Brunhild's land, as part
Of our good name and fame on this trip to sea?
Thirty thousand we can have and readily."

340   "Whatever troops we take," was his reply,
"So fearsome is the queen, that they would die
At the mercy of her pride. But I submit,
Brave lord, there is a better way of doing it.

341   Go down the Rhine like knights adventure bound—
I'll name you the only lords that need be found,
Four in all, to go with us to sea,
And we shall win the queen, whatever else may be.

342   I shall be one, the second one is you.
Let Hagen be the third. And Dankwart too—

That valiant man shall be the fourth to go.
In war with us, a thousand men won't stand a show."

343   "Another thing I'd like to have you say
Before we leave (I'd gladly be on our way!):
What sort of clothing we should take to wear
Before Brunhild. Tell me what is proper there."

344   "The best of clothes that can be found they wear
Always in Brunhild's land. Let us take care,
Therefore, to let her see us richly dressed,
That when they tell of us we need not be distressed."

345   Said the noble knight, "Then I shall go and see
If I can get my mother to agree
To set her maids at work on such array
That we may go before this queen in a fitting way."

346   Said of Hagen of Trony (his words bespoke refinement):
"Why do you give your mother this assignment?
Let your sister know what you intend.
Your trip will profit from the help that she can lend."

347   Word was sent to his sister they would call—
Sigfrid and he—to see her. But first of all
The lovely maiden dressed in perfect taste,
Not displeased at the gallant visitors she faced.

348   Suitably adorned was all her court.
The two princes came. At this report,
She rose from her chair, in perfect form and breeding,
And went to give her noble guest and brother greeting.

349   She spoke, "I welcome my brother and his friend,
And I am curious, what does this portend,
Your visit here at court? So let me hear,
My great and gentle lords, how both of you may fare."

350   Gunther spoke, "My lady, you shall know.
We face with pride and courage the risk of woe.
Far in foreign lands on chivalry
We ride and must be dressed for the journey splendidly."

351   The princess said, "Sit down, my brother dear.
Who are these women—I do so want to hear—
Whose love you seek in other monarchs' lands?"
With this the lady took the lucky heroes' hands.

352   She walked with them back to her former seat,
       On a couch with splendid pillows, all complete
       With pictures, rich in gold, a lovely thing.
       They found good entertainment, here in the women's wing.

353   Friendly glances and sweet meeting of the eyes
       Between the couple then—and no surprise!
       Her image was in his heart; much as his life
       Was she to him, this lovely woman, soon his wife.

354   The mighty king then spoke, "Without your aid,
       Sister dear, our trip could not be made.
       We go to Brunhild's land, in search of pleasure;
       Before these ladies we need clothes of richest measure."

355   "Believe me, dearest brother," she replied,
       "My fullest help shall never be denied,
       If in any way it may avail you,
       And I should be displeased if any one should fail you.

356   Do not ask, hesitant or fearing,
       Command of me, in high and noble bearing!
       Whatever you wish of me, I shall do,"
       This the charming princess added, "and gladly, too."

357   "Dear sister, we must have fine clothes to wear.
       Let preparations be in your gracious care.
       Your maids must do their work with never a slip
       In fit and good appearance. Our hearts are set on this trip."

358   The princess replied, "Remember just one thing.
       I have the silk; your men, however must bring
       Jewels to us in their shields. That's all we need
       To make the clothes you want." Gunther and Sigfrid agreed.

359   "And who are the friends," she asked, "who go with you,
       For whom such splendid courtly dress is due?"
       Gunther answered, "I am one of four.
       Two vassals, Dankwart and Hagen, go with us—no more.

360   And take good note, my lady, of what I say.
       The four of us must have, for every day
       Of four, three changes of clothes, in perfect taste,
       Lest when we leave Brunhild's land we go disgraced."

361   The lords now said good-bye. To the separate hall
       Where the women lived, the queen sent out a call

For thirty maids in waiting, every one
Renowned for special skill whenever such work was done.

362   Silks from Arabia, white as the winter snows,
And green from Zazamanc, as the clover grows—
Into such fabric they worked the precious stone,
For lovely clothes, cut by the fair princess alone.

363   A picture strange to see: on the undersides
A marvelous lining made of otter hides.
This they covered with silk (it is worn that way).
Now listen to the wonder of their bright array.

364   Silks from the lands of Morocco and Libya, the best
That ever any king or queen possessed,
In lavish stock: thus Kriemhild, for her part,
Made known to all the sweet affection of her heart.

365   With the lofty purpose of their trip now sure,
Ermine trim alone seemed much too poor,
Hence the woolen cover, black as coal—
Fitting still for heroes in their festive role.

366   On a ground of Arabian gold the brilliant light
Of jewels played. The cost was nothing slight
In women's work—and seven weeks all spent,
But now it was done and with it, too, their armament.

367   And while the women toiled, a sturdy ship
Was swiftly in the building, to speed their trip
Upon the Rhine, and take them down to the sea.
What weariness for women of noble pedigree!

368   But now they could tell the knights that what they
       willed
In the way of elegant clothes was all fulfilled,
Ready for them to wear. They did not choose
To tarry by the Rhine, once they had heard this news.

369   To friends went out a message, to inquire
If they would come and view their new attire—
And say if they thought the fit too short or long.
The ladies earned their thanks, their friends found nothing
       wrong.

370   And everyone who saw must needs agree
No better clothes in this world did he ever see.

So they could wear them there at court with pride—
The best that knights have ever owned, no one denied.

371   Great was the gratitude that they expressed.
But now in courtly style they made request
That the ladies grant them leave, these merry peers,
And eyes that once were bright were moist and sad with tears.

372   Kriemhild said, "You still could stay, dear brother
(I'd think it wise), and seek the hand of another.
Your life would not be wagered in the try.
You'll surely find as noble a wife—and nearer by."

373   I think their hearts foretold what the future kept.
No matter what was said, the women wept,
Until the gold upon their breasts was flecked
And tarnished by the tears that fell from their eyes unchecked.

374   The princess said, "Sir Sigfrid, I commend
My brother to your care. Your favor attend
His ways in Brunhild's land, lest ill ensue."
Which, on Kriemhild's hand, he boldly swore to do.

375   "So long as I shall live," the warrior said,
"From your heart, my lady, banish dread!
I shall bring him back, as surely as I have vowed,
In safety to the Rhine," The lovely maiden bowed.

376   Down to the beach they carried their shields of gold,
And took along their clothes. Their men they told
To bring the horses, for they were ready to ride.
Great was the weeping then, as lovely women cried.

377   Beautiful damsels stood at the windows watching.
The sails of the ship were moved by a strong breeze catching.
The proud companions now put out from land
And royal Gunther spoke, "Who shall take command?"

378   "I will," Sigfrid said, "since I can guide
Your way across the sea. Be satisfied,
My friends, I know the way by water there."
And so they left from Burgundy, without a care.

379   Sigfrid took a pole, with it began
To shove away from the shore; a sturdy man;
And Gunther the bold himself took up an oar,
Off from the land they went, these valiant men of war.

380 They had good food with them, and excellent wine.
The best that they could find along the Rhine.
Their horses were quartered well, in a decent stall,
The ship rode an even keel, they had no trouble at all.

381 The powerful stays of their sails were stretched out tight.
They had covered twenty leagues before the night,
Down with a favorable wind, down to the sea.
(From all of their haughty labor, grief and misery!)

382 Twelve mornings after that, so goes the tale,
The wind had borne them far, until their sail
Was in sight of Isenstein, in Brunhild's realm
(Familiar only to the hero at the helm).

383 When royal Gunther saw so many towers,
And the size of the place, he cried, "Good friends
   of ours,
Tell us, if you know, whose might they be,
All these many towers, the splendid land we see?"

384 Sigfrid replied, "I know, for the truth is plain.
This is Brunhild's people, her domain,
And the fortress Isenstein, as you've heard me say.
There are lovely women there—you'll see this very day!

385 And here is some advice I have for you:
All of you say the same and carry it through.
(This I think is best.) If we are seen
By her today, take care how we approach the queen.

386 Before her court and the lovely lady's throne,
No two reports, my sirs, but this alone:
That Gunther is my lord, and I am one
Among his many vassals, and what he wills is done."

387 He bade them swear to this, and they complied.
And not a one that failed, for all their pride.
They spoke as he desired, when Gunther was bid
Before the lovely Brunhild, and it was well they did!

388 "Not so much for love of you I take
This step, as for your lovely sister's sake,
Who is like my soul to me, my very life.
For this I gladly serve: that she should be my wife."

SEVENTH ADVENTURE

How Gunther Won Brunhild

389   Meanwhile their ship had come so close to land
The king could see the fairest maidens stand
Far above in the windows of the city—
But none he recognized, which seemed to him a pity.

390   He turned to question Sigfrid his companion:
"Who might these maidens be, in your opinion,
Looking down at us on the ocean tide?
Whoever their lord may be, there's spirit there and pride."

391   Noble Sigfrid answered, "Cast a glance,
In secret, among these girls. Given the chance,
Now tell me, which would you choose to be your bride?"
"All right, I shall," bold and eager, Gunther cried.

392   "I see one now, by the window over there,
Dressed in a snow-white dress, of such a rare
And lovely form—my eyes would never err,
If they had the chance to choose, and I would marry her."

393   "The light of your eyes served you well in the choice,
For that is noble Brunhild, the lovely prize
Toward which your heart and mind and will, unceasing,
Urge you." Her very gesture seemed to Gunther pleasing.

394   The queen soon ordered her maids to stand away
From the window ledge: it was not right to stay
Where strangers could stare at them. And they obeyed her.
But we shall also hear of them what they did later.

395   With the strangers in mind, they put their finery on,
Like lovely women always, and were gone
To the narrow windows where, looking through,
They had seen the heroes stand—all this for a better view.

396   But they were only four who came to the land.
Sigfrid led Gunther's horse out on the sand—
Maidens watched from the window as he did it,
Which seemed to Gunther all to his greater fame and credit.

397   He led him by the bridle, the graceful steed,
Big and strong and handsome, of perfect breed.

Royal Gunther rose to the saddle then,
This was Sigfrid's service, soon forgotten again.

398   He went to the ship and brought his horse to land.
No common thing was this, that he should stand
Beside the stirrups of another knight,
And from the windows highborn ladies watched the sight.

399   In perfect harmony the princely pair:
White as the snow the clothes they brought to wear
And of their steeds the same; their shields well made,
From which, as they held them high, the bright reflection
      played;

400   Their saddles studded with jewels; fine and small
The gauge of their martingales. To Brunhild's hall
They came in splendor. Bells of bright red gold
Hung on their saddles. They rode to this land as suits the
      bold,

401   With newly whetted spears and well-made swords
Broad and sharp, held by the handsome lords
So that the point reached down to the very spur.
This fair Brunhild watched, nothing escaping her.

402   With them came Sir Dankwart, and Hagen came,
Their noble vassals, wearing garments the same,
Richly made, in color black as the raven.
Their shields were things of beauty—massive, broad, and
      proven!

403   From India came the splendid jewels fastened
Upon their clothes, which with their moving glistened.
Unguarded they left their craft by the waterside,
And turning toward the castle now, began to ride.

404   Eighty-six towers they saw in all,
Three palaces, and a nobly fashioned hall
Of marble green as the grass, and it was here
That with her lords and ladies dwelt Brunhild the fair.

405   The city was open wide, the gates unlocked,
Toward them quickly Brunhild's vassals walked,
Eager to welcome guests in their mistress' land.
They took their horses in charge, the shield from each one's
      hand.

406   A chamberlain said, "Now give your weapons over,
And your suits of mail." Said Hagen, "That's one favor
We will not do you. We'll keep them close at hand."
Sigfrid answered: "Let me explain how matters stand.

407   That is their custom at court. They let no guest
Carry weapons here. So it is best
To let them take our arms and lay them aside."
Much against his will, Gunther's man complied.

408   Wine was poured for them; the guests were made
To feel at home. At court a bold parade
Of warriors dressed to suit their princely station,
Still the strangers got their share of admiration.

409   The news had been conveyed to Brunhild, the queen,
That unkown men in elegant clothers were seen
Arriving at court, bornc by the ocean tide.
Now the lovely maiden asked of this; she cried:

410   "These men, these strangers, tell me who they are,
Coming all unkown and from afar,
To stand so proudly here within my walls—
And to whose honor and credit this heroes' voyage falls."

411   One of her retinue spoke, "This much I can say:
None have I ever seen until this day—
Except that one among them I can tell
Looks like Sigfrid. Truly I counsel you: welcome him well.

412   The second is a man of such good breeding
That hc would be a king—only needing
Wide lands to rule. Perhaps he really is—
To stand among those men with dignity like his!

413   The third among these men appears so gruff,
And yet in form, my Queen, handsome enough;
Look at those flashing eyes and the angry stare.
I'll wager anything there's a fierce temper there.

414   The youngest of the group is most refined—
His bearing and his breeding seem the kind
We cherish in maidens, such his gentle charm.
Things would go hard with us if he ever came to harm.

415   For all his handsome form and gentle tone,
Many a winsome wife would weep alone

If he ever turned to rage. He seems indeed
A bold and dauntless man, a knight of the noble breed."

416   The queen cried out: "My dress, my battle-gear!
If mighty Sigfrid has made this journey here
With thought of winning my love, he'll pay with his life.
I'm not so afraid of him that I mean to be his wife."

417   Soon the fair Brunhild, in fitting dress,
Came with her beautiful maids, surely no less
Than a hundred in all, fair and handsomely clad.
Here they could see the strangers—at which their hearts
       were glad.

418   As escort for the ladies, Iceland's lords,
Vassals of Brunhild, came, bearing their swords—
Five hundred, and maybe more. Alarmed by that,
The doughty guests arose from the couches where they sat.

419   And now would you like to hear the words that passed,
When Brunhild saw the prince of the Rhine at last?
"Welcome to Iceland, Sigfrid," said the queen,
"And will you tell me, please, what does this voyage
       mean?"

420   "Your gracious favor, Lady, has reversed
The order of your greeting. He is first
Who stands before me here, this noble lord,
My liege—I must decline the honor you accord.

421   Born to the Rhenish throne—what more to say?
And all for the love of you we are here today.
He means to marry you, at any cost.
Reflect on this! My lord will not yield, and you are lost!

422   Gunther is his name, a glorious king.
In all the world he wishes this one thing:
To gain your love. This trip I did not choose,
But that was his command and I could not refuse."

423   "If you are a vassal, and he the one who bears
The crown, the challenge is his. In case he dares
To take it up and wins, I'll be his wife.
But if I vanquish him, all of you lose your life!"

424   Hagen spoke, "Lady, let us see
These might contests. Awesome they must be

Before you hear surrender from Gunther, my king.
For you are the sort of beauty he thinks of marrying."

425 "He shall throw the stone, and jump, and shoot the spear.
Before you answer rashly, let this be clear;
Life and honor both you stand to lose,"
The beautiful woman said. "Think before you choose."

426 Sigfrid said to the king, as he stepped up near,
"Say what you feel like saying. Have no fear
Because of the queen or the hurt you might incur.
I know some tricks to keep you safe enough from her."

427 Said royal Gunther, "Gracious lady, decree
As suits your pleasure. If more—so let it be!
For I shall brave it all for your sweet sake.
I must have you in marriage—for this my life is at stake."

428 Now that Brunhild knew the king's intent,
She told them to hasten the start of the games and sent
To get good armor for the battlefield:
Mail of red gold, and a hard-bossed shield.

429 Here was the silken tunic that she wore
In many battles. No weapon ever tore
Its lovely Libyan wool, carefully made
With light designs in shining woven work and braid.

430 During this time, arrogant taunt and threat
Were the strangers' lot. Dankwart was much upset,
And Hagen worried over Gunther's fate.
They thought: "The good we get from this trip will not be great."

431 Meanwhile crafty Sigfrid walked away,
Unnoticed, back to where their vessel lay,
And took the Mantle from its hiding place,
And quickly slipped it on, so none could see his face.

432 Returned, he found a crowd of knights, who came
To hear the queen decree her lofty game.
He wisely came upon them unaware.
Not a soul could see him, of all the people there.

433 The place for the game was set, the ring was drawn,
Ready for the host of lookers-on—
More than seven hundred referees,
For they would say who won; in armor all of these.

434   Brunhild now had come, weapons in hand,
       As if she meant to conquer some monarch's land—
       In silks with golden brooches fastened in,
       Beneath which gleamed the shining whiteness of her skin.

435   Then came her retinue of knights, to hold
       The mighty breadth of shield, of pure red gold
       With heavy straps as hard as steel and bright,
       Under the guard of which the lovely maid would fight.

436   The enarmes upon her shield were a noble braid,
       With precious stones, green as the grass, inlaid,
       Their many gleams competing with the gold.
       The man who won her love must certainly be bold.

437   People say that, at the boss, her shield
       Was three hands thick, and this the maid could wield!
       A splendid mass of gold and steel so great,
       Four of her chamberlains could hardly bear its weight.

438   When mighty Hagen watched them bring the shield,
       His mood of bitterness was unconcealed:
       "What now, King Gunther? A nice farewell to life!
       This woman you hope to marry is surely the devil's wife!"

439   But listen, too, how ample her attire!
       A tunic of silk from Azagouc, with the fire
       Of many precious stones, whose color shone
       From the rich and noble cloth and the queen who had it on.

440   They also brought the maiden a mighty spear,
       Enormous in size, yet part of the battle gear
       She always used. The stock was heavily made,
       The point was sharp and true, a fearsome cutting blade.

441   I tell you, amazing tales have made the rounds
       About how heavy it was. A hundred pounds
       Of metal alone, they say, went into the spear;
       It was all three men could lift. Great was Gunther's fear.

442   He thought to himself, "Is our whole plan amiss?
       How could the devil in hell get out of this?
       If I were back alive in Burgundy,
       She'd wait a long, long while for any love from me!"

443   Now Hagen's brother spoke, the brave Dankwart:
       "I rue this trip from the bottom of my heart.

They call us knights—is this the way we die,
Here, at the hands of women, under this foreign sky?

444   I'm sorry that I ever came to this land!
But if my brother had his weapons in hand,
And I the use of mine, they'd soon dispense,
All these men of Brunhild's, with some of their insolence.

445   They'd learn to watch their step, take that from me!
This beautiful woman here—before I'd see
My master die, her own life-breath would cease,
Though I had sworn a thousand oaths to keep the peace!"

446   "They'd never stop our getting out of here,"
His brother Hagen said, "if we had the gear
We need when the fighting breaks, and swords at our side.
We'd teach this mighty woman a humbling of her pride!"

447   The noble lady heard what Hagen said.
With a smile about her lips, she turned her head,
And looking back she spoke, "If he feels so brave,
Give them back the armor, the sharp swords they gave."

448   When at the lady's behest they got their swords,
Dankwart flushed with joy. "And now, my lords
We'll take the game as it comes. Since we are armed,"
The valiant warrior cried, "Gunther cannot be harmed,"

449   But Brunhild's strength was clearly an awesome thing.
They brought a heavy stone up to the ring,
A mammoth piece of rock, huge and round.
It took a dozen men to lift it off the ground.

450   She used to throw it after she threw the spear.
The men of Burgundy were filled with fear.
"Great God," said Hagen, "he's chosen his lover well!
She ought to be the cursed devil's bride in hell."

451   Back from her white and gleaming wrist she rolled
Her sleeves, and took her shield in hand to hold,
And lifted up her spear. The games were on.
At the thought of Brunhild's wrath, their confidence was gone.

452   If Sigfrid had not come to Gunther's aid,
The king would have lost his life to the mighty maid.
Now secretly he went and touched his hand.
Sigfrid's strategem left Gunther all unmanned.

453   "What touched me?" Gunther thought. He looked around
And all about him no one to be found!
"It is I, Sigfrid, your loyal friend.
As for the queen, let all your fears be at an end.

454   Hand over now your shield for me to hold
And make a careful note of what you're told.
You go through the motions, the work is mine."
Gunther knew his man; this was a welcome sign.

455   "Keep my trick a secret. Tell no one of it.
The queen shall not increase her fame nor profit
At your expense—which is what she wants to do.
Look how that woman stands undaunted in front of you!"

456   The maiden made her throw, a mighty one,
Against the great new shield that Siglind's son
Held in his hands. As if a wind had chanced
To sweep across the steel, the sparks of fire danced.

457   Clear through the shield the mighty blade-point came,
And over the rings of mail there flashed a flame.
Both of the heroes staggered under the blow—
But for the Magic Cape it would have laid them low.

458   Blood burst from Sigfrid's mouth, but he was swift
In leaping back to the ring, there to lift
The spear she had hurled with force enough to cleave
His shield, and send it back at her with a mighty heave.

459   "I do not want to kill the girl," he thought.
He turned the blade of the spear around and shot,
Shaft first, and straight at her tunic he aimed the throw.
Her coat of mail rang loud with the powerful force of the blow.

460   Out of the rings of mail the fire swirled
Like sparks in the wind. The son of Sigmund hurled
A mighty spear; her power gone, she fell
Beneath the blow. Never would Gunther have done so well.

461   How quickly the fair Brunhild sprang to her feet!
"My compliments, Gunther! The noble lord I greet
Who made that throw." (For so she thought him to be.
But she was tricked at her game by a mightier man than he.)

462   Straight to her place she went, with an angry frown;
High in the air the maiden raised the stone.

She gave it a mighty heave—and how it flew!
Her armor clanging, she jumped after the stone she threw.

463   The stone had traveled twenty yards or so,
and still the jump she made surpassed her throw.
Now the hero Sigfrid walked to the stone.
Gunther hefted it, but Sigfrid threw it alone.

464   Sigfrid was tall and powerfully built. He threw,
And the stone went farther. His jump was farther, too.
His vast skill and cunning made him so strong
That he could make the leap and carry Gunther along.

465   The jump was over, the stone was on the ground,
And none in sight but Gunther, all around.
Beautiful Brunhild flashed an angry red:
Except for Sigfrid's feat, Gunther would be dead.

466   Now that she saw him standing safe and sound
At the end of the ring, she shouted, "Gather 'round,
Kin of mine, men of my retinue,
You shall be in liege to Gunther, all of you."

467   And all the warriors laid their weapons down,
And knelt in obeisance to the Burgundian crown
Of Gunther the mighty, thinking the while, of course,
That he had won the contest by his own sheer force.

468   He greeted her graciously, like a perfect knight.
She placed her hand in his, granting the right
Of command to him and giving him full domain—
Much to the joy of Hagen, his great and valiant thane.

469   She asked the noble king to come with her
Into the palace, this time to confer
Upon the warriors services multiplied
(Which Dankwart and Hagen had to accept and be satisfied).

470   Sigfrid was not the least ingenious of men.
He took his mantle back to store it again.,
And then returned where all the women sat,
And asked the king a question (a wise precaution, that):

471   "What do you wait for, sir? Why do we need
Delay these many games the queen decreed?
Let's see what kind they are!"—all this a show
He cunningly put on, as if he didn't know.

472 The queen inquired, "How could it possibly be,
Sigfrid, my lord, that you should fail to see
The victory which the hand of Gunther gained?"
Hagen of Burgundy it was who thus explained:

473 "True, my lady, by some unhappy slip
Our good companion here was down at the ship
When the lord of all the Rhineland conquered you,"
Gunther's man went on, "and so he never knew."

474 "I'm glad to hear that news," Sigfrid cried.
"So now at last someone has leveled your pride;
A mortal man has proved he could best you. Fine!
And now, my noble lady, follow us back to the Rhine!"

475 The fair maid answered, "Not yet! Before I go,
All my kin and all my men must know.
I cannot lightly leave my native land;
First I must have my friends and family close at hand."

476 So out on every path her heralds flew
Till all her troops, her kith and kin all knew
That they were summoned to court without delay.
For them she ordered splendid clothing given away.

477 And every day they came, from dawn to late,
Down to Brunhild's castle, like streams in spate.
"Hello," said Hagen of Trony, "what have we here?
This waiting for Brunhild's men is apt to cost us dear.

478 What if they now descend on us in force—
(We don't know what she has in mind, of course,
What if she's mad enough to plot our death?)
Then an evil day for us was the day she first drew breath!"

479 Stalwart Sigfrid said, "Leave this to me,
The thing you fear will never come to be,
For I shall bring you help, to Iceland here,
Knights you have never seen, men who have no peer.

480 Now I shall go and do not ask me where.
Meanwhile your honor stands in God's good care.
I'll not be long. You'll have a thousand men,
The finest fighters I know, when I come back again."

481 "Just so you aren't too long!" replied the king.
"We're duly grateful for the help you bring."

"I shall be back in hardly more than a day,
Tell Brunhild that it was you who sent me away."

EIGHTH ADVENTURE

How Sigfrid Went to Get the Nibelung Warriors

482   Sigfrid walked to a gate by the waterside,
Wearing his magic cape. There he spied
A boat and, boarding secretly, was gone.
As though a swift breeze blew, he pushed the vessel on.

483   No one saw the pilot. The boat moved off
By Sigfrid's strength alone—great enough
To make it seem there blew some special wind.
But no, this was the work of the son of fair Siglind.

484   In what remained of day and one brief night
He reached the land he sought, so great his might—
A trip of a hundred miles and even more.
These were the Nibelungs, here was his treasure-store.

485   All alone he landed on an isle,
Gaily moored and tied his boat meanwhile,
And walked ahead to a castle on a hill,
And sought for lodging there, like tired travelers still.

486   He came before the gate. They had it locked,
A guard of their good name, and so he knocked,
Unknown, upon the door. The one he tried
He found was guarded well. A giant stood inside,

487   The guardian of the castle. Always near,
In readiness, he kept his battle gear.
"Who's beating on the door like that?" he cried.
Sigfrid changed his voice and waited there outside.

488   "A wandering knight," he said, "adventure-bound.
And any man who'd rather lie around
And take his ease today—I'll stir him up!
Open the gate!" It vexed the guard that he would not stop.

489   That giant now had put his armor on,
His helmet on his head, and swiftly drawn
His heavy shield. He opened wide the gate,
Rushing out at Sigfrid, fierce and full of hate.

490   How dare he come and wake so many men?
And from his hand the blows descended then,
Like rain. The splendid stranger parried back.
The giant warder used an iron mace to hack

491   His shield-rim off. Thus was the hero harried.
The chance of dying even had him worried,
Since his giant gateman fought so hard,
And yet, as master, he was proud of such a guard!

492   They struggled so, the castle echoed 'round
And in the Nibelungs' hall they heard the sound.
Sigfrid won, and tied him foot and hand.
The news of it soon spread through all the Nibelung land.

493   Far across the hill the fearful clash
Had roused up Alberich the dwarf, wild and rash.
He put his armor on, ran and found
The noble stranger there, the giant warder bound.

494   The dwarf was fierce, and anything but frail.
He had his helmet on, his coat of mail,
And in his hand, all made of gold, a knout.
In search of Lord Sigfrid he boldly sallied out.

495   This knout had seven iron-knotted bands.
The shield before courageous Sigfrid's hands
He struck so violently it smashed apart.
Fear for his very life laid hold on the stranger's heart.

496   Sigfrid threw aside his broken shield
And sheathed his long blade, which he would not wield
To kill his chamberlain; and thus restrained,
Preserved his perfect breeding, as worthy knights are trained.

497   He ran at Alberich with those hands men feared,
And grabbed the grey-haired fellow by his beard,
And brought him up so short that Alberich screamed—
A hero's bringing-up, and painful, so it seemed!

498   Alberich cried aloud, "Let me live!
If my oath of bondage were free to give
To any but the master I swore to cherish"—
Craftily he spoke—"I'd be yours before I'd perish."

499   Sigfrid bound the dwarf, like the giant before.
The knight's great power left him hurt and sore.

The dwarf inquired, "What's your name, pray tell?"
He said, "My name is Sigfrid. I thought you knew me well."

500   The dwarf replied, "That is good news to hear!
Your warrior's handiwork has made it clear
That you have every right to rule this land.
Only let me live—I'll do what you command."

501   Sigfrid answered, "Quickly go and call
A thousand Nibelung knights, the best of all,
And have these men report to me today."
What he wished them for, no one heard him say.

502   The giant and the dwarf he let go free.
Alberich ran where he knew the knights would be,
Anxiously woke the Nibelung retinue:
He cried, "Get up, you men, Sigfrid summons you!"

503   They leaped from bed, a thousand of the best,
Eagerly prepared, and quickly dressed,
And hurried where they found Lord Sigfrid waiting.
Then, in words and actions, came a handsome greeting.

504   Candles were lit and spiced wine was poured.
For such a swift response he gave reward
Of thanks to all. "You and I shall go,"
He said, "across the sea." And who would answer no?

505   Thirty hundred knights had come in all
Of whom a thousand men received the call.
To these—the best—they carried sword and helm,
For he was about to lead them back to Brunhild's realm.

506   "At court, my lords—this much I'll tell you here—
Have on your finest clothes when you appear.
Many charming girls must see us there,
And so provide yourselves with splendid things to wear."

507   By early morning, men were journey-bound.
Bold companions these, that Sigfrid found.
They took the finest clothes, and steeds to ride.
They came to Brunhild's land in full chivalric pride.

508   Winsome maidens lined the parapet.
"Does anyone recognize these travelers yet?"
The queen inquired. "They ride the waterflow,
And the sails they fly are rich, whiter than any snow."

509   Replied the king of the Rhine, "Those are my men!
En route, I left them near; I sent again
To bid them come, my queen, and here they are."
All eyes were turned upon the strangers from afar.

510   There was Sigfrid standing at the bow
In splendid dress, with many men, and now
The queen inquired: "Say what course to choose:
To greet these guests, my lord, or silently refuse?"

511   "Go out to meet them on the palace ground,
That they may know what welcome they have found,"
The king replied. She did as Gunther told;
She greeted all the rest; to Sigfrid she was cold.

512   They found them rooms and put their things aside.
So many strangers came—there seemed a tide
Of pushing crowds, wherever they might be.
But now the knights would leave for home and Burgundy.

513   "All thanks to any man who might divide
My store of gold and silver," Brunhild cried,
"Among my guests and his—so much is there."
Answered Dankwart, thane of royal Giselher:

514   "Let me have your keys in custody,
And I'll divide it well, depend on me!
Oh noble queen, let me take any blame."
(He clearly proved that he deserved his generous name.)

515   When Hagen's brother took in charge the key
He gave with a hero's hand, so fast and free
That he who wanted half a pound was given
All a poor man needs to think himself in heaven!

516   Times untold, he offered a hundred pounds—
Or more; and many left the palace grounds
In better clothes than they had ever possessed.
This the queen found out, and she was much distressed.

517   She cried, "My lord, this goes a bit too far.
The way your steward gives, what clothes there are
Will all be gone, my gold—he will have spent it!
My thanks to any person who can now prevent it.

518   He must assume I've sent for Death to come,
Such gifts he gives. I'd thought of keeping some,

And spending what my father left to me."
(No queen's steward could match his generosity!)

519 Hagen of Trony said, "You should be told
That Gunther has so much in clothes and gold
To give away that we can well afford
To take no single garment out of Brunhild's hoard."

520 Said she, "But let me fill, for my own sake,
Twenty trunks with gold and silk to take
And give away as gifts, from my own hand,
When all of us have reached our goal in Gunther's land."

521 They filled the trunks with jewels—and not a flaw!
Gunther and Hagen laughed at what they saw:
Chamberlains of hers must needs be there,
For she refused to trust the thane of Giselher!

522 The queen now thought to whom to leave her lands:
"This should be confirmed by our two hands,
Before we go." "Bid the man appear
Who seems most fit," he said. "We'll make him regent here."

523 She saw her uncle standing close beside,
High in rank among her kin. She cried,
"I here commend to you my towns and land
Until the whole be ruled by royal Gunther's hand."

524 Two thousand men she chose as company
From all her court, to sail to Burgundy,
Besides the thousand knights from Nibelung land.
Prepared for the journey now, they rode along the strand.

525 Eighty-six matrons she took from here,
Perhaps a hundred maids, in person fair,
They wished to hurry now—no more delay,
The ones they left behind, how full of tears were they!

526 In perfect courtly grace she left her land.
She kissed her friends who waited close at hand.
They took their formal leave and left the shore—
Her father's land to which the queen would come no more.

527 En route they played at every kind of game,
And every pastime known. There also came,
To speed their sail, a fair and steady breeze.
They left the lady's land in joy and pleasant ease.

528   She'd not embrace her lord upon the way—
    Pleasure saved until another day:
    At Worms, the castle, and the festive night—
    Where soon they all would be, in joy and much delight.

NINTH ADVENTURE

How Sigfrid Was Sent to Worms

529   When they had been nine days upon the way
    Lord Hagen spoke, "Hear what I have to say!
    We've sent no one to Worms to tell our story;
    Heralds by now should be in Burgundian territory."

530   Gunther answered, "What you say is true;
    No better man for such a trip than you,
    My friend, so ride ahead to Burgundy!
    Finer herald of our journey could never be."

531   "I'm no good as messenger," Hagen cried.
    "I'll watch the stores and be at the ladies' side,
    Guard their lovely things, and stay at sea
    Until we bring them home to the land of Burgundy.

532   Ask Lord Sigfrid to carry back the news,
    He's more than man enough. Should he refuse
    To make the journey, then politely frame
    Your same request again, in your dear sister's name!"

533   They sent to find him and he came. "And now,"
    Said Gunther, "we are nearing home, somehow
    Word must be dispatched to kin of mine,
    My sister and the queen, that we approach the Rhine.

534   This I ask of you. If you will do
    My bidding, I'll always be obliged to you."
    Sigfrid, stalwart lord, would not agree
    Till urgently the king began to press his plea:

535   "I beg you make this ride for me," he prayed
    "And for my sister's sake, the lovely maid,
    That she may join with me in fair reward."
    When Sigfrid heard these words, he spoke, in full accord:

536   "Anything you ask, I'll undertake,
    And do it gladly, too, for her sweet sake.

Why should I refuse the very one
My heart holds dear? Ask in her name and it is done."

537   "Then to Uta the queen, my mother, say
That on this trip of ours our hearts are gay.
Let my brothers know how we fared.
Seek out our friends as well, and let the news be shared.

538   Let my lovely sister hear from you.
Pledge her my regard and Brunhild's too.
Tell all the court, the vassals in my hire,
To what a perfect end I brought my heart's desire.

539   Tell my cousin Ortwin he shall see
To having places set at Worms for me.
And look up all my other friends and say
Brunhild and I intend to hold a gala day!

540   Tell my sister also, when she hears
My company of guests and comrades nears,
That she shall take good care to greet my lover;
I'll not forget my gratitude for Kriemhild's favor."

541   At once the hero sought, from Brunhild's hands,
The formal leave that etiquette commands,
And from her court as well. He rode to the Rhine—
Never in all the world a herald half so fine!

542   With twenty-four good knights he came to Worms—
Without the king. Reported in these terms,
The news alarmed the court with grief and dread;
They feared their royal lord was left afar and dead.

543   His men dismounted now, their spirits high,
How soon the fine young Giselher came by!
His brother Gernot, too—how quick to shout,
Seeing Sigfrid there, the king nowhere about:

544   "Welcome, Sigfrid! Tell me everything!
Tell me where you left my brother, the king.
Have we been robbed by Brunhild's mighty arm?
If so, her lofty love has brought us fearful harm."

545   "Discard your fears! To you and every friend
The lord I journeyed with bade me extend
His loyal word of greeting. I left him well.
He sent me here as herald, and gave me news to tell.

546 Arrange it any way, but this you must do:
Let me see the queen—your sister, too,
For they must hear this embassy of mine
From Brunhild and the king (both of whom are fine)."

547 "Well," said Giselher, "go pay your call;
The favor you do my sister is far from small.
Gunther's trip has caused her much disquiet.
She'll gladly give you welcome, I swear she'll not deny it!"

548 Sigfrid said, "However I may serve her,
It shall be done in willing faith and fervor.
Now who will tell the ladies I am here?"
They sent the word by Giselher, that handsome peer.

549 And this bold knight announced, when he had seen
His sister and his mother, Uta the queen:
"The prince of Netherland has reached the Rhine,
Dispatched to visit us, by Gunther's own design.

550 Of his condition now he brings report,
So let this lord appear before your court,
For he will tell of Iceland." Still the minds
Of noble ladies weighed with fears of many kinds.

551 They ran to get their clothes and quickly dressed.
And bade the lord appear, with which request,
In joy to see them both, he soon complied.
Noble Kriemhild spoke, in greeting sweetly cried:

552 "Accept our welcome, Sigfrid, master sword!
Where is my brother Gunther, king and lord?
I fear, by Brunhild's mighty power torn
From us and dead! Alas that I was ever born!"

553 "Messenger's reward, I ask no less!"
He said, "You have no cause for such distress,
My ladies, hear! I left him safe and well.
This is the very news they sent me here to tell.

554 He and his love, in warm and kindred meeting,
Send you, noble lady, cordial greeting.
Have an end of tears. They'll soon be here!"
Not in a long, long time had she heard such words of cheer.

555 She wiped her lovely eyes, after her tears,
With a fold of her snow-white hem. She filled his ears

With thanks for the news that he as herald brought;
Her sorrow and her woe were all reduced to naught.

556 She bade him sit, which he was glad to do.
Charmingly she said, "I'd give to you
My gold as herald's pay, but this would be rude
To one so mighty. You'll always have my gratitude."

557 "If I alone were lord of thirty lands
I still should welcome presents from your hands,"
Said he, and the princess spoke: "So be it then,"
And after herald's pay she sent her chamberlain.

558 Two dozen armlets set with jewels she gave
As his reward. His thought was not to save
But give them all away, with none to spare,
To members of her court, in her apartment there.

559 Her mother, in kindly greeting, wished him well.
The knight replied, "There's more I have to tell:
On coming home, one thing that he would ask—
And he will love you much, if you will do this task:

560 Receive them well—for thus he spoke his mind—
These splendid guests of his. Be so kind,
And ride to meet him on the beach by Worms.
This the king required in fair chivalric terms."

561 "I shall," the lady said, "with joy comply.
No favor I can do will I deny;
It shall be done in friendly faith and trust."
And for the pleasure that she felt the lady blushed.

562 What prince's messenger has better fared?
She would have kissed him, too, if she had dared.
He took his leave from the ladies, gallant and bold.
Men of Burgundy went to do as Sigfrid told.

563 Sindold, Hunold, Rumold—all these three
Had very little time for leisure free.
They built the stands at Worms, along the strand;
Among the royal staff was not an idle hand.

564 Ortwin, too, and Gere would not miss
The chance to tell their kin and friends of this—
Inform them of the coming celebration.
Lovely ladies planned for dress and decoration.

565   For honored guests the palace, walls and all,
Was richly hung and trimmed, and Gunther's hall
Redone for the many strangers coming here.
The grand event began upon a note of cheer.

566   They rode the many paths across the land.
Kin of three great kings, at high command
To wait attendance on the crowd that neared.
Out of wardrobes then resplendent garb appeared.

567   Word was passed: men approach, on horse—
Brunhild's train! Excitement ran its course
Through all the gathered mass of Burgundy.
On either hand, what a host of knights, what gallantry!

568   "The maids who join with me in welcoming,"
Said lovely Kriemhild now, "I ask to bring
The finest clothes of all from the garment chests,
That we may gain esteem and praise from all our guests."

569   And now the knights arrived, and men were told
To bring the saddles worked with splendid gold
For ladies at Worms to ride to the river Rhine.
Nowhere has anyone seen harness quite so fine.

570   How bright a flash of gold from the horses shone!
From gleaming reins with jewels fixed thereon,
And golden stepping stools on carpets laid,
Which serving men had brought for each vivacious maid.

571   The noble ladies' mounts, as I said before,
Were ready in the yard, and each one wore
About its chest a silken martingale
As good as you will find in mine or any tale.

572   In formal headgear all the matrons came,
Eighty-six of them, in Kriemhild's name,
Ladies comely in their gleaming dress,
And beautifully appareled winsome maids, no less

573   Than fifty-four, from all of Burgundy,
The country's highest aristocracy,
Blond of hair beneath their shining bands.
Such was the eager crowning of the king's commands.

574   They wore for their guests the richest silks on earth—
So well arrayed as to reflect the worth

Of their great beauty. The man who would disdain
A single one of them could hardly pass for sane.

575   Sable wraps and furs of ermine graced
Many arms and hands, in charming taste,
And over the satin, golden rings extended.
No one could tell you all the effort they expended.

576   Rich and long the artful girdles placed
By many hands on many a lovely waist;
Made of Arabian silk the farandine
On their noble coats—and joy in noble maidens' mien!

577   Pretty girls were sweet in lacing framed
Across their breasts, and each would be ashamed
If her clothes outshone the brightness of her skin.
No finer retinue for any king or kin!

578   Now the lovely ladies all were dressed.
Their escorts soon arrived, the very best
Of haughty knights, a company large and good;
Shields they carried there, and spears of ashen wood.

TENTH ADVENTURE

How Brunhild Was Received at Worms

579   Across the Rhine, as far as the eye could reach,
The train of the king and his friends approached the beach.
Here too were soldiers leading by the reins
Many maidens riding. Their welcome spared no pains.

580   When those from Iceland and the Nibelung host,
Sigfrid's men, had reached the waiting boats,
They sped across (never an idle oar!)
For there were Gunther's people, lining the other shore.

581   Hear now my words of Uta the glorious queen,
How when she left the town her maids were seen
To follow her on horse as she appointed.
(And thus would many ladies and knights become acquainted.)

582   Duke Gere held the reins of Kriemhild's steed,
But just to the gate, where Sigfrid came to lead
The lovely princess on, so to afford
The service of chivalry, and sweet was his reward.

583 Ortwin rode along at Uta's side—
   Maidens and men in pairs, a social ride.
   Never were lovely women, safe to say,
   Seen in such multitudes on so gala a welcoming day!

584 And lovely Kriemhild watched the great behourds
   Staged along the road by worthy lords,
   All the way to the ships—their joy and duty.
   They lifted from their steeds women of fairest beauty.

585 The king and his worthy guests were now across.
   In crowded joust the crash of boss on boss
   Echoed loud, and shield on shield-rim battered—
   The ladies were looking on—and sturdy lances shattered.

586 The graceful maidens stood by the landing quay,
   As Gunther and his guests debarked. And see!
   Brunhild came herself, on Gunther's arm.
   Costumes shone and jewels gleamed in rival charm.

587 Kriemhild came, as perfect ladies do,
   To welcome Brunhild and her retinue.
   Bright hands lifted ladies' veils
   For the sweet exchange of kisses etiquette entails.

588 Kriemhild spoke, gently bred, polite:
   "I bid you welcome here, in my own right,
   And for my mother, too, and all the dear,
   Devoted friends we have." Brunhild bowed to hear.

589 Often now the regal pair embraced.
   Never such kind regard and perfect taste
   As Uta and Kriemhild showed the bride-to-be.
   And on her sweet mouth they kissed her repeatedly.

590 When Brunhild's maids were all upon the beach,
   In courtly fashion they were taken each
   By a handsome knight in hand. With pleasing grace,
   Before their lady Brunhild the maidens took their place.

591 A long time passed before their words could tell
   The joy of welcome there, and kisses fell
   On rose-red lips. Together still they stood,
   Two princesses. To heroes' hearts the sight was good.

592 Men who once had heard that in all their days
   No lovelier sight would ever meet their gaze

Than these two women, found that judgment fair.
(Nor did they see a trace of make-up anywhere.)

593   Connoisseurs of woman's charm and grace
Lauded Gunther's wife for her lovely face.
Yet men who looked with more experienced eyes
Vowed that Kriemhild, more than she, deserved the prize.

594   Ladies and maids drew near—and what a sight
Of lovely figures gaily decked and bright!
Silken canopies and tents galore
Graced the town of Worms and filled the fields before.

595   Great was the crush among the royal kin.
They bade Brunhild and Kriemhild now turn in
And all the ladies, where the shade was fair.
Knights of Burgundy had come to lead them there.

596   Now they had all come up, the guests on horse,
And lances shot through shields with all the force
Of mighty jousting, and clouds rose from the field,
As if the earth were aflame. Valor stood revealed.

597   These deeds of theirs were all the ladies' concern.
I picture Sigfrid riding many a turn
Before their tents, up and back again,
With his handsome Nibelung troop (he had a thousand men).

598   Then Hagen of Trony came, at the king's request,
In courtesy to call an end to the test,
And stop the joust lest too much dust should fly
And cover the pretty girls. The guests were glad to comply.

599   Gernot spoke, "Let the horses rest,
Until the cool of evening. Then we'd best
Pay our ladies court before the hall.
When Gunther decides to ride, be ready one and all!"

600   Over the whole field the tilt was spent.
Now, for entertainment, warriors went
To the tall tents, and the pleasant life inside,
And so they passed the time, until the word to ride.

601   The hour was near to evening, and setting sun;
The day was growing cool, delay was done:
The time had come for man and maid to rise.
Lovely women shared the fond caress of eyes.

602   Valiant heroes rode their clothes to tatters,
After the country's custom in such matters,
Until the king dismounted by the hall.
They served the ladies well, men of spirit all.

603   Here at the palace they parted, queen from queen
Uta and her daughter left the scene,
Went to a grand apartment, with both their trains—
Everywhere such noise as comes when pleasure reigns.

604   Seats at the table were set, to be occupied
By king and royal guests. There at his side
Lovely Brunhild stood, wearing her crown
Within the king's own land, befitting her renown.

605   A very host of chairs, tables broad
And set with many foods! It would be odd
To find this meal were lacking any thing
To suit the lofty guests who gathered 'round the king.

606   Water was brought, in basins made of gold,
By the royal chamberlains. If anyone told
Of service more refined, seen or heard
At any prince's feast, I'd not believe his word.

607   Before the lord of the Rhine had dipped his hand
In the finger bowl, Sigfrid made demand,
As well he might, recalling the promise made
Before in distant Iceland he sought the lovely maid.

608   He spoke, "Remember now what on your hand
You swore to me: when Brunhild came to this land,
You'd give me your sister. What's become of the oath?
Your journey cost me much in labor and trouble both!"

609   Said Gunther, "Justly you recall my vow.
In this my hand shall not turn perjurer now,
And I shall help you out as best I may."
They called the princess in to audience straightway.

610   With lovely girls of her train she neared the hall.
Giselher sprang to the foot of the stair, to call:
"Send these maidens back. None shall appear,
Except my sister alone, before his Highness here."

611   And so they brought the princes where she found
The king with knights from royal lands around.

In the vastness of the hall they bade her stand.
Lady Brunhild came to the table, close at hand.

612   Gunther spoke; these are the words she heard:
"Sister, by your goodness redeem my word!
I promised you in marriage. Will you fulfill,
By granting him your hand, the tenor of my will?"

613   "Dearest brother," the noble maid replied,
"You need not plead with me. As you decide,
So I would do—and thus is your promise kept.
The man you choose for me I willingly accept."

614   Eyes he loved were on him, his color warmed.
As Sigfrid vowed his service a circle formed,
Which now they bade them walk together toward.
They asked her then if she would have this handsome lord.

615   Maidenly breeding made her seem embarrassed,
But such was fate and Sigfrid's star, she cherished
No desire at all to turn him down.
He swore to be her husband, the heir to Netherland's crown.

616   When each to the other they had pledged their troth,
He took her in his arms—and was not loath
To hold in sweet embrace the lovely princess.
He kissed the fair young queen, with many knights as witness.

617   Lords in waiting parted. Opposite,
In the place of honor, Sigfrid went to sit
With Kriemhild and receive great homage rendered.
(Along with Sigfrid all the Nibelung knights had entered.)

618   The king was seated. Brunhild, too, was there—
This was her greatest sorrow, to see this pair
Sitting together. Her eyes began to well,
Over her bright cheeks the hot tears fell.

619   "What troubles you, my dear," said the king at last,
"That eyes so bright should be thus overcast?
You've better cause for joy; my lands and castles
Stand in liege to you, and many handsome vassals."

620   "I've cause enough for tears," the lady cried,
"I'm sick at heart for your sister! Here at the side
Of your own vassal she sits; I must weep
At seeing her degraded thus and sunk so deep."

621   "Take this all in silence," said the king.
"Another time I'll tell you everything—
Why I gave my sister as Sigfrid's wife.
Well may she live with him, happy all her life!"

622   "I pity her, so nobly bred and fair!
I'd run away, if only I knew where,
And never sleep with you, unless you say
Why it is that Kriemhild was given him this way."

623   "I'll tell you the truth of it," came his reply.
"He has castles and lands as well as I.
Of this be sure: that he is a mighty king;
I gladly grant him the princess, for his love and marrying."

624   In spite of his words, her mood was far from bright.
Now from the tables rose many a knight.
The castle rang with din of melees and tests,
Until the host was irked with all his many guests.

625   He thought he'd like it better, to lie at her side.
The hope within his heart would not subside
Of all the pleasant favors she would render.
He looked at lovely Brunhild—his glance was long and tender.

626   The guests should cease their jousting now, they said—
Time for the king and queen to go to bed.
Kriemhild and Brunhild met, there in the palace
Before the stairs—neither yet with trace of malice.

627   Their courtiers followed. Mindful of what was right,
Chamberlains lit the way with candlelight.
The two kings' men now took their separate course.
All eyes watched as Sigfrid's knights withdrew inforce.

628   The two lords came to where their sleep would be,
And each one thought of lover's victory
Over lovely women, by which their state
Of mind grew gentler—and Sigfrid's pleasure then was great.

629   By Kriemhild's side he found his resting place.
The offices of love, with noble grace,
He tendered her. As much as his life was she,
And more to him than could a thousand others be.

630   I'll say no more of what he did with her,
But listen now and hear what things occur

Between the king and Brunhild! Gunther might,
With someone else, have spent a far more restful night.

631 His retinue had left, and soon the door
Was closed and locked. The sweet embrace in store
He pictured to himself. The time was wrong.
She was not yet his wife, and still his wait was long.

632 She walked to the bed in a gown of linen-white.
"Here and now I have," so thought the knight,
"All that in all my days I ever desired!"
Great must be the joy such beauty as hers inspired.

633 The king reached out and put the light away.
He turned and walked to where his lady lay,
Himself lay down beside her, in pure delight.
He took his love into his arms and clasped her tight.

634 He would have pressed caress upon caress,
Had his noble spouse allowed. To his distress,
She turned instead in anger, so irate,
That where he looked for a friend, he found a foeman's hate.

635 "You must stop it now, my lord," cried she,
"What you are hoping for, cannot be.
I mean to stay a virgin—of that be sure—
Until I know the truth." Then Gunther turned on her.

636 He struggled for her love, and disarrayed
The gown she wore. Then the marvelous maid
Reached for the girdle of braid she wore at her waist—
And treated him so that he was hurt and left disgraced.

637 She tied him, hand and foot, nor was that all;
She found a nail and hung him on the wall!
He spoiled her sleep, and she withheld her love—
A cruel show of strength he nearly perished of.

638 He who would be master now must plead:
"Untie me, noble queen! If I am freed,
All my hopes of winning you are through
Never, never again will I lie so close to you."

639 She cared not how he felt, her sleep was soft.
All the night till dawn he hung aloft.
Till into the room the light of morning shone.
If ever strength was his, now it was surely gone.

640   "Now tell me, royal Gunther, would you mind
If chamberlains of yours should come and find
Their master strung up here, by a woman's hand?"
"They'd think it ill of you," replied the lord of the land;

641   "And little credit to me!" the warrior said.
"So out of your goodness, let me back in bed.
Since my attentions cause such bitterness,
I swear my hands shall never so much as touch your dress."

642   She loosed and let him down. He made his way
To the bed again, where his fair lady lay,
And stayed so far from her, her lovely clothing
Was safe from his touch. (She would have greeted that
    with loathing!)

643   The servants came to bring their change of clothes,
The numerous things held ready when they rose.
Perhaps all those around were light and gay—
The king was filled with gloom, though he wore his
    crown that day.

644   After the country's custom—rightly so—
Gunther and Brunhild did not forgo
The early trip to church, where mass was held.
Sigfrid also came, the multitude was swelled.

645   Clothes and crown were ready, before their eyes,
All that royal privilege implies.
Then came the rites of anointment! The crowd around
Beheld the happy sight of four sovereigns crowned.

646   A good six hundred youths (an honor paid
The two great kings) received the accolade.
Joy in Burgundy beyond compare!
The shock of shafts in hands of lancers filled the air.

647   In the windows sat the pretty girls and gazed,
As the light from countless shields before them blazed.
The king had left his men and stood apart.
Whatever others did, he stood with a gloomy heart.

648   Sigfrid's mood and his were not the same.
The warrior knew what the trouble was; he came
To where the monarch stood and asked outright:
"Tell me truthfully, how did you fare last night?"

649 His host replied, "With shame and injury!
I've brought the very devil home with me.
I had in mind to love her, that was all.
And she tied me up and hung me on a nail in the wall!

650 There I hung, in danger, till dawn of day
When she untied me—how quietly she lay!
I tell you this for help and sympathy,
And as a friend." "This truly troubles me,"

651 Sturdy Sigfrid said. "If you agree,
I promise—and tonight I'll guarantee—
She'll lie so close to you that never again
Will she withhold her love." The words were balm to his pain.

652 Sigfrid went on, "Things will be all right.
I gather we fared differently last night.
Your sister now means more to me than life,
Before this night is out, Brunhild shall be your wife!"

653 He said, "I'll come to your room this very day,
Wearing my Magic Cloak, by a secret way,
That not a soul shall see my stratagem.
Your chamberlains must go home, be sure to get rid of them.

654 I'll blow the candles out in the page's hand.
That shall be the sign; you'll understand
That I am there to help. I'll tame your wife
For you to love tonight, or else I'll lose my life!"

655 "Providing you don't make love," the king replied,
"To my wife—otherwise I'm satisfied.
So do whatever you please. If it should be
The death of her, I'd let it pass, so fearsome is she."

656 "You have my word that I won't touch your queen.
Of all the women I have ever seen
Your sister is the only one for me."
Gunther put his faith in Sigfrid's guarantee.

657 They took their pleasure now in strenuous joys,
Until they called a halt to joust and noise,
For soon the ladies were about to ride
Back to the hall, and chamberlains ordered folk aside.

658 The courtyard soon was cleared of horse and men.
Each of the queens was led by a bishop then,

In the king's presence to the dining tables.
And they were followed to their seats by handsome nobles.

659 The king's fond hope and happy humor grew.
He thought of what his friend had pledged to do.
This day seemed like a month! His lady's love—
That was the only thing that he was thinking of.

660 He could hardly wait until the meal was through.
But then the time was come—the queens withdrew
To privacy, each to her own apartment
With valiant knights attending, men of bold deportment.

661 Sigfrid sat by his wife, as lovers sit,
In perfect joy, with hate no part of it.
She stroked his hands with her own white hand.
But suddenly he was gone—she could not understand.

662 As she was caressing him he disappeared.
She turned to his men and said, "How very weird!
I wonder now, where could the king have gone?
Who took his hand from mine?" But she did not go on.

663 He made his way meanwhile until he found
Chamberlains with lights, all standing 'round.
In the pages' very hands he blew them out.
Thus did Gunther know his friend was close about.

664 He knew why he was there. Gunther bade
The maids and ladies leave, and when they had,
The vaunted king himself then locked the door,
And quickly threw the heavy double bolts before.

665 He hid the light behind the canopy,
And now began the struggle that had to be:
Fair maid and mighty lord. Whatever pleasure
Gunther felt was matched by pain in equal measure.

666 Sigfrid now lay down, close to the queen.
"Stop it, Gunther," she cried, "unless you mean
To get yourself in trouble once again."
Before the night was out she hurt this prince of men!

667 He hid his voice and uttered not a word.
Though he could not see, still Gunther heard
No sound of wantonness from them at all.
Indeed, the comfort such a bed could give was small.

668   He acted just as if it were Gunther there,
And put his arms around the lady fair.
Then all at once she threw him out of bed.
He crashed against a stool, hitting it with his head.

669   Up he jumped again with all his might,
To make one more attempt, and when he tried
He paid with hurt and pain for this violence.
I doubt if woman ever put up such defense!

670   When he would not give in, she sprang from bed.
"I will not have you touch a single thread
Of my white gown. For your rudeness you will be
A sorry man," she cried. "I'll show you—wait and see!"

671   She closed her arms around the marvelous knight,
And meant to pack him off, thus fastened tight,
As she had before, in peace to have her sleep.
He disarrayed her clothes, and her revenge ran deep.

672   What good his mighty strength of muscle and bone?
She proved to him the measure of her own,
She dragged him off (he had no choice at all)
And rudely squeezed him between a cupboard and the wall.

673   "Good Lord," he thought, "am I to lose my life
At a maiden's hands? If so, how many a wife
Will turn in scorn and pride against her lord,
Who otherwise would not do it of her own accord?"

674   What his Highness heard did not assuage
His worry! Sigfrid turned in shame and rage,
Fighting back again with main force,
Wildly, trying her strength. His was a risky course.

675   It seemed an age to the king, before he won.
She crushed his hands, making the blood run
Gushing from his nails. His joy was scant!
Shortly though he made the glorious queen recant

676   What once she vowed—her rude and harsh intention.
(The king had heard, though neither word nor mention
Came from Sigfrid.) He pinned her on the bed—
She screamed aloud! For now his strength hurt her instead.

677   She reached down at her side and found the sash,
To tie him up. He gave her such a lash

With his hand, her body cracked in every bone.
With that the fight was done, and she was Gunther's own.

678   She cried, "Oh noble sovereign, let me live!
Whatever I have done to you, I'll give
Full payment back, your love shall not be spurned,
For you can master a woman, as oh so well I've learned."

679   She lay upon the bed, and Sigfrid rose
As if he intended taking off his clothes.
But first he slipped from her hand a golden ring—
All the while the queen did not perceive a thing.

680   He took her girdle, a sash of silk and gold.
(I cannot say if being overbold
Made him do this. He gave it to his bride—
To his later grief.) Now Gunther lay at Brunhild's side.

681   Rightfully he lay there, making love.
Much she had to be forgetful of:
Both wrath and modesty. She paled at the touch
Of his embrace. Ah, love ebbed her strength so much!

682   No stronger than any woman then was she.
He caressed her lovely body tenderly,
Nor could she now by fighting back demur.
This is what the love of Gunther did to her.

683   With what sweet charm at Gunther's side she lay,
In tender love, until the break of day!
Meanwhile Sigfrid left to seek his bride—
A lover's welcoming, at a lovely lady's side.

684   He brushed aside the question she had thought
To ask of him, and hid what he had brought,
Until she took the crown in his own land.
But what he was destined to give he gave with open hand.

685   The king next morning felt much more cheerful far
Than he had felt before. The only bar
To perfect joy in all his land was gone,
And all his noble guests were nobly waited on.

686   The celebration lasted fourteen days,
And all the while no end of the noise men raise
In following after every sort of pleasure—
A heavy burden, too, on royal Gunther's treasure!

687   To further the king's repute his friends were told
         To give the poets there shining gold
         And silver, clothes to wear, steeds to ride.
         If they came in hope of gifts, they left there satisfied.

688   The lord of Netherland, his thousand men—
         Why, all the clothes they brought were gone again,
         Given away, till nothing was left to give—
         Horses and saddles, too. They knew how to live!

689   Before their great largess had ceased its flow,
         It seemed an age to those who wished to go.
         Never guests received more elegant care.
         So Gunther willed, and that was the end of the festival there.

ELEVENTH ADVENTURE

How Sigfrid Went Home with His Wife

690   When all the foreign guests had gone their way,
         Sigmund's son addressed his friends to say:
         It's time that we made ready to return."
         This was the sort of news his wife was pleased to learn.

691   She asked her husband then, "When shall we go?
         Not in haste—I should not like it so.
         My brothers first must share with me our lands."
         (He was not pleased to find her making these demands.)

692   The princes came to him and spoke, all three:
         "Know this, my lord: our services shall be
         In fealty yours, as long as she shall live."
         He bowed to them in thanks for the love they pledged to give.

693   "We shall divide with you," said Giselher,
         "The castles and lands we own, and you will share
         With Kriemhild then, as full and rightful gain,
         In all the far-flung lands that make up our domain."

694   The son of Sigmund said, as he saw and heard
         How much the princes meant their every word,
         "God save you all your heritage intact,
         And all your subjects, too! If Kriemhild ever lacked

695   For anything, it's not this proffered share.
         Her wealth at home, where the crown is hers to wear,

Shall pass (if I live to see it), all power known
To mortals. In all things else, your wishes are my own."

696 Said she, "My dower perhaps you cannot use—
Burgundian knights are harder to refuse!
A king would gladly take them to his land.
And I should like my share from my dear brothers' hand."

697 "Take your pick," said Gernot, when she was through.
"You'll find no lack of men who'll ride with you
Of our three thousand thanes we'll give a third
To be your men-at-arms." Kriemhild now sent word

698 To Hagen and Ortwin, asking if they would agree,
With all their men, to bear her fealty.
Anger filled the answer Hagen hurled:
"The king has no right to give us to anyone in this world!

699 Let others of our courtiers follow you.
Well you know what men of Trony do:
Our job it is to stay with the kings at court;
We followed them here. We cannot cut our duty short."

700 There they left it. Kriemhild, going through
With her plans to leave, gathered her retinue:
Thirty-two young maids, five hundred men.
Count Eckewart went with them, following Sigfrid then.

701 Now they asked their leave—as form requires—
All the dames and maids, knights and squires.
They kissed farewell, for time had come to part.
They left the land of Gunther, gay and happy at heart.

702 Their kinsmen rode along, to guide them right.
Instructions were that they might spend the night
In the king's domain, wherever they cared to stay.
Heralds to royal Sigmund started on their way,

703 Bearing word to him and Siglind, too:
Their son and lovely Kriemhild soon were due,
Uta's child, from Worms across the Rhine.
No other news in all the world could be so fine!

704 "Thank God," said Sigmund, "I shall be around
When lovely Kriemhild walks our land, and crowned,
Shall add her glory to my dominions' fame.
My son, the noble Sigfrid, shall rule in his own name."

705 Siglind gave a weight of gold away,
Silver, and red velvet—herald's pay—
For what she heard had brought her happiness.
Eagerly her maids gave thought to proper dress.

706 They asked who else was coming to their land,
And had the seats erected and the stand,
From which his friends would see the prince appear,
New crowned. Sigmund's men rode out to bring him here.

707 I never heard of such reception yet
As these great knights in Sigmund's country met.
The lovely Siglind rode to meet Kriemhild,
Escorted by charming ladies and lords. The journey filled—

708 Before they met the strangers—one whole day.
They suffered great impatience on the way,
Friend and stranger alike, until they found
The mighty castle Xanten, where they would soon be crowned.

709 Siglind and Sigmund, laughing in joy and pleasure,
Gave Kriemhild many kisses—in equal measure
To Sigfrid too. Gone was all their pain.
They granted heartfelt welcome to them and all their train.

710 They asked that the guests be brought to Sigmund's hall.
Now they came to lift the maidens all
Down from their steeds. And many men were there,
Serving the lovely ladies with every zealous care.

711 Great as was the tourney by the Rhine,
Here they gave the heroes clothes so fine
They never had the like in all their days—
What wonders I could tell you about their wealthy ways!

712 They lived in splendor, with all they wished and more.
Such golden-colored skirts her ladies wore,
With pearls and jewels woven through and through.
On such a scale the queen maintained her retinue.

713 Among his friends assembled, Sigmund came
And spoke, "To the kin of Sigfrid I proclaim:
Before these lords my crown shall be his to wear."
This news the men of Netherland rejoiced to hear.

714 He commended him his crown, his courts and land.
All who came to justice at his hand

He truly judged, and so maintained the law,
The name of Sigfrid soon was held in general awe.

715   In splendor passed ten years of Sigfrid's life,
Of law beneath his crown, and then his wife,
The lovely Kriemheld, bore to him a son—
Kin or friend, a source of joy for everyone.

716   Soon the christening and then his name:
After his uncle, Gunther—no cause for shame
Should he take after him, how good and right!
They brought him up with zealous care, as well they might.

717   In these same days Dame Siglind passed away.
Uta's daughter now held rightful sway,
Mighty mistress in all the land was she.
Death had taken the queen. They mourned her grievously.

718   And far by the Rhine, as soon all people knew,
A son was born to mighty Gunther, too,
By lovely Brunhild, queen of Burgundy—
For love of Sigfrid christened, and so his name should be.

719   They watched and cared for him with zealous joy.
Gunther picked out tutors for the boy
Who brought him up to be a stalwart lord.
What awful toll of friends he paid as fate's reward!

720   Many tales were told, on many days,
How cheerful warriors lived a life of praise
In Sigmund's country always. They said the same
Of royal Gunther's courtiers, men of peerless fame.

721   Nibelung's land and Shilbung's thanes and all
The wealth of both now stood at Sigfrid's call.
(The power of his greatest kin was nothing near it—
Even prouder pleasure to his valiant spirit!)

722   To him belonged the greatest treasure hoard
That, but for its former owners, any lord
Had ever won, the prize he had fought to gain
By the mountainside, at cost of many warriors slain.

723   The honors men desire he possessed.
But lacking these, he still must be confessed
One of the best who ever sat a horse.
People had good cause to fear his potent force!

TWELFTH ADVENTURE

How Gunther Invited Sigfrid to the Festivities

724   Gunther's wife kept thinking all the while:
"How can Kriemhild live in such high style?
Her lord is after all our vassal, and yet—
Much time has passed and little service do we get."

725   This she held in silence in her heart,
Embittered that they kept themselves apart,
That Sigfrid's people rendered service due
So rarely. How this came about she wished she knew.

726   She tried her way with the king, hoping to find
Some chance to see Kriemhild. Set in her mind,
She plotted what she wished, in confidence.
But what she said, in Gunther's view, made little sense.

727   He answered her, "How can we bring them here?
The impossibility of that is clear.
I dare not ask them, the distance is so huge."
Brunhild countered this with a cunning subterfuge:

728   "However great the power in a vassal's hands,
He cannot fail to do as his king commands."
Gunther smiled at her words. When Sigfrid came,
One could scarcely say he did it in duty's name.

729   She spoke, "My dearest lord, to this for me:
Help me to arrange that I may see
Lord Sigfrid in this land, and your sister, too.
There is no dearer favor I could ask of you.

730   In mind and manners your sister is so well-bred.
How sweet it is whenever my thoughts are led
To the time I spent with her, when we were wedded.
Surely Sigfrid's love for her is to his credit!"

731   She urged so long he said at last, "No guest,
I swear, was ever so welcome, and your request
Falls on willing ears. Heralds of mine
Shall go to both of them, bidding them come to the Rhine."

732   The queen replied, "Will you please then say
When you mean to send them—or by what day

Our dear friends are to come here? Those who go
On such a mission I should also like to know."

733 "Gladly," said the prince. "I plan to call
On thirty men to ride." He summoned all,
Telling in Sigfrid's land what news to recite.
Brunhild gave them splendid clothes, for their delight.

734 "My lords," the king declared, "repeat for me,
Omitting nothing, all my embassy
To sturdy Sigfrid and my sister, thus:
They have in all this world no better friends than us.

735 And ask them both to visit us by the Rhine,
Which I and my queen will greet with every sign
Of gratitude. By solstice time he'll see,
As shall his vassals, many who laud his courtesy.

736 Give King Sigmund my regards, and tell
How I and my kin as always wish him well,
And tell my sister not to fail this journey
To see her friends. She'll never find more fitting tourney."

737 Brunhild, Uta, and ladies on every hand
Sent their greetings on to Sigfrid's land,
To charming ladies, to men of war, stout-hearted.
With royal friends' assent, the messengers departed.

738 They rode as on campaign, with steeds and dress
For all of them. They left the land, to press
Their journey forward, ever the same direction,
With royal safeguard for his messengers' protection.

739 In three weeks' time at last they made their entry
Into the March of Norway and the country
Where Nibelung Castle was and the knight they sought.
The long trip had tired the steeds the heralds brought.

740 Sigfrid and Lady Kriemhild both were told
Of men-at-arms arriving, whose clothes recalled
The way Burgundian men by custom dressed.
They quickly rose from the couch where they had been at rest.

741 They sent to the window a maid, who soon had spied
In the courtyard valiant Gere, and at his side
All his companions who were ordered there.
What pleasant news to still her homesick heart's despair!

742   She cried to the king "See them there below,
Walking the yard with Gere, to and fro.
My brother Gunther sent to us these men,
Down the Rhine." Said he, "May they be welcome
then!"

743   Out ran all the courtiers, offering each
As best he could in turn a kindly speech
Of welcome to the heralds, whose coming here
Filled the heart of old King Sigmund with good cheer.

744   Lodging was found for Gere and his men,
Their horses cared for. In went the heralds then,
Where at Kriemhild's side Lord Sigfrid sat
(They had been invited, hence they ventured that.)

745   The host and his wife arose immediately,
With kindly welcome to Gere of Burgundy
And Gunther's vassals who came with him there.
They asked the mighty Gere to come and take his chair.

746   "Grant us our mission first before we sit,
Way-weary guests. Let us stand a bit,
For we must tell you all the news we bear
From Gunther and Lady Brunhild—proudly and well
they fare!

747   Also the word we have from Uta, your mother.
Young Giselher and Gernot, too, his brother,
Have sent us here, and your excellent family.
They send you pledge of service from lands of Burgundy."

748   "God bless them," Sigfrid said. "With joy I accord
Good faith and wealth to them, the due reward
Of friends—as does their sister. But now go on
And tell if our friends at home are somehow put upon.

749   Has someone since we parted offered ill
To my lady's kin? Let me know! I will,
In faith and always, help them bear the blow,
Until their foes shall weep at the loyalty I show."

750   Margrave Gere cried, "Truest merit
Abides with them; proud and high their spirit!
To the Rhine they bid you, for certain festivities,
They truly want to see you—set you mind at ease.

751   They also ask that my lady come with you
As soon as the present wintertime is through
And hope to see you by next solstice day."
"Hardly," powerful Sigfrid said, "I see no way."

752   Cried Burgundian Gere, in reply:
"Your mother Uta begs you: don't deny
Gernot and Giselher! Every day
I hear them all complain that you're so far away.

753   My Lady Brunhild and all her company
Rejoice to think of this: for should it be
That they may see you, in joy their hearts would rise."
(And all of this found favor in lovely Kriemhild's eyes.)

754   The host asked Gere to sit—he was her kin—
And ordered wine for his guests. They rushed it in.
Sigmund also came, having seen
Burgundian heralds, and spoke to them with a friendly
    mien:

755   "Welcome, men of Gunther! Ever since
Kriemhild was married to my son the prince,
We surely should have seen you more often now,
Here in our land, if you mean the friendship you avow."

756   They said whenever he wished they'd gladly come.
Their great fatigue they felt delivered from
By all this pleasure. They had the heralds sit
And brought them food, in plenty—Sigfrid ordered it.

757   Nine full days, perforce, the knights remained,
And then at last the gallant men complained
At not returning back to their dominions.
King Sigfrid called his friends, seeking their opinions:

758   "Do you advise my going to the Rhine?
I am asked by Gunther, kin of mine,
And by his family, for a festive day.
I'd go there gladly but his land is far away.

759   They ask that Kriemhild come with me as well.
How is *she* to get there, friends, pray tell?
Had I to fight for them through thirty lands,
Of course they'd have the trip as service from Sigfrid's hands."

760   "If this," they said, "is how your mind now lies—
To make the journey—here's what we advise:
Take a thousand knights and ride to the Rhine.
Thus in Burgundy shall your fame and glory shine."

761   Cried Lord Sigmund, "If you mean to go
To these festivities, why not let me know?
I'll ride with you, if you think it worth your pains,
And thus increase your party by a hundred thanes."

762   "My dear father, if you would join our ride
I should be delighted," Sigfrid cried.
"We'll leave the land when twelve full days have passed."
Now they gave apparel and steeds to all who asked.

763   And since the highborn king had set his heart
Upon this trip, they had the heralds depart
For home again, back to the Rhine to tell
His lady's kin: to join their fete would please him well.

764   The story goes that Kriemhild's and Sigfrid's gift
To the heralds leaving was more than they could lift
On their steeds to carry home—so rich was he.
They urged their pack-train off, driving them merrily.

765   Sigfrid and Sigmund gave whatever it took
To clothe their men. Count Eckewart had them look
For women's dress, the best they had on hand
Or could find anywhere in all of Sigfrid's land.

766   Saddles and shields were ready. Gifts they gave
To every knight and lady about to leave,
Whatever heart desired, in nothing short.
He took as guests to his friends a large and splendid court.

767   The heralds made their way home, eagerly.
Gere the warrior came to Burgundy,
Where he was welcomed, and they dismounted all
From charger and steed, in front of good King Gunther's
        hall.

768   The wise and the simple ran, as is the way,
To ask for news. The good knight stopped to say:
"Wait till I tell the king and you will hear!"
He went with his companions, finding Gunther near.

769 For joy the king jumped up from where he was seated.
Their swift return the lovely Brunhild greeted
With thanks. Gunther called the heralds over:
"How is Sigfrid, who has done us such great favor!"

770 Valiant Gere spoke, "His face was glowing,
As was your sister's. Never such bestowing
Of love, and true regard, has any friend
Had from mortal man as he and his father send."

771 The queen addressed the margrave, "Tell me though,
Is Kriemhild coming? Has she kept some show
Of that refinement which so graced her pure
And lovely form?" Said Gere, "She will come, be sure!"

772 Uta quickly called the messengers
And one could tell from every word of hers
How eager she was: How did her daughter fare?
He told her how they found her, that soon she would
            be there.

773 What Sigfrid gave they did not try to hide
From the three kings' men, but opened wide
The clothes and gold they had for all to see.
Great was their praise for all this generosity.

774 But Hagen said, "It's nothing for him to give.
With all he owns, if he had forever to live
He could not spend it—the Nibelung treasury!
Ah, if only that should come to Burgundy!"

775 All the court looked forward to the day
When they would come. Men in the three kings' pay
Found they had no leisure early or late
Setting up the stands to hold a crowd so great.

776 No idleness for Hunold, surely none
For Sindold either, with all these things to be done—
Serving and pouring, setting up benches of wood.
Ortwin helped, and Gunther gave his gratitude.

777 Kitchener Rumold managed his underlings
With skill: a multitude of cooking things—
Kettles, and pots, and pans—there on hand
To fix the food for those who headed toward their land.

THIRTEENTH ADVENTURE
How They Came to the Festival

778 Let us leave their busy ways and turn
To Lady Kriemhild and her maids, to learn
How they made their way from Nibelung land to the Rhine.
Never did horses bear garments half so fine.

779 Saddle-boxes set for the journey, they started
For where they hoped to find it happy-hearted,
Sigfrid, his friends, and the queen. The time was brief
For all of them before it turned to bitter grief!

780 They left Lord Sigfrid's little child, the son
Of Kriemhild, home—what else could they have done?
Out of this courtly journey came great pain:
The child would never see father or mother again.

781 Sigmund rode along. Had he been aware
Of what in aftertime would happen there,
He would have had no part of the tournament.
On what man's kin was such affliction ever sent?

782 They ordered heralds ahead to give report.
Uta's many friends and Gunther's court
Rode out to meet them in a gay procession—
Guests for whom he spent much time in preparation.

783 Gunther went where Brunhild sat. "When first you came,
How did my sister greet you? You owe the same
In welcome to Sigfrid's wife." "Well and good,"
She said, "I'll do it gladly. I love her as I should."

784 The great king said, "They come tomorrow forenoon.
If you would welcome them, be at it soon.
We mustn't wait in the castle till they are due.
Never have I had guests I so looked forward to."

785 She told her maids and matrons to be quick
And look for good apparel, the very pick
Of all things fit to wear before their guests.
Need I tell you this: that there were no protests?

786 And Gunther's men ran out to offer aid
And homage while his summons were relayed

To all his knights. The queen rode out in splendor—
As vast a welcoming of guests as they could tender.

787   Beloved friends and joyously received!
This was a day exceeding (so they believed)
Kriemhild's welcome of Brunhild in Burgundy.
Meeting them was to meet the pride of chivalry.

788   Sigfrid now had brought his men to ride;
Back and forth they went, from side to side
Across the field—so vast his retinue.
Who could avoid the confusion and all the dust that blew?

789   The king, seeing Sigfrid and Sigmund there,
Was moved by his affection to declare:
"My best of welcome to you—to all my friends.
What pleasure to our spirit your courtly journey lends!"

790   "God bless you," answered Sigmund, a man whose joy
Lay in honor. "Ever since my boy,
Sigfrid, became your friend, my thoughts have turned
On meeting you." Said Gunther, "Much pleasure have I
    earned!"

791   Sigfrid they received, in fitting state
With greatest homage. No one bore him hate.
Gernot and Giselher, perfect in breeding,
Joined their welcome. Have any guests had kinder greeting?

792   And so the two kings' wives approached, and saddles
Stood empty there as men of many battles
Lifted ladies down upon the grass.
Many served and gladly, the time was quick to pass.

793   The charming ladies-in-waiting then drew near
One to the other, and knights were filled with cheer
To see on either hand a greeting paid
With such perfection, as warrior stood by lovely maid.

794   These splendid folk, they took each other's hands
With all the bowing etiquette demands
And fairest ladies' kisses, charmingly!
(A joy for Gunther's men—and Sigfrid's men—to see.)

795   They waited there no more, but rode to town.
They host gave orders that his guests be shown

How very welcome they were in Burgundy.
They charged with lances couched for all the ladies to see.

796 Hagen and Ortwin and all—they left no doubt
What mighty men they were. And who can flout
Whatever challenge such a knight suggests?
They rendered worthy service to all their welcome guests.

797 One heard their shields, echoing thrust and blow,
Before the castle gate. They tarried so,
Guest and host, a while before they entered.
The day sped by, with all their thoughts on pastime
    centered.

798 They rode before the palace, full of pleasure,
Artful robes, cut to perfect measure,
Hung beneath the saddles of the fair
And handsome ladies all. Gunther's men were there.

799 They ordered that the guests be shown their lodging.
Meanwhile people noticed Brunhild watching
Lady Kriemhild—her beauty was untold,
Bright against the shining of the very gold.

800 All about the town of Worms one heard
The noise of people. Gunther issued word
To have his Marshal, Dankwart, take in charge
Their retinue and find them a goodly place to lodge.

801 Food was served them, out of doors and in;
Better treatment of guests had never been.
Whatever thing they wanted—that was done
(So rich the king) without refusing anyone.

802 They served them as friends, with not a trace of malice.
His Highness sat at table in the palace
With his guests. He showed Sigfrid the chair
He had before. Handsome knights were with him there.

803 About his circle sat twelve hundred men.
It seemed to Queen Brunhild that never again
In any vassal could such power be vested.
(As yet, she liked him enough to leave him unmolested.)

804 That evening, where the king sat, rich clothes
Were wet with wine, as many bearers rose

To make their rounds from table on to table—
The fullest service done as fast as they were able.

805   They found, as is the way at celebrations,
For maids and ladies fine accommodations—
Helped by their host, whatever their country be.
And courteous people served them well and liberally.

806   At end of night, when day appeared, there glowed
From traveling cases precious jewels sewed
In lovely dresses, touched by woman's hand,
As splendid clothes were chosen and fair attire planned.

807   Day had not quite dawned when knights and men
Came to the hall and noise grew loud again,
Before the king's own morning mass was through.
Young lords jousted, for the royal praise they drew.

808   The mighty crash of trombones swelled around,
And drums and flutes gave out so great a sound
That with it echoed all the wide extent
Of Worms. Lords were mounted, proud and confident.

809   Then in this land began a lofty game
Of numerous able knights. How many came,
Armed with shields in hand, men of parts
And handsome, whose pride and spirit came from
        youthful hearts!

810   Splendid ladies sat in each window niche,
And many lovely maids, their figures rich
With ornament, watching valiant heroes' sport,
When now the king himself rode out, with kin and court.

811   Thus they passed their time—it seemed not long—
Until from out of church they heard the song
Of many bells. Now ladies left on horse,
And noble queens escorted by valiant men in force.

812   On the grass before the minster they dismounted,
All the guests, whom Brunhild still accounted
Friends of hers. They entered church in state,
Crowned as queens—their love soon torn by bitter hate.

813   When they had heard the mass, they all went back,
And later then to table—still no lack

Of joy and honors, pleasure holding sway
Unbroken at the feast until the eleventh day.

FOURTEENTH ADVENTURE
How the Two Queens Hurled Insults at Each Other

814   One vesper time the castle yard was loud
With tumult rising from the eager crowd
Of knights intent on the pleasures of chivalry.
Many men and women hurried up to see.

815   There together sat the mighty pair,
Their queenly thoughts on two whose names were fair,
And Kriemhild spoke, "My husband's hand
Should rightly rule the width and breadth of this land."

816   The lady Brunhild cried, "How could this be?
If no one were alive but you and he,
No doubt our kingdom might be his domain.
As long as Gunther lives, that hope is all in vain."

817   Kriemhild answered, "See how well he stands,
How proud, before the warriors he commands,
Like the shining moon before a starry sky.
For this my heart has every right to swell with joy!"

818   "However fair and charming your lord may be,
However brave and strong, you must agree
Your noble brother Gunther still is best.
In company of kings, be sure, he leads the rest."

819   Kriemhild again: "My lord is proud and strong.
Surely praising him I do no wrong.
His glories are manifold. Never fear
That I deceive you, Brunhild: he is Gunther's peer."

820   "My dear, you must not take my words amiss.
Not without good right do I say this:
When first we met, I heard them both declare
(When the king imposed his will on mine, and there,

821   In knightly contest, won my love) he came
As Gunther's vassal. Sigfrid said the same;
I take it he's my thane, since he agreed."
Said Kriemhild, "If that were so, I'd be ill-served indeed!

822   What trick do you suspect my brothers of,
That they should let me be a vassal's love?
I ask you, Brunhild, as one of my family,
Stop this talk, in kindliness, for sake of me."

823   "I cannot drop the matter," replied the queen.
"Should I give up these many men, you mean,
Who stand, as Sigfrid does, in our vassalage?"
The lovely Kriemhild answered her, in terrible rage:

824   "Don't think he'll ever serve you! He never can,
In any way, for he is a greater man
Than my good brother Gunther could ever be.
And now you'd best take back the words you said to me!

825   Another thing—it's strange, if he's your thrall
And both of us are at your beck and call,
That he has never bothered to set aside
A penny's tribute! I really should be spared your pride!"

826   "You raise yourself too high," cried the queen.
"Very well, then, let it now be seen
If you are honored equally with me."
The wrath of both these queens was a fearful thing to see.

827   Lady Kriemhild said, "Then come what must,
Since you called my lord your bondsman! Let us trust
The two king's own retainers to decide:
Dare I go to chapel before a monarch's bride?

828   You'll see this day that I am noble and free,
That my lord is better than yours could ever be.
And I do not intend to be cried down;
This night you'll see your bondmaid go before the crown

829   And court of Burgundy, with knights to wait her.
I intend to be acknowledged greater
Than any queen this land has ever known."
And so between them seeds of bitter hate were sown.

830   Said Brunhild, "If you deny your vassalage,
Don't come to church with me—the privilege
Of my attendants! You and your maids must leave me."
To which Kriemhild replied, "That I will, believe me."

831   "Now dress, my ladies," she said, "dress for church;
My honor's not for anyone here to besmirch.

If you have elegant clothes, don't be accused
Of hiding them. We'll make her rue the words she used."

832   They hardly needed urging, but chose their best,
Ladies and maids alike, richly dressed.
With all her suite now, Sigfrid's consort neared:
The lovely Kriemhild, in lavish garb, appeared

833   With the maids she brought to the Rhine, all forty-three.
Gleaming silks they wore from Araby.
These lovely maidens came to the minster then;
Before the building waited all of Sigfrid's men.

834   The people wondered why it was they saw
The queens in separate companies withdraw
And not together walking as before—
This sight, for many men, held grief and woe in store.

835   Before the minster Gunther's lady stood.
Many warriors thought to themselves how good
Their fortune was to see such beauty there.
Then came Lady Kriemhild, her suite beyond compare.

836   The best that ever royal maidens wore
Compared to this was nothing. Such a store
Of wealth was hers, no thirty queens could add
All their goods together to match what Kriemhild had.

837   With all the will in the world, no man could say
He ever saw such clothes as these today
In which her winsome maidens now were seen.
In this she had no purpose but to hurt the queen.

838   They met at the minster steps. For the hate she bore,
The queen of the land bade Kriemhild walk no more.
She spoke, her words were sharper than a knife:
"Never shall bondmaid go before the king's own wife."

839   Then Lady Kriemhild cried, to anger stung:
"You'd be better off to hold your tongue!
You've sold your beauty cheap and shamed your life.
How can a vassal's mistress pass for a king's own wife?"

840   "Whom are you calling mistress?" the queen outburst.
"You!" said Kriemhild, "The one who loved you first
Was Sigfrid, my own dear lord and good.
Indeed it was not my brother who took your maidenhood.

841   And what a base deception! Where were your brains?
      Why did you let him love you—one of your thanes?
      All of your complaint is build on air!"
      Answered Brunhild, "I'll tell Gunther this, I swear!"

842   "And what is that to me? By your own pride
      You stand betrayed. With your own words you tried
      To make me out your servant. Honestly,
      I hate it all. You'll have no silent friend in me."

843   Then Brunhild wept. And Kriemhild paused no more.
      Ahead of the queen, she entered the minster door
      With all her train. The mighty hate began
      For which, from shining eyes, so many sad tears ran.

844   However God was praised, whatever the song,
      The time that passed to Brunhild seemed too long,
      For will and body both were dark with gloom—
      The price of which in time was noble heroes' doom.

845   She wept with her maids and waited at the door.
      She thought, "I must hear from her, if there is more
      To the noisy libel of her bitter tongue.
      If Sigfrid boasted this, I swear I'll have him hung."

846   Now with her warriors, Kriemhild came outside.
      "Stand where you are!" Lady Brunhild cried.
      "You say that I'm a harlot. Prove what you say!
      You know what pain you've caused me—to talk of me
          that way."

847   Said Kriemhild, "You'd do better to let me go!
      This gold upon my hand is the proof I show;
      My lover brought me it when he lay with you first."
      Of all of Brunhild's days this was far the worst.

848   "This precious ring—someone made bold to steal it,"
      She said, "and long maliciously conceal it.
      Now I see too well who was the thief!"
      The rage and fury of both these women passed belief.

849   Said Kriemhild, "I will not play your stealing game
      And you would hold your tongue if your good name
      Meant much to you. Who says I lie, be cursed!
      The proof is the belt I wear: my Sigfrid had you first."

850 From Nineveh the silk that made the sash
  She wore about her. On it played the flash
  Of splendid gems. When Brunhild saw, she wept.
  Not from Gunther nor Burgundy could this be kept.

851 "Ask the prince of the Rhine to come," she cried.
  "He shall hear how I am vilified
  By his own sister—giving me the name
  Of Sigfrid's mistress." He and his retainers came.

852 He saw his own dear lady weeping greatly.
  "Tell me now," he questioned her most sweetly,
  "Who it is that has hurt you so, my dear."
  She said to the king, "I stand bereft of joy and cheer.

853 Your sister has tried her best to slur and taint
  My good repute. I bring you my complaint:
  She says her husband Sigfrid slept with me."
  King Gunther spoke, "If so, she acts most evilly."

854 "And here she wears my belt, which I had lost,
  My red gold ring. I rue the bitter cost
  That I was born. Defend me, Sire, and set
  An end to this disgrace, or I shall not forget!"

855 King Gunther spoke, "Let him come forward now.
  If he has made this boast, he must so avow
  Or else he must deny what here you say."
  They sent for Kriemhild's lord to come without
    delay.

856 Sigfrid saw their tears, their patience tried,
  And had no notion why. He quickly cried,
  "Why do these women weep, I'd like to know
  And by what cause I get the royal summons so."

857 King Gunther answered, "I am deeply pained.
  My lady Brunhild here has just complained
  You boast you conquered her and first became
  Her paramour. Or so at least your wife would claim."

858 Sigfrid answered, "Would she? If this is true,
  She will be very sorry before I'm through.
  I'll swear there's nothing to be offended at.
  Your men shall hear my oath: I never told her that."

859   "Let us see," announced the king of the Rhine;
"If you will swear this oath you offer, fine!
I'll judge you free of every evil thing."
They bade the proud Burgundians join to form
    the ring.

860   Sigfrid swore the oath with upraised hand.
Said mighty Gunther, "I fully understand
Your innocence, and I declare you quit
Of all my sister's charge: you've done no part of it."

861   Said Sigfrid, "If my wife has got some gain
Or comfort out of causing Brunhild pain,
Believe me, I am moved to deep regret."
At this the dashing courtiers turned, and their
    glances met.

862   "Women should be trained in a proper way,"
Said Sigfrid, "to curb the haughty things they say.
Warn your wife, and I will do the same.
Their immoderate conduct fills my heart with shame."

863   Many women's tongues were now at rest,
But Gunther's men beheld their queen depressed
And full of gloom, and pity at what they'd seen
Stirred their hearts. Hagen came and spoke to the queen.

864   He asked what the trouble was. In tears she told
What just had happened. He swiftly vowed to hold
A pledge that Kriemhild's husband should be
    punished—
Else from his life all joy should be forever banished.

865   Ortwin and Gernot joined the plotting twain,
As they discussed how Sigfrid might be slain.
And Giselher, the highborn Uta's son,
Came and heard their talk; he spoke as the loyal one:

866   "Noble warriors, why should you do this?
Does he deserve such hate, to prejudice
His very life? The things that women find
To get upset about are a vain and petty kind."

867   "Shall we raise cuckoos then?" Lord Hagen cried.
"That would give us little cause for pride.

He has boasted of my lady, my king's wife.
For that I swear to die unless he pays with his life."

868 The king spoke up: "What did he ever give
But good and glory? Let him live.
What use if I become his enemy?
He was always loyal and served us willingly."

869 "Indeed," said Ortwin, warrior knight of Metz.
"From all his mighty strength small good he gets!
I'll see that he's hurt—if you permit, my lord."
So most wrongfully the men gainsaid their word.

870 None but Hagen pressed this counseling.
He, at every moment, urged the king
That with his death the lands that Sigfrid had
Would surely fall to his crown. The king grew troubled
  and sad.

871 But there they left it. Again the jousting sounds,
As lances broke on shields, from the minster grounds,
As Sigfrid's wife went forth, to the castle hall—
With many of Gunther's men in no good mood at all.

872 The king declared, "Forgo this mortal fury.
He was born for our good, our greater glory.
He is, besides, a man of strength so grim—
If he should find this out, who'd dare face up to him?"

873 "He won't," said Hagen. "You shall keep it quiet.
I have in mind a secret plot and by it
He'll pay in sorrow for my lady's weeping.
Hagen has no further bond with him worth keeping."

874 King Gunther said, "How could that ever be?"
"I'll tell you how," said Hagen. "We shall see
That heralds come to our land declaring war,
In public, men whom no one here has seen before.

875 Then you, before your guests, bid every one
Take up our arms and march. When that is done,
He'll surely pledge his help—and lose his life!
I'll get the facts we need—straight from his own wife."

876 The king fell in with Hagen's evil plan.
Without a soul suspecting, they began

To shape their perfidy, these men of pride.
From two women's wrangling many heroes died!

<h2 style="text-align:center">FIFTEENTH ADVENTURE</h2>

How Sigfrid Was Betrayed

877   The fourth day dawned; thirty-two men were sighted
Riding to court. News was soon recited
To mighty Gunther, of truce revoked, and war—
A lie that held for women bitter woe in store.

879   The men were granted audience and told
How they were men of Liudeger the Bold.
The monarch bested once by Sigfrid's hand
And brought by him as hostage to royal Gunther's land.

879   He welcomed them and bade them take a seat.
"Let us stand," said one, "till we repeat
The message we have brought. This you must know:
That many a mother's son, my lord, is sworn your foe.

880   Our king and Liudegast call off the truce,
Who suffered at your hands such grave abuse.
They mean to ride in force against your land."
When Gunther heard the news it seemed his wrath was fanned.

881   They sent to their lodgings now the traitorous crew.
What could Sigfrid—what could any man do
To guard against this plotting? They would in time
Themselves be forced in pain to suffer for their crime.

882   The king took whispered counsel with his kin.
Hagen would not let his lord give in.
Though many would have willingly forgot,
Trony refused to hear of giving up the plot.

883   Sigfrid passed them once as they conspired
In whispered tones. The valiant lord inquired:
"Why are king's and courtier's faces so long?
If any one has harmed you, I'll help avenge the wrong."

884   "If I am pained, I have good cause to be,"
Said Gunther. "The Danish kings have challenged me.
They will, in open war, invade my land."
The stalwart warrior cried, "That let Sigfrid's hand

885 Prevent for you—as royal honors bid,
I'll deal with them as once before I did.
Their castles and their lands I'll level flat
Before I rest my hand. My life is pledge for that.

886 You and all your men can stay right here.
I and mine shall ride, and thus make clear
How willingly I serve. Bitter woes,
Be sure of that, shall come through me to all
     your foes!"

887 "This is good news to me!" And Gunther made
As if he honestly were glad of aid.
The faithless man, all in deceit, bowed low.
And Sigfrid cried, "You need have little worry now."

888 They mobilized the men of their company—
All this for Sigfrid and his men to see.
He ordered his Lowland troops in readiness.
The knights of Sigfrid sought their gear and battle dress.

889 "Father Sigmund, stay. There is no need
For you to go," he said. "With God's good speed
The shortest time will see us back again.
You'll have a pleasant stay, here with the king and his men."

890 They fixed the banners on, as if to go.
Many of Gunther's vassals did not know
The true account of all these steps they took.
A crowd was there with Sigfrid, gathered around to look.

891 Helmet and corselet tied upon their horse,
Stalwart knights prepared to set their course
Away from home. And now Lord Hagen went
To Kriemhild, ready to leave, asking her assent.

892 "How lucky for me," she said, "that I should win
The sort of man who dares, for friends and kin,
To be defender, as Sigfrid does for mine!
In the pride and joy of this," she cried, "my heart shall shine.

893 Lord of Trony, loyal friend, reflect!
I never bore you hate, but full respect.
Grant me reward of this in my husband's name!
If I insulted Brunhild, he should not bear the blame.

894 Whatever I did, I've since regretted roundly,
And he himself it was who thrashed me soundly
For saying what so weighs upon her mind.
My lord exacted penance, and that of the strictest kind."

895 "The two of you will shortly reconcile
Your differences, oh Queen. But say meanwhile
How by helping him I might serve you—
None I'd rather help, and nothing I'd rather do!"

896 "I should never fear," replied Kriemhild,
"In any battle-storm his being killed,
Had he not this rash and headstrong will,
For then my gallant lord could never suffer ill."

897 Said Hagen, "Lady, if you have cause to feel
That he is vulnerable, do not conceal
By what devices this may be averted.
Afoot or riding then I'll be on guard, alerted."

898 "You are kin to me, and I to you.
I commend to you my lord, and this I do
In faith that you may guard the one I love."
She told him things that better were not spoken of.

899 She said, "My lord is bold, and strong as well.
By the mountain when he fought and the dragon fell—
He bathed himself in its blood, and never since,
In any battle waged, could weapons wound my prince.

900 Still, whenever he fights, I have my fears,
Where warriors hurl so many heavy spears,
That I shall lose my dearest husband there.
Alas, he causes me such great and frequent care.

901 I tell you now, upon your charity—
And may you ever keep your faith with me!—
Where my beloved husband may be hit
And hurt. In trust to you, my friend, I utter it.

902 When in the dragon's wounds, and in the well
Of steaming blood he bathed himself, there fell
Between his shoulder blades a linden leaf.
There he can be hurt. This is my cause for grief."

903 Hagen of Trony said, "If you will sew
A little mark on his coat, then I shall know,

When we are fighting, where to shield my friend."
She thought to save his life—she caused his bitter end!

904 "With finest silk I'll sew upon his cloak
A secret cross, and there," the lady spoke,
"Protect my husband when the battle flows
Around him violently, and he must face his foes."

905 "Dear lady," Hagen answered, "I will do it!"
And so she thought her lord would profit through it,
But thus is was instead he stood betrayed.
Hagen took his leave, his happiness was made.

906 The spirits of the court were gaily keyed.
I doubt if ever knight will do such deed
Of treachery as by his will occurred,
When Kriemhild put her trust in Hagen's faith and word.

907 In all good cheer, at dawn the following day,
His thousand men and Sigfrid rode away,
Avenging, as he thought, his friends' distress.
Hagen rode so close that he could scan his dress.

908 When he had seen the cross, he sent two men,
In secret, to tell a different tale again:
How peace should be restored to Gunther's land,
And how they came to him at Liudeger's command.

909 Sigfrid now rode back, in sad dismay;
His friends were not avenged in any way.
They hardly talked him into turning 'round.
He rode to see the king. What words of thanks he found!

910 "Sigfrid, noble friend, may God reward
Your willingness to do what I implored.
I'll always give you thanks, as I should do.
More than all my friends, I place my trust in you.

911 Since this campaign has ceased to be our care,
Let us hunt the Vosges for boar and bear,
As I have often done." This was a plan
That Hagen first proposed, the false and faithless man.

912 "Send to all my guests and let them know:
We'll make an early start. Prepare to go,
All those who wish to hunt. And those who stay
To pay the ladies court will please me well that way."

913   With perfect sense of form, Sigfrid cried:
"Whenever you call the hunt, I shall ride.
Lend me a beater then, and if you could,
Some hunting dog, and I shall ride with you to the wood."

914   "Do you want only one?" the king replied.
"If you wish I'll lend you four, well-versed and tried
In woods and forest paths, the tracks of game.
They'll get you safely back to the camp from which you
        came."

915   The dashing warrior rode to see his wife.
Hagen took his plot on the hero's life
Straightway to the king—through and through
A deed of faithlessness, and more than man should do.

SIXTEENTH ADVENTURE
How Sigfrid Was Slain

916   Gunther and Hagen, bold, but with the face
Of false deceit, proposed a forest chase:
To hunt with sharpened spears the wild swine,
The bison and the bear—is there any sport so fine?

917   They took with them supplies of every kind.
Sigfrid rode, in grace and noble mind.
Beside a cooling spring he lost his life—
This was the work of Brunhild, royal Gunther's wife.

918   To Kriemhild's side the stalwart knight had gone.
His hunting gear and theirs was loaded on,
Ready to cross the Rhine. Never before
In all her days, had Kriemhild cause to suffer more.

919   He kissed his love upon her lips and cried,
"God grant I see you safe again, my bride,
And may your eyes see me. Now you must find
Diversion with your kin, I cannot stay behind."

920   She thought of the words she spoke in Hagen's ear
(And dared not now repeat). In pain and fear
The princess grieved that she was ever born—
Kriemhild wept, her tears unnumbered, all forlorn.

921   "Give up this hunt!" she cried. "Last night I dreamed
A painful thing. Two wild boars, it seemed,
Pursued my lord across a field. In sleep,
The flowers all turned red. I have my right to weep;

922   I fear from many hands an evil plot—
What if someone here should think he'd got
Ill use from us and turned this thought to hate?
Dear lord, I say, turn back, before it is too late."

923   "I'll soon return, my dear, I swear I will.
I know no persons here who wish me ill,
For all your kin are well disposed to me,
And I have always acted so that this should be."

924   "Oh no, my lord, I fear it can't go well.
Alas, I dreamed last night two mountains fell
On top of you, and I never saw you again.
If you should leave me now, my heart will be heavy with pain."

925   He held his perfect wife in arms' embrace,
With lover's kiss caressed her lovely face.
He took his leave and soon he went away.
Alas, she never saw him safe beyond that day.

926   They rode to a certain heavy wood, in quest
Of hunt and sport, and many of the best
Were they who followed Gunther's party there.
The only ones who stayed were Gernot and Giselher.

927   The horses went ahead, across the Rhine,
Full laden with the hunters' bread and wine,
Their fish and meat, and other good supplies
To suit a wealthy king in full and fitting wise.

928   At the forest edge they had their camp site placed.
By this device the haughty hunters faced
Where game would run, there on a spacious isle.
They told the king that Sigfrid had ridden up meanwhile.

929   The hunters' stations now were occupied
At every major point. Lord Sigfrid cried,
That stalwart man, "And who shall show the way
To the woods and the waiting game, you lords in bold array?"

930   Hagen said, "Before the hunting starts,
Why not split our group in several parts?
Thus my lords and I may recognize
Which hunter masters best our forest enterprise.

931   All the men and hounds we shall divide.
And each one choose the way he wants to ride.
Whoever hunts the best, his be the praise!"
The hunters did not wait, but went their separate ways.

932   "One dog is all I need—more's a waste,"
Lord Sigfrid said, "a hound that's had his taste,
To help him hold the scent through all this wood."
Thus said Kriemhild's lord: "This hunting will be good."

933   His ancient huntsman chose a goodly hound
Who soon had led them to a spot of ground
Where game in plenty ran. They bagged at will
Whatever rose from cover—experts do it still.

934   All the hound could flush fell to the hand
Of valiant Sigfrid, prince of Netherland—
So fast his horse that nothing got away.
His was the greatest praise for work in the hunt that day.

935   In all respects a skilled and sturdy man!
He made the kill with which the hunt began:
A mighty boar that fell at a single blow.
Shortly then he saw a monstrous lion go.

936   He strung and shot as the dog flushed his prey.
The sharp and pointed arrow sped its way.
The lion sprang three times—then it fell.
His fellow huntsmen praised him, saying he hunted well.

937   He added elk and bison to his bag,
Aurochs—four of them—and a giant stag;
His horse was fast, it never fell behind,
And they could not escape—no hope for hart or hind.

938   The hunting dog now found a giant boar.
It fled, the master hunter on the spoor
Without a moment's pause, and sticking tight.
The angry pig turned back and rushed the gallant knight.

939   What other hunter could have drawn his sword
To slay as easily as Kriemhild's lord?

After the kill they brought the hound-dog in.
Now the Burgundians learned how good his luck had been.

940   His fellow sportsmen said, "If you don't mind,
You might, my lord, just leave a few behind.
You've emptied hill and forest all this while.
Please let something live!" At this he had to smile.

941   There still was noise and clamor all around
Of hunters, and hunting dogs, so great a sound
That hill and forest answered. (The men released
A full two dozen packs, to hunt the forest beast.

942   And many animals would not survive.)
The other hunters thought they might contrive
To win the prize—an honor not for earning
With hardy Sigfrid there, where hunting fires were burning.

943   The chase was over now—and yet not quite.
Returning hunters brought to the camping site
Hides of many beasts, a host of game.
And ah, what wonderful things for the royal kitchen came!

944   The king was ready now to take repast,
And ordered the hunt informed. A single blast
Upon a horn sufficed to signify:
The noble prince had come to the camping site nearby.

945   A hunter of Sigfrid's cried: "My lord, I hear
By the sound of horns they want us all to appear
At camp again. I'll send an answer back."
(They blew for the other hunters, by way of keeping track.)

946   "We'd better leave the woods," Sir Sigfrid cried.
They hurried on, his horse at an even ride.
Their noise aroused a savage beast who broke
And ran—an angry bear. The hero, turning, spoke:

947   "I think we'll have some sport for our comrades there.
Let go the hunting dog, I see a bear.
He'll come to camp with us—as good as done!
He cannot save himself, unless he can really run."

948   The hunting-hound was loosed, the bear took flight.
Off to ride him down went Kriemhild's knight.
He came where trees lay felled and blocked the path.
The mighty beast now felt secure from the hunter's wrath.

949 The haughty warrior leapt at once from his steed
And ran on foot. The bear, forgetting heed
And caution, failed to run and soon was caught
And swiftly tied—and not a scratch had Sigfrid got!

950 The captured beast could neither claw not bite.
He tied him to the saddle, the fearless knight,
And mounting, rode to camp. The feat was done
In a hero's pride of heart and all for the sake of fun.

951 He came to camp arrayed in his splendid gear:
Broad-bladed and massive, his mighty spear,
Down to his very spurs a handsome sword,
And a horn of reddish gold in the hand of the gallant
   lord.

952 Of finer hunting garb I never heard.
He wore a black silk cape; his cap was furred
With sable skins and very richly made.
He had a quiver, too, adorned with costly braid,

953 And covered with panther hide—by purpose so
Because its smell was sweet. He had a bow
No man except himself could bend an inch,
If he were asked to draw, without an archer's winch.

954 His suit was made throughout of otter's skin
With patches sewn from head to hem therein.
The gleaming pelts had golden buckles on;
At the hunter's right and left the clasps of red gold shone.

955 He carried Balmung, too, his handsome sword,
So broad and sharp as never to fail its lord
In helmet strokes, its edges true and tried.
This was a huntsman great in confidence and pride.

956 And since I have the full account to tell:
The choicest arrows filled his quiver well,
Spliced with gold, the blades were a good hand wide.
Whatever felt their cut, so stricken, swiftly died.

957 He rode with spirit, the way of hunting men.
Gunther's thanes could see him coming then.
They hurried out to hold his tourney-mare.
There at his saddle, tied, was a big and vicious bear!

958   Jumping down, he loosed the ropes that bound
The bear by foot and maw. The dogs around,
As many as saw the beast, gave tongue and bayed.
The bear was all for the woods; the men—a bit afraid!

959   Into the kitchens he went, confused by the noise.
Ho, but that place was not for the kitchen-boys!
Kettles were tumbled, hardly a fire was whole.
And oh, what foods were strewn among the ash and coal!

960   Men were leaping up on every hand.
The bear was angry now. At the king's command
The dogs that still were leashed they cut away.
With a better end that would have been a merry day.

961   No waiting now, but up with spear and bow
And after the bear, to see where he would go.
They dared not shoot with all the dogs around.
They raised a fearful racket and made the hills resound.

962   The bear, pursued by dogs, began to flee.
Kriemhild's lord kept up—and none but he.
He ran him down, with his sword he struck him dead;
Later they brought him back to camp and the fire-stead.

963   All that saw it praised a mighty deed.
They bade the noble hunters come and eat.
The whole assemblage sat on a pleasant sward.
What marvelous foods were set before each noble lord!

964   The stewards took their time in bringing wine.
Otherwise no service quite so fine
Was ever seen. These men would have no reason
To fear a word of censure, but for their stain of treason.

965   Sigfrid said, "It gives me some surprise
When they sent us from the kitchen such supplies
Of excellent food, and no one brings the wine.
If they serve their huntsmen thus, the next time I'll
      decline.

966   I think I merit better service," he cried.
Falsely spoke the king, from the tableside:
"We'll make up later what you missed at first.
This is Hagen's fault—he'd let us die of thirst."

967   Said Hagen of Trony, "Listen, my lord, to me.
       I thought the hunt today was meant to be
       In Spessart and that is where I sent the wine.
       We missed our drinks today; I'll not forget next time."

968   "Confound them," answered Sigfrid then, declaring:
       "They should have brought me seven sumpters bearing
       Spiced wine and mead. And failing that,
       Was there no place closer to the Rhine we could have sat?"

969   Said Hagen of Trony, "Noble knights, my king.
       Not far from here I know a cooling spring.
       Do not be angry now—why not go there?"
       (Counsel fraught, for many, with sorrow and grievous care).

970   The pang of thirst was all that Sigfrid feared.
       He ordered the table that much sooner cleared,
       That he might go to the hills and find the spring.
       There they worked their plot—a black and faithless thing.

971   They placed on carts the game Sigfrid had killed
       To have it carried home, and all who beheld
       Granted Sigfrid honor in high degree.
       (Hagen broke faith with him—and he broke it
           wretchedly).

972   As they were about to go to the linden tree
       Lord Hagen said, "They're always telling me
       How nothing is fast enough to keep the pace
       With Sigfrid running. I wish he'd show us how he can race!"

973   Cried the Prince of the Low Lands, Sigmund's son:
       "Find out for yourself, my friend! If you want to run
       A race to the spring, all right. Whoever's faster
       To the finish we shall all acknowledge master."

974   "Very well," said Hagen then, "let's try."
       Stalwart Sigfrid made a bold reply:
       "I'll first lie down in the grass before your feet."
       Royal Gunther smiled, the words he heard were sweet.

975   Sigfrid had more to say: "I'll tell you what.
       I'll carry every bit of clothes I've got,
       My spear and shield, and all my hunting gear."
       He put his quiver next to his sword and laced it there.

976   Gunther and Hagen removed their clothes and stood
       In their white underwear. It did no good.
       Across the clover like two wild panthers burst
       The pair of running men, but Sigfrid got there first.

977   (In all, from many men, he won renown!)
       He loosed his sword, and put his quiver down
       And leaned on a linden branch his giant spear.
       The splendid stranger stood by the waters flowing
             clear.

978   With perfect sense of form in everything,
       He laid his shield on the ground beside the spring
       And would not drink, however great his thirst
       (Evil thanks he got!) till Gunther drank there first.

979   The spring was pure and good and cool.
       Gunther bent his head above the pool
       And after drinking rose and stepped away.
       Ah, if Sigfrid could have done the same that day!

980   He paid the price for the courteous thing he did.
       His sword and bow Lord Hagen took and hid
       And hurred back where the spear had lain before.
       He looked for a certain mark on the cape that Sigfrid
             wore.

981   As Sigfrid leaned to drink, he took his aim
       And hurled it through the cross. The heart-blood came
       Welling from the wound, richly to spill
       On Hagen's clothes. No knight has ever done so ill.

982   He left the spear embedded by Sigfrid's heart.
       Never in all this world did Hagen start
       And run so fast from any man before.
       When good Lord Sigfrid knew the vicious wound he bore,

983   He leapt from the spring like a man out of his mind.
       Up from his heart and towering out behind
       Rose the shaft of the spear. His bow and sword
       He sought in vain, or Hagen would have his due
             reward.

984   The wounded man could find no blade to wield,
       And nothing left to fight with but his shield.

He snatched it up and after Hagen he ran—
Even thus he still caught up with Gunther's man.

985   Mortally wounded as he was, he hit
So hard with his shield that from the edge of it
The precious jewels spun, and the shield was shattered.
For that most splendid knight revenge was all that
      mattered.

986   Hagen stumbled and fell at Sigfrid's blows—
So violent all the island echoes rose!
Had Sigfrid sword in hand, he would have killed him.
What rage in the wounded man, as hurt and anger
      filled him!

987   The color of Sigfrid's skin had turned all pale.
He could not stand. His strength was doomed to fail;
He bore the mark of death in all his pallor.
Many lovely women later mourned his valor.

988   So Kriemhild's husband fell where flowers grew.
They saw the blood that left his wound burst through,
And then from bitter hurt he cursed them all,
Whose faithless plotting first designed his cruel fall.

989   Cried Sigfrid dying, "Cowards, knave on knave!
Is murder your reward for the help I gave?
I kept my faith with you, and so I pay!
A shame upon your race, what you have done today.

990   Every child that's born to you will bear
The stain of this forever. Far too unfair
Is this revenge you take for your hate of me!
You should be banned in shame from decent
      company."

991   The other knights ran up where he lay slain.
It was, for many there, a day of pain,
For he was mourned by all that ever served
A loyal cause—no more than a gallant man deserved.

992   Another mourned: the king of Burgundy.
The dying man looked up; "What need has he
To weep for hurt who caused it? Scorn of men
Is all it earns," said he. "Why not forget it then?"

993   Cried Hagen, "I don't know what you're mourning for.
Our fears are at an end. How many more
Will dare to stand against us? A fortunate hour,
I say, when I destroyed his pride and all his power!"

994   Cried Sigfrid, "Boasting is an easy art.
If I had seen the murder in your heart,
I should have taken care to guard my life.
I worry not so much for me as for my wife.

995   And God have pity that my son was born,
Whom men in later days will heap with scorn
For having kin who bear the murderer's taint.
If only I had strength!—I have a just complaint."

996   Said the dying man, in anguish: "Noble king,
If you intend to do a loyal thing
In all this world for any man, then take
My wife in your protection, for grace and mercy's
         sake.

997   And let it profit her that she's your sister,
As you are a well-born prince, in faith assist her.
My father and men have a long time to wait.
Never did woman's pleasure end in pain so great."

998   The flowers all around were wet with blood.
He fought with death but not for long—what good?
Death has always owned the sharper sword.
He had no longer strength to speak, that gallant lord.

999   Soon, when the warriors saw the knight was dead,
They placed him on a shield all golden red,
And then debated how they might proceed
Best to conceal the fact that Hagen did this deed.

1000   And many spoke: "We have seen evil done.
Hide it then, and all shall speak as one
That Kriemhild's husband rode a forest lane
To hunt alone, was met by bandits there, and slain."

1001   "I'll take him back," said Hagen. "Have no doubt:
It's all the same to me if she finds out.
She caused my lady Brunhild misery—
Now let her weep as much as she wants, for all of me!"

SEVENTEENTH ADVENTURE

How Kriemhild Wept over Her
Husband and How He Was Buried

1002   They waited for night and crossed the Rhine in force.
Truly, heroes never hunted worse:
The game they slew—a cause for women's tears.
Many warriors paid the price in later years!

1003   Of overweening pride you hear me sing.
And awful vengeance. Hagen had them bring
The murdered lord of the Nibelungs, had him laid
Before the women's hall where Lady Kriemhild stayed—

1004   In secret, by the door where she would pass
And find him as she left for matin mass,
Before the day had dawned. (And rare indeed
The call to such a mass that Kriemhild failed to heed.)

1005   By custom now they rang the minster bell.
The lovely lady roused her maids to tell
What light to bring, what special clothes to wear.
Then came a chamberlain and found Lord
        Sigfrid there.

1006   He saw him red with blood, his clothing wet,
But who it was he had not fathomed yet.
He took the light in hand to the women's room—
To bring his lady Kriemhild a tale of death and doom.

1007   As she and her maids were about to make their way
To church and mass, the chamberlain shouted, "Stay!
Before your chamber lies a warrior slain."
And Kriemhild now began to weep in boundless pain.

1008   Before she knew it was her husband there
She thought of Hagen's query, his pledge of care
To save his life. Her hurt now passed all measure.
Upon his dying she forswore all joy and pleasure.

1009   Without a word she fell to the floor and lay,
In all her beauty, shorn of joy, the prey
Of endless pain. At last she raised her head
And shrieked till all the chamber echoed. Servants said:

1010 "What if this should be some stranger, though?"
Blood welled from her lips in her heart's woe:
"It is Sigfrid, my own dear lord, I know it.
Hagen did this deed and Brunhild made him do it."

1011 There where he lay she asked that she be led.
In her white hands she lifted his handsome head.
She knew at once, for all the blood and red,
The hero of Nibelung land lay wretched there and dead.

1012 The gracious queen cried out in misery,
"O Lord, my sorrow! Look, your shield is free
Of any mark of swords. They murdered you!
I'd have the death of him who did it, if I knew."

1013 All her attendants mourned with her and cried,
Sad at heart because their lord had died,
Their noble master whom they now had lost—
Brunhild's rage avenged by Hagen, at bitter cost!

1014 The wretched woman spoke, "I ask you, go,
And wake up Sigfrid's men. Tell my woe
To Sigmund too, and ask if he will shed
His tears with mine and help me mourn my husband
        dead."

1015 A herald went where the Nibelung warriors slept,
Sigfrid's men. His painful tidings swept
Their spirits bare of joy. Until they heard
The sound of weeping, they could not believe his word.

1016 And soon the herald came where lay the king.
Sleep for Sigmund was a foreign thing.
I think his heart had told him what befell:
Never again to see his son alive and well.

1017 "My lord, wake up! I come as Kriemhild's thane
Sent to tell the hurt she bears, whose pain
Beyond all other pain strikes to her heart.
Help her mourn this hurt, of which you bear your part."

1018 Sigmund rose. "What hurt is this?" he cried,
"You say the queen has suffered?" The man replied,
In tears, "I should keep the news from you in vain;
Gallant Sigfrid, Lord of Netherland, is slain."

1019   "Now stop your wicked tales," Lord Sigmund spoke,
"For sake of me. This is no time to joke,
Telling somone that his son is slain.
My life would be too short to overcome such pain."

1020   "If you will not believe what I report,
Listen!—you can hear them, queen and court,
Mourning over Sigfrid slain and dead."
Great fear struck King Sigmund then. He sprang from bed.

1021   His hundred men rose up, their hands in haste
Upon their long and pointed blades, they raced
Toward the sound of weeping, all distraught.
The thousand also came whom gallant Sigfrid brought.

1022   They heard the ladies weep their great distress.
Some imagined they should even dress
To visit them; their very senses strayed
With so much sorrow. They went, in their deepest hearts
        afraid.

1023   Sigmund came to Kriemhild. "I curse this land
And the trip that brought us here. What murderer's hand—
Here among such friends a cruel reward—
Has robbed me of my son and you of your dear lord?"

1024   "If I found out," she cried, "my heart and hand
Would be his enemies until I planned
Mortal hurt for him. His every friend
Would weep and, weeping, know who caused his sudden end."

1025   Sigmund the king embraced the prince, his son.
Such sadness then took hold on every one
That palace and hall were filled with a great noise;
The whole town of Worms echoed with their cries.

1026   No none could console Lord Sigfrid's lady.
They now removed the clothes from his fair body
And washed his wounds and placed him on a bier.
In hurt and misery his followers paid dear.

1027   Then cried his men-at-arms from Nibelung lands:
"He shall be avenged by willing hands.
The man we want is in this castle here."
And Sigfrid's warriors ran to get their battle-gear.

1028   Eleven hundred knights with shield in hand
Approached in force, King Sigmund's whole command.
He wanted vengeance gained for the death of his son,
And truly, he had cause enough to wish it done.

1029   They did not know on whom to turn their swords,
Unless it be on Gunther and Gunther's lords,
With whom he rode to hunt. For war arrayed
Lady Kriemhild saw them come. She stood dismayed.

1030   However deep her hurt or great her dread
She feared still more to see the Nibelungs dead
At the hands of her brother's men. To thwart this end,
She warned them out of kindness, as friend to loyal friend.

1031   The wretched woman cried, "What could you do,
Sigmund, my lord? Oh if you only knew!
King Gunther has so many fearless men—
The knights you send against them will not return again."

1032   Helmets donned, battle was their heart's need.
And yet the noble queen began to plead
And even to command that they desist.
Great her sorrow when it seemed they might insist.

1033   She cried, "Wait until some better time,
My lord, and you and I shall avenge this crime
Against my husband. Once I am satisfied
I know who took him from me, he shall be destroyed.

1034   The Rhineland has its arrogant men—no lack.
That is why I say do not attack.
For they have thirty men to your one.
(God give them just reward for the evil they
        have done!)

1035   Stay here and share my pain. At break of day,
Men of noble heart, help me lay
My dear lord in his coffin, I beg of you."
The warriors answered, "What you ask, we shall do."

1036   No one could tell you how vast it was, the crowd
Of knights and ladies weeping now—so loud,
The sound of lamentation roused the town,
Whose goodly people all in haste came running down.

1037   They mourned with the many guests their painful loss.
No one yet had told them by what cause
Sigfrid the noble warrior lost his life.
So noblewoman wept, and good burgher's wife.

1038   They ordered smiths, out of silver and gold
To build a coffin, large and strong, and told
The men to make the straps the finest steel.
(How sad at heart his passing made the people feel!)

1039   The night was past, and day, they said, would break.
Then the noble lady bade them take
Her dear lord Sigfrid to the minster square.
They walked, weeping, all the friends he counted there.

1040   They brought him to the church. Bells rang,
And everywhere many priests sang.
Then King Gunther came with his retinue
To join their lamentation—and fierce Hagen, too.

1041   "My dear sister, alas! what pain you bear!"
Said Gunther. "Oh, that something could repair
Our loss! We'll mourn forever that Sigfrid died."
"You have no reason to," the wretched woman cried.

1042   "If you had cared, all this would never be!
I say it now: you gave no thought to me
When I was torn from my dear husband," she said.
"I would to God it had been me, and I were dead."

1043   And now, as Gunther's men cried out denial:
"Who says he has no guilt, submit to trial!
He shall, before this crown, approach the bier.
For such is the quickest way to make the truth appear."

1044   A mighty marvel, this, which still is done,
For if beside the corpse you see the one
Who bears the mark of murder, the wounds will
        bleed.
And so it was they knew that Hagen did the deed.

1045   The wounds poured out their blood, as they had
        before.
Those who once wept greatly now wept more.
And Gunther cried, "I will have this clearly said:
Bandits struck him down. This is nothing Hagen did."

1046   "Well I know who the bandits are," she cried.
        "God grant his own good friends be not denied
        Their vengeance. Gunther and Hagen, you did this!"
        Men of Sigfrid waited battle—in eagerness.

1047   Then Kriemhild spoke, "Help me bear my pain."
        And both the men came by where he lay slain,
        Her brother Gernot, Giselher the youth.
        They mourned him with the others in honest faith and truth.

1048   Their tears welled deep for him. Time for mass
        Had now arrived, one saw the people pass—
        Man, woman, child—to church where they,
        For whom the loss was less, wept too for him that day.

1049   Both brothers said, "As you are sister to me,
        Take heart in face of death, for this must be.
        We'll make amends to you as long as we live."
        But solace now was more than all the world could give.

1050   His coffin stood complete by noon that day,
        They took him from the bier on which he lay,
        And still his lady would not have him buried—
        By which the people all were pained and sadly
                worried.

1051   They wrapped his body in finest silk. I doubt
        That any eyes were dry. The queen cried out
        In her heart's grief, Uta the noble born,
        Over the handsome knight. Her ladies helped her
                mourn.

1052   They heard from the minster now the sound of song.
        He lay in state. There came a mighty throng—
        What offerings they brought for his soul's repose!
        He still had loyal friends, here among his foes.

1053   Poor Kriemhild spoke to her chamberlain. Said she:
        "Let them take this trouble because of me,
        All of those who wished him well and hold
        Some love for me. For Sigfrid's soul, give out his gold!"

1054   No child of age to use his wits at all
        Was left at home. Before the burial
        They sang that day a hundred masses or more.
        Crowds of Sigfrid's friends thronged the minster door.

1055   Mass was sung and done, the people gone,
And Kriemhild spoke, "Do not leave me alone,
To watch beside my perfect lord tonight.
All my joy is gone with him, and my delight.

1056   Three days and nights I wish him here in state,
To fill my heart with my sweet lord and mate.
And what if God command that death take me?
That at least would end my wretched misery."

1057   The townsfolk started on their homeward way,
But priests and monks the lady asked to stay,
And all his retinue who served her hero.
The night they spent was troubled, the day was full of
      sorrow.

1058   Many stayed with not a thing to eat
Or drink. For those who wished, a lavish treat
Of food was set, proclaimed and all supplied
By royal Sigmund. Nibelung hearts were sorely tried.

1059   For all three days, they say, the clerics there,
Who knew the chants of mass, were forced to bear
The brunt of toil, but their reward was great.
Those who once were poor were now in rich estate.

1060   Needy men who had no gold were sent,
With money from Sigfrid's store, to the sacrament.
Since it was not his lot to live, they told
His treasure out for his soul, thousands of marks
      of gold.

1061   She granted in usufruct the lands around,
Wherever cloisters were or poor men found;
Silver and clothing she gave to those in need,
Proving her high esteem for him by her gracious deed.

1062   When the third morning came, and matinsong,
The square before the minster seemed to throng
In all its breadth, with weeping folk who brought
Homage even after death, as dear friends ought.

1063   In the space of four days, or so they say,
Thirty thousand marks were given away—
Maybe more—in alms for his soul's rest,
For now his manly beauty and his life lay waste.

1064 When God was served and mass was sung no longer,
Many struggled mightily to conquer
Pain untold. They had his body borne
From church to grave—for those who missed him most
to mourn.

1065 With loud cries the crowd walked with him there—
No joy in man or woman, anywhere.
Before they buried him they sang and read.
The best of priests was there, for burial of the dead.

1066 Before his wife had reached the grave she fought
With grief so great that often people brought
Fresh water to bathe her face, for this affliction
Sent upon her spirit was harsh beyond description.

1067 It seems a miracle that she recovered,
Though many helped her mourn the loss she suffered.
Cried the queen, "By your fidelity,
Men of Sigfrid, grant this proof and grace to me:

1068 One little pleasure after all my pain,
That I may see his noble face again."
She begged in such a piteous way, so often,
They were forced at last to break his splendid coffin.

1069 They brought the queen to him. She took his head
In her white hands to raise it. Though he lay dead
She kissed him now, noble knight and good.
Because of all her pain, her shining eyes wept blood.

1070 This was their wretched parting. Now they bore
The queen away for she could walk no more
But lay in a deep swoon, his stately wife,
From sorrow that nearly cost her sweet and comely
life.

1071 Now that they had buried him, a pain
Beyond all measure fell on every thane
From Nibelung land who had followed Sigfrid there,
And seldom did one see Lord Sigmund free of care.

1072 Some, for sorrow, three days long refused
To eat or drink at all, but so ill-used,
The body could not long endure, and then
Worry gave way to eating, as often it is with men.

EIGHTEENTH ADVENTURE

How Sigmund Returned Home

1073 And then it was that Sigmund chose to come
To Kriemhild, saying: "We are going home.
We seem unwelcome guests here by the Rhine;
Beloved lady, come where all the land is mine!

1074 You and I have lost through breach of faith,
Here in this land, your husband done to death—
Why should you pay for that? I'll be your friend
For love of my son, so let your doubts be at an end.

1075 And you shall also have the power and might
That Sigfrid showed you once, that valiant knight.
Crown and country shall be at your command
And Sigfrid's men to serve you, whenever you demand."

1076 They told the men to ready their departure—
And now a hurried search for steed and charger,
For they were loath to stay with bitter foes.
They ordered maids and ladies to gather up their clothes.

1077 Now that Sigmund wished to be away,
Kriemhild's family pled with her to stay.
Remaining in her mother's company.
The gracious lady answered, "That could hardly be.

1078 How could my eyes endure the constant sight
Of him who hurt me so?" "It is only right,
By reason of loyalty if by no other,
My sister," said Giselher, "to stay here with your mother.

1079 You have no need of those who tried to rend
Your heart with care and grief. You shall depend
On my resources!" "I can't," she said. "The pain
And hurt would kill me if ever I saw Hagen again."

1080 "I'll see that you don't have to, sister dear,
Stay with Giselher your brother here,
And I shall make amends for your husband's fate."
Wretched Kriemhild cried, "Truly my need is great!"

1081 While Giselher in kindly words besought her,
Uta came, with Gernot, to beg her daughter

(As did her loyal friends) that she might stay:
Sigfrid's men were not her kin in any way.

1082 Gernot said, "You and they are strangers.
And no man lives so strong but time or dangers
Bring him down. Dear sister, ease your heart.
Reflect—and stay with your kin; this is the better part."

1083 She promised Giselher that she would stay.
Out the horses came; they were on their way.
Sigmund's men, to the land of Nibelung,
With all the gear of warriors loaded to take along.

1084 The king, Lord Sigmund, went to Kriemhild then
And said to her, "My lady, Sigfrid's men
Wait by their mounts—it is time for us to ride.
Burgundy is not for me." The lady replied:

1085 "The counsel all my loyal kinsmen give
Is to stay with them. I have no relative,
They say, in all the Nibelung domain."
What Sigmund heard from Kriemhild filled his heart
        with pain.

1086 King Sigmund said, "Let no one tell you so!
You'll have the crown as before, and the powers that go
With wearing it, in presence of my kin.
I don't want you to suffer for our losing him.

1087 For sake of your boy, my lady, come with us.
You have no right to leave him fatherless.
Your growing son will be a comfort to you.
Meanwhile you'll have knights to serve you, brave and true."

1088 "Lord Sigmund, I cannot ride with you," said she.
"I must stay here, whatever happens to me—
Here with my own kin, to help me mourn."
(Words, it seemed to them, not to be lightly borne!)

1089 "Let us say to you," they all agreed,
"That we should feel most pained and wronged indeed
If you decide to stay here with our foes.
Heroes' journey never came to sadder close."

1090 "Go without fear," she said, "in God's kind hands!
Escort shall be yours to Sigmund's lands,

That you may ride in safety. I give to you
My dearest child in trust, believing you are true."

1091 Hearing thus that she would never leave,
All of Sigmund's men began to grieve—
Truly, a wretched parting this, the queen's
And royal Sigmund's for now he learned what anguish
    means.

1092 "Cursed tourney!" cried the noble king.
"The pleasure of chivalry will never bring
The like on any king or his family
Never again will you see us here in Burgundy."

1093 Sigfrid's men spoke plainly: "This country yet
May see us on the march if we should get
Certain proof by whom our lord was slain.
They shall not look for foes among his kin in vain!"

1094 Sigmund kissed Kriemhild and spoke in grief,
To know in truth that she would never leave:
"We ride, then, homeward. Our joys are scattered far.
And now at last I know how great my sorrows are."

1095 They rode from Worms to the Rhineland, unescorted.
You may be sure that they were so stout-hearted,
If they were set upon by enemies
They'd well defend themselves—valiant Nibelungs, these!

1096 They did not go to say farewell nor claim
Their leave of anyone. But Gernot came,
In kindness, to see the king, and Giselher.
His loss had touched them—of this they made him well
    aware.

1097 Gernot the prince spoke up, a man well-bred:
"God in heaven knows, though Sigfrid's dead,
I bear not even the blame of having known
Who hated him. To your lament I add my own."

1098 Young Giselher, who gave them good escort,
Led from the land the king and all his court
Of knights, in sorrow home to Netherland.
Little happiness they found in kin or friend!

1099 How their journey fared I cannot say,
But those at home heard Kriemhild every day
Weeping, and solaced by none in heart or mind—
Unless by Giselher, for he was staunch and kind.

1100 Brunhild the fair still held forth in pride.
Little did she care how Kriemhild cried—
For her she had no love or faith to offer.
(At Kriemhild's hands, in later days, she too would suffer!)

NINETEENTH ADVENTURE

How the Treasure of the Nibelungs Came to Worms

1101 With Kriemhild left a widow, Eckewart stayed
At home with her, with all his men, and paid
Daily homage and service, so to afford
His lady help in frequent mourning of his lord.

1102 In Worms, by the church, they built her a building there;
Wide it was and large, costly and fair.
Here with all her suite she dwelt most sadly,
Though often she went to church, reverently and gladly.

1103 She hardly left the place her love was buried.
There in sorrow of heart she always hurried,
Asking the good Lord's mercy on his soul.
This was the hero's mourning—constant and heart-whole.

1104 Uta and her ladies tried to keep
Her spirits high; her heart's wound ran so deep
That nothing came of all their sympathy.
She longed for her beloved more insatiably

1105 Than ever woman for man, before or since.
(In this you see her proven excellence!)
She mourned till the end, as long as life endured,
But what a bold and thorough vengeance she secured!

1106 After the pain of her lord's death, it appears
She lived alone for three and a half long years,
Never to speak to Gunther; never to see,
In all of the long time, Hagen her enemy.

1107   Said Trony now, "What of some arrangement
Devised to end your sister's long estrangement,
And bring the Nibelung gold to our domain?
If she were well disposed there might be much to gain."

1108   "We'll try," said Gunther. "Let my brothers, who spend
Much time with her, persuade her to be our friend—
Perhaps we'll get it without offending her."
"I do not think," said Hagen, "that such will ever occur!"

1109   He sent to court Sir Ortwin, then, for one,
And Margrave Gere another—which being done,
They brought in Gernot and young Giselher,
Who did their best to urge her, both with a friendly air.

1110   Bold Gernot of Burgundy addressed her so:
"You mourn too long. The King would have you know
It was not he by whom your lord was slain;
And yet we hear you mourn, my lady, in awfullest pain."

1111   "No one accuses him. Hagen got
From me the secret of the fatal spot—
And killed him! How," she cried, "was I to know,
When he came to me, that Hagen hated Sigfrid so?

1112   Else I should never have betrayed his life
And should not now be weeping—his wretched wife!
I'll never forgive the ones who did that deed."
Then the handsome Giselher began to plead.

1113   At last she promised, "I shall see the king."
With that, they saw him come to her and bring
His closest friends, but Hagen did not dare,
For he had done her harm, and the guilt was his to bear.

1114   When she renounced her hate for Gunther, this
(And doubly!) was the moment for his kiss.
Had she not been undone by schemes he laid,
He might have come before her lightly and unafraid.

1115   Never with more tears was peace regained
Among old friends, and still her sorrow pained.
But she forgave them all—all but one!
(Except for Hagen, there'd have been no murder done.)

1116   They so arranged it shortly afterward
That Lady Kriemhild got her treasure-hoard

From Nibelung land and brought it back to Worms.
This was her dowry money, and hers by any terms.

1117   Gernot went to get it, with Giselher.
Kriemhild bade eight thousand men prepare
To fetch the treasure from its hiding-place,
Where Alberich stood guard, and the best of Alberich's
race.

1118   The valiant dwarf soon saw the men of Rhine
Come for the hoard, and to his friends made sign:
"This treasure here we do not dare withhold.
The noble queen will claim it as her dowry gold.

1119   But this would not have happened," Alberich spoke,
"If we had never lost the Magic Cloak,
And Sigfrid, too, by wickedness and crime,
For Lady Kriemhild's lover wore it all the time.

1120   And now he falls a prey to evil thus,
Because he took the Magic Cloak from us
And forced this land to bear him fealty."
With this the steward turned and went to get the key.

1121   Kriemhild's vassals stood by the great hill,
With her several kin. Down to the sea, to fill
The little ships, they bore the treasure in line
And carried it over the waves, up the river Rhine.

1122   Now hear the wondrous measure of the hoard:
All that twelve wagons could load aboard,
In four days and nights, and haul away
From the mountains, each one making three good trips a
day!

1123   Nothing but jewels and gold! And had they paid
Every person there, it would have weighed
Not less than half a pound, each portion of it.
Such treasure Hagen had no lack of cause to covet!

1124   (The best lay underneath: a wand of gold—
Understand its nature and you would hold
The world in sway and every man therein!)
Now Gernot left, and with him many of Alberich's kin.

1125   When they had got the treasure to Gunther's land
And Lady Kriemhild took it all in hand,

It filled the palace rooms and many a tower.
Never had people known such endless wealth and power.

1126 Yet had there been a thousand times as much—
If Sigfrid were restored to sight and touch,
With empty hands she would have stood at his side.
No warrior ever found himself a truer bride.

1127 She drew to the land, now that she had the treasure,
Unnumbered foreign knights. She gave in measure
So unstinting they never in all their days
Saw such bounty. For merit and worth they sang her praise.

1128 To poor and rich she now commenced to give
So freely Hagen said if she should live
For any time she'd soon have every stranger
Bound to her in service—for them a mortal danger.

1129 Said Gunther, "Her person is hers, and her property.
Whatever she does with it, don't look to me
To interfere! We two are barely friends.
Forget who shares her silver and gold, and what she
          spends."

1130 Hagen said to the king, "A prudent man
Would leave no part of this hoard to a woman who can,
With generous giving, bring about the day
That bold men rue it all—as we of Burgundy may!"

1131 "I swore to her an oath," cried Gunther the king,
"That I would cause her no more suffering.
She is my sister. That oath I'll not disclaim!"
Hagen spoke once more, "Then let me take the blame."

1132 All their oaths were broken. Her vast wealth
They took from her, a widow; Hagen, by stealth,
Got the key to it all. When Gernot learned
The true account of this, a brother's temper burned.

1133 Said Giselher, "Hagen has done my sister wrong.
I should have stopped it! He'd not live for long,
I swear, if he were not blood-kin to me."
Kriemhild renewed her tears. Said Gernot, "Are we to be

1134 Forever weighted down beneath this blanket
Of gold? We'd do better if we sank it

In the Rhine—and let it be no man's!"
The queen had come to her brother; she spoke with a
    piteous glance:

1135   "Dear Giselher, my brother, remember me,
And be my guardian in life and property!"
"It shall be so, I promise," he replied,
"When we come back again. But first we mean
    to ride."

1136   And now the king and his kinsmen left the country,
And with them rode all the finest gentry,
But Hagen alone, who stayed, for the enmity
He bore the Lady Kriemhild—he did it willingly!

1137   Before the mighty king returned once more,
Hagen had taken all the treasure-store
To Locheim, there to sink it in the Rhine.
(He hoped to use it later—that was not fate's design.)

1138   The princes now, and their many men, returned,
As Kriemhild with all her maids and ladies mourned
For her great loss; it pained them bitterly.
Giselher would gladly have proved his loyalty.

1139   All together said, "He has done great wrong."
But Hagen, evading the princes' wrath so long,
At last regained their favor. They let him be;
But never had Kriemhild hated him more bitterly.

1140   Before the lord of Trony hid the gold
They pledged with mighty oaths that they would hold
The treasure secret till every man was gone—
Never one of them to have it, nor pass it on.

1141   The pain of her husband's death revived and throbbed
Within her breast, as now they even robbed
Her wordly goods. This plaint was never stilled
In all her life, until her span of days was filled.

1142   After Sigfrid's murder, it appears,
She lived in deepest grief for thirteen years,
And never could forget her master's death.
Her faith to him was known the country's length and
    breadth.

TWENTIETH ADVENTURE

How King Attila Sent to Burgundy for Kriemhild

1143   This was the time when Lady Helke died
And King Attila sought a second bride.
His friends proposed a noble widow who came
From the land of Burgundy—and Kriemhild was her name.

1144   Since lovely Helke now had left his life,
They urged, "If ever you would win a wife,
The best and noblest any king has won,
Then take this lady, once the wife of Sigmund's son."

1145   The king replied, "I don't see how I can,
For I am unbaptized, a pagan man.
And she who is a Christian will not agree.
What a miracle if that could ever be!"

1146   But his bold knights rejoined, "Perhaps she would;
Because your wealth is great and your name is good.
One ought at least to venture asking her.
Think of the happy feeling so sweet a love would stir!"

1147   The king inquired, "Who among you knows
Land and people where the Rhine flows?"
Good Ruedeger of Pöchlarn spoke, "I've known
That high and gracious queen since she was a girl half-grown;

1148   And Gunther and Gernot, highborn, worthy lords;
The third is Giselher. In deeds and words
They strive to merit glory and high fame,
And always in the past their forebears did the same."

1149   Attila said, "Tell me this, my friend:
Is she the one to wear the crown in my land?
For if she is as fair as I hear say,
My closest friends and kin will not regret the day."

1150   "In beauty she is like my lady, sir,
Like mighty Helke; none to rival her
Among the queens of all the world around.
Whoever wins her hand—his happiness is crowned."

1151   "Then as you love me, Ruedeger," he cried,
"Take up this task. If ever at my side

The lady lies, I'll give, as best I can,
A fit reward. You will have well fulfilled my plan.

1152   Out of my stores I'll see that they provide
All the clothes you want and steeds to ride,
To keep you happy—and the men of your company.
All this I order done for you on your embassy."

1153   Ruedeger replied, the great margrave,
"Such help would be a shameful thing to crave.
I'll be your messenger to Rhenish lands
At my own cost in goods, which I have from your hands."

1154   Asked the mighy king, "When will you go
For my fair queen? May God in glory bestow
Safety to you on the trip—to my lady, too;
And Fortune grant me this, that she should smile on you."

1155   Said Ruedeger, "Before we leave the land,
The arms and dress we take must first be planned,
To gain from kings respect and dignity.
I want five hundred men to take to the Rhine with me,

1156   That Burgundy, in seeing me and mine,
May then concede: Never were sent to the Rhine
By any king so many men, so far,
Or better fitted out than these of Attila's are.

1157   Not wishing, Sire, to turn your purpose aside—
She was Sigfrid's once, his noble bride—
The son of Sigmund, you have seen him here;
One says but simple truth to make his glory clear."

1158   "What if she was his wife?" the king returned.
"Such was the great distinction Sigfrid earned.
That I could never think her of low degree.
And for her loveliness she greatly pleases me."

1159   "I'll tell you then," Ruedeger went on,
"Twenty-four days from now, and we'll be gone.
Soon I shall see my wife and say to her:
Your word shall go to Kriemhild with me as messenger."

1160   He sent to Pöchlarn news for the margravine
That he would leave to sue for the hand of a queen,

A wife for Attila. Sad, yet happy too,
She thought of lovely Helke and the sweet love they knew.

1161 So Gotelind heard of the trip, and sorrow swept
Upon her at the thought. She rightly wept.
What lady could be like her queen before?
Whenever she thought of Helke, her inmost heart was sore.

1162 In seven days the margrave rode away
From Hungary. Attila's heart was gay.
There in Vienna town their clothes were made,
So Ruedeger was loath to have his trip delayed.

1163 In Pöchlarn they were waiting, margravine
And margrave's daughter both, the child all keen
To see her father, the men of Ruedeger—
Many lovely girls happily waiting there!

1164 Before the margrave left Vienna behind,
To go to Pöchlarn, clothes of every kind
Were loaded on their beasts. Little wonder,
Escorted as they were, that nothing fell to plunder.

1165 Reaching Pöchlarn now, the lord requested
Shelter for his friends, Soon they rested,
By his kindness, each in a decent room.
Gotelind was glad to see her master home.

1166 And his dear daughter, the young margravine—
For her his coming never could have been
Sweeter than now. And the Huns—with what delight
She met these knights! The maiden cried, her spirits
        bright:

1167 "All welcome to my father and his men!"
She earned a burst of gracious thanking then
From many zealous knights. And Gotelind
Herself was well aware of her master's state of mind.

1168 She lay that night at the side of Ruedeger.
With tender questioning, she asked him where
The King of Huns had ordered him to go.
"My lady Gotelind, I shall gladly let you know.

1169 My mission is to seek another bride
For my liege-lord, since lovely Helke has died;

I ride to where the Rhine river runs—
For Kriemhild, who shall be the great queen of the Huns."

1170 "Such favor," Gotelind said, "may God confer!
We hear so many splendid things of her,
We may in time place her in my lady's stead
And gladly see the Hunnish crown upon her head."

1171 The margrave spoke, "My dear, these men who go
To the Rhine with us—to them I beg you show
Your generous wealth and sweet desire to share it.
When heroes travel richly, they travel bright in spirit."

1172 "To every one of them, if he will choose,
I'll gladly give whatever he can use,"
Said she, "before you leave with your company."
The margrave said, "Your kindness greatly pleases me."

1173 What silks they brought from her chambers, splendid furs
In linings neatly sewn from neck to spurs,
And these she gave the knights in generous share,
For they were the men he wanted, the choice of Ruedeger.

1174 They rode from Pöchlarn at dawn of the seventh day,
The host and his knights, well laden on their way
With arms and clothing through Bavarian lands,
Yet they were not attacked en route by robber bands.

1175 Within twelve days they reached the Rhine, and word
Of this could not be hid; they soon had heard,
The king and all his men, that guests had come
From foreign lands. The king then asked if there were some

1176 Who knew these men, that they should tell him so.
The heavy load their sumpters bore would show
That they were men of wealth. They brought them
      down
Without delay to lodgings in the ample town.

1177 And when they had the strangers settled there
They all began to wonder, most aware
Of these new men, whence they might have come.
The king of the Rhineland asked if Hagen knew their home.

1178 "I have not seen them yet," said Trony's lord,
"But soon we shall, and I give you my word:

Wherever they came here from, these mounted men,
They must be foreign indeed, to be beyond my ken."

1179   The strangers now were lodged and settled down,
The messenger got dressed in his splendid gown,
His company as well, and rode to court—
Cut by a master, theirs were clothes of the finest sort.

1180   Bold Hagen spoke, "As far as I can tell—
I have not seen this man in a long, long while—
The way they look it might be Ruedeger
Of Hunnish lands, a lord most valorous and fair.

1181   "What?" said the king. "Am I to understand
That Pöchlarn's lord has come to this, my land?"—
A question Gunther the king had barely broached
When Hagen saw indeed that Ruedeger approached.

1182   He and all his friends went out in force,
As five hundred men got down from horse.
Lords from Hunnish lands were welcomed well.
Of clothes more elegant than theirs no man could tell.

1183   Hagen of Trony's words were loud and clear:
"God give welcome to all you warriors here,
Regent of Pöchlarn, men of your company!"
(A greeting for Hunnish heroes, in honor and dignity.)

1184   The king's own next of kin drew near the place
Where Ortwin spoke to Ruedeger, face to face:
"Never in all our days—I swear it's true—
Have we seen guests," he said, "as welcome here as you."

1185   For greetings given now they thanked them all
And with their suite entered the door of the hall.
There they found the king and his company;
He rose up from his seat, in greatest courtesy,

1186   And went to them. What perfect form in greeting!
He and Gernot showed their zeal in meeting
Properly their guest and his noble band.
The king took Ruedeger and led him by the hand.

1187   He brought him to his seat, at his own side
And bade them serve (which they did with pride)
Excellent mead, and the very finest wine
That ever they could find in lands around the Rhine.

1188 Giselher and Gere both appeared.
Dankwart and Folker heard, their hearts were cheered
By news of the strangers there. They came to bring
Their greetings to well-born knights, in presence of the king.

1189 Hagen of Trony spoke, and said to his lord,
"Our vassals here should render fit reward
For kindness done us by the margrave's aid.
The husband of fair Gotelind deserves to be repaid."

1190 Gunther spoke, "One thing I must say:
Tell me how it goes with them, I pray—
King Attila and Helke of Hungary."
Margrave Ruedeger spoke, "I'll tell you willingly."

1191 With all his men he rose and left his seat,
Addressing the king, "If it is right and meet
To give me leave, my lord, abandoning
My silence now I'll gladly tell the news I bring."

1192 Gunther said, "Whatever news you have
For me and my men, speak! I give you leave
To tell us—I'll not call my friends in session,
But grant you full respect, to carry out your mission."

1193 Boldly the messenger spoke, "My sovereign sends
His loyal faith to you and all the friends
That you may have, here by the river Rhine.
My mission to you is also a true and faithful sign.

1194 My king has asked that his grievous case be said:
His people joyless, and my lady dead.
Mighty Helke, wife of my noble lord,
And orphaned by loss of her, many a maid, her ward;

1195 Children of highborn princes, reared by her hand!
From this the misery stems that fills our land,
For they have none to care and none to tend.
My sovereign's sorrow, I think, will have no early end."

1196 "God's grace to him," said Gunther, "that he sends,
With such good will, to me and all my friends
His pledge of faith. I'm pleased to hear from him.
We hope to merit his regard, my men and kin."

1197 Champion of Burgundy, Lord Gernot, said,
"Helke's death the world may well regret,

With all the excellence that she displayed."
Hagen and others seconded the speech he made.

1198   Said Ruedeger, the noble emissary,
"Since you permit, my lord, the message I carry
From my beloved master I shall speak.
For him, since Helke's dying, everything is bleak.

1199   They tell him Sigfrid is dead, and in his place
Kriemhild has no husband. If this is the case
And if you grant permission, she shall wear
The crown among his knights. This is the message I bear."

1200   The great king spoke (his manner most refined):
"She'll hear my wishes, if she is so inclined;
Within three days from now I'll let you know.
Before I question her, why should I say no?"

1201   Meanwhile they saw to the comfort of every guest.
So well they served them, Reudeger confessed
He found good friends in Gunther's men of war.
Hagen was kind to him, as he to him before.

1202   So Ruedeger remained till the third day.
The king requested counsel—the wisest way—
Whether it seemed to his kin a proper thing
That Kriemhild should be married to Attila the king.

1203   All advised him so, but Hagen not.
He spoke to Gunther the king, "If you have got
Your wits about you, this will never be.
And she must be prevented, even if she agree!"

1204.   "And why," said Gunther, "should I not concur?
Whatever pleasant thing can come to her
I ought to grant. She is after all my sister.
Whatever serves her greater good we ought to foster."

1205   Hagen replied, "This much and I am through:
If you could know Attila as I do—
Let her marry him as you have said,
And you'll be inviting troubles heaped upon your head!"

1206   "And why?" said Gunther. "I shall take good care
To stay away from him, and need not fear
His enmity, though she should be his wife."
"I'll never agree to that," said Hagen, "in all my life."

1207   They sent for Gernot and Giselher, to see
Whether these two lords would not agree
That Kriemhild ought to wed the mighty Hun.
Hagen still opposed, but not another one.

1208   Spoke young Giselher of Burgundy,
"Now is the chance to show your loyalty,
Friend Hagen; make up to her for all the pain
You caused nor grudge her what good fortune she may gain.

1209   So numerous are the wrongs that you have done
To hurt my sister," Giselher went on,
"That if she hates you, what could surprise you less?
Never was woman robbed of so much happiness."

1210   "One thing I know, and tell you," Hagen said.
"Should she live long enough to go and wed
King Attila, her plotting will bring us harm,
For she will then be served by many a man's strong arm."

1211   In answer to Hagen, valiant Gernot cried,
"It may well not occur until they've died
That we should ever go to Attila's land.
For sake of our noble name, lend her our loyal hand!"

1212   Hagen said, "No man can talk me down.
If ever Kriemhild wears Queen Helke's crown
She'll do us ill, however she may start it.
All you lords would be far better advised to thwart it."

1213   Giselher, Uta's son, in anger gave
His answer: "All of us needn't play the knave.
If honors come to her, our hearts should fill
With joy. I'll serve her truly, Hagen, say what you will."

1214   Hagen listened, in a somber mood.
Gernot and Giselher, proud and good,
And powerful Gunther joined at last to advise
Consent without ill will, if Kriemhild found it wise.

1215   Prince Gere said, "I'll tell my lady this:
Not to take Attila's suit amiss—
Lord in awful liege of many a knight,
Whatever wrong she suffers, he can make it right."

1216   He went to Kriemhild then. In gentle meeting
She received him. "Well may you grant me greeting,"

He cried, "and herald's pay for what I bring.
Good fortune comes to ease you of all your suffering.

1217 For sake of your love, my lady, one of the best
Who ever wore a crown or yet possessed
A king's domain in honor has sent to us
Noble lords as suitors. Your brother informs you thus."

1218 "May God forbid," this wretched woman cried,
"That you or any of my kin deride
My sorrow. What would a man want of me,
If ever his heart enjoyed a good wife's company?"

1219 And so she was opposed. But later came
Her brothers Gernot and Giselher, to claim
That she should be consoled and not demur:
If she were to wed the king, all would be well with her.

1220 That she should ever give a man her love
Was more than they could all persuade her of.
The lords then begged, "To this at least defer,
If nothing else, and deign to see your messenger."

1221 The noble lady said, "I shall not claim
I do not wish to see him, since Ruedeger came,
So excellent a man. If it were not he,
But any other herald, he'd not lay eyes on me.

1222 Tomorrow morning ask if he will be
At my apartments. He shall hear from me
My will in this, which I shall then declare."
And thus it was all renewed, her tears and
        great despair.

1223 Noble Ruedeger wished for nothing more
Than to see the gracious queen, for on this score
He knew himself so skilled, that if she waited
For his visit, she could surely be persuaded.

1224 Next morning early, after matin-song,
The noble heralds came, a mighty throng.
With Ruedeger to court—and what a sight
To see in such apparel so many a splendid knight!

1225 The gracious Kriemhild, sad of heart, was there
To wait the noble herald, Ruedeger.

He found her in mourning dressed as for every day,
While all her suite was clad in the most expensive way.

1226 She went to meet him, standing by the door,
Welcoming King Attila's men—no more
Than twelve in all went in. What courtesies
Were offered them! She never saw such heralds as these.

1227 Lord and vassals sat, upon her order.
Standing before the queen, two Counts of the Border,
Eckewart and Gere, took their place.
Because of their lady-liege, there was not a cheerful face.

1228 Lovely women sat at her feet, while she,
In constant plaint, renewed her misery.
The clothes before her breasts were wet with tears.
(And none of this escaped the margrave's eyes and ears.)

1229 "Child of a noble king," said the messenger,
"On me and those who came with me confer
Permission to stand before you and declare
The tidings we bring to you, for which we journeyed here."

1230 "Say what you wish, you have the leave you require,
Noble herald. Such is my desire
That I shall gladly hear." But all the rest
Could clearly sense: she seemed unwilling and distressed.

1231 The prince of Pöchlarn spoke, "A glorious king,
Noble Attila, loyally bids us bring
Expression of his regard to you in this land.
My lady, he sends good knights to ask for your love and
      hand.

1232 He offers you affection, sweet and free
Of any pain, and pledges constancy
Such as he had for Helke, his heart's love,
Whose merit he spends bitter hours thinking of."

1233 The queen replied, "Margrave Ruedeger,
If anyone knew the sharp pain I bear,
He would not ask that I should marry again:
I lost the finest husband a woman could ever win."

1234 "What makes up for pain," the prince declared,
"But joy of friendship, if one be so prepared,

And find another one who suits the part?
For nothing so avails against distress of heart.

1235   And if you deign to wed my noble lord
The power of twelve great crowns is your reward.
He'll give you thirty princes' share of land,
All of whom were conquered by his most valiant hand.

1236   Many worthy men will acknowledge you
Their mistress, who once were Helke's retinue,
And many ladies born of princely rank,
Over whom she ruled." He spoke on, bold and frank:

1237   "If you consent, my lord the king assures,
To wear the crown at his side, this too is yours:
Of powers that Helke had, the uttermost,
The mighty fealty of all of Attila's host."

1238   The queen replied, "How in all my life
Should I desire to be a hero's wife?
In one, death hurt me so that I shall cherish
In my heart the grievous pain, until I perish."

1239   The Huns spoke up, "Queen of power and grace,
Your life with him will be so full of praise
That you will have great joy, if it comes to be;
For the king has many lords of charm and dignity.

1240   If Helke's maids in waiting and yours could be
Together in a single company,
Heroes' hearts would glory in the sight.
Take our word, oh queen, all things will turn out right."

1241   With perfect presence she said, "Let this be all
Until tomorrow morning, then pay your call,
And I shall give you the answer you ask of me."
(What could gallant warriors do except agree?)

1242   When they had all returned to their quarters there,
The lady sent for Uta and Giselher.
She told them both, her mother and her brother:
The one right course for her was weeping—there was no
        other.

1243   Giselher answered, "Sister, I am told—
And would believe—that all your pain of old

King Attila would banish, once you wed.
I think you should, whatever others may have said.

1244 His power to give redress or aid," said he,
"Extends from Rhone to Rhine, from Elbe to sea.
There is no other king of equal might.
If he espouses you, rejoice, with every right!"

1245 "Brother dear, why give me such advice?
Mourning and tears are far the better choice.
In courtly life how could I carry on?
Perhaps I once had beauty, that is past and gone."

1246 Lady Uta addressed her daughter, too:
"What your brother counsels, dear child, do!
Follow your friends, and see if good may be.
I've seen you live so long in the depths of misery."

1247 She asked and begged of God that he not withhold
The means to be generous: silver, garments, gold,
As it was when he was alive, her lord the prince;
Never had she enjoyed such happy moments since.

1248 She thought in her heart, "Christian as I am,
Can I betroth myself to a pagan man?
As long as I live I'd feel the great disgrace.
Though he gave me all his realm, it is more than I can face."

1249 And there she left it. All the night till day
Deep in many thoughts, the lady lay
Upon her bed, her bright eyes never dried,
Until she went to matins again, at morningtide.

1250 They came in time for mass, the kings of the land,
Meaning to take their sister again in hand;
They counselled her to marry the royal Hun,
But all of them found that lady a most unhappy one!

1251 They now sent out to gather Attila's men,
Who wished for leave to go back home again,
With yes or no, however it might be;
Ruedeger came to court, met by his company.

1252 To make the test of the noble prince's mind,
And do it soon—so were they all inclined.

Back home, they said, was a long way to fare.
They found where Kriemhild was and took Lord
   Ruedeger there.

1253   The knight began to entreat, but gently so,
Begging the noble queen to let him know
What answer to King Attila she would choose.
It seemed that she could still do nothing but refuse;

1254   For she would never love another man.
The margrave cried, "That is the poorest plan!
Why should you want to ruin so fair a life?
With honor and homage still you can be a good man's wife."

1255   Their pleading did no good, till Ruedeger
Assured the queen, in trust alone with her:
Whatever wrongs she suffered, he'd requite,
On the darkness of her grief there seemed to fall some light.

1256   He said to the queen, "Let this weeping be.
If you had among the Huns no one but me,
Beside my loyal kin, and my retinue,
A man would pay for any harm he did to you."

1257   Her mind was now relieved in good degree.
"Swear me an oath, whatever is done to me,
That you will be the first to avenge my hurt."
The margrave said, "On that, milady, you have my word."

1258   The margrave joined with all his men, in swearing
To serve her loyally for ever, declaring
She would never lack, in Attila's land,
For homage of excellent knights, the pledge of Ruedeger's hand.

1259   The faithful woman thought, "Since I have found
So many friends, let people all around,
Who see me wretched, say what they wish to say.
What if my lord's dear life should be avenged some day?

1260   If Attila has as many men as these
And they are mine to command, I'll do as I please;
And surely he's so rich that I can be free
In giving, though evil Hagen took my wealth
   from me."

1261   She said to Ruedeger, "Could I but know
That he was not a heathen, I'd gladly go,

Following his will, and we'd be wed."
"Speak no more of this, my lady," the margrave said.

1262 "So many of his knights are Christians now,
You'll suffer no remorse with him—and how
If you should bring about that he were christened?
Your reason to marry the king is not in this way lessened."

1263 Her brothers cried again, "Sister, agree,
And let this show of your displeasure be."
They begged so long, until the sorrowful one
Promised in their presence she would wed the Hun.

1264 "Poor queen that I am," she said, "I will comply
And go among the Huns, but I must try
To find some friends to take me to his land."
On this, in heroes' presence, Kriemhild gave her hand.

1265 Margrave Ruedeger spoke, "If you have two,
I have more beside, and that will do
To take you across the Rhine in propriety.
Lady, you should no longer stay in Burgundy.

1266 Five hundred of my men and kin will afford
Good service here, and will at home accord
With every wish, milady, and I the same,
Whenever you remind me, that I may bear no shame.

1267 Have them now prepare your riding gear—
You shall never regret what I counseled here—
Inform the maids you want to take with you;
For excellent knights will join us as we travel through."

1268 They still had jeweled harness they used to use
In Sigfrid's time. In honor, she could choose
Many maids to go, when she was ready.
They found a perfect saddle for every lovely lady.

1269 Whether they ever wore rich clothes before,
They had a plenty now for the trip in store,
Because of the king, of whom all people talked.
They opened boxes now which always had been locked.

1270 No idle hour till nearly the sixth day!
They took from garment bags whatever lay
Within their folds. Kriemhild came to unbar
Her treasury, making Ruedeger's men richer by far.

1271   She still had some of the gold from Nibelung land—
She wished the Huns to have it from her own hand—
More than any hundred horses could hold.
This was Kriemhild's plan, and Hagen heard it told.

1272   "She'll never waste her love on me, that's plain,
So Sigfrid's gold must not leave our domain.
Why should I hand my foes such revenue?
With treasure like this," he said, "I know what she
      would do.

1273   If once she got it there, it's plain to see,
It soon would be paid out for hate of me.
Beside, they don't have horses to carry the gold.
Hagen will keep it all—so let Kriemhild be told."

1274   She heard this news; it pained her bitterly.
The same was also told the kings, all three,
Who gladly would have stopped it. This came to naught,
But noble Ruedeger proposed this happy thought:

1275   "Mighty queen, why lament your gold?
Attila has for you a love untold,
And when his eyes shall once behold you there,
He'll give you more than you can ever spend, I swear."

1276   "Good Ruedeger," the queen replied at last,
"No king's daughter ever had so vast
A wealth of riches as Hagen took from me."
But then her brother Gernot went to her treasury,

1277   And set to the door, by royal right, the key,
Passed out her gold, as great a quantity
As thirty thousand pounds, or more, and bade
The guests receive it all. This made Gunther glad.

1278   Lord of Pöchlarn, Gotelind's husband, cried,
"Now if my lady wants it kept aside—
All that was ever taken from Nibelung land—
It need not ever be touched by mine or the queen's own
      hand.

1279   So have it put away, for I want none.
I brought along with me so much of my own
That we shall have, for the road, a good surplus.
Fare for the journey back stands splendidly with us."

1280 Her maids had packed a dozen boxes full
      Of golden things, in all this interval—
      The best there were; and these they carried thence,
      And for the ladies' journey many ornaments.

1281 Stunned by the force of fierce Hagen's works,
      She kept as an offering a thousand marks
      And spent it for her beloved husband's soul,
      Playing, to Ruedeger's mind, a loyal woman's role.

1282 Spoke the mourning queen, "Where are my friends,
      Who, for me, will live beyond the ends
      Of home and ride to the land of Huns with me?
      Take my money and buy them horses and livery."

1283 Kriemhild heard the Margrave Eckewart call:
      "Since I became your vassal first of all,
      I've served you loyally," the warrior cried,
      "And will, until the end, continue at your side.

1284 I'll take five hundred of my men, in faith
      And trust to grant you service. But for death,
      No force shall ever make us separate."
      For the words he spoke she bowed to him. Her need was
          great.

1285 Then they brought the steeds, for they were leaving;
      One heard their many friends deeply grieving,
      Uta the mighty and many a fair maid,
      So great was the pain at losing her which they displayed!

1286 A hundred splendid maids she too, attired
      In every way as dignity required;
      The tears ran coursing down from their bright eyes.
      (Attila's court would one day bring her many joys.)

1287 Then, as breeding willed and courtly manners,
      Came Gernot and Giselher with their retainers,
      On their dear sister's leaving, to give escort.
      They brought a thousand handsome men, knights at court.

1288 Neither Gere nor Ortwin stayed behind,
      Nor Kitchener Rumold either. Night would find
      They'd reached the Danube, there to settle down.
      (The farthest Gunther rode was just outside the town.)

1289 Before they left the Rhine, they'd sent ahead
The swiftest heralds to the Huns, who said
To royal Attila: Ruedeger had seen
And won as wife for him the high and gracious queen.

TWENTY-FIRST ADVENTURE

How Kriemhild Went among the Huns

1290 Let the heralds ride, and we shall say
How through this country Kriemhild made her way
And where Gernot and Giselher retired,
Having served her well, as loyalty required.

1291 They rode along to the Danube shore at Pförring,
There to take leave of her, no longer caring
To be kept from riding back—except
That even this must have its cost, and good friends wept.

1292 Said Giselher, a man of bravery:
"Whenever, sister you have need of me—
If ever you're in trouble, I shall go
To Attila's land to help you—only let me know."

1293 Kin of hers she kissed upon their lips.
Numerous sweet farewells for homeward trips
There were for Margrave Ruedeger's men-at-arms
The queen had many maids along, of many charms!

1294 How richly dressed they were, all hundred four,
In ornate, patterned silks! And warriors bore,
As they walked along the path, where the ladies were,
Broad shields in hand; till the gallant lords took leave of her.

1295 Down through Bavarian lands their journey stretched,
News of unknown guests advancing reached
The place where a cloister-house has always been,
Down where the Danube takes the waters of the Inn.

1296 A bishop dwelt in the town of Passau there,
But princely court and burgher's house stood bare,
As people sought their guests, in haste to get
Up to Bavaria, where Bishop Pilgrim and Kriemhild met.

1297 Knights of the land were not annoyed to see
The comely maidens in her coterie—

Their eyes paid court to daughters of high lords.
(They found for these noble guests good lodging after-wards.)

1298   The bishop rode to Passau with his niece.
They soon informed the burghers of the place
That Kriemhild came, his sister Uta's daughter—
And what a flood of greetings all the merchants brought
    her!

1299   It was the bishop's hope they might remain
But Eckewart said, "That wish is all in vain.
We have to go on down to Ruedeger's lands:
Many lords expect us—the news is in their hands."

1300   Of this the lovely Gotelind was aware,
Who with her highborn child made haste to prepare,
As Ruedeger asked and as to him seemed right:
That they might thus provide the queen with much delight,

1301   Riding out to meet her, with his thanes,
As far as the river Enns. Roads and lanes
On every hand were far from standing idle,
While they went out to meet their guests, on foot or saddle.

1302   By now the queen had come to Eferding.
Bavarian folk, had they a mind to cling
To ancient custom, could have brought the dangers
Of highway robbery and harm upon the strangers.

1303   This the margrave took good care to prevent.
He had at least a thousand knights who went
With him and Gotelind his wife. She, too,
Had many noble thanes in her splendid retinue.

1304   When they had crossed the river Traun and reached
The field beside the Enns, tents were pitched
And awnings, for the guests to spend the night—
Ruedeger provided for his guests' delight.

1305   Fair Gotelind had left her house behind;
Many steeds of noble stature lined
The roads and walked along with jingling reins.
Ruedeger was pleased, their welcome spared no pains.

1306   On either side, riding to merit praise,
Came many warriors, honoring the ways

Of chivalry, in games that maidens attended—
An office of knighthood by which the queen was not
    offended.

1307 When Ruedeger's men came into the strangers' view,
In spirit of knighthood a host of splinters flew
From warriors' hands high in the very skies—
They rode for praise and glory, before the ladies' eyes.

1308 In kindness now these many knights forsook
Their games to greet each other. Then they took
The lovely Gotelind to see Kriemhild,
As men who honored women found every moment filled.

1309 The lord of Pöchlarn rode to see his wife.
That he'd returned unharmed, in health and life,
From the Rhine, was no regret to her, for now
Her sorrow seemed removed, and joy in its place some-
    how.

1310 She greeted him. He bade her be dismounted
Upon the turf, with all the women she counted
In her company. For men of birth,
No idle moments—of service to ladies, little dearth!

1311 Now that Lady Kriemhild once had seen
With all her retinue the margravine,
She'd not go on, but drawing her horse's rein,
Asked to be lifted quickly from the saddle again.

1312 Now the bishop, leading his sister's daughter,
With good Count Eckewart as escort, brought her
To Lady Gotelind. With backward steps,
The crowd made way, as Kriemhild kissed her on her lips.

1313 Said Ruedeger's lady, sweetly, "How I prize
Dear lady, this good fortune that my eyes
Behold you here in this land. Past or present,
Truly, I can think of nothing half so pleasant."

1314 Said Kriemhild, "Noble lady, may God bless you.
If I stay safe and well—and Attila too—
For our encounter you may sometime be glad."
(Neither woman knew what shape the future had!)

1315 Now came, politely meeting, many a maid,
Receiving knightly homage, gladly paid.

Their greeting done, they sat on the clover lawn—
Friends to many now they never before had known.

1316 Wine was served the ladies. The time was noon;
The court would stay no longer. Riding soon,
They came where many spacious tents were ready—
Willing service there for strangers, lord and lady.

1317 They rested through the night, till break of day.
Men of Pöchlarn had to find some way
To shelter all their august visitors.
If little enough was lacking, the credit was Ruedeger's.

1318 Along the walls, the windows stood ajar—
The town was open wide! Guests from afar,
And welcome there, rode in through Pöchlarn's gate.
Their noble host provided shelter in fitting state.

1319 Ruedeger's own daughter went to greet
The queen most graciously, with all her suite.
Her mother, too, the margrave's wife, attended.
How kind a welcome to these maidens they extended!

1320 They took each other by the hand and went
To a most lovely palace of vast extent,
Beneath which flowed the Danube. Here with the breeze
To blow on them they sat and took their pleasure and ease.

1321 What other things they did I cannot say.
The knights of Kriemhild chafed at this delay
Which slowed their trip—it cast their spirits down.
What stalwart men went with them when they left the town!

1322 The margrave was kind in offer of homage and honor.
His daughter took what the queen bestowed upon her:
Lovely clothes and twelve red-gold armbands,
Gifts as good as any she took to Attila's lands.

1323 Though she had been deprived of the Nibelung gold,
All who saw her there were soon enrolled
In her support, for with the little left,
She gave her host's retainers each a generous gift.

1324 Lady Gotelind in turn conferred
Such honors on her Rhenish friends one heard
Of scarcely any guest who did not wear
Some splendid dress of hers or precious jewel there.

1325   When they had eaten and prepared to go,
The mistress of the palace came to show
Most loyal homage to King Attila's bride;
And she in turn embraced her lovely child, who cried:

1326   "My Queen, whenever you are so inclined,
I know my dearest father would not mind
Sending me to you, among the Huns."
The girl's sincere devotion Kriemhild felt at once.

1327   Their steeds were ready now and stood in view
Of Pöchlarn's gates. The queen now bade adieu
To Ruedeger's wife and daughter. Demoiselles
Of greatest beauty took their leave with sweet farewells.

1328   (Rarely, in time to come, would they behold
One another!) From Melk, in cups of gold
Flashing on outstretched arms, men carried wine
For the strangers on the road—this was their welcome
        sign.

1329   The lord who lived there was Astold by name—
He pointed out the road by which they came
To Austria, down the Danube, toward the spot
Called Mautern. What a royal welcome Kriemhild got!

1330   The bishop parted fondly from his niece.
How eagerly he wished her joy and peace,
And honor there to equal Helke's honor.
Oh, what splendid homage the Huns would shower
        upon her!

1331   They took the strangers to the banks of Traisen,
With Ruedeger's men to guide, till in due season
Came the Huns, riding overland.
There she found what lavish honors they had planned.

1332   Beside the Traisen was a castle-town
Owned by the Hunnish king, widely known
And called Traismauer—where Helke lived before
In perfect merit such as the world would see no more,

1333   Except for Kriemhild, who could give in measure
Such that after all her pain some pleasure
Still was hers—and homage rendered, too,
By King Attila's men, in full and generous due.

1334   Attila's power was granted far around,
Whence at all times in his court were found
The most courageous knights that Christendom
Or heathen countries knew—and all of these had come.

1335   Under his rule (but scarcely any more)
Men lived by Christian faith or pagan lore,
As they might choose. Whatever life each led,
On all alike the bounty of the king was shed.

TWENTY-SECOND ADVENTURE
How Attila Married Kriemhild

1336   At Traismauer she stayed four days as guest.
The dust upon the road was never at rest—
Like smoke from fires swirling, on every hand;
Attila's men came riding through the Austrian land.

1337   The king soon let his happy thoughts dispel
All trace of sorrow, from what they had to tell
Of Kriemhild in splendor crossing the countryside.
Attila hurried out to meet his lovely bride.

1338   Many valiant knights, of many tongues,
Rode the ways before the king in throngs,
Christian men and heathens far and wide,
Coming to his lady in splendor and in pride.

1339   Many men were riding, Greek and Russian;
On perfect mounts they came, in swift procession,
Strong on their steeds, Wallachian and Polish
Warriors playing all their native roles with relish.

1340   Many horsemen rode from Kiev land,
And savage Kangli tribes. And many spanned
Their bows to shoot, for sport, at birds in flight;
Back to the fullest draw they drew their arrows tight.

1341   In Austria on the Danube lies a town,
Its name is Tulln. Customs all unknown
To her before she saw for the first time there,
And many welcomed her, whom later she did not spare.

1342   Retainers rode ahead on Attila's way,
In might and cheerful mind, polite and gay,

Great and august princes—twenty-four!
They wished to see their queen, desiring nothing more.

1343   Duke Ramung, with his troop of seven hundred,
From Wallach land—before her eyes they thundered,
Riding as fast as flying birds almost.
Then came Gibech the prince with all his splendid host.

1344   And now Hornbow the brave, with a thousand men
Turned from the king to his queen, raising then
A loud noise, as is by custom done
Within that country. How they rode, those men of the Hun!

1345   Then, from Denmark, valiant Haward came;
Iring the bold, free of the traitor's blame,
Fair Irnfrid from Thuringia, sharing the honor
Which came from such a welcome as they urged upon her.

1346   They had twelve hundred warriors in their band.
Attila's brother Bloedel of Hunnish land
With his three thousand warriors now appeared
Where the queen was waiting. In splendor Bloedel neared.

1347   And then Attila came, and Theodorich
With all his friends. High in praise, the pick
Of noble-lineaged knights, a stalwart crowd,
And all of this made Kriemhild's spirit light and proud.

1348   "His Majesty will," said Ruedeger to the queen,
"Welcome you, my lady, upon the scene.
Whomever I bid you kiss, so let it be—
You may not greet his vassals all in like degree."

1349   They lifted the gracious queen down from her mount.
Attila now would wait on no account
But with his valiant lords sprang to the ground
And walked toward Lady Kriemhild—the happiest man
    around.

1350   The train of the princess' dress, so people say,
Was borne by two great princes on the way,
As King Attila came to her, and she,
In turn, kissed the noble prince most tenderly.

1351   She raised her wimple; her lovely color shone
In all that gold. And many men looked on

And swore that Helke could have been no fairer.
Now Lord Bloedel, brother of the king, came nearer.

1352   To him the margrave said a kiss was due,
And royal Gibech. Theodorich stood there too.
Attila's lady kissed, in all, twelve lords,
And then to many knights extended welcome words.

1353   Attila stood by Kriemhild. The whole time through,
Young knights rode, as people still will do,
In splendid jousts and tilts, both Christian lords
And, after their several ways, men of the pagan hordes.

1354   In true chivalric form, Theodorich's knights
Made lances fly in splinters, over the heights
Of shields from hands of men as fine as live—
Shields the Germans left with holes more like a sieve!

1355   The breaking of lances raised a mighty sound.
All the knights of the land had gathered 'round,
And the royal guests, many noble men.
The glorious king arrived with Lady Kriemhild then.

1356   Beside them stood a pavilion of great expense,
And all the field around was filled with tents,
For men to rest in after all their pains;
There many maids were ushered by stalwart lords and
        thanes.

1357   And there the queen was brought, to take her seat
Upon the tapestried chair; and this was sweet
To Attila's mind; to see how people prized
This throning of the queen his margrave had devised.

1358   Just what Atilla said I do not know—
In his own right hand lay her white hand, though,
And lovingly they sat—but Ruedeger
Would still not leave the king alone and free with her.

1359   Then they bade the jousting be suspended;
So in honor all the tumult ended.
Attila's men repaired to the tents; they found
Good lodging for their guests, near and far around.

1360   The day was over now, and rest in store,
Until they saw bright morning shine once more—

And then to horse, and many men were mounted,
Honoring the king with pleasures and games uncounted.

1361   Attila told his Huns to act in manner
Suiting them. They journeyed to Vienna,
Leaving Tulln, and found there, well arrayed,
Ladies to greet Atilla's bride, and homage paid.

1362   All they needed was there in fullest measure.
Crowds of cheerful knights foresaw with pleasure
All the tumult. Search for lodging started.
Attila's feast began, gay and happy-hearted.

1363   Not all could stay within the city borders.
All but foreign guests should take their quarters,
Ruedeger said, out among the peasants.
I dare say one could find in Lady Kriemhild's presence,

1364   At any moment, Lord Theodorich
And many others. Rest for them was quick
To yield to labor—heartening to see
For all the guests, and sport for the margrave's company!

1365   The celebration fell in Whisuntide,
When King Attila lay beside his bride
In the city of Vienna. (Did her first wedding
Ever bring so many men to do her bidding?)

1366   By gifts she made herself well known to folk
Who'd never seen her, and many among them spoke,
"We thought that Kriemhild must have nothing left,
And here she works amazing things with every gift."

1367   The celebration lasted seventeen days.
I know of no king winning greater praise
For grander feast—of such we never hear.
And everyone had brought his newest clothes to wear.

1368   I doubt if she had sat with such a host
Of vassals in Netherland. For all the boast
Of Sigfrid's power, I think he never won
The number of noble knights she saw before the Hun.

1369   Nor has any king bestowed so many capes,
For his wedding feast, in wide and ample shapes,

With many other splendid clothes, to make
A sum so large as here was given for Kriemhild's sake.

1370   Both friends of theirs and guests were so inclined
As not to stint in wealth of any kind.
They gladly gave whatever people chose,
Till many stood, for their largess, bereft of clothes.

1371   Her life beside the Rhine she thought of yet—
Beside her noble husband. Her eyes grew wet
With tears which she concealed that none might see—
After so much pain to be honored in such degree.

1372   The merest trifle, all the giving done,
Beside Theodorich's! What Botelung's son
Had granted him was spent and given away.
And generous Ruedeger's hand did wonderfully that day.

1373   By order of Bloedel, prince of Hungary,
His many traveling chests were emptied free
Of gold and silver, all of which was spent.
Attila's heroes lived in joy and merriment.

1374   Werbel and Swemmel, minstrels of the king,
Got each a thousand marks—if anything,
I gather, more—upon this high occasion
When Kriemhild sat with Attila at their coronation.

1375   They left Vienna on the eighteenth morning.
Chivalric practice left their bucklers yawning
Wide with the cut of spears they bore in hand,
Thus King Attila came to his own Hunnish land.

1376   They stayed at ancient Hainburg overnight.
Who could guess the crowd or tell aright
The force with which they rode across the face
Of Attila's land? What beauties graced his native place!

1377   At mighty Wieselburg they had to embark.
The waters there, with horse and men, were dark
As solid ground, as far as the eye progressed.
Women weary of travel now found comfort and rest.

1378   Numbers of sturdy boats were lashed together,
Protected thus from harm by wave or weather,

And over all, their many tents were spanned,
As if they had beneath them open field and land.

1379   The news had come to Attila's fort at Gran,
And everyone there rejoiced, woman and man.
This was the suite where Helke once held sway;
They saw, with Lady Kriemhild, many a happy day.

1380   Numerous highborn maidens waited there,
Who since Helke's death had suffered care
And sorrow; daughters of seven kings she found,
Who graced in beauty all of Attila's land around.

1381   Mistress Herrat had the suite in charge,
Daughter of Helke's sister, her merit large,
Theodorich's betrothed, and royal child
Of King Nentwin, on whom in time great honor
        smiled.

1382   Her heart was glad to see the strangers come.
Money too stood ready, a mighty sum.
How Attila lived—who could describe the scene?
The Huns had never fared so well with any queen.

1383   As king and wife now rode up from the beach,
Noble Kriemhild heard the name of each,
And so could welcome him with better grace.
(With what a show of power she sat in Helke's place!)

1384   They rendered loyal services untold.
The queen, in turn, gave clothes away and gold.
And gems and silver, all she brought with her
Across the Rhine to the Huns—all this she must confer.

1385   Attila's kin and all his men became
Her subjects soon, to serve in Kriemhild's name;
And Lady Helke never had such power,
Since they were sworn to serve till Kriemhild's dying
        hour.

1386   Such honored excellence in court and nation,
That everyone found pleasant occupation,
According as his taste and mind might lean—
All for love of the king and of his gracious queen.

TWENTY-THIRD ADVENTURE

*How Kriemhild Planned to Avenge the Wrong
She Suffered*

1387 The truth of the matter is, till the seventh year
They lived together in much splendor here.
And then it was the queen gave birth to a boy.
Nothing else could have brought Attila greater joy.

1388 The queen would not give in till she realized
Her purpose to see Attila's son baptized
In Christian rites, Ortlieb to be his name.
Great was the pleasure reigning in Attila's domain.

1389 Every point of excellence that lay
In Helke's life she strove day after day
To equal, in mastery of manners led
By exiled Herrat, mourning in secret for Helke dead.

1390 She became well known alike to stranger and friend,
Who said no lady ever ruled king's land
So well and generously—this truth was clear.
She lived amid praise of the Huns until the thirteenth year.

1391 She now had seen that no one flouted her
(As any king's retainers still defer
To a prince's wife) and that she had twelve kings
Always before her. She thought of many painful things,

1392 Done to her at home. She also thought
Of the glories of Nibelung land, once hers, all brought
To nothing by Hagen's hand, in Sigfrid's death—
And whether that might once be turned on him in wrath.

1393 "It might, if I could bring him to this land."
She dreamed that Giselher walked, close at hand,
Her brother, and she kissed him all the while,
Often, in gentle sleep. (There would come a time of trial!)

1394 I think the Devil counseled her to break
With Gunther's friendship, whom she kissed for sake
Of peace restored in the land of Burgundy.
But now her hot tears fell and dulled her finery.

1395   Night and day, there weighed on her heart the question,
Why she was forced to love not a Christian
But a pagan, through no fault of her own.
This is what Lord Hagen and Gunther the king had done.

1396   One intention never left her mind:
She thought, "I have power of such a kind,
And wealth enough, to hurt my enemies badly—
This I swear I'd do to Hagen of Trony gladly.

1397   Often my heart cries out for loyalty.
I wish I were near to those who injured me—
Vengeance then would come for my lover's life.
For that I can hardly wait." So thought Attila's wife.

1398   Attila's vassals loved her, every knight
Of Kriemhild's court—which was no more than right.
Eckewart managed her treasure. Thus he made
Good friends for her, and what she willed no one
        gainsaid.

1399   She held this constant thought: to ask the king
That he, in kindness of heart, might let her bring
Her kin to the land of Huns. Not one man
Among them ever fathomed the queen's malignant plan.

1400   There by Attila's side one night she lay.
He had her in his arms, as was his way,
Embracing his beloved, dear as his life—
When thought about her foes came to his regal wife.

1401   And now she said to the king, "My dearest lord,
By your favor, I'd ask that you afford
Some sign, If I should merit it, to show
If you are truly fond of my family or no."

1402   The mighty king replied in honest mind,
"But I assure you, anything good and kind
That might befall them I'd be happy of,
For never have I gained such friends through woman's
        love."

1403   The queen cried, "That is good of you to say,
But I have noble kin, hence my dismay
That they have never deigned to visit me;
And I am called 'the stranger' among your citizenry."

1404   "Dear wife," said Attila, "if they do not mind
So great a distance, whomever you are inclined
To have as guests I'll ask across the Rhine
To my country here." She heard his wish, and that was fine!

1405   "If you would serve me well and truly, my lord,
Send messengers to Worms on Rhine with word
Of what I have in mind, and you shall see
Within our borders knights of high nobility."

1406   He answered, "When you command, so let it be.
Your kin you could not more desire to see
Than I the sons of Uta. Far too long
Have they been strangers to us; I think it very wrong.

1407   And my dear lady, if it pleases you,
This is what I'd be prepared to do:
Send to Burgundy my fiddlers here
To get your friends." He bade his minstrel lords
        appear.

1408   Soon they hurried where the king was seated
Beside his queen. He told them they were needed
As messengers to Burgundy, and ordered
That as heralds they be splendidly accoutered.

1409   They made up clothes for twenty-four knights, whose
        task
The king disclosed to them, for they must ask
Most royal Gunther and all his men to ride.
(Lady Kriemhild later spoke to them, aside.)

1410   Then said the king, "I'll tell you what to do.
Wish them fortune and say my heart is true,
And may they not refuse to ride our way!
Rarely have I known such welcome guests as they.

1411   If they would pay my wishes due respect,
These kin of Kriemhild, may they not neglect,
This summertime, to come to my tourney here.
My lady's kin account for much of my good cheer."

1412   Proud Swemmel the fiddler cried, "When is the day
Of tournament time in our land, so we may say
The word to your friends?" King Attila replied,
"Let the date be set at next solstice-tide."

1413   "We'll do as you command us," Werbel said.
The queen gave secret orders they be led
To her room among the chambers of the women,
To speak with them—for many knights no pleasant omen.

1414   She said to both the heralds, "Do my will
In kindly fashion, and earn yourselves a fill
Of worldly goods, with messages home to our lands;
I'll put splendid clothes and riches in your hands.

1415   Whatever kin of mine you two may meet
In Worms by the river Rhine, do not repeat
That you have ever seen my spirits low;
Say this to those gallant knights: to them my
        greetings go!

1416   Ask that they comply with the king's desires
Freeing me from all that so conspires
To hurt me. I have no friends, the Huns would say.
Oh, if I were a knight, I'd get to them some way!

1417   My noble brother Gernot—tell him too
No one loves him more the whole world through,
And I would have him bring to me the best
Of all our friends to make our greatness manifest.

1418   Tell Giselher that he must not forget:
Never through fault of his have I suffered yet.
And sight of him would please my eyes to see,
I should like to have him here, for his great loyalty.

1419   And tell my mother that I live in splendor.
And if Lord Hagen stays, who then shall tender
Escort through these lands? He has known the ways
Here to the Huns ever since his youthful days."

1420   The heralds did not know why this was done—
Why Hagen of Trony should be the very one
Not to be left by the Rhine. They learned it late,
In sorrow; his challenge meant for many a cruel fate.

1421   They had their charge, by letter and spoken word.
They traveled rich in goods and could afford
The best of living, and a splendid show
Of things to wear, for they had royal leave to go.

TWENTY-FOURTH ADVENTURE

How Werbel and Swemmel Carried Out Their Sovereign's Mission

1422 Attila sent to the Rhine his messengers riding
With news that flew from land to land, inviting
(And commanding) by heralds bold and fast
Attendance at his fete—for many to be their last.

1423 Out of the land of Huns his riders went
To the land of Burgundy, where they were sent
For three most noble kings and their retinues,
Asked to Attila's court. They had no time to lose.

1424 First they rode to Pöchlarn, finding there
Unstinted care and service. Ruedeger,
His wife, and child made sure that every sign
Of their respect should go with them to the river Rhine.

1425 They did not let them leave without bestowing
Gifts on Attila's men, so that their going
Might be more pleasant. Ruedeger bade them tell
Uta and her sons no margrave loved them so well.

1426 They sent to Brunhild pledge and kindly word,
Constant faith and friendship. Having heard,
They wished to go forth on their job of herald.
The margravine prayed God to speed them
                unimperiled.

1427 They had not passed through all Bavaria yet
When Werbel met the bishop. I forget
What message to his Rhenish friends he sent—
Except he gave the heralds gold, which he spent

1428 Out of kindness, and so he let them ride.
Bishop Pilgrim said, "What delight
If I should have them here, my sister's sons!
I cannot go to the Rhine to see them, even once."

1429 I don't know by what route they sought their goal,
Through all those lands to the Rhine; but no one stole
Their clothes or silver, fearing so the anger
Of their noble lord, than whom no king was stronger.

1430   Werbel and Swemmel reached the Rhine, and the spot
Where Worms is, in twelve days. News was brought
To kings and men, of foreign heralds nearing.
Now the lord of the Rhineland Gunther spoke, inquiring:

1431   "Who can tell us from what place they are,
Riding here, strangers from afar?"
No one knew, until Lord Hagen came
And saw them there, at which the king heard him exclaim:

1432   "I want to tell you this, that there will be
Great news. Those are Attila's fiddlers I see,
Sent to the Rhine by your sister. They deserve
A kindly welcome here, for sake of the lord they serve."

1433   That very moment up to the palace they rode—
Such splendor no king's minstrels ever showed!
Now they were met and welcomed by Gunther's suite,
Who stored their clothes and found them places to lodge
and eat.

1434   Their traveling clothes were rich and so well made,
At court thus dressed they might with honor have stayed
But would not go before the king that way.
"Who wants these clothes?" the heralds cried, "Come
and say!"

1435   This was the case with many, who were glad
To take what they were given. The guests were clad
In better garments now by far, the sort
A great king's heralds wear for sake of fair report.

1436   By Gunther's leave, Attila's men repaired
Where he was seated. In pleasure, people stared.
Hagen ran, as chivalry requires,
To greet them with affection, thanked by both the squires.

1437   He sought for information—asking how
Attila fared, and his men. "Better than now,"
The fiddler said, "our countries never were,
Nor the people so happy, of that you may be sure."

1438   They sent to the king. The palace now was filled,
For such reception of guests as custom willed,
The kindly welcome to lands of another lord.
(Werbel found a host of knights at Gunther's court.)

1439   Gunther greeted them in courteous words:
       "Welcome to you both, minstrel lords
       Of Hunnish lands, and to your company!
       Did mighty Attila send you here to Burgundy?"

1440   They bowed to him. Said Werbel, "To you we bring
       The loyal greetings of our beloved king,
       His pledge of service—from Kriemhild your sister, too,
       For they have sent us here in all good faith to you."

1441   The great prince answered, "This I am glad to hear.
       And how," the king went on, "does Attila fare?
       And my sister Kriemhild, far in the land of Huns?"
       To this the fiddler spoke, "I shall tell you that at once.

1442   Never yet have people prospered more
       Than do these two—be certain on this score—
       And all their courtiers, too, kin and man.
       We left them very happy, as our trip began."

1443   "My thanks for the loyal greeting he extended
       My sister too, since any doubt has ended
       That now both king and men live happily—
       Because I asked for news with some anxiety."

1444   The two young kings had come, just now aware
       Of what had happened. In youthful Giselher
       The happy sight of the heralds there awoke
       Great joy for love of his sister. With kind regard he
              spoke:

1445   "You heralds would be very welcome here
       Beside the Rhine, if you were to appear
       Much more often; you'd find such friends as warm
       Your hearts to see, and in our country meet no harm."

1446   "We trust in your high favor," Swemmel spoke.
       "Not with all my powers can I evoke
       The loving manner of King Attila's greeting—
       And your great sister's, whose ways are honored as is
              fitting.

1447   The queen recalls to you your gratitude
       And trust, your hearts and persons once imbued
       With love for her. But first is our command
       To see the king and ask that you should ride to our land.

1448   Great King Attila said, at all accounts,
To ask you this, bidding us announce,
If you would not submit to your sister's view,
He then would like to know what he has done to you,

1449   That you shun his land and him. Even suppose
You never knew the queen—your honor owes
At least a visit granted to the king,
Which, if it should occur, he'd find a pleasant thing."

1450   "Seven nights from now," the king replied,
"And I shall let you know what I decide
In council with my friends. Meanwhile repair
To your hostelry, and may you have good resting there."

1451   Werbel answered, "Would you be averse
To our seeing noble Lady Uta first,
Before we seek the comfort of our rooms?"
Said Giselher, with the breeding chivalry presumes:

1452   "No one shall hinder. Seek your audience.
In seeing Uta thus you suit the sense
Of her desire; she'll see you willingly,
For sake of my sister Kriemhild. How welcome you will be!"

1453   Giselher took them to the queen at once.
Glad to see these heralds from the Huns,
She greeted them sweetly, so fine her character.
The heralds spoke their message, courtly and kind, to her.

1454   Said Swemmel, "My lady sends her loyalty
And pledge of faith to you. And might it be
That she could see you often, believe of her:
No greater joy than this could all the world confer."

1455   Said the queen, "It cannot be, however gladly
I'd see my daughter often; I tell you sadly,
She lives too far away, your great king's wife.
I can only wish for her and the king a prosperous life.

1456   But now before you leave: do let me know
When you return! It never cheered me so
In a long time to see such heralds as you."
This the herald-squires gave their word to do .

1457   Now the Huns went back where they were quartered.
Highborn Gunther, mighty king, had ordered

His kinsmen to him, asking how they inclined
To judge the present matter. More than one opined

1458   That he could well proceed to Attila's land.
Indeed the best among them took this stand,
Except for Hagen (to him, a baleful thing!).
"You call down war on yourelf," he whispered to the
        king.

1459   "After all, you know what things we did.
With Kriemhild there, we never can be rid
Of worry and fear. I killed her lord with these hands.
What makes you think we dare to ride to Attila's lands?"

1460   Said the king, "She quit her anger, with a kiss,
And lovingly. What hurt we caused her, this
She had forgiven us, before she went—
Unless, my lord, her hate for you is not yet spent!"

1461   "Do not be fooled," said Hagen, "whatever they say,
These heralds of the Huns. You may well pay
For seeing Kriemhild there, with loss of life
And honor both. Revenge is long with Attila's wife."

1462   Adding his word to the council, Gernot cried,
"You fear your death—and that is justified—
But if for that alone we fail to travel
To Hunnish lands to see our sister, our course is evil."

1463   Prince Giselher addressed his knight, to say:
"Then since you know your guilt, friend Hagen, stay
And take good care of yourself! Let those who face
The trip with courage go with us to my sister's place."

1464   Then the lord of Trony was angry. He cried,
"I don't intend that you should take this ride
To court with men of purpose any stronger
Than mine which I'll prove to you, since you will wait
        no longer."

1465   Rumold, Master of the Kitchen, spoke:
"Here you can entertain familiar folk
And strangers as you will—with all your stores.
Would Hagen hold you here like captives in the wars?

1466   If you won't listen to him, take my advice;
I'm bound to you by liege, and loyal ties,

And I tell you: stay here for sake of me.
Attila's safe with Kriemhild now—there let him be.

1467 How could things be better in all the earth?
You have protection here when foes come forth;
Excellent clothes to adorn you, the finest sort
Of wine to drink, the fairest of charming women to court.

1468 Besides, the food you get is a favor earned
By no other king on earth—and if it weren't,
Still you should stay for your lovely ladies' sake,
Not go and place your lives on a risk no child would take!

1469 And so I say to stay. Your lands are rich;
Here at home, if you make some foolish pledge,
We're better set for bail than with the Hun.
Who knows how things are there? Stay, say I for one."

1470 "We shall not stay," said Gernot. "So kind a word
From my sister and the king as we have heard,
Inviting us—why should we fail to come?
Whoever doesn't want to go, can stay at home."

1471 Hagen answered this: "Whatever you do,
Don't let what I say appear to you
A pointless thing. If you would not be harmed,
I tell you this sincerely, go to the Huns well-armed.

1472 Send for your men, if you won't change your mind—
Send for the best you have or can ever find,
Then I shall pick among them a thousand knights,
And you need not fear the harm her wicked heart incites."

1473 "I'll gladly do as you say," the king replied.
He sent his heralds far through the countryside,
Till they brought back three thousand men or more,
None of whom imagined the fearful hurt in store.

1474 They rode to Gunther's land in great good cheer,
Where they were given steeds and clothes and gear,
All of those preparing to depart
From Burgundy. (And many he found with a willing
heart!)

1475 Hagen bade his brother Dankwart summon
Eighty of the knights they had in common,

Here to the Rhine. Gallantly, with helm
And clothes and armor they rode, into Gunther's realm.

1476 Valiant Folker came, of noble birth,
A minstrel, with thirty men and clothing worth
A king's wearing. Off to the Hunnish court
He meant to go, and sent to Gunther this report.

1477 I'll tell you more of Folker: nobly born,
A lord of Burgundy, to whom were sworn
In liege some of the best of that domain,
He played the fiddle, too, hence his minstrel name.

1478 Hagen chose his thousand. He knew them well,
The work of their hands where battles rose and fell—
All the many things they had done he knew.
Call them valiant men, no other word will do.

1479 Kriemhild's messengers grew much concerned,
Fearful over their master. Daily they yearned
For leave to go, which was denied to them
By Hagen of Trony. This was a cunning stratagem.

1480 He said to his master, "We should take good care
Not to let them ride till we prepare
To leave for Attila's land, one week hence.
If someone bears us malice, we'll have a better chance

1481 To find it out and Kriemhild has no time
To turn this plot of hers to someone's crime
Against us—though if that is her intent
She may get hurt. The men we bring are excellent!"

1482 Shields and saddles, clothes, and everything
That they would take to the land of the Hunnish king
Stood ready now for all these valiant men.
They told the heralds of Kriemhild: go see Gunther again.

1483 The heralds came, to hear Lord Gernot cry:
"Attila asks and Gunther will comply;
We shall come to his festival and tourney,
And see our sister. Have no doubt, we welcome the
            journey."

1484 Gunther asked them, "Can you say perhaps
When the festival is, what time should elapse

Before we ought to leave?" Swemmel replied,
"The truth is this, it is to be next solstice-tide."

1485 He granted them what never yet had been:
An audience, if they wished it, with the queen,
Lady Brunhild—he would not forbid it.
But Folker held them back, and she was glad he did it.

1486 "My lady's humor is not such of late
That you can see her," Folker said. "So wait
Until tomorrow, then we'll let you pay
Your visit to her." (They went there and were turned
away.)

1487 In courtesy, the prince, who seemed to hold
The heralds in good esteem, brought forth his gold,
For he had much, and the shields they put it in
Were broad. They also had rich presents from his kin.

1488 Gere and Ortwin, Gernot and Giselher
Gave proof of their largess. Indeed so fair
And costly were the gifts that they presented,
The Huns did not dare take them; fear of their lord
prevented.

1489 "Great king," declared Lord Werbel the messenger,
"Keep your gifts in your own country, sir.
We cannot take them, my master won't permit
The taking of gifts—and we have little need of it."

1490 The Lord of Rhineland found it most unpleasant
That they refused so great a monarch's present,
And so they had to take his gold in hand,
And clothes, to carry back with them to Attila's land.

1491 They sought the queen before they left again.
Giselher ushered both the minstrel men
Before his mother. She sent with them this word:
By honors paid her daughter her own joy was assured.

1492 The queen presented them with gold and braid
For Attila's sake and Kriemhild, whom she paid
Her loving respect. The minstrels had no fear
To take the gifts from her; her giving was sincere.

1493 And so the messengers had taken leave
From men and women there, nor did they grieve

As they rode to Swabia, given escort through
By Gernot's men—who kept them free of trouble, too.

1494 When those who went to give them escort left,
The power of the Hun made safe their ways—no theft
Of clothes or steeds at anybody's hands.
They made all haste they could to mighty
        Attila's lands.

1495 Where they had friends, they halted to proclaim
That from the Rhineland men of Burgundy came
To the land of the Huns—and little time to lose!
(Thus did Bishop Pilgrim also hear the news.)

1496 As they rode down the road by Pöchlarn town,
They did not fail to make the story known
To Ruedeger and Lady Gotelind,
Who looked to their visit there, both in a joyful mind.

1497 The minstrels with their tidings hurried on,
Finding Attila in the town of Gran.
They told him the friendly things so many said,
Their many greetings. He flushed with joy, all
        pleasure-red.

1498 When Kriemhild heard in truth that Uta's sons,
Her brothers, were on their way to the land of Huns,
Her heart was light. Her minstrels she presented
With costly gifts—her reputation thus augmented.

1499 "Werbel and Swemmel, tell me both of you,"
She said, "which of my next of kin are due
To come to our feast, of those we asked to this land?
And what did Hagen say, hearing what we planned?"

1500 "He came to council," they said, "early one day,
And very few kind things did he have to say!
When they spoke of coming here and gave their word,
It seemed the name of Death that fierce Hagen heard.

1501 The kings will make the journey, your three brothers,
High in spirit; as to all the others—
To tell so great a sum would be too hard.
But Folker promised to ride with them, the gallant bard."

1502 "Folker," she answered, "I can do without,
Or the sight of him anywhere about!

Hagen I like—a man of hero's measure.
If we are to see him here, my heart is filled with pleasure."

1503　The queen then went to the king. Her words were sweet
That now she spoke to him. "And do you greet
This news, my dearest lord, with joy—or how?
All my will desired will be accomplished now."

1504　"Your will is my delight," replied the king.
"I should not take more joy in the journeying
Of kin of mine to my land. Worry ends,
And cares are banished by the kindness of your friends."

1505　The king's officials set out everywhere
In hall and palace benches to prepare
For welcome guests about to pay their call—
Who soon enough would leave the king no joy at all.

TWENTY-FIFTH ADVENTURE

How the Lords All Traveled to the Land of the Huns

1506　No more of this, of what the Huns were doing.
So proud a sight, of splendid heroes going
To any monarch's land, rarely happens.
They took whatever they chose of armor and of weapons;

1507　The lord of the Rhine equipped his warriors well—
A thousand and sixty knights, so I heard tell,
And nine thousand squires, on their festive way.
(The ones they left at home would later mourn the day.)

1508　Across the courtyard at Worms they took their gear.
And ancient bishop of Speyer encountered here
The lovely Uta: "Our friends will now repair
To the tournament—may God preserve their honor there."

1509　Then the noble Uta spoke these words
To all her sons: "Stay here, most excellent lords!
I had a dream last night, of things I dread
And fear to see: for all the birds in the land were dead."

1510　"He who goes by dreams," Lord Hagen cried,
"Cannot in any rightful way decide
What fully suits his honor and good report.
I hope my lord will go and ask for leave at court,

1511   And we should gladly ride to Attila's land,
Where kings may well be served by hero's hand,
When we have gone to Kriemhild's tournament."
Hagen spoke for a trip he later would repent—

1512   And would have then opposed, had Gernot not,
In violent words, provoked him with the thought
Of Sigfrid, Kriemhild's husband. These words he cried:
"That's why Hagen wants to miss our courtly ride!"

1513   "I do not act from fear," Lord Trony said.
"Whatever you will, my lords, go right ahead!
I shall gladly ride with you to Attila's realm."
(In time to come he shattered many a shield and helm.)

1514   The ships were set, and many men were there;
They took aboard them all their things to wear.
Till evening time they had no moment free;
Soon they would leave their homes in the greatest gaiety.

1515   Awnings and tents they pitched upon the grass,
Across the Rhine. When that was brought to pass,
His fair wife came and begged the king to stay—
Embracing her handsome lord the night of that same day.

1516   The morning came, and flutes and trumpets blew
For them to leave, which they prepared to do.
For those who lay in love, one more caress—
Parted soon by Attila's wife in bitterness.

1517   The sons of lovely Uta had a thane,
Bold and true; when they would not remain,
He told the king his feelings secretly.
He said, "Your trip to court is a cause of grief to me."

1518   This was Rumold, man of mighty hand.
He spoke, "To whom will you leave people and land?
Why, my lords, can no one change your mind?
The good in Kriemhild's plan is more than I can find."

1519   "My lands I commend to you, and my little son,
And serve the ladies well. Let this be done.
Whomever you see weeping, bring him solace.
Great King Attila's wife will do us no deed of malice."

1520   Kings and men, each one found his charger,
And then with tender kisses took departure,

All of them with spirits proud and high.
For many lovely wives there would come a time
    to cry.

1521   As valiant warriors mounted, one perceived
That many women stood about and grieved.
Their thoughts foretold that being long apart
Would end in awful loss—a balm to no one's heart.

1522   The bold Burgundians set out to ride;
The country stirred with action. On either side
Of the mountains people wept. All unworried
By men and women's lot at home, away they hurried.

1523   With them knights of the Nibelung treasure had come,
In a thousand hauberks. They had left at home
Lovely ladies, never again to be seen.
The hurt of Sigfrid's wound weighed hard upon the
    queen.

1524   They set their course to the Main River then,
Up through East Franconia, Gunther's men,
With Hagen leading (he knew what the route should be).
Dankwart was their marshal, hero of Burgundy.

1525   Riding from East Franconia to Swaleveld
They showed to what high sense of form they held,
Kings and kin—and were so lauded for.
And on the twelfth morning they reached the Danube
    shore.

1526   Hagen of Trony rode the forwardmost,
A help and solace to the Nibelung host.
Dismounting now, upon the river sand,
He quickly tied his charger to a tree, to stand.

1527   The waters were in flood, no boat in sight.
The men of Nibelung worried how they might
Cross the river—it ran too wide a course.
Many a dashing knight dismounted from his horse.

1528   "My lord of the Rhine," said Hagen, "this may be
Ill luck for you; as you yourself can see,
the water is over the bank, the current is strong.
We'll lose good fighters here today, unless I'm wrong."

1529   The king said, "What do you reproach me for?
For good of your name, discourage us no more.
Seek us out the place for fording here,
So we can bring across our horses and our gear."

1530   "I'm not so tired of life," Sir Hagen said,
"That I should want to drown myself in the bed
Of these broad waves. Rather my hand should kill
Men in Attila's land—for that I have the will.

1531   Stay by the water here! I'll follow the river
And look for a ferryman to take us over,
My noble lords, into Gelfrat's land."
Now the sturdy Hagen had his buckler in hand.

1532   Well armed he was! He took a shield along,
And tied his helmet on, bright and strong,
And over his byrnie carried a sword so wide
That it could take a fearful cut with either side.

1533   He looked all around for the boatman. A sudden sound
Of splashing met his ears; he listened and found
Wise sorceresses at a lovely pool,
Who made the noise, bathing there to make them cool.

1534   Hagen saw and crept up stealthily.
At sight of this, they were in haste to flee—
And glad to get away! All their clothing
Hagen took from them, but otherwise did nothing.

1535   He heard Hadeburg, one of the mermaids, cry:
"Noble Hagen, we will prophesy—
If you, bold knight, will give us back our things—
And tell your trip to the Huns, and what that journey
        brings."

1536   Seeing them float like birds upon the water,
He felt they must have magic truths to utter,
So much the more believing what they would tell—
And what he wanted of them, they told him all too well.

1537   She spoke, "Ride on in trust to Attila's land;
On this assurance to you I pledge my hand,
That greater honors never were conferred
On warriors riding to any realm. Believe my word."

1538 Her speech made Hagen in his heart so gay
He gave them back their things without delay.
When they had donned their wondrous clothes anew,
They told his trip to Attila's land—and told it true.

1539 Another mermaid, Sigelind, began,
"I warn you, Hagen, child of Aldrian:
To get our clothes my aunt has lied to you.
If you go to the Huns, you're deluded through and
   through.

1540 While you still have time, turn back again,
And do it soon. You go, as valiant men,
Invited there to die in Attila's land.
Those who make this journey Death will take in hand."

1541 "Don't play tricks on me," came Hagen's reply.
"How could it ever happen that we should die,
All of us there, through anybody's hate?"
Then, more fully now, the mermaids told their fate.

1542 The first of them spoke up, "It must be so.
No single one of you—and this we know—
Except the king's own chaplain shall survive
Unscathed, to come again to Gunther's land alive."

1543 Dauntless Hagen cried, with an angry shout:
"A fearful thing to tell my lords about—
That every man of us in Hun land dies.
Show us the way over the waters, if you are so wise!"

1544 "Since you insist upon your trip," she cried,
"Upstream there stands a house by the waterside,
With a boatman—nowhere else." He had learned enough
From all his questioning now, and quickly broke it off.

1545 She cried as Hagen left, in anger and worry,
"Wait a moment, you're in too great a hurry!
Listen how you cross to the opposite beaches.
A man whose name is Else rules these border reaches.

1546 His brother is Gelfrat, lord in Bavaria land.
In his domains are dangers to withstand.
If you pass through, be on your mettle there.
And as for the ferryman, handle him with care.

1547 Your life is in danger—so fierce his disposition—
Unless you treat him with consideration.
If you want his services, pay him his fee.
He guards this land for Gelfrat in loyal fealty.

1548 If he should take too long, then give a shout
Across the flooding water, making out
You're Amelrich, who left when this became
A hostile land for him. He'll come when he hears the
        name."

1549 Haughty Hagen thanked the women, bowed,
And fell to silence, saying nothing aloud.
He walked by the water, heading upstream more,
Until he found a house that lay on the other shore.

1550 He called with a great voice across the wave:
"Come and get me, ferryman, you shall have
As pay an armband made of gold, all red.
I need this crossing badly—let the truth be said!"

1551 The ferryman had such wealth that it would look
Unseemly for him to work, and so he took
But seldom pay, and his men were men of pride.
So Hagen stood there all alone on the other side.

1552 He called till the water echoed in reply—
So vastly great his power: "It is I,
Amelrich, Else's man; in enmity
I left this country once. Come and ferry me!"

1553 High on his sword he put a ring, to show,
Bright and fair, all gold and red aglow,
That he might ferry him to Gelfrat's land.
The haughty ferryman himself took oar in hand.

1554 Now he was a troublesome man, no easy friend,
And greed for wealth will bring an evil end.
He wanted to earn Hagen's gold, all red;
For this the warrior left him sword-stricken and dead.

1555 Quickly now the ferryman rowed over.
He'd heard a name and now did not discover
The one he thought, but Hagen. His wrath was stirred.
He spoke to the lord before him, anger in every word:

1556   "Knight, maybe Amelrich is your name—
The one I thought of doesn't look the same,
He was my brother—sire the same, and mother.
Since you tricked me, stay on this side, not the other!"

1557   "No, by mighty God," said Hagen then.
"I am a foreign knight, in charge of men.
Take my payment as a friend would do,
For carrying me across. I'll be obliged to you."

1558   The ferryman said, "That cannot be, for these,
The lords I serve and love, have enemies;
I take to this land no strangers any more.
In case you wish to live, step back at once on shore!"

1559   "Not that!" said Hagen. "My heart is full of worry,
Take this gold for love of me, and ferry
Our thousand horses across and as many men."
"That shall not be done," the fierce thane said again.

1560   He lifted a heavy oar, big and broad,
And fetched unhappy Hagen a blow so hard
He fell to his knees in the boat. This was as yet
By far the fiercest boatman Hagen ever met.

1561   To give his haughty guest a better right
To hurt and anger, he swung his pole at the knight,
And broke it over his head; his strength was vast.
But the ferryman of Else suffered for this at last.

1562   In fury Hagen reached for his sheath and took
The weapon he found in it, and off he struck
The boatman's head, which he plunged to the riverbed.
Among the proud Burgundians news was quickly spread.

1563   Just as he hit its pilot, the boat took off
To drift downstream, and he had trouble enough
To bring it back, growing tired and sore
Before he did. Hagen pulled a mighty oar.

1564   With rapid strokes he turned the boat about
Until the great oar in his hand gave out
And broke in two. He wanted to reach his friends,
On shore, but his pole was gone. Swiftly he took the ends

1565   And tied them with a shield-strap, a narrow thong.
He turned now towards a wood and went along

Till he found his liege-lord standing by the shore.
They all came out to meet him, handsome men of war.

1566 The bold lords gave him welcome. Then their eyes
Saw within the boat the warm steam rise
Out of the blood from the wound, cruel and grim,
That slew the boatman. They had questions to ask of him!

1567 And when King Gunther saw the blood, all hot
And rolling in the boat, he quickly sought
Answer from Hagen: "Where is our boatman, friend?
I gather that thanks to your valor he has met his end."

1568 Hagen denied it. "By a wild willow I found
This vessel here which then my hands unbound,
But I have seen no ferryman here today.
No one's been hurt through fault of mine in any way."

1569 Gernot spoke, lord of Burgundy:
"Thought of dear friends dying worries me.
We have no boatman and did not prepare
To get ourselves across; I stand here in despair."

1570 "Servants, lay our harness on the grass.
By the Rhine, as I recall, I used to pass
For the best by whom a boat was ever manned.
I trust I can ferry you," said Hagen, "to Gelfrat's land."

1571 To get across the river fast they struck
The horses and drove them in. They had good luck:
In swimming, the great waves failed to make them founder.
Some drifted far—with their weariness, it was little
        wonder.

1572 They took to the boat all their clothes and gold,
Determined to go no matter what they were told.
Hagen managed things. To the opposite sand
He brought them, all the powerful knights, to a foreign
        land.

1573 First he ferried over fifty score
Of splendid knights, and then his own, and more:
Nine thousand men he took across the way—
The gallant lord of Trony was busy enough that day!

1574 When he had got them over safe, he thought
(Fearless lord) of strange tidings brought

To his ear before, told by a wild mermaid;
For this the royal chaplain's life was all but paid.

1575   He found the priest among his chapel gear,
Leaning on his hand, with the altar near.
Little good it did him! When Hagen saw,
It meant great harm for him, poor servant of God's law.

1576   He threw him out of the boat—it was quickly done.
And many cried, "Grab him, men, hold on!"
Young Giselher was angered and annoyed,
But Hagen would not stop till the chaplain was destroyed.

1577   Gernot spoke, "Hagen, what profit to you
Is the chaplain's death?—which if another should do
Would make you angry with him at the very least.
What reason did you have to turn against the priest?"

1578   The cleric tried hard to swim: he might pull through
If someone helped, but that no one could do—
With Trony fierce and angry there, no wonder!
But all of them stood aghast when Hagen pushed him
        under.

1579   Now that the poor priest saw no help in store,
With great travail he turned about once more.
He could not swim, and yet by God's own hand
He still came out, unhurt back again to land.

1580   There the poor priest stood and shook his clothes.
And thus did Hagen see no force could oppose
The things he heard the mermaids prophesy;
And Hagen thought to himself, "All these men must die."

1581   When they had emptied the boat and took the things
They had aboard, these men of the three great kings,
Hagen smashed it and threw it on the wave.
They all were taken aback, bold as they were and brave.

1582   "Why did you to that, brother?" Dankwart cried.
"How shall we cross from Hun land when we ride
Back from the Rhine to home and family?"
(Later Hagen told him this could never be.)

1583   Said Trony's hero, "I did it in this hope,
If on our journey now we have to cope

With any coward who wants to run in fear,
That he should meet his shameful end, by the waters
here."

1584   They had with them one lord from Burgundy,
A man of deeds, called Folker. Eloquently,
The fiddler spoke, stating in full his view,
And all that Hagen did he gave approval to.

1585   Their steeds were ready, the pack-horse train
Was loaded well. The journey brought no pain
Or hurt for any but the chaplain to meet.
He had to go back to Rhineland on his own two feet.

Twenty-Sixth Adventure

How Gelfrat Was Slain by Dankwart

1586   Now they all had come to the waterside;
And Gunther asked, "Who is here to guide
Our travel through this country, lest we miss
The proper way?" Said Folker, "Let me take care of this."

1587   "Stop, all of you," said Hagen, "squire and knight!
You follow friends in trust, and that is right.
But this is an awful thing to hear from me:
Never again shall we return to Burgundy.

1588   Two mermaids told me early this very day
We'll not come back. But here is what I say:
Warriors, arm yourselves, stay clear of hurt!
Our foes are powerful here; ride on, and keep alert.

1589   I thought to catch them lying, wise as they are.
They said not one of us would get as far
As shore again, except the chaplain alone.
And that," he said, "is why I wished to see him drown."

1590   From company on to company went the tale,
And valiant heroes, in their pain, turned pale,
To think of bitter death upon the way
To Attila's court. They had good cause for their dismay.

1591   At Mehring, where the boatman's life was lost
(Else's man), there they all had crossed.

And Hagen spoke once more, "Since I have made
Enemies en route, we'll doubtless be waylaid.

1592   I killed the ferryman early this very day,
As well they know. Prepare, without delay—
If Gelfrat and Else choose this time and place
To hit our forces, let them see what losses they face!

1593   I know these men have courage; they'll not forget.
So make your horses march more slowly yet—
Let no one think we use these roads to flee."
"This word," said Giselher, "is good enough for me!"

1594   "Who shall guide us overland?" they cried
"Let Folker! Road and byway, far and wide,
The gallant minstrel knows." They'd not expressed
But half the wish, when there before them full dressed

1595   In armor stood the fiddler, his helmet fastened.
The colors of his battle-garments glistened;
He fixed a red device upon his lance.
(He and the kings were soon to fall on evil chance.)

1596   The boatman's death had come by true account
To Gelfrat. Mighty Else too had found
What happened there; they both were pained and angered.
They summoned their knights to readiness—and no one
        lingered.

1597   I tell you this, the time was very brief
Before they came a-riding. Monstrous grief
And hurt they caused, when mighty war was made.
Seven hundred or more had come to Gelfrat's aid.

1598   As they rode to meet the savage foe they faced,
Their masters led. They were in too great haste,
Seeking such valiant guests, to vent their wrath.
For this they lost a goodly toll of friends in death.

1599   Now Hagen, lord of Trony, well had planned
(Could hero better guard his friends?) to stand
At the army's rear on watch with his allies,
And with his brother Dankwart, too. This course was wise.

1600   The light of day was spent, there was not more.
He feared for his friends great pain and hurt in store.

Across Bavaria they rode, shields up-drawn
And held at ready. Shortly they were set upon.

1601   On either side of the road and close behind
They heard the beat of hooves—a foe inclined
Too much to haste. "They mean to strike us here.
Fasten your helmets on! The need for that is clear."

1602   Thus spoke Dankwart. As it must, the stream
Of travel ceased. They saw through dusk the gleam
Of shining shields. Hagen could not sit by:
"Who hunts this road for us?" Gelfrat had to reply,

1603   The margrave and Bavaria's overseer:
"We look for foes, and we pursued them here.
Who killed my boatman today, I do not know—
A stalwart hero, his loss has left my spirits low."

1604   "And was the boatman yours?" his answer came.
"He would not ferry us. Mine is the blame,"
Said Hagen. "I killed him, but it had to be;
Your champion's hands were very nearly the death of me!

1605   To reach your land I offered him in payment
To ferry us over, milord, gold and raiment.
That so angered him he struck me a blow
With a heavy pole—at which my gall began to flow.

1606   I got my sword and settled his angry whim
With a mighty wound, and that was the end of him.
I'll make amends to you, as you think right."
Their hearts were set and hard. It ended in a fight.

1607   "When Gunther and his men came riding along."
Said Gelfrat, "I knew that we should suffer wrong
From Hagen of Trony, and he shall not go free.
For the boatman's death, this man shall be our surety."

1608   Lance over shield they lowered for the thrust,
Gelfrat and Hagen; each one had a lust
For meeting the other. Dankwart and Else were curious
Who was braver. They rode in splendor; the fighting was
         furious.

1609   How could ever lords compete as well?
A mighty charge, and over backwards fell,

Unhorsed, valiant Hagen, at Gelfrat's hand.
His martingale was broken; he came to understand

1610 What fighting is. The sound of lances shivered
Rose from their armies. Hagen had recovered,
Who before had fallen, thrust to the earth.
He thought of Gelfrat, I dare say, with little mirth!

1611 I do not know who took their steeds in hand,
But now they both were down, upon the sand,
Hagen and Gelfrat, charging. Either knight
Had friends to help him—and show the others how to
fight.

1612 Hagen sprang at Gelfrat, fierce and wild,
And yet the noble margrave struck from his shield
A mighty piece, and made the fire dance,
And Gunther's vassal almost died from this mischance.

1613 He called upon Lord Dankwart, "Help, dear brother!
This man who set upon me is no other
Than a hero. He'll never let me go."
Bold Dankwart cried, "Let me decide if that is so."

1614 He sprang up close and struck him a blow so hard
He lay there dead, victim of his sharp sword.
Else wanted vengeance for him, but he—
And all his troops—left there in hurt and injury.

1615 His brother was slain, and he had many wounds.
Eighty of his knights had passed the bounds
Of bitter death. Thus compelled to flee,
Their master turned and ran from Gunther's company.

1616 As the Bavarians fled the battleground
One could hear close after them the sound
Of awful blows, as knights of Trony chased
Foemen eager not to suffer, all in haste.

1617 Lord Dankwart raised his voice in their flight, to say:
"We ought to turn and ride the other way,
And let them go, for they are soaked with blood.
Let's hurry to our friends. This word of mine is good."

1618 When they came back where all the hurt took place,
Hagen of Trony spoke, "Men, let us trace

What friends are missing here, or whom we've lost
In this engagement, counting what Gelfrat's anger cost."

1619 Four were lost, but there is an end to pain,
And they were well atoned, for they had slain
In turn a hundred Bavarians—perhaps more yet;
The shields of the knights of Trony were dark with blood
    and wet.

1620 The bright moon broke a moment from the cloud.
And Hagen said, "Let no one say aloud
To my good masters what we managed here.
Let them go along till morning, safe from fear."

1621 When they who fought caught up with all the rest,
Fatigue had left their ranks so much oppressed
That many asked, "How long are we to ride?"
Bold Dankwart answered, "What shelter can we provide?"

1622 You all must ride till daybreak." Folker the bold,
In charge of the servants, sent one whom he told
To ask the marshal, "What place tonight affords
A rest for all our mounts, and my beloved lords?"

1623 Brave Dankwart answered, "How am I to say?
We cannot rest until the break of day.
We'll camp whatever grassy spot we find."
They heard this news, and more than one was sad in mind.

1624 And so, the red of warm blood undisclosed,
They stayed till over hills the sun proposed
Its brilliant light to morning, and the king
Perceived that they had fought. He said an angry thing:

1625 "What's this, my friend? It seems that you disdained
My company when coats of mail were rained
With soaking blood. Who did this thing to you?"
Said Hagen, "Else did, before last night was through.

1626 We'd been attacked because of all the bother
Over his boatman. Gelfrat fell to my brother,
Else fled us, forced by his awful plight:
A hundred of his and four of us lay dead in the fight."

1627 Where they camped, we have no information;
Later, word reached all the population

That highborn Uta's sons were on their way,
To visit at court. Passau received them well that day.

1628   Bishop Pilgrim, uncle to all three
Of these high kings, was filled with joy to see
His nephews come to the land with a complement
Of so many knights. His kindness soon was evident.

1629   Friends ran out in welcome along the way:
Passau could not provide a place to stay,
They had to cross the water, where they found
A field to set up tents and shelters all around.

1630   They stayed there one whole day, till night had ended.
The treatment they received was truly splendid.
Then it was time to leave for Ruedeger's land.
The margrave had the tidings soon enough in hand.

1631   Travel-weary men had found their rest.
Onward toward the Hunnish land they pressed,
And there at the border found a guard, asleep.
Hagen of Trony took his mighty sword to keep.

1632   This same good knight was called Sir Eckewart;
But he was now oppressed and sad at heart
To lose his sword to this heroes' expedition.
(The watch on Ruedeger's border they found in poor
        condition!)

1633   "Oh, the shame!" he cried. "I rue the cost
Of this Burgundian journey. When I lost
My lord Sigfrid, my days of joy were through.
Alas, Lord Ruedeger, what have I done to you?"

1634   When Hagen saw his doleful circumstance,
He gave him back his sword and six gold bands.
"Take these, milord, in kindness! And may you own
Yourself my friend—you're bold to stand this border
        alone."

1635   "May God repay your gift of rings," said he.
"And still your trip to the Huns disquiets me.
You killed Sigfrid, and you are hated here.
Be on your guard, I tell you—believe that I'm sincere."

1636   "The Lord watch over us!" said Hagen then.
"The only thing that much concerns these men

Is a place to stay, for king and squire and knight—
Where in these domains we spend the present night.

1637 Our steeds have come to ruin on such far ways;
Our food is gone. And where does one buy who pays?
What we need is a host," Hagen said,
"Who for his good name tonight would give us bread."

1638 "I'll show you a host," Lord Eckewart exclaimed,
"And you will rarely be so entertained
As guest in any land, as you will fare
If you bold men will come and visit Ruedeger.

1639 He lives beside the road, the finest host
That ever owned a house. His heart may boast
Such virtues as, in sweet May, the grass does flowers.
He spends, in heroes' service, his most happy hours."

1640 "Will you bear my message," Gunther cried,
"To see if for my sake he will provide
For all my kin and our men?—and I'll repay
My good freind Ruedeger for this, as best I may."

1641 Eckewart spoke, "I'll gladly bear your message."
With willing spirit he set out on passage,
To tell Lord Ruedeger what he had heard.
Not in a long, long time had come such pleasant word.

1642 He ran to Pöchlarn, first identified
By Ruedeger. "That's Eckewart," he cried,
"A vassal of Kriemhild, hurrying along."
(He thought at first that enemies had done him wrong.)

1643 He went before the gate where he espied
The herald undoing his sword to lay aside.
The news he had to bring was not concealed
From either host or kin of his, but soon revealed.

1644 He said to the margrave, "They who ordered me
To find you here are Gunther of Burgundy,
And Giselher his brother; Gernot, too,
Each of whom has pledged his high regard for you.

1645 From Hagen you hear the same, Folker as well,
In loyal zeal. But I have more to tell.
The royal marshal sends this word by me;
His excellent squires need your hospitality."

1646   Ruedeger said with a laugh, "What welcome news
That these most noble, gracious monarchs choose
To seek my service—which shall not be slighted.
If they will visit my home, I am pleased and most de-lighted."

1647   "The marshal, Dankwart, asked that you be told
How many—and whom—your house was asked to hold;
Sixty valiant champions; in rank of knight,
A thousand, and nine thousand men." This was his de-light.

1648   "What luck for me, these guests," said Ruedeger.
"These champions here in my house! The times are rare
That I have any chance to nobly treat them.
Kin and men of mine, ride out now to meet them!"

1649   They hurried to their chargers, squire and knight,
For what their lord commanded seemed most right.
They sped their service, eager not to be slow.
(Gotelind, in the ladies' suite, still did not know.)

TWENTY-SEVENTH ADVENTURE

How They Arrived at Pöchlarn

1650   The margrave went to where the ladies waited,
His wife and daughter, quickly then related
The pleasant news which he had taken to mean
That they should have as guests the brothers of their queen.

1651   "Dear love," said Ruedeger, "go, in kindness meet
These highborn, gracious monarchs and their suite
As soon as they approach our court and castle.
Greet with kindness also Hagen, Gunther's vassal.

1652   With them comes a lord called Dankwart—he,
And one named Folker, models of gallantry.
You and my daughter too shall grant these six
Your kisses and in gentle courtesy shall mix

1653   Among the champions." This they gladly vowed.
They chose from boxes garments costly and proud
To wear in meeting the knights when they went out.
How eagerly the lovely women hurried about!

1654   These ladies had but little make-up on.
Upon their heads, golden chaplets shone,
Costly garlands, lest breezes disarray
Their lovely hair. (The simple truth is all I say.)

1655   There let us leave the women occupied—
Here the margrave's friends made haste to ride
Out where the princes were, across the plain.
They found a good reception in Ruedeger's domain.

1656   When valiant Ruedeger saw them coming near,
The margrave called aloud in great good cheer,
"Welcome, lords, and all your retinue,
Here in my land! What pleasure I have in seeing you!"

1657   In homage free of hate the champions bowed.
He loved them well, and this he freely showed.
Hagen he knew, and greeted specially,
And did with Folker likewise, knight of Burgundy;

1658   And gallant Dankwart, too, who came to ask,
"If you give aid to us, whose is the task
To care for the men we brought, our retinue?"
The margrave said, "I promise a good night's rest to you.

1659   And I shall place such guard on all the force
You brought with you to my land, armor and horse,
That nothing shall be ruined, nor incur
So much as the loss to you of one single spur.

1660   Servants, out to the field, erect the tents!
And any loss you have, I'll make amends.
Let the horses free, remove the reins!"
Seldom before had host of theirs taken such pains.

1661   And the guests were glad of this. When all was done,
The lords rode off, the servants every one
Lay down in the grass and rested in comfort there.
I doubt if they had on all their trip such kindly care.

1662   Now with her comely daughter the margravine
Came before the palace, where were seen,
Beside her, winsome ladies, fair and tender
Maidens wearing many rings and clothes of splendor.

1663 How far the gems of their costly garments shone!
How fair of form they were! Riding on,
The guests had now arrived and soon dismounted.
In men of Burgundy, true courtesy abounded.

1664 Thirty-six maids and many matrons too,
Figures as lovely as one could wish for, flew
To meet them there, and valiant lords attended.
What kindly welcome the noble womenfolk extended!

1665 The margravine's daughter kissed the kings, all three
(As did her mother). And Hagen—there was he.
Her father said to kiss him, but she thought,
Staring at him: he seems so fearsome, I'd rather not.

1666 Still her lord commanded, so she must.
Her color changed; by turns she paled and blushed.
She also kissed Lord Dankwart; the minstrel, too.
For valor and mighty prowess, this greeting was his due.

1667 The youthful margravine took by the hand
Giselher the prince of Burgundy land;
As did her mother, Gunther the gallant peer.
And so they left with the heroes, full of the greatest cheer.

1668 The host, with Gernot, entered a spacious hall,
Where knights and ladies sat. Now came the call
To have for all their guests good wine obtained.
Never were any heroes better entertained.

1669 Loving glances fell from many eyes
On Ruedeger's child, her beauty so fair a prize
That in his fancy many a knight embraced her—
As was her merit, too; highest spirits graced her.

1670 (Let them think as they would, it could not be.)
Much the glancing, back and forth, to see
The maids and ladies, in such a multitude,
The noble fiddler paid the host his gratitude.

1671 By custom then they went their different ways,
Knights and ladies each to a separate place.
They set the tables in the ample hall,
Nobly serving guests they had scarcely known at all.

1672 For love of her guests the margravine had deigned
To come to table. Her daughter, though, remained

Among the maidens, her proper place to sit.
The guests, unable to see her, did not like this a bit!

1673 After they had drunk and eaten all,
They led the lovely women back to the hall.
There was no lack of merry small talk there,
Of which the gay and gallant Folker did his share.

1674 Loud and plain the noble minstrel cried:
"Most powerful margrave, God has not denied
His grace to you, in giving you a wife
Of such great beauty—and this as well: a blessed life.

1675 If I were a prince, sometime to wear a crown,
Then I should want your daughter for my own
To be my wife—suiting my wish and mood,
For she is sweet to look at, nobly born, and good."

1676 "What chance is there," Margrave Ruedeger cried,
"That any king could ever want as bride
My darling daughter? We live afar, exiled,
My wife and I. What good is beauty to the child?"

1677 Gernot answered this, a man of breeding:
"If I could have a lover truly meeting
My every wish, I'd be most satisfied
With such a wife." And Hagen cordially replied:

1678 "After all, Lord Giselher must marry.
She comes of so noble a line hereditary
That few of us would grudge the margravine
Our service in Burgundy, should she become our queen."

1679 What he said seemed good to Ruedeger
And Gotelind, and pleased their hearts to hear.
With this, the nobles soon arranged her marriage—
Befitting Giselher as a king and man of courage.

1680 Who can hinder what is bound to be?
They bade the maiden join their company
And promised him this lovely girl as bride.
He vowed in turn to keep her lovingly at his side.

1681 She was granted palaces and land,
Secured by oath and the noble monarch's hand,
And Gernot's too, that this would soon be done.
The margrave spoke, "Castles, I have not a one.

1682   I pledge you the love and loyalty I hold,
       And give my daughter dowry of silver and gold
       As much as a hundred loaded sumpters carry,
       To suit this hero's kin, their sense of honor and glory."

1683   They formed a circle and bade them enter it,
       For that is the custom. Standing opposite,
       There was a group of youths—their cares were few,
       And they let their fancies play, which young men like to do.

1684   They asked if she would have him. Much embarrassed
       Though she was at this, still she cherished
       Thoughts of him as husband. So for shame
       The maiden blushed (as many have) when the question
           came.

1685   Her father counseled her that she say yes,
       And that she gladly take him. Soon the press
       Of his white hand, and there he stood beside her,
       Giselher—though joy of him would be denied her.

1686   "High and mighty kings," the margrave cried,
       "When, as custom has it, you shall ride
       Home to Burgundy, I'll give to you
       My child to take along." This they vowed to do.

1687   After their noise, silence was now in order.
       The maiden was asked to go to the women's quarter,
       The guests to sleep and rest until the day.
       Then he fed them again, their host, in his generous way.

1688   When they had eaten they wished for leave to go
       To the land of Huns. "I would not have it so!"
       Their noble host declared. "Stay here with me,
       For rarely have I gained such pleasant company."

1689   "That surely cannot be," Lord Dankwart said.
       "Where would you get the food, the wine and bread,
       With all these many men you'll need it for,
       Even tonight?" The margrave answered, "Say no more!

1690   Dear lords and friends of mine, do not refuse.
       I'd give you all the food that you could use
       In two week's time, for all your company.
       Little indeed has Attila taken away from me."

1691   They had to stay (much as they would not yield),
Until the fourth morning. Their host revealed
Such generosity, men spoke of his deeds
      Far and wide. He gave his guests both clothes
          and steeds.

1692   But this could last no longer; they must go.
And still Lord Ruedeger could never slow
His generous hand. Whatever anyone wanted—
      One had to humor him—ask and it was granted!

1693   The servants brought their steeds, with saddles set,
Before the palace gate, where they were met
By many foreign knights, with shield in hand,
      For they were eager to ride, off to Attila's land.

1694   The margrave urged his gifts on each and all,
Before his noble guests could leave the hall—
A generous man, his ways were honored there.
      His lovely daughter he had given to Giselher.

1695   He gave to Gunther, champion noble praised,
What he could wear with honor undisgraced,
Rarely as he took gifts: an armor suit.
      Gunther bowed to Ruedeger's hand in gratitude.

1696   Then he gave to Gernot a noble sword,
With glory borne in battles afterward—
Generous giving which pleased the margrave's wife.
      Yet Ruedeger, by the gift, was doomed to lose his life.

1697   Now Gotelind—rightly, since even the king
Accepted presents—offered some loving thing
As gift to Hagen, lest with no favor from her
      He leave for the festival. At first he'd not concur.

1698   But then he said, "Of all I have chanced to see
I wish for nothing more to take with me,
Except that shield which hangs upon the wall.
      That I'd like to have when we pay the king our call."

1699   These words of Hagen fell on Gotelind's ears
And turning her mind to sorrow, led to tears.
She thought of her love for Nudung, whom Witich slew—
      And from whose loss her pain and lamentation grew.

1700   She said to Hagen, "I will give you the shield,
Would God that he whose once it was to wield
Were still alive! In battle he was killed—
For me, poor woman, a cause for tears and never stilled."

1701   The margravine arose from where she sat
And took the shield in her white hands; with that
She brought it to Hagen, who took it in his hand,
A gift of honor given and placed at his command.

1702   A cover of brilliant silken cloth concealed
Its color, bright with jewels—a better shield
The sun has never seen. Should one desire
To buy it, its worth would be a thousand marks or higher.

1703   Hagen ordered the shield carried away.
Now Dankwart came to court, receiving that day
Costly clothes the margrave's child presented,
Which later he wore among the Huns, proud and splendid.

1704   All these many gifts they took, which never
Would be theirs without their host's kind favor,
Who freely proffered all. (So hostile to him
They became one day, that in the end they slew him.)

1075   Folker came with his fiddle, having his mind
On courtly form, to stand by Gotelind
And play her his sweet tunes and sing a lay—
Saying farewell to Pöchlarn as they turned away.

1706   The margravine now had them bring a casket.
(This is a tale of friendly giving—ask it,
And you shall hear!) From this she took twelve rings
And wound them on his wrist. "I want you take these
        things.

1707   To Attila's land with you, to wear at court
For sake of me, that I may have report,
When you return, what deeds of service you did
At this high feast." How well he accomplished what she
        bid!

1708   The host announced, "Travel at ease the more
As I shall escort you, making very sure
That no one does you damage on the road."
His train of sumpters soon was ready with its load.

1709   He too prepared. Five hundred men, with steed
       And dress for each, were set to follow his lead,
       Off to the festival the Huns were giving,
       Gay at heart. Not one returned to Pöchlarn living.

1710   Their host took leave with a loving kiss, likewise
       Lord Giselher, heeding his heart's advice.
       They held their lovely women in arm's embrace—
       A thing for many maidens to mourn in coming days.

1711   On every hand were windows opened wide.
       Host and men were ready to mount and ride.
       I think their hearts foretold some awful woe,
       For all these ladies and charming maids lamented so.

1712   Many longed for friends they'd never see
       In Pöchlarn town again; yet cheerfully
       They rode away, down by the sand where runs
       The Danube in its valley, far to the land of Huns.

1713   Cried noble Ruedeger, the merry knight,
       To the men of Burgundy, "It is not right
       To keep from the Huns news of our visit in store.
       Attila never received a message to please him more."

1714   Down through Austria a herald hastened,
       Telling everywhere as people listened—
       Attila's court was never so gratified—
       How knights were come from Worms, on the farther
            Rhenish side.

1715   Heralds ranged ahead to tell their story:
       Nibelung men in Hunnish territory!
       "Greet them well, Kriemhild, this you must do.
       Your loving brothers come in honor and homage to you."

1716   Lady Kriemhild stood in a window watching,
       As friends will do, for her kin. She saw them marching,
       Men from her father's land. This came to the king,
       Who when he heard it smiled as at some pleasant thing.

1717   Kriemhild cried, "How sweet is my delight!
       My kinsmen bring new shields, and hauberks white
       And shining. Whoever has a wish for gold,
       Recall my pain. My gratitude will be untold."

TWENTY-EIGHTH ADVENTURE
How the Burgundians Came to the Castle of Attila

1718   And so the Burgundian warriors entered the land—
News which soon had reached old Hildebrand.
He told his lord of Verona, who grieved to hear it
But said to welcome them, as men of valor and spirit.

1719   Wolfhart, quick of courage, got their steeds.
There rode with Theodorich men of might deeds;
Out to the fields and the place of welcome they went,
Where men were packing on horses many a splendid tent.

1720   When Hagen of Trony saw them far ahead,
He called his lords, in courtly manner said,
"Men of courage, I'll tell you what to do:
Get up and go to meet these men who welcome you.

1721   There rides a troop that I know well," he said,
"Sturdy Amelung warriors, they are led
By the lord of Verona, men of spirit and pride.
Whatever service they offer should not be turned aside."

1722   All of them dismounted, as was right,
Theodorich and many a squire and knight,
And went where the guests, like heroes, took their stand.
They gave an affectionate welcome to men of Burgundy
    land.

1723   Theodorich spoke. (You may be curious to hear
This warrior's words, as he saw them drawing near,
These sons of Uta, whose journey here he dreaded.
Lord Ruedeger knew the truth, he thought, and could
    have said it.)

1724   "Gunther and Giselher, welcome, my lords, to you!
To Gernot and Hagen welcome, and Folker, too,
And Dankwart the bold! But are you informed so ill
You do not know that Kriemhild weeps for Sigfrid still?"

1725   "She can weep a long time, can't she?" Hagen said.
"That man has lain for years, slain and dead.
She ought to save her love for the Hun she married.
Sigfrid won't come back. He is dead and long since buried."

1726   "Let us speak no more of Sigfrid's death.
Harmful things can happen so long as breath
Is in her body," cried Verona's lord.
"Prince and shield of the Nibelung host, be on your guard!"

1727   The great king answered, "What should I watch out for?
He sent us heralds—should I inquire more?—
And brought us word that we should not refuse
To ride to Attila's land; and my sister sent good news."

1728   Said Hagen again, "In this I counsel you well:
Ask Theodorich and his knights to tell
Their story in more detail, that you may find
The truth from them: what Lady Kriemhild has in mind."

1729   The great kings went, conferring privately,
Gunther and Gernot, Theodorich, all three:
"Excellent lord of Verona, be so kind
And tell us what you know of the queen's true state of
        mind."

1730   The lord of Verona spoke: "What more should I say?
I hear the wife of Attila every day,
Her heart in misery, weeping and crying the love
She had for stalwart Sigfrid, to mighty God above."

1731   A valiant man, Folker the fiddler, cried,
"What we have heard cannot be turned aside.
Ride to court and let us see what fate
For gallant men like us among the Huns may wait."

1732   And so to court the brave Burgundians came,
With all the splendor due their country's name.
Hagen of Trony, among the Huns, could strike
The wonder of many valiant men—what was he like?

1733   Reason enough: because their ears were filled
With tales of him by whom Sigfrid was killed,
That warrior peerless in strength, their queen's, first lord,
So Hagen was the cause of many questions at court.

1734   A man of heroic build, truth to say:
Broad in the chest, his hair all streaked with gray;
His legs were long, a look that terrified
Flashed from his face; he walked along with a splendidstride.

1735   They found a place for the knights of Burgundy
And put up Gunther's servants separately—
This was the work of the queen, whose heart was filled
With hate for which the men in the inn would soon be
    killed.

1736   Dankwart, Hagen's brother, was marshal there.
The king assigned the servants to his care,
That he might be their guard, supplying their needs.
He was well disposed to them, and a man of noble deeds.

1737   Kriemhild the fair, taking her retinue, went
To welcome the Nibelungs—with false intent.
Giselher she kissed and took by the hand;
Hagen of Trony saw—and tightened his helmet band.

1738   "After a greeting like that," Hagen cried out,
"Men of valor have some cause to doubt.
For kings and men their welcome seems to differ.
Our trip to this tournament has little good to offer."

1739   "Have welcome from someone to whom your sight is dear!"
She cried, "Not as a friend do I greet you here.
Tell me what you bring from Worms on Rhine
That you should merit any welcoming of mine."

1740   Said Hagen, "If I had known that this was the way—
That vassals should bring you presents, I dare say
I'm rich enough—had I given this more thought,
There would have been some gift for you I could have
    brought."

1741   She cried, "There's more I want to know from you:
The treasure of Nibelung—what did you do
With that which was mine, as well you understand?
You should have brought it here to me, to Attila's land."

1742   "I assure you, milady, many days have passed
Since I was guardian of that treasure last.
My lords had it sunk in the Rhine, all the way
To the bottom, and there it must remain till Judgment Day."

1743   To this the queen replied, "That's what I thought.
It's very little for me that you have brought,
Though it's all mine and once was in my power.
For this my days are filled with hour on wretched hour."

1744 Said Hagen, "The devil a lot I'll bring to you,
To carry my shield is all that I can do,
And my byrnie here, my helm, with its brilliant hue.
The sword I have at my hand I'll never bring to you!"

1745 The queen cried out to the warriors one and all:
"No weapons shall be carried in this hall.
Hand them over to me, my lords, I'll see
That they are stored." Cried Hagen, "That will never be.

1746 Kind lady and prince's love, I do not mean
To covet such honor—that you, who are a queen,
Should carry my shield and armor to the inn.
That's not what my father taught me. I'll be chamberlain."

1747 Then Kriemhild cried, "Oh, the pain of it!
Why will my brother and Hagen not permit
Their shields to be stored? Some warning has
              been spread,
And if I knew the one who did it I'd see him dead."

1748 Theodorich answered, in his voice was anger:
"I am the one who warned these kings of danger—
And Hagen their vassal of Burgundy. Go to it,
Evil woman, you're not the one to make me rue it."

1749 At this, Attila's wife was struck with shame
And bitter fear of Theodorich. Quickly she came
Away from them and had no more to say,
But looked upon her enemies in a baleful way.

1750 And then two men shook hands, Hagen the one,
The other Theodorich; which being done,
The lord of light heart spoke in words well bred
And gallant: "I'm deeply sorry you came to the Huns,"
              he said,

1751 "The way the queen has talked." Said Trony's knight:
"We'll see. Things may still turn out all right."
Thus they spoke together, two brave men.
This King Attila noticed and inquired then:

1752 "I'd surely like to know who that might be,
The knight to whom Theodorich courteously
Is giving welcome. He's proud and confident—
Whoever his father was, a knight most excellent!"

1753 One of Kriemhild's thanes replied, "That man
Was born of Trony, his father was Aldrian.
He's fierce enough, however gay he acts.
You'll see that what I say are the plain and simple facts."

1754 "You say he's so fierce, but how am I to know?"
Still the king was unaware what woe
The queen had plotted for her kindred ones,
Such evil that, living, none of them should leave the Huns.

1755 "Aldrian I knew, from early days,
A vassal who gained with me both honor and praise.
I made him a knight, and granted him my gold,
And faithful Helke loved him more than could be told.

1756 So I know Hagen well, and his career.
Two handsome boys I had as hostage here,
They grew to manhood, he and Walter of Spain.
Walter ran off with Hildegund, Hagen I freed again."

1757 He thought of long ago and what occured,
Recognizing his friend of Trony, his ward,
Who served him well as a youth—and now by whom,
A man full grown, beloved friends would meet their doom.

TWENTY-NINTH ADVENTURE

How Kriemhild Accused Hagen and How He Did Not Rise When She Approached

1758 So they parted, two knights whom all men praised,
Theodorich and Hagen. Gunther's vassal gazed
Over his shoulder then, looking around
For one of his companions, whom he soon had found.

1759 There stood Folker, master of minstrel-song,
By Gunther's side. He asked him to come along,
His spirit of fierceness in mind, and he was right.
He was in all respects a brave and perfect knight.

1760 Their lords still waiting in the courtyard there,
These two set off alone across the square
To go before a far-off, spacious palace—
Knights of the highest order, fearing no man's malice.

1761   Down they sat on a bench in front of it,
With the rooms of Lady Kriemhild opposite,
Their garments gleaming so brightly as to show them
In all their splendor. Many who saw them were eager to
       know them.

1762   The Huns were gaping as if each haughty knight
Were some wild beast. Attila's wife caught sight
Of both of them through her window, a sight designed
To sadden and trouble deeply lovely Kriemhild's mind.

1763   Recalling her sorrow and pain it made her cry.
Attila's men began to wonder why.
What, they asked, had cast so deep a pall
Upon her heart? "Brave heroes, Hagen did it all!"

1764   They asked her, "How is that? A moment ago
We surely saw you happy. But tell us so—
Bid us avenge it, and no man lives so brave
Who, if he did this to you, shall escape the grave."

1765   "Whoever avenged my wrong I should repay
With all he wished, and gladly. Pleading, I lay
Myself at your feet." Thus cried Attila's wife.
"Give me vengeance on Hagen, that he may lose his life."

1766   Sixty valiant men, for Kriemhild's sake,
Got ready, swift to venture out and take
The life of brave Lord Hagen and his friend
The fiddler, too; and this was done with base intent.

1767   But when the queen perceived her troop so small,
She came to the warriors, full of wrath, to call:
"You'll miss the mark in what you hope to do—
You'll never take the measure of Hagen with so few!

1768   Whatever may be Hagen's valor and power,
Folker the fiddler at his side will tower
Higher than he in strength—a dangerous man.
You'll not fight them with ease, and do not think you can."

1769   Hearing this, more men came on the scene,
Four hundred stalwart lords. The gracious queen
Was bent on causing harm and spared no pains.
Serious trouble was in store for all these thanes.

1770   Seeing her brave retainers armed and ready,
        She spoke to the warriors thus, the royal lady:
        "Wait a while, do not break your rows;
        With crown upon me I shall go before my foes.

1771   Then hear what he did, and what reproach I throw
        At Gunther's vassal, Hagen. This I know,
        That he is proud beyond denying it.
        What happens to him in turn I do not care a whit."

1772   The fiddler, gallant bard, was now aware
        Of the noble queen descending by a stair
        That led from the building. Folker the valiant man
        Turned to Hagen his friend and, watching this, began:

1773   "Look, friend Hagen, there she comes, the one
        Who asked us here—in poor faith that was done.
        I never saw king's wife accompanied
        By so many men with sword in hand, warlike indeed.

1774   Have they something against you, Hagen my friend,
        Do you know? If so, I say you'd best attend
        To life and honor—a sound idea, I find.
        Unless my eyes deceive me, they come in an angry mind.

1775   And some of them are rather broad in the chest—
        If one would be on guard, it might seem best
        To do it soon; I think they wear bright mail
        Beneath their silk. For whom they mean it I cannot tell."

1776   Then Hagen the fearless answered angrily:
        "I know that all of this is meant for me,
        The shining weapons they carry there in hand—
        For all of them, I'd still get back to Burgundy land.

1777   Tell me now, my friend, do you stand with me,
        If I am set upon by this company
        Of Kriemhild's men? As you love me, let me know,
        And you shall have forever the loyal thanks I owe."

1778   "I'd help you just as surely," the minstrel said,
        "If I saw here a king approach at the head
        Of all his knights; there is, while I may live,
        No inch I yield in fear, no help I will not give."

1779   "God bless you, noble Folker! If they fight
        Against me here, I need no other knight,

Since you will help me as you said you would,
Let them come this way, and may their guard be good!"

1780   "Let's get up from this seat," the minstrel said,
"She is a queen—and let her come ahead,
Showing our respect for her noble birth,
And thus enhancing both of us in fame and worth."

1781   "Over my dead body," Hagen said.
"These thanes would think I acted out of dread
And apprehension here, if I retreated.
Not for one of them would I rise, when I am seated.

1782   Better indeed by far if we did not.
Why give honor when hate is all I've got?
That I never will, while I have life.
What do I care for the malice of King Attila's wife?"

1783   Across his knees the arrogant Hagen laid
A shining weapon from whose pommel played,
In light as green as grass, as jasper stone.
Kriemhild knew at once that it was Sigfrid's own.

1784   She saw the sword—how heavy her sorrow weighed!
The hilt was made of gold; the sheath, red braid.
It called to mind her pain, and all this ended
With her weeping—just, I think, what Hagen intended.

1785   There on the bench, bold Folker drew to his side
A mighty fiddle-bow, long and wide,
Much like a sword, sharp and heavily made.
And there the merry warriors sat, unafraid.

1786   They thought themselves so much without a peer
That they would not arise from their seats in fear
Of anyone. Before their very toes
Stepped the highborn queen, and greeted them as foes:

1787   "Tell me, Hagen," she said, "who sent for you,
That you ride to this country—which you dare to do,
Knowing well what you have brought on me?
If you had any sense, you would have let it be."

1788   "No one sent for me," said Hagen. "There came
An invitation for three who are by name
My lords in liege, and I by this same token
Am their vassal. No trip with them have I forsaken!"

1789 She cried, "Go on and tell me why you did
The deed by which my hate is merited.
You killed Sigfrid, my lord and beloved one—
Sufficient cause to weep until my days are done."

1790 "Why go on? We've talked enough, I'm through.
I am Hagen still, the one who slew
The mighty hero Sigfrid. How he suffered
For the slur on Brunhild's name that Kriemhild offered!

1791 Mighty queen, there shall be no denying:
All the guilt is mine, for doom and dying.
Woman or man, avenge it whoever will.
Either I lie to you, or I have done you ill."

1792 "Listen, my lords, hear this man confess
All my hurt! What happens to him for this,
Men of the king, that is my least concern."
And now the haughty warriors looked at each other in turn.

1793 If someone had started fighting, what ensued
Would have brought the two men fame and praise renewed.
In battle, they would have made their merit clear.
The Huns laid plans in pride, they gave them up in fear.

1794 One of their warriors cried, "Don't look at me.
I intend to go back on my guarantee,
And not to lose my life for anyone's gift.
Great King Attila's wife would cast us all adrift."

1795 "The same for me," another one near him said.
"Give me towers of solid gold, all red,
I wouldn't fight this fiddler, just for the grim
And terrible look I see upon the face of him.

1796 Also, I've known Hagen since he was young,
And I don't need to hear his merit sung.
On twenty-two occasions I've seen him fight,
In battles where women's hearts were left as dark as night.

1797 They took the road on more than one campaign
Here with Attila, he and the knight of Spain,
When they fought so well for the honor of the king.
Credit rendered Hagen is only a rightful thing.

1798 Then he was just a child in years but they
Who once were young with him are now turned gray,

And he is a man mature, a fearsome lord.
Besides he carries Balmung, his ill-gotten sword."

1799 That was the end of it, no one would start
The fighting now. The queen was sick at heart.
The heroes turned about, fearing to die
At the hands of the fiddler. Well they knew the reason why!

1800 "Now we have clearly seen," said Folker the bold,
"That we find enemies here, as we were told.
The kings are in court, and we had best go back
And keep our masters safe from any new attack.

1801 A man will often neglect a thing from fear;
Just so will friend aid friend, if his mind is clear,
And in his friendship do nothing of the kind.
Hurt to many a man is saved by presence of mind."

1802 Said Hagen, "I'll follow you and go along."
They went where brilliant warriors stood in a throng
At court reception. To his lords in the crowd
Folker the valiant knight began to call aloud:

1803 He said, "How long do you mean to stay and let
Yourselves be surrounded. Go to the court and get
Straight from the king's own mouth his state of mind."
Now you could see brave warriors move, in pairs aligned.

1804 The ruling prince of Verona took by the hand
Mighty Gunther, lord of Burgundy land,
And Irnfrid, valiant Gernot; also there
Was Margrave Ruedeger, off to court with Giselher.

1805 However they were paired in going to court
Folker and Hagen never drew apart—
Till once in battle when their end was come;
And that was many women's tearful martyrdom.

1806 People saw the kings on the way to the castle.
A thousand bold retainers, liege and vassal,
Sixty champions, too, who made the ride,
Recruits of dauntless Hagen from his own countryside.

1807 Haward and Iring, two men beyond compare,
Walked along with the kings, a friendly pair,
And Dankwart with Wolfhart (a worthy man was he),
Each impressing the others with his dignity.

1808   The lord of the Rhineland entered the palace gate.
Mighty Attila would no longer wait;
Seeing him, he ran from where he was seated.
No man has been by any king so nobly greeted.

1809   "Gunther my lord; Gernot, and Giselher,
Your brothers, welcome! I sent—and did not spare
Good faith or zeal—my pledge of service to you,
To Worms on Rhine. And welcome to all your retinue!

1810   To you two knights a special welcome word,
Folker, man of valor, and Hagen my lord,
From me and my lady too, upon your entry
Into our land. She sent you heralds to Rhenish country."

1811   Hagen replied, "I've heard that more than once.
Had love of my lords not brought me to the Huns,
In homage to you I'd have ridden to your land."
The highborn host now took his dear guests by the hand,

1812   And led them to sit where he himself was sitting.
They poured for their guests—with eagerness most fitting—
Vessels of wide gold full of wine and mead
And mulberry drink, making the strangers welcome indeed.

1813   Said King Attila, "I would have you know:
No greater pleasure could this world bestow
Than you have given me in coming here.
You've made the queen's great burden of sorrow disappear.

1814   For I have wondered what I did to you—
Seeing my many noble guests who do—
That you have never cared to visit here.
Now that I see you before me, the end is joy and cheer."

1815   Said Ruedeger, man of pride and confidence,
"Well may you welcome them! A noble sense
Of loyalty has always been the forte
Of my lady's kin. What handsome knights they bring to
        your court!"

1816   The lords had come the eve of solstice-tide
To the court of mighty Attila. Far and wide,
No welcome ever heard of matched their greeting.
Soon came dinner; he sat with them at table, eating.

1817   No host has sat with guests more splendidly.
       They gave them all they wished, in quantity,
       Of food and drink—most gladly, for they had heard
       About these heroes, long ago, most wondrous word.

THIRTIETH ADVENTURE
How Hagen and Folker Stood Watch

1818   Now the day was done and night drew near,
       And travel-weary men began to fear
       Lest they might have no rest nor get to bed.
       Hagen talked of this; word was quick to spread.

1819   Gunther cried to his host, "God save you, sir!
       We wish to have our sleep. If you prefer
       We'll come tomorrow morning. So give us leave."
       The king and his guests were parting; there seemed no
            cause to grieve.

1820   But now the guests were being crowded 'round,
       And valiant Folker cried to the Huns, "Give ground!
       How dare you come and tread on our very toes?
       If you don't stop you'll have your share of pain and woes.

1821   My fiddle-bow will fetch you a blow so smart—
       If you have one loyal friend, it'll break his heart.
       Get out of our way—you'd better! They share the name
       Of warrior, all of them—but their hearts are not the same."

1822   And when the fiddler spoke so angrily,
       Valiant Hagen turned around to see.
       "That's good advice you hear our minstrel give.
       Go back, you men of Kriemhild, back to where you live!

1823   No one will do what you are counting on.
       If you want trouble, come back tomorrow at dawn.
       Tonight, let us as strangers rest in peace.
       Men of such a mind as yours do that at least."

1824   They took their foreign guests to a spacious hall
       Prepared for courtly taste with beds and all,
       Long and wide and splendid. But there the queen
       Had plotted them the bitterest woe the world has seen.

1825   There were many quilts of Arras, skillfully made
Of shining satin cloth, with covers laid,
Of very best Arabian silk, thereon;
And all around the edges lovely bindings shone.

1826   Some had coverlets of ermine fur
Or black sable, under which they were,
That night, supposed to sleep till light of day.
No king or king's retainers ever slept that way.

1827   Young Giselher cried, "Alas for this night we spend,
For those who came with us, our every friend!
Think of the kindly things my sister said—
And yet because of her I fear we'll soon lie dead."

1828   Hagen the warrior spoke, "Do not take fright.
I myself will stand shield-watch tonight.
I think that I can keep you safe till dawn—
Have no fear. Tomorrow—let him who can live on!"

1829   They bowed in thanks to him, and off they went
To seek their beds. Little time they spent,
These handsome lords, before they all had gone
Sound asleep. Bold Hagen put his armor on.

1830   Folker the fiddler spoke, "If you're not scorning
Offers of help, I'll stand with you till morning,
Hagen, taking my share of tonight's watch."
For this the chivalrous hero thanked Lord Folker
    much:

1831   "The Lord in Heaven bless you, Folker my friend,
I wish for no companion but you to spend
My anxious moments with, when trouble is near.
I'll pay you back, unless my death should interfere."

1832   Then they both put on their shining clothes
(Taking each his shield in hand) and rose
And left the house, to stand before the door
And guard the guests—out of the loyalty they bore.

1833   Valiant Folker took his trusty shield.
Leaning it by the palace wall, he wheeled

And went inside, to get his fiddle there.
Thus he served his friends, for this was his rightful care.

1834 Beneath the doorway, seated on the stone,
The boldest of fiddlers played, and when the tone
Rose sweetly from the strings, out of the ranks
Of warriors far from home Lord Folker had his thanks.

1835 His strings were loud, and all the hall resounded,
For in this man both valor and art abounded.
He began to play more sweetly and softly then,
Lulling to sleep upon their benches anxious men.

1836 When he could see that they were sleeping fast
He took his shield in hand again and passed
From out of the room, to stand before the tower,
And guard the homeless wanderers from Kriemhild's power.

1837 No earlier than the middle of the night,
I think, bold Folker saw the play of light
From helmets in the darkness. (All too gladly
Would Kriemhild's men have reached their guests and
used them badly.)

1838 The fiddler said, "Hagen, my friend, this trouble
Might be better borne if we bore it double.
I see men in armor by the palace.
So far as I can judge, they mean to fight and kill us."

1839 "Quiet then," said Hagen. "Let them near.
There'll be helmet-cases jolted here,
By our two swords in hand, before we're seen.
We'll send them back in poor condition to the queen."

1840 Suddenly one of the Huns had looked about:
The door was guarded! He was quick to shout,
"What we thought of doing cannot be.
Someone's standing watch—that's the fiddler I see.

1841 On his head he has a helmet, shining,
Bright and hard, of sound and strong designing,
His mail is glowing like a fire reflected—
And Hagen by his side! Our guests are well protected."

1842   When Folker saw the men retrace their path,
He turned to his companion, full of wrath:
"Let me leave the house and follow behind,
And speak to Kriemhild's men—I have questions on my
        mind!"

1843   "No," Lord Hagen cried, "for my own sake!
Leave the house, and these brave men would take
Their swords to you. Such trouble they'd have you in,
I'd have to help you, though it cost me all my kin.

1844   If both of us went out, to wage this war,
In no time two of them, or maybe four
Would rush the hall together. The havoc wrought
Among our men asleep would never be forgot."

1845   Said Folker, "One thing at least we should do then:
Let them know I saw them. Kriemhild's men
Shall never have the chance to go about
Denying the treachery they hoped to carry out."

1846   Folker shouted at them, "How does this happen,
That valiant men of Kriemhild come, a weapon
In every hand?—riding out to rob?
You need my friend and me to help you with the job!"

1847   No one answered that. His anger grew;
The hero spoke, "You worthless cowards, you!
While we were sleeping, you'd have murdered us?
Not often have such worthy men been treated thus."

1848   The queen was duly told her messengers
Had failed their mission. Greatest grief was hers.
Fierce of heart, she thought of other ways.
For this, courageous lords would perish in coming days.

THIRTY-FIRST ADVENTURE
How They Went to Church

1849   "My armor," Folker said, "is cooling fast.
I do not think this night has long to last.
I can tell by the breeze, day is about to dawn."
They went to wake the rest, still sleeping soundly on.

1850   Now bright morning came to the guests in the hall.
       Hagen went to the knights and woke them all,
       And would they go to church and hear mass sung?
       According to Christian custom, many bells were rung.

1851   (Clearly, they did not sing in harmony,
       Christian and pagan, there seemed no unity.)
       Gunther's heroes wished to be up and gone
       To the minster now, and rose from where they slept, as one.

1852   The knights got dressed in clothes the like of which
       Heroes never brought (they were so rich)
       To any king's land—hard for Hagen to bear.
       "Warriors," he said, "these are not the clothes to wear.

1853   There's more than one among you here who knows.
       Carry a sword in your hand, and not a rose!
       And take your solid shining helm in lieu
       Of jeweled chaplets. We know what evil she means to do.

1854   And we must fight today, I give you my word.
       Wear your hauberk instead of a silken shirt,
       Take your good broad shield and not your cape.
       If anyone raises trouble, be in fighting shape!

1855   My dear lords, kin, and men, do not be loath
       To go to church—your sorrow and trouble both
       Complain to mighty God! Let this be clear
       In all your minds: the hour of our death is near.

1856   Do not forget the things that you have done,
       And stand in earnest before the Almighty One,
       For I will warn you this, my splendid men,
       Without God's special help, you'll never hear mass again."

1857   To go to the minster, princes and vassals rose,
       But valiant Hagen stood within the close
       Sacred to God and bade them stop and thus
       Remain together. "Who knows what the Huns will
              do to us?

1858   My friends, place your shields before your feet,"
       Said Hagen. "If anyone should basely greet
       Your presence here, repay with the fatal sword.
       There's my advice!—so act that praise be your reward."

1859   Ahead of the others Folker and Hagen went
In front of the wide minster, with this intent:
To be quite sure the queen must crowd in past,
In order to enter. The rage within their hearts was vast.

1860   Now came the lord of the land, in company
Of his lovely wife. Adorned in luxury
Were the knights one saw with them, walking along.
A cloud of dust rose high from all of Kriemhild's throng.

1861   Great King Attila, seeing them armed this way,
The kings and their retinue, was quick to say,
"What's this I see? My friends with helmets on?
I honestly regret if any harm's been done.

1862   And I will make amends as they see fit,
For hurt to mind or heart because of it,
To make it clear to them how bad I feel.
Let them but ask, and I shall answer their appeal."

1863   Said Hagen, "No one's done a thing to us.
My lords by custom go in armor thus
For three full days at any festival.
Hurt to us would be relayed to you in full."

1864   Clearly Kriemhild heard what Hagen spoke,
And cast at him a hostile look that broke
From lowered brow; yet she would not declare,
Well as she knew it from Burgundy, the custom there.

1865   However fierce her hate for them, or bitter,
Had someone told the king the truth of the matter,
He might well have stopped what yet occurred.
In their great arrogance, they told him not a word.

1866   A crowd came with her. A space but two hands wide
Was more than these two men would stand aside.
This was what the Huns felt wary of,
As there was nothing left to do but push and shove.

1867   Attila's chamberlains did not approve.
They would have gladly gone ahead to move
These knights to wrath—which they hadn't the courage for,
With Attila there. They jostled about and nothing more.

1868   When church was over and time had come to go,
The Huns made for their steeds—and were not slow.
Maidens stood by Kriemhild, fair to see,
And seven thousand thanes rode in her company.

1869   There by the windows with the mighty king,
She sat with her maids—for him a pleasant thing—
To watch at riding lords of such good cheer.
How many foreign knights rode in the courtyard here!

1870   Dankwart the bold, as marshal, now came back
With the serving-men. He had been keeping track
Of all the staff of the king of Burgundy.
Horses were fitly saddled for Nibelung chivalry.

1871   Now that kings and men were all on horse,
Folker the strong proposed they joust in force
As was their custom at home. This gave the tip
To all the heroes to show their brilliant horsemanship.

1872   So he proposed what they were not against.
The jousting and the noise were soon immense,
As many men approached the spacious court.
Kriemhild and King Attila turned to watch the sport.

1873   Six hundred thanes arrived, drawn by the tests—
Theodorich's knights who came to face the guests
And share the fun with the men of Burgundy.
Had he allowed, they would have done so willingly.

1874   What knights rode after them! The eager news
Was passed to Theodorich; he did not choose
To let them vie with Gunther's retinue.
He worried for his men and had good reason to.

1875   Now that the knights of Verona had left the field,
Ruedeger's men from Pöchlarn, under shield,
Five hundred strong, approached the front of the hall.
The margrave himself would rather they had not come at all.

1876   He rode through the ranks of his men, wise and cautious,
Saying they must have noticed how ferocious
Gunther's warriors were, their anger stirred,
and he'd be pleased if they'd not ride in this behourd.

1877   And when these merry knights had left them, then,
Our story runs, there came Thuringian men,
And a thousand valiant lords from Denmark entered,
Brandishing spears; and pieces flew from lances splintered.

1878   Irnfrid and Haward rode to join the melee.
The Rhinelanders waited in their stately way
To offer joust to the men of Thuringia and give
Such thrusts that many a splendid shield was left a sieve.

1879   Bloedel and his three thousand men approached.
The king and Kriemhild saw him, as they watched
The scene before them, the games of chivalry.
The queen was pleased at this, for the hurt of Burgundy.

1880   Shrutan and Gibech, Ramung and Hornbow joined
In jousting, for so the Huns are always inclined,
Facing the men of Burgundy, heroes all.
Shafts went whirling, high as the royal palace wall.

1881   (All this was nothing more than sport and sound.)
The crash of shields made house and halls resound
Loud with the echoing noise of Gunther's lords.
His retinue was first in glory and high awards.

1882   So fast and violent did their pastime get
That through the saddle cloths the shining sweat
Ran from the fine horses the heroes rode.
They tried their luck with the Huns, in an overbearing mood.

1883   The minstrel cried, "It seems these men would rather
Not attack us now. From what I gather,
They bear toward us some hateful prejudice.
Well, there never was a better time than this!"

1884   And Folker went on, "Have our chargers led
Back to quarters. We'll ride toward evening instead,
Whenever the time is ripe. What will you bet
The queen must give the prize to men of
            Burgundy yet?"

1885   No man could match in pomp one of the chaps
Whom they saw riding up. He had, perhaps,
A sweetheart on the parapet, to ride
In clothes so elegant, just like a knight's new bride.

1886   Folker cried, "How can I let that go?
This lady's man deserves a whacking blow.
Let no one hinder me, he pays with his life;
And what do I care if this should anger Attila's wife?"

1887   "No, for my sake don't," said Gunther in haste.
"If we should launch the attack, we'd stand disgraced
In people's minds. Let the Huns, as is more fitting."
Attila still was there with his queen, quietly sitting.

1888   Hagen said, "I'm going to join the battle.
Let these lords and ladies see the mettle
Of our riding. This is the best we can do—
They won't give any prizes to Gunther's retinue."

1889   Folker the valiant rode behourd again,
Destined soon to be a cruel bane
To many women, for his spear impaled
That wealthy Hun, at which both maids and ladies wailed.

1890   Hagen and his men, with sixty thanes,
Rode off in a mighty rush, taking pains
To follow the fiddler where the games were run.
Attila and the queen saw clearly what was done.

1891   The kings were loath to let their minstrel go
Without protection there among the foe,
So a thousand heroes rode to show their skill,
Doing all as they pleased, with a proud and haughty will.

1892   Now when the rich and mighty Hun was slain,
His kinsmen all were heard to weep and complain.
And those of his household asked, "Who struck the blow?"
"That was the minstrel Folker, man of the fiddlebow!"

1893   They shouted for their swords and shields at once,
The kinsmen of this margrave of the Huns,
Wishing the death of Folker. Leaving his post
In the window niche he rushed to the scene, their royal
        host.

1894   All the people raised a great to-do.
By the hall the kings leaped down, with their retinue.
Burgundians too had pushed their horses back.
Attila intervened lest either side attack.

1895   Nearby, a friend of the Hun happened to stand.
        Attila snatched a weapon from his hand
        And beat them back, for he was very mad.
        "What a way to ruin the welcome these knights have had!

1896   If you should kill this minstrel before me here,
        What a wicked thing! My view was clear;
        I saw the way he rode when the Hun was humbled.
        That was no fault of Folker's; it happened because he
            stumbled.

1897   You'll have to leave my guests in peace," he said,
        And gave them his protection. Now they led
        Their horses back to the inn; servants there
        Stood in readiness to give them zealous care.

1898   The host and all his friends entered the palace;
        And he'd allow no further show of malice.
        They set out tables, serving them water on these—
        But here the men of Rhine had many enemies.

1899   Before they all were seated, a long time passed.
        Fear of Kriemhild's plotting held them fast.
        She cried, "Prince of Verona, I seek your aid,
        Your guard and counsel. I'm in peril and afraid."

1900   Answered Hildebrand, a worthy lord,
        "The man who kills the Nibelungs for reward
        Need not count on me. He may regret
        The step he takes. These knights have not been conquered
            yet."

1901   Theodorich added, a man of courteous air:
        "Mighty queen, do not renew that prayer.
        Your valiant kin have done no wrong to me,
        That I should turn on them in open enmity.

1902   Your wish does you little credit—as the wife
        Of a noble prince, to plot against the life
        Of your own kin. In trust they sought this land.
        Sigfrid will have no vengeance from Theodorich's hand."

1903   Finding Theodorich free of perfidy,
        She gave vast marches once in Nudung's fee

In pledge to Bloedel's hand—her move was swift!
(Dankwart slew him soon, and he forgot his gift.)

1904   She said, "Help me, Bloedel! Here in this house
Are foes of mine, by whom my lord and spouse
Lord Sigfrid died. Whoever helps me get
Revenge for that, to him I stand in constant debt."

1905   Bloedel answered, "Lady, this is a fact:
I dare inflict on them no hostile act,
Because of the king. He loves to see them here,
And he would not forget if I should interfere."

1906   "Not so, Lord Bloedel, you'll always have my aid.
I'll give you silver and gold in pay, and a maid
Of greatest beauty, Nudung's bride intended,
A charming maiden in whose arms you'll be contented.

1907   Land and castles, everything I'll give,
Most noble knight, to you that you may live
In joy forever, if you become the heir
Of Nudung's march. I'll keep in faith, what now I
     swear."

1908   Now that Bloedel had his pay revealed
And found that in her beauty she appealed
So much to him, he thought in war and strife
To win her love. For this he soon would lose his life.

1909   "Go back to the hall again," he said to the queen.
"And I shall raise the alarm before you're seen.
Hagen will pay for what he did to you.
I'll hand him over, bound and tied, when I am
     through."

1910   He turned: "Now arm yourselves, men of mine,
We go to our foes in the inn, by her design
From which she will not release me, Attila's wife.
That is why each one of us must risk his life."

1911   Leaving Bloedel in spirit battle-fit
The queen now went to table, there to sit
With Attila and his warriors, all of them.
She had devised for her guests a fearful stratagem.

C1963*The princes at long last were seated all
     And now began to eat, when into the hall
     To join their party entered Attila's child—
     For which the mighty king would grieve, unreconciled.

1913 Quickly, four of Attila's vassals there
      Went to bring Ortlieb, his son and heir,
      To the princes' table, where also Hagen sat.
      There was murder in his hate—the child would die for that.

1914 And when the great king saw his son, he cried
      To all his kin-in-law, in kindly pride:
      "Look, my friends, here is my only son,
      And your sister's too, a sign of good for everyone.

1915 A valiant man, if he takes after his race,
      Rich and noble, strong, and fair of face!
      If I shall live to give them, twelve whole lands
      Shall all be his. You'll be well served in Ortlieb's hands.

1916 So I am pleased to ask, dear friends of mine,
      That when you travel home, back to the Rhine,
      You take your sister's son with you, and ever
      Let the boy be granted your most gracious favor.

1917 And rear him in the way of excellence,
      Till manhood. Should anyone do violence
      In your dominions, he will help you repay it,
      When he is grown." The wife of Attila heard him say it.

---

* Here the translation follows manuscript C. B reads:

> Since otherwise the fighting would not start—
> Her ancient pain deep buried in her heart—
> Kriemhild brought to table Attila's son.
> No woman has sought revenge through a deed more cruelly done.

These verses are a holdover from sources in which Kriemhild not only has Ortlieb thus brought to sacrifice, but incites the youth to strike Hagen, who then kills him. In the *Nibelungenlied* Ortlieb is obviously too young to fit into this pattern, and the poem has besides a more reasonable if less traumatic occasion for the outbreak of war: Dankwart's report of the death of all the squires. With this the version of C is in accord, while B's strophe is gratuitous. In affectionate tribute to its grisly impact, B apparently kept it anyway.

1918   Cried Hagen, "These knights might well give him their trust
If he should grow to manhood, yet it must
In truth be said the prince has a fated air.
The times I'll come to this young prince's court are rare."

1919   Attila looked at Hagen. The words had hit.
A cheerful man, he did not speak of it,
And yet his heart was sad, and grave his mind.
This was no jest, not so was Hagen's will inclined.

1920   The princes, like their king, were shorn of joy,
At what Lord Hagen said about the boy,
Annoyed that they must take it—still not knowing
All of what was yet to come of that man's doing.

THIRTY-SECOND ADVENTURE
How Dankwart Killed Bloedel

1921   Bloedel's knights stood ready. All aligned
In a thousand hauberks, they set out to find
Dankwart at table with the squire's train.
There, among heroes, awful hate began its reign.

1922   For when Lord Bloedel came where they were seated,
He was met by the marshal, and duly greeted:
"Welcome, sir, to this house. and yet I doubt
If I fully understand—what is this all about?"

1923   "You need not greet me," Bloedel said. "I came,
But my coming means your end—for this the blame
Is your brother Hagen's, by whom Sigfrid was slain.
You'll pay the Huns for that, with many another thane."

1924   "Oh no, Lord Bloedel," said Dankwart. "We should clearly
Regret our journey then. But I was merely
A youth and no more, when Sigfrid lost his life.
Tell me, what cause of reproach am I to Attila's wife?"

1925   "I tell you this, and this is all I know:
Your kinsmen Gunther and Hagen did it. And so,
Outcast men, on guard! There is no path
To safety here; you'll be my lady's bond in death."

1926   "If you will not relent," Dankwart declared,
"I rue my pleading. It were better spared."
Up from the table leapt the valiant lord
And drew his mighty blade, his sharpened sword,

1927   And struck Lord Bloedel such a violent blow,
His head rolled off and lay at his feet below.
"Now let that be your dowry," Dankwart cried,
"For the one whose love you hoped to win, for Nudung's
      bride!

1928   Marry her tomorrow to another —
We'll do the same for him, if he wants to bother
For his dowry." (It seems he'd been appraised
By loyal Huns of the terrible harm the queen devised.)

1929   Bloedel's men, seeing their master slain,
Could not forgive their guests or bear such pain.
Their swords held high, they rushed with fierce intent
Upon the pages, a step which many would soon lament.

1930   Loudly Dankwart cried to the household hands,
"Good squires and pages, you see how your future stands.
On guard, my outcast men! Our need is clear.
And yet most noble Kriemhild sweetly asked us here."

1931   Some had no swords; they reached beneath the table,
Seizing the long footstools—now unable
Longer to bear the great affront they felt.
Even through helmets those heavy chairs could raise a welt.

1932   How fiercely the youths resisted this attack!
The men in armor soon were driven back
Leaving within a good five hundred dead.
All the serving men were drenched with blood and red.

1933   This fearful piece of news was soon made plain
To Attila's knights (causing them bitter pain):
That Bloedel himself was killed, and all his crew,
Which Hagen's brother did, with men of the retinue.

1934   Before the king found out, two thousand or more
Of the Huns made ready, and for the hate they bore,
Fell on the squires—for so their doom took shape.
Of all of these retainers they let not one escape.

1935   The traitors brought to the hall a mighty host.
Bravely the foreign squires stood their post.
What good their valor? Their death was now ordained.
In all too short a time, most frightful havoc reigned.

1936   Now your ears shall hear both wonders said,
And monstrous things. Nine thousand men lay dead,
Besides a dozen knights of Dankwart's own.
He himself stood up, among his foes, alone.

1937   The din of battle stilled, the tumult died.
Looking over his shoulder, Dankwart cried,
"Alas for all the friends I had to lose;
Now sadly I must stand alone among my foes."

1938   Swords fell heavy on him. (Women would weep
For this in time.) In order now to keep
His shield up higher, he set his enarmes low.
On many suits of mail he made the wet blood flow.

1939   Cried Aldrian's son, "Alas, this pain and despair!
Step back, you Hunnish men, and give me air.
The breeze shall cool my battle-weary frame."
They watched him come ahead, and splendidly
              he came.

1940   Out of the house, battle-worn he sprang.
And how the fresh swords on his helmets rang!
They rushed upon the lord of Burgundy land—
Men who had not seen the wonders done by his hand.

1941   "Would to God above I had a herald
To tell my brother Hagen how, imperilled,
I stand and face these knights," Lord Dankwart said.
"He'd help me get away or lie beside me, dead."

1942   Hun lords cried, "Herald? There'll be no other
But you, when we carry you before your brother,
Dead. Gunther's vassal then will know
At last what pain is, for you have hurt Attila so."

1943   "Stop the threats," he said, "and stand aside!
I'll keep the armor yet from getting dried
On some of you. I go myself to reveal
The truth at court and tell my lords the grief I feel."

1944   He soon was such a bane to Attila's lords,
They did not dare resist him with their swords.
They hit his shield with their spears, in number so great
He had to set it down for all the added weight.

1945   They thought to conquer him, now that he bore
No shield in hand, but what deep wounds he tore
Through helmets then! Heroes sank before him.
What a harvest of praise Lord Dankwart's valor bore him!

1946   They rushed him from either side, but of these some
Who joined the fray had been too quick to come.
He faced his foes, like a wild boar held at bay
By dogs in a forest. Could he be braver in any way?

1947   Once again his very path was wet
With steaming blood. Lone warrior never yet
Has better fought against his foes than he.
Hagen's brother strode to court, and splendidly!

1948   Bearers of wine and stewards heard the sound
Of swords at work, and cast their drinks to the ground,
Their food for the court, which they were about to bear,
And—foemen savage enough—met him at the stair.

1949   Said the weary man, "Stewards, what's amiss?
You ought to take much better care than this
Of all your guests, and feed those lords good things—
Letting me tell my tale to my beloved kings."

1950   On those who in their courage blocked the stair
He swung his sword so fiercely through the air
That they moved higher up the steps in fear.
With strength and courage he accomplished wonders here!

THIRTY-THIRD ADVENTURE

How the Burgundians Fought the Huns

1951   Valiant Dankwart stepped inside the door,
Making the Huns move back a little more.
His clothes were run with blood. He took his stand,
Holding a mighty weapon naked in his hand.

1952   Dankwart shouted loud to all the throng:
        "Hagen my brother, sir, you sit too long.
        To you and God above I cry our doom.
        Our knights and all our squires lie dead in the hostel room."

1953   "Who did it?" Hagen shouted back again.
        "Bloedel did it, Bloedel and his men.
        I tell you this, he's paid a heavy fine,
        For I struck off his head with these two hands of mine."

1954   "Little harm in that," his brother said.
        "People say that if a man be dead,
        And if it be at the hands of some great hero
        So much the less excuse for lovely women's sorrow.

1955   But tell me, brother Dankwart, why so red?
        You seem in pain from all the blood you shed.
        If he who did it is still in this countryside
        There'll be his life to pay—or the devil save his hide."

1956   "You're looking at a healthy man, this wet
        Is blood from others' wounds. That's what I get
        For all the men that I have killed today.
        How many I left dead, I swear I could not say."

1957   "Dankwart, watch the door, and look about!
        Do not let a single Hun get out.
        I'll have a word with them," Lord Hagen said.
        "We have no choice but this. Our guiltless men lie dead."

1958   Said he, "If I'm to be the chamberlain,
        Why, I know how to serve such worthy men,
        And I shall tend the stairs as suits my fame."
        To Kriemhild's thanes more gloomy tidings never came.

1959   "I wonder here," said Hagen, "what the Hun
        Is whispering about? I gather it's the one
        Who stands by the door, the one who brought in the news.
        They'd not mind getting rid of him, if they could choose.

1960   They tell the tale of Kriemhild—I've known it long—
        That she was one to nurse her heart's wrong.
        Now drink a toast for the dead and pledge the wine!
        The scion of the Huns shall be the first in line."

1961 He struck the boy Ortlieb, Hagen the lord;
Down to his hands the blood ran on the sword.
And the head flew straight to the queen's lap.
Bitter murder broke about like a thunderclap.

1962 With his two hands he launched a blow that caught
Off guard the man by whom the lad was taught.
By the table there, his head rolled to the floor.
That was the wretched fee he paid to the tutor's score.

1963 Before King Attila's table he saw a bard.
Hagen dashed across—his heart was hard—
Straight from the fiddle severed his right hand.
"Take that for your message next when you go to
  Burgundy land!"

1964 "Oh Lord, my hand!" cried Werbel. "What shall I do?
Hagen of Trony, what have I done to you?
I came in all good faith to your master's land.
How shall I play my songs, now that I've lost my hand?"

1965 Little Hagen cared if he ever played.
In mortal rage and savage hurt he made
His way through Attila's house and host and slew
Great numbers of them. Enough were dead when he was
  through.

1966 Up from the table leapt Folker the strong.
The bow in his hand gave out its noisy song—
Harsh the fiddle play of Gunther's bard.
He earned his fill from the Huns of hate and ill-regard.

1967 The three great kings got up and came at a run
To stop the fight before more harm was done,
But all their wise restraint had no effect,
While Folker and Hagen both poured out their rage unchecked.

1968 When Gunther saw the fight could not be stopped,
The lord of the Rhine drew sword himself and chopped
Wide wounds through the bright mail of his foe—
A hero with his hands, as he gave them all to know.

1969 Now the sturdy Gernot joined the fray,
And many Huns lay dead from his swordplay
With the sharp blade, his gift from Ruedeger.
He dealt the knights of Attila hurt beyond repair.

1970   Uta's youngest son sprang to the battle;
His sword rang through helmets, in glorious mettle,
Upon King Attila's knights from the land of the Hun—
Where, by Giselher's hand, amazing things were done.

1971   Of kings and men, whatever show of daring,
Giselher stood forth, beyond comparing,
Against the enemy—an excellent man.
Many he felled there, wounded, into the blood as it ran.

1972   Bitterly the Hunnish side fought back.
One could see the foreign warriors hack
With shining swords, a path through Attila's hall.
And soon one heard sounds of moaning over all.

1973   The men without would join their friends inside—
A poor reception waited when they tried.
The ones within were not contented there,
But Dankwart let no one go up or down the stair.

1974   By the towers at the door was such a crowd,
And the sound of sword on helmet grew so loud,
That Dankwart found himself in perilous straits.
His brother showed his concern—as loyalty dictates.

1975   "Comrade, do you see," he shouted back
To Folker there, "my brother under attack,
Before the Huns, with heavy blows to bruise him?
My friend, go save my brother for me, before we
        lose him!"

1976   "Trust me," the bard replied. "It shall be so."
He played his way through the hall with his fiddle-bow.
(A tempered sword made music in his hands.)
They paid their thanks to him, knights of Rhenish
        lands.

1977   Dankwart heard courageous Folker say,
"I see you've had no easy time today.
Your brother said that I should help you out.
So I shall stand within, if you will watch without."

1978   Brave Dankwart stood outside the entry there
And barred the way to all who approached the stair
(And you could hear the sound of weapons plied
By heroes' hands), while Folker did the same inside.

1979   Over the heads of the crowd the minstrel talked:
       "Hagen my friend, this hall is shut and locked.
       Attila's door is barred, and it will hold
       By the swords in two men's hands, which bolt it a
              thousandfold."

1980   When Hagen saw such a guard upon the door,
       He put his shield behind him, squaring the score
       With greater fury now, for what they'd done.
       His foes had not a hope to see the light of sun.

1981   When now Verona's governor perceived
       How many helmets mighty Hagen cleaved,
       He rose upon a chair, and they heard him call:
       "Hagen here serves out the bitterest wine of all!"

1982   The host was worried now, and no surprise.
       So many friends were lost before his eyes—
       And a bare escape the best that luck could bring!
       He sat, an anxious man. What good that he was king?

1983   Mighty Kriemhild begged the noble lord,
       "Theodorich, protect me with your sword,
       "For all the princely glory in Amelung land!
       If Hagen gets me now, my death is near at hand."

1984   "How shall I help you?" Theodorich said.
       "When I have worries enough on my own head,
       Oh queen, with Gunther's men in such an anger,
       Right now I can't protect a single soul from danger."

1985   "No, Theodorich, no, great knight of merit
       And high birth—prove your noble spirit
       By helping me escape, or I am dead."
       In worry over this the queen was struck with dread.

1986   "I will try to see what help may be.
       But not in a long, long time did my eyes see
       In such a bitter rage so many lords.
       Here is blood, burst from helmets, by force of swords!"

1987   And he began to shout, the nobly born,
       His voice resounding like a bison horn,
       Till the great castle shook through all its length
       By dint of him—a massive thing, Theodorich's strength!

1988   Gunther heard him call, through all the row
And battle din around. He listened now,
And spoke, "Theodorich's voice rings in my ear.
Our men have done away with one of his, I fear.

1989   I see him on the table, waving his hand.
Friends and kinsmen here, of Burgundy land,
Call off the fighting now; let's hear and see
Just what this lord's complaint against my men
      may be."

1990   They carried out what Gunther asked them for,
And held their swords at rest, in midst of war.
This was greater power: that no one fought.
He lost no time in asking what Theodorich sought.

1991   "My noble lord," he said, "what have my friends
Done to you? I promise to make amends
And pay the bill in full and willingly.
And harm to you is deepest grief to me."

1992   Lord Theodorich spoke, "No harm is done.
Let me leave this house, and everyone
Of my command, with guarantee of peace,
From this ferocious war. My thanks will never cease."

1993   Said Wolfhart, "Why so quick to plead? This knight,
The fiddler, hasn't barred the door so tight
We couldn't open it to let us through."
"Quiet!" Theodorich said. "Devil a lot you do."

1994   King Gunther spoke, "This much I grant to you:
Take them out as you will, many or few,
But not my enemies. They shall stay.
They've done me bitter wrong among the Huns this day."

1995   Hearing that, on one protecting arm
He took the queen, who feared for further harm,
And led upon the other Attila then.
Out with Theodorich went six hundred handsome men.

1996   Now the noble margrave Ruedeger cried,
"If any more may make their way outside,
With gratitude to you, then tell us that news.
Loyal friends deserve the firmest pledge of truce."

1977   Answered Giselher of Burgundy:
"Since you and all your men in loyalty
Stand firm and true, we here proclaim our peace.
You may therefore withdraw—and all your worries cease."

1998   As Ruedeger the knight now left the hall,
Half a thousand followed him in all—
These the men of Pöchlarn, thane and friend,
From whom King Gunther drew great sorrow in the end.

1999   A Hunnish warrior saw his monarch come,
With escort which he tried to profit from—
But Folker struck him such a fiddle-beat
As made his head fly off and fall to Attila's feet.

2000   Once the lord of the land had got outside,
He turned and, looking back at Folker, cried:
"My curse upon these guests—a thing of dread,
A scourge is this, that all for them my knights lie dead.

2001   And a curse upon this feast," Attila swore.
"There's a man in there who fights like a wild boar—
By name, Folker; by work, a bard no less!
I thank my lucky stars I fled this devil's mess.

2002   His song has an evil sound, his bow is red;
His melodies have left my warriors dead.
What reason had this bard to be distressed?
I never had such bitter fill of any guest!"

2003   All they ever would they'd now let out.
Within the hall arose a mighty shout.
For what they had suffered the guests would now extract
Their full revenge. How many helmets Folker cracked!

2004   The sound attracted Gunther's notice soon;
He cried, "Hagen, do you hear the tune
Our friend is fiddling for the Huns who head
To the doorway now? The rosin he puts on his bow
        is red."

2005   Said Hagen, "This I rue beyond all measure,
That while he fought I sat here at my leisure.
I was his good friend, and he was mine.
And so we'll be again, if ever we see the Rhine.

2006 My king, Folker is staunch and true; behold!
How zealously he earns your silver and gold,
And what hard steel his fiddle-bow will slice
And how it will crush a helmet's shining bright device.

2007 I never saw a minstrel yet display
The splendid courage Folker has shown today.
Through shield and helm his music fills the air.
For this he should ride good steeds, and have the best to
    wear!"

2008 Whatever Huns had been within the hall,
There now was not a person left at all.
The sound was quiet now of their discord.
Cheerfully the valiant men laid down the sword.

THIRTY-FOURTH ADVENTURE

How They Threw the Corpses Out

2009 The men sat down to take what rest they could,
Folker and Hagen left the hall and stood,
Leaning on their shields, haughty lords,
Both with much to say, in proud and mocking words.

2010 Giselher of Burgundy addressed
His men and said: "My friends, we cannot rest—
Not yet. Let's get these dead men out of here.
We'll have to stand and fight again. Let that be clear!

2011 They must not lie around here under foot.
Before the Huns destroy us we shall put
Out swords to work, letting their wounds renew
Our cheerful spirits. That's what I intend to do."

2012 "For such a king," cried Hagen, "praise to Heaven!
This advice that my young lord has given
Is of the kind that only heroes voice.
For this you men of Burgundy may all rejoice!"

2013 They did as they were counseled, casting in all
Seven thousand bodies from the hall,
To lie by the castle steps, where they were thrown.
And from their friends and kinsmen rose a wretched moan.

2014 So minor were the wounds of some that fell,
With gentler care they might have gotten well.
Instead, by this high fall, they all were killed—
Due cause for all the grief with which their friends
   were filled.

2015 Shouted the fiddler Folker, cheerful knight:
"Now I see that what they say is right,
About the Huns: What cowards! They are wailing
More like women, when they should help their hurt
   and ailing."

2016 One took him at his word, a margrave who found
A kinsman fallen in blood; he bent to the ground
To pick him up and save him from his foes.
The warrior minstrel shot and killed him as he rose.

2017 The others saw. With that began the flight,
And as they fled they cursed the fiddler-knight.
He seized a spear, a sharp and tempered one
Which had been hurled at him up there by a certain Hun.

2018 He shot it across the courtyard, over the welter
Of fleeing people, pointing safer shelter
To the men of Attila, not so close to the hall.
They feared the fiddler's violent prowess most of all.

2019 Many thousand stood before the building.
Folker and Hagen spoke, not withholding
Anything they felt from the Hunnish chief,
Great King Attila, much to their later fear and grief.

2020 "It would seem," said Hagen, "the place for the People's Shield
Is in front of the people, first on the battlefield,
And this is the place no king of Burgundy shuns.
Helmets they hew; their swords fall—and the blood runs!"

2021 The bold king seized his shield. Cried his wife:
"Be careful, Sire, take no risk with your life!
Offer your warriors gold, in shields to the rim.
If Hagen catches you, you'll have your death from him."

2022 So dauntless was the Hun, he would not yield
In his intent, until by the strap of his shield

They held him back—such valor now a thing
Most rare in princes. And yet fierce Hagen mocked the king:

2023   "A distant sort of kinship, this," he said,
"That Attila shares with Sigfrid! Kriemhild's bed
Was his before she ever looked at you,
Oh coward king, why plot for me the evil you do?"

2024   The great king's wife had heard his calumny.
Incensed that by his daring she should be
Before the king's own court thus vilified,
She tried once more her scheme against the guests. She cried:

2025   "There is Hagen of Trony. Whoever will kill
That man and bring me his head, for him I'll fill
Attila's shield to the rim with good red gold,
And give him many lands and castles in freehold."

2026   "What are they waiting for?" the minstrel cried.
"I never saw more soldiers stand aside,
Craven, at the offer of such high pay.
Attila has no cause to praise his men today—

2027   Thankless eaters of the king's own bread,
False in his great need, full of dread,
I see them skulk around, assuming the name
Of valiant men, this to their everlasting shame."

THIRTY-FIFTH ADVENTURE

How Iring Was Slain

2028   "I've always," Danish margrave Iring cried,
"Aimed at excellence in all I tried.
When armies fought, my deeds were of the best.
Bring my armor—I'll put Hagen to the test."

2029   I counsel you, don't do it," Hagen cried.
"Or tell your Hunnish thanes to stand aside!
If any of you rush the hall—in pairs,
Or threes at a time—I'll send you aching down the stairs."

2030   "I'll not stop for that," rejoined Lord Iring.
"I've attempted things as awe-inspiring.

I'll take you on alone, in a test of swords.
What good will be your vaunting, all of which is words?"

2031   Iring was swiftly armed. There came along
Thuringia's bold young Irnfrid and Haward the strong
To join him, with a thousand men beside.
They wished to stand with him, whatever Iring tried.

2032   Now the fiddler looked and saw the swarms
That came along with Iring, all in arms,
With many handsome helmets tied and ready.
Valiant Folker could not keep his temper steady.

2033   "Look, friend Hagen, here is the Iring who vowed
To meet you alone, with swords. Are knights allowed
By custom to lie? This I must deplore:
He has with him, in armor, a thousand knights or
        more."

2034   "Don't make a liar of me!" cried Haward's thane.
"I mean to do as I vowed. I'll not refrain
Out of apprehension. I take for granted
Hagen is fearsome—still I'll meet him singlehanded."

2035   He fell to his knees, begging men of his own,
Retainers and kin, to let him fight alone
Against proud Hagen. They would not willingly,
For well they knew that arrogant knight of Burgundy.

2036   He begged so long, it happened. His retinue,
Perceiving his intent, and that his view
Was all on honor, let him go ahead.
And what a battle both men waged, fierce and dread!

2037   Iring, worthy knight of Denmark, held
His spear on high; covering with his shield,
He dashed at Hagen, up to the palace door.
And now the heroes raised a mighty clash and roar.

2038   With violent hands they hurled their spears to sail
Through solid shield and strike the shining mail;
The shafts went spinning. Both the mighty lords
(Fiercely bold they were) reached now for their swords.

2039   Though valiant Hagen boasted strength unbounded,
When Iring hit him, all the house resounded;

Towers and palace echoed with their blows,
And still the knight could not accomplish what he chose.

2040   He left Lord Hagen standing there, uninjured,
And rushed at the fiddler-knight, for Iring ventured
To think his savage blows might lay him flat.
But handsome Folker knew the right defense for that!

2041   The fiddler swung his sword, the buckles scattered
From the shield that Folker's arm had battered.
Iring left him—too hard a man was he!—
And next he ran at Gunther, King of Burgundy.

2042   Each of them was fierce enough in war,
Yet all the blows that both of them could score
Brought no flow of blood from any wound—
Prevented by their armor, which was strong and sound.

2043   He left King Gunther now, off to assail
Lord Gernot, striking from his coat of mail
Sparks of fire, and yet the valiant Dane,
Meeting the savage Gernot there, was nearly slain.

2044   He sprang away from the prince—oh, he was fleet!—
And quickly slew four knights of the noble suite.
Of Burgundy, from Worms on the Rhenish shore.
Young Sir Giselher was never angered more.

2045   The prince cried out, "The Lord in Heaven knows,
Lord Iring, you will pay to me for those
Who here and now lie dead!" In his attack,
He struck the Dane a blow which stopped him in his
        track.

2046   He fell to the ground before him, into the blood.
They all assumed that in the battle-flood
He'd strike no further blow of any sort—
But Iring lay at the feet of Giselher unhurt.

2047   What with clangor of helm and crash of sword,
His wits had gone all faint, the valiant lord;
He lay unconscious, like a lifeless one.
This the strength of mighty Giselher had done.

2048   The ringing in his head, which he had got
From the mighty blow, subsided now. He thought:

"I'm still alive—not wounded anywhere!
But now I really know the strength of Giselher."

2049 He heard his foes, on either side of him.
And had they known the truth, how much more grim
Would be his fate! And he heard Lord Giselher.
How could he flee his foes and get away from there?

2050 Out of the blood he sprang, like a man possessed,
And he could well give thanks that he was fast.
He ran from the hall, meeting Hagen again.
Savage blows fell from his powerful arm like rain.

2051 "You are meant for death!" Hagen thought.
"Unless the foul fiend saves you, you are caught."
Yet Iring, striking straight through Hagen's casque,
Wounded him with his good sword which men called Waske.

2052 When noble Hagen felt the sudden pain,
The sword in his hand thrashed wildly. Haward's thane
Gave way to him and had to turn in flight,
Down the stairs, in full pursuit, came Gunther's knight.

2053 Bold Iring swung his shield over his head,
And if these stairs had been three flights instead,
Hagen would not have let him strike a blow
In all that way. The red sparks made his helmet glow!

2054 Still, sir Iring got to his friends unhurt.
When Lady Kriemhild heard the true report
Of what he did to Hagen in that affray,
The queen gave him her thanks in the very fullest way.

2055 "God reward you, Iring, worthy knight!
In heart and mind you comfort me with the sight
Of Hagen's armor, red with the blood he spilled."
The queen herself, for joy, took from his hand the shield.

2056 Said Hagen, "Keep your thanks on a modest plane.
It would better suit a hero to try again.
Call him a valiant man, should he return.
He wounded me, but little the profit you will earn!

2057 To have you see the rings of my armor red
Has set me hungering for many dead.
Now I am really mad at Haward's knight—
And all the hurt he's done me up to now is slight."

2058 Iring of Denmark turned to face the breeze,
   To cool himself in his coat of mail and ease
   His helmet straps. And all the people cried
   That his strength was great, which filled the margrave's
     heart with pride.

2059 Again said Iring, "Friends, I want you to know
   That you must arm me soon. I mean to go
   And force, if I can, this haughty man to yield."
   Since his was hacked to bits, they brought him a better
     shield.

2060 Soon he was fully armed. In hostile mind
   He seized a vicious spear and went to find
   Lord Hagen once again and force the fight.
   There, in anger, waited a mortally savage knight.

2061 He ran at Iring—Hagen was past restraining—
   Ran with thrusting spear and sword blows raining,
   Down the flight of stairs, their whole length.
   His rage was great. Small joy to Iring, all his strength.

2062 Through shields they smote until it blazed and roared
   Like winds of red fire. Hagen's sword
   Dealt out a mighty wound to Haward's thane,
   Through shield and byrnie, from which he never rallied
     again.

2063 He raised his shield—when he felt the wound at first—
   Up to his chin-strap, thinking this the worst
   In way of hurt that he had in store,
   But royal Gunther's man was soon to hurt him more.

2064 He seized a spear from the ground where it had lain
   Before his feet, and shot at Iring the Dane,
   And there the shaft protruded from his head.
   Hagen had wrought his bitter end; he'd soon be dead.

2065 Iring fled to the Danes. Before they could take
   His helmet from his head they had to break
   and pull the spear; and now his death drew near.
   His kin began to weep—the cause for that was clear.

2066 And now the queen stood over him to mourn
   For mighty Iring, and for the wounds he'd borne.
   It was bitter pain to her. Once bold and gay,
   That warrior now addressed his kinsmen there, to say:

2067   "Leave your mourning, glorious queen! What use
     Is all your weeping now, for I must lose
     My life from the wounds I have, and death no more
     Will let me serve the king and you, as I have before."

2068   To the men of Thuringia, too, he spoke, and the Danes:
     "Let each of you be sure his hand refrains
     From taking the queen's reward, her gold, bright red.
     If you encounter Hagen, men will see you dead."

2069   The color had fled his face, and Iring had
     The sign of death upon him. Their hearts were sad,
     And Haward's knight was doomed to lose his life.
     With this the Danes were all compelled to join the strife.

2070   Irnfrid and Haward rushed in front of the hall
     With a thousand knights or more, and over all
     There rose a violent noise, monstrous and vast.
     They fell on Burgundy—what mighty spears they cast!

2071   Irnfrid ran at the minstrel—but he would gain
     At Folker's hands the greatest hurt and pain.
     The fiddler struck the landgrave such a blow
     As split his solid helmet; he was a savage foe.

2072   Then Sir Irnfrid struck at Folker so hard
     The rings of his coat of mail burst apart,
     Spraying his byrnie with a fiery red.
     Yet soon the landgrave fell before the fiddler, dead.

2073   Haward and Hagen met; and he who saw,
     Saw marvels done. With heroes' hands to draw,
     Swords fell fast indeed and furiously.
     But Haward perished, slain by the lord of Burgundy.

2074   When Danes and Thuringians saw their master slain
     Before the hall came strife and fearful pain,
     Until, with valiant hands, they gained the door.
     Shields and helms were hacked to pieces by the score.

2075   "Back!" Lord Folker cried. "Let them come on,
     And what they think to do will be undone;
     Once inside the hall their time is short,
     And they must perish—and reap in death the queen's reward."

2076 They entered the hall, proud and insolent,
But many a warrior's head was lowly bent,
And under fearful blows he perished there.
(King Gernot fought with glory, as did Sir Giselher.)

2077 A thousand and four of them went into the hall.
One saw the glowing swish of sword-blades fall,
And every man of them was soon struck down.
What marvels one could tell, to Burgundy's renown!

2078 There came a silence, as the noise subsided.
Through the drains and down the gutters glided,
Everywhere, the blood of warriors killed.
Thus was the valor of the men of Rhine fulfilled.

2079 Burgundians sat down to rest and laid
Their shields and arms aside. And still he stayed
Before the door, the valiant minstrel-knight,
And watched to see if others came to join the fight.

2080 Bitterly the king and queen lamented.
Women scourged themselves, their hearts tormented.
Death, I think, at last had sworn their doom.
The strangers' toll of knights was fated to resume.

THIRTY-SIXTH ADVENTURE

How the Queen Caused the Hall to be Set Afire

2081 "Take your helmets off," Hagen said.
"My friend and I will stand you watch, instead;
If Attila's men have in mind returning,
As quickly as I can, I'll bring my lords the warning."

2082 Many a worthy knight now bared his head,
As they sat on the maimed bodies lying dead
In blood before them, work their hands had done.
The guests had gained the angry notice of the Hun.

2083 They made another try before night fell,
Spurred by the king and by his queen as well,
Who before their eyes had still the sight
Of twenty thousand Huns—now compelled to fight.

2084 The storm rose hard upon the strangers then.
   Hagen's brother Dankwart, best of men,
   Left his lords and ran to the door to face
   His foes—and death, they thought. Unhurt, he reached
      his place.

2085 The savage fighting lasted till the night
   Prevented more. As was for heroes right,
   They fought against the Huns the summer-long day.
   How many valiant warriors they were fated to slay!

2086 This awful slaughter came one solstice-time
   When Kriemhild took her vengeance for the crime
   That pained her heart, against her closest kin
   And many more—which Attila took no pleasure in.

2087 The day ran out. Their fears were newly stirred.
   They thought swift death a thing to be preferred
   To long and tortured wait for awful pain.
   Proud lords of highest spirit longed for peace again.

2088 Asked to seek the king and bring him back,
   Heroes red with blood and tarnished black
   Left the palace, three most splendid kings.
   They knew not whom to blame for all these bitter things.

2089 Attila soon appeared, and Kriemhild too.
   The land was theirs, and so their numbers grew.
   Attila spoke, "What do you want of me?
   If you have hopes of peace, that can scarcely be.

2090 For this great hurt you caused me (which shall give
   No profit to you while I still may live),
   For my child you slew, my kinsmen killed—
   Your hope of peace and respite shall never be fulfilled."

2091 Gunther answered, "Greatest need compelled
   The deeds we did. My men lay dead, all felled
   By yours at their lodgings. Did this deserve to be?
   I came to you in trust, thinking you honored me."

2092 Young Giselher spoke, "Whom are you reproving,
   Men of Attila, you who still are living?
   Why is it me? What have I done to you?
   I rode to this land of yours as a friendly man and true."

2093   "My palace is full of your kindness, wretched woe
Is in our land. If we could have it so,
We'd wish you had never come from Worms on Rhine.
You and your brothers leave my land to an orphaned line."

2094   Warlike Gunther answered angrily,
"Turn this bitter hate to amnesty
For us, exiled—a favor all around.
For what Attila does to us he has no ground."

2095   The lord of the land replied, "My pain and yours
Are most unlike. The insult done, and worse,
The injury that here has been my lot—
For that no one of you, alive, shall leave this spot."

2096   Mighty Gernot spoke to the king of the land,
"Then may you act as a friend by God's command.
Kill us, your foreign guests, but let us come down
To the open court with you. That would suit your
        renown.

2097   Whatever may be our fate, let it be brief.
You have fresh troops. We have had no relief
From the storms of battle. Our hope of living fails
If they attack. How long shall we suffer these ordeals?"

2098   In this Attila's men almost concurred,
And let them leave the palace. Kriemhild heard,
Bitterly distressed, and they were driven
Soon to end the truce these outcast men were given.

2099   "No, Hunnish lords, this thing you plan to do,
In faith I counsel not to carry through.
Let those vengeful killers out of the hall,
And you and all your kin will suffer mortal fall.

2100   Suppose no one were left but Uta's sons,
My noble brothers—let the breezes once
Cool their coats of mail, and you are fated!
Never in all this world were braver men created."

2101   Young Giselher replied, "Fair sister of mine,
How poorly I placed my trust when over the Rhine
You asked me here to face these perils! And why,
By what offense to the Huns, do I deserve to die?

2102   I always brought you friendship, never hurt.
In this good faith I journeyed here to court:
That, noble sister, you held me in some regard.
Think mercifully of us—all other hope is barred."

2103   "I feel no mercy; I am merciless!
Hagen caused me pain and bitterness
Which shall be unforgiven all my life,
And all of you must pay," answered Attila's wife.

2104   "Hagen alone as hostage I ask you give,
And I may not refuse to let you live
But try to make these warriors reconciled,
Since I am sister to you, and one mother's child."

2105   "God in Heaven forbid," Lord Gernot said.
"If we were a thousand here, we'd all lie dead,
Kin of your blood, before we'd give to you
One single man as hostage. That we will never do."

2106   "We die," said Giselher, "but none prevents
Our fighting here like knights, in self-defense.
Whoever longs for battle, here we are!
And I have never left a loyal friend so far."

2107   It wasn't right for Dankwart not to speak:
"My brother is not alone. Those who seek
To thwart the peace may suffer for it, too.
We'll give you proof of that, truly I promise you."

2108   Cried she, "Men of spirit, move along
Up to the steps with you, avenge my wrong!
I promise the recompense your actions merit.
The price of Hagen's pride is high, and he shall
          bear it.

2109   Let no one leave the building there at all!
At the four corners I shall have the hall
Set on fire, avenging my every wrong."
Attila's men were ready; it did not take them long.

2110   The ones that stood outside they drove back in
With sword and spear, making a mighty din,
But prince and man they could not drive apart.
One would not leave the other, out of loyal heart.

2111 Then she had the building lit, a pyre
To torture warrior's bodies in its fire.
The house was burning soon, with the breeze that blew—
The greatest terror, I think, an army ever knew.

2112 There were many cries within of "Help!" and "Woe!"
"Much better die in fighting than perish so.
May God have pity how we all are lost!
She takes her anger out on us, at fearful cost."

2113 A man cried out inside, "And so we die.
What good the words that we were welcomed by?
By thirst and this awful heat I am so punished,
That in these perils, I think, my life will soon have
  vanished."

2114 Hagen of Trony spoke, "Great lords and good,
If you are plagued by thirst, drink this blood—
In heat like this, finer than wine by far;
At least you'll not do better now, the way things are!"

2115 One of the warriors went where a man lay dead,
And kneeling by the wounds, untied from his head
The helmet-case, and drank the flowing blood.
Strange though it was to him, it seemed exceedingly good.

2116 "God bless you, Hagen," said the tired knight,
"For teaching me to drink with such delight.
Rarely have I been served a drink so fine.
And should I live a while, I'll thank you for this wine."

2117 After the others heard he found it pleasing,
Many more drank up, the blood increasing
The strength of all who did so—for which perished,
In return, men whom lovely ladies cherished.

2118 Now fire was falling on them all around.
They used their shields to ward it to the ground,
Smarting from the awful smoke and heat.
Did heroes ever have more wretched fate to meet?

2119 Hagen of Trony cried, "Stand close to the wall,
Do not let your helms be hit when firebrands fall,
Kick them with your feet where the blood is deep.
This is an evil feast the queen would have us keep."

2120   In misery like this they passed the night.
Still before the house the minstrel-knight
And his companion Hagen, the valiant ones,
Leaned on their shields, waiting more harm from the
         Huns.

2121   The fiddler spoke, "Let's go back in the hall.
The Huns will think that we have perished all,
Dead from the torment done us. We shall greet them
With the sight of men of battle, come to meet them."

2122   Giselher spoke, "Signs of day are growing,"
Said the prince, "there is a cool wind blowing.
May God above see fit to let us live
To better times. A wretched fete for my sister to give!"

2123   Another man remarked, "I see the day.
Since we shall fare no better anyway,
Put on your armor, men, and think on life!
She'll be here far too soon for us, Attila's wife."

2124   The king had thought his guests must soon expire
From their ordeals and from the dreadful fire.
Six hundred gallant men were living yet
Within the hall, as good as any king could get.

2125   The guards who watched the guests had noted well
That they were still alive, despite the hell
Of pain and hurt, alike to man and lord.
They saw them in the room, sound and well
         restored.

2126   Many men survived, they told the queen,
But she asserted that could not have been,
That any man survived that fire. She said,
"I find it far more likely that all of them are dead."

2127   Men and princes would have liked to live,
If anyone was willing there to give
The gift of mercy—but not in the Hunnish land!
So they avenged their death with more than willing hand.

2128   Toward morning then they paid them their respects
In bitter battle, a thing which came to vex
Heroic men. Heavy spears were hurled
Against the bold defense of the bravest knights in the world.

2129   Excitement hurried through Attila's ranks,
To earn the gifts and pay of Kriemhild's thanks
And carry out their king's command in war.
Quick death it was that many had to settle for.

2130   What tales of gifts and offers could be told!
She had them bring on shields her red gold
And gave to whoever would take it. Such an amount
Has never yet been paid against a foe's account.

2131   Then did a host of men in arms appear
And gallant Folker said, "We still are here!
I never saw heroes come more willingly
To fight, taking the king's gold for our injury."

2132   Many called to the warriors, "Closer, friend,
And quickly, let us bring this to an end.
No one falls but who is doomed to die."
Soon their shields were stuck with spears, towering high.

2133   What more can I say? A good twelve hundred Huns
Attacked repeatedly, but the foreign ones
Dealt them wounds enough to cool their ardor.
Neither side prevailed, and so the blood flowed harder

2134   From all the many wounds, that cut life-deep,
For friends now lost they all were heard to weep.
Slain were all the stalwart men of the king,
And loving kin were filled with bitter sorrowing.

THIRTY-SEVENTH ADVENTURE

How Margrave Ruedeger Was Slain

2135   The foreign knights kept up the fight till dawn.
Then it was that Gotelind's lord had gone
To court, to find great hurt and misery
On either hand. The loyal man wept inwardly.

2136   "Alas," said Ruedeger, "that I was born!
Alas that no one has the power to turn
This evil aside. I want to try for peace—
But not the king, who sees his many woes
        increase."

2137   Reudeger sent to Theodorich to see
If they together might save the royal three.
The lord of Verona sent word: "We're all too late.
The king will not let any of us arbitrate."

2138   A man saw Ruedeger standing thus, some Hun—
His eyes were moist from all the weeping he'd done—
And cried to the queen, "Now see how he stands there;
He has of all King Attila's power the greatest share,

2139   And holds in liege all this—land and vassals.
Why does Ruedeger have these many castles,
Of which the king permits him so great a show?
In all our fighting yet he's struck no worthy blow.

2140   I'd say he doesn't care what goes on here,
He has his fill of all that he holds dear.
They say he's braver than any man could be.
We've had poor proof of that in our great misery!"

2141   Sad at heart, the loyal margrave sought
A glimpse of the man who said these words. He thought:
"You'll reap the harvest! You say fear has me cowed.
But you have told this tale of yours in court too loud."

2142   He tightened his fist and ran at him and hit
The Hun so hard a blow, by force of it
He lay in a second dead before his feet —
One more grave misfortune for the king to meet.

2143   "Down, you bare-faced coward!" said Ruedeger.
"I have pain and hurt enough for my share.
Why rebuke me that I do not fight?
I'd be sworn the foe of these guests, with every right;

2144   And everything I could, I should have done,
Except I brought them here, and was the one
Who gave them escort to my master's land,
And so I must not raise against them my wretched
          hand."

2145   Attila spoke to Margrave Ruedeger:
"So this is how you help us, noble sir!
With so many doomed men here, we have no need
Of any more, and you have done an evil deed."

2146 Said the noble lord, "He made me ill at ease,
Slandering all the honors and properties
I have from your hand and in such generous portion—
Which worked out rather to that lying man's misfortune."

2147 Then Kriemhild came, and she had also seen
What for the warrior's rage his fate had been,
Her eyes were moist and bitterly she lamented:
"Through what fault of ours," she said, "have you
          augmented

2148 My suffering and the king's? Always before,
Oh noble Ruedeger, you vowed and swore
To risk for us your life and honored fame.
And I've heard many knights who greatly praise your name.

2149 I bid you recall your pledge of favor when,
Urging the choice of Attila, best of men,
You swore to serve me till one of us should go—
Help that I, poor woman, never needed so."

2150 "That I do not deny, great king's wife.
I swore to risk for you both honors and life,
But not to lose my soul—I've never sworn.
I brought to your tourney here these warriors, royally born."

2151 "Remember, Ruedeger, your loyalty,
Your constant faith, and the oath you gave to me
To avenge my hurt and all the pain I bore."
The margrave answered, "I have not refused before."

2152 But then great King Attila joined her pleas.
They both fell down before him on their knees;
And one could see the margrave's sad distress,
As now the faithful knight spoke in his wretchedness:

2153 "Unhappy man, that I should live to see
My honors forfeit, my inner loyalty
And the decent breeding God enjoins—surrendered!
This, oh Lord in Heaven, I wish my death had hindered.

2154 Whichever course before me I reject,
To do the other, I've done a cursed act.
If I do neither, I face the people's wrath
And their reproach. Counsel me now, who gave me breath!"

2155 They pled with force, the monarch and his wife—
   For this, in time, knights would lose their life
   At Ruedeger's hands, who also perished there.
   Listen, you will hear his deeds of great despair.

2156 Foreseeing harm and awful suffering,
   He would most gladly have refused the king,
   And his queen as well. Of this his fear was great:
   If he killed one of the guests, the world would bear him hate.

2157 The brave man cried to the king, "Your Majesty,
   Take back everything you gave to me,
   Land and castles; let all I had be vanished.
   I will go on foot to foreign countries, banished."

2158 "Who would help me then?" Attila cried.
   "I'll give you your castles and your lands outright,
   If you'll bring vengeance on my enemy.
   You'll stand beside me then—a mighty king like me."

2159 "How can I do that?" Lord Ruedeger said.
   "I asked them home to my house. Drink and bread
   I offered them in kindness, and I gave
   My gifts to them. How can I send them to the
     grave?

2160 How easy for men to think that I'm afraid!
   But I refused no single service, no aid
   To noble prince or man. The very bond
   Of kinship we concluded makes me now despond.

2161 I gave to royal Giselher my daughter.
   No match in all the world could so have brought her
   Trust and manners, honors, and property.
   I never saw a young prince so perfect in chivalry."

2162 Kriemhild cried, "Most noble Ruedeger,
   Take pity on the hurt we both must bear,
   The king and I, and think: no country's master
   Ever gained from guests such harvest of disaster."

2163 The margrave spoke again to the king's high wife:
   "Today the cost is paid with Ruedeger's life.
   The kindness you and my lord have done to me—
   I now must die for that. What cannot wait, must be.

2164   I know this very day my towers, my land,
Must all revert to you through someone's hand.
My wife and children I commend to your care,
And the many men of Pöchlarn, now left lordless there."

2165   "May God reward you, Ruedeger," said the king,
He and the queen no longer sorrowing,
"Your people shall be safe in our loyal care,
And I trust you too will live, as I count on my own
        welfare."

2166   He placed upon the balance soul and life.
Then it was she wept, Attila's wife.
"What I have vowed," he said, "I must fulfill.
Alas for my friends whom I must fight, against my will."

2167   They saw him leave the king, sad of eye.
He found his warriors standing there, close by:
"Arm yourselves, my men. I now must leave
To fight the bold Burgundian knights—for which I grieve."

2168   They had men hurry out for armor and bring
Their helmet or their shield, whatever thing
Each warrior needed, squires brought it here.
What proud Burgundians heard was news of little cheer.

2169   Five hundred men were armed, with Ruedeger,
And twelve more knights he found to help him there,
Fighting to gain renown in peril of war.
They did not know the truth: that death lay close before.

2170   The guests saw Ruedeger, his helmet on,
The margrave's vassals with their sharp swords drawn,
Bright broad shields in their hands. When he perceived
This sight before his eyes, the fiddler greatly grieved.

2171   Giselher watched his father-in-law as he went,
Walking with helmet fixed. What other intent
Could he imagine but help in fullest measure?
At this the youthful prince's heart was filled with pleasure.

2172   "Thank God for such good friends and kin," he cried,
"As we have gained on our journey. Now my bride
Will bring us great good fortune. Take my word:
I am more than glad our wedding feast occurred!"

2173 "I don't know where you get your comfort from,"
Said Folker. "When have you seen heroes come
For peace with helmets fixed and sword in hand?
The margrave means to use us to earn his towns and land."

2174 Before the fiddler finished speaking, there,
In front of the hall, stood noble Ruedeger.
And set his good shield down before his feet,
Facing the friends he now could neither serve nor greet.

2175 The noble margrave shouted into the hall:
"Look to your defense, Nibelungs all;
I ought to bring you good, I bring you bad.
We once were friends. I now revoke the bond we had."

2176 These tidings left the troubled men dismayed,
For there was little comfort here or aid,
If he would fight them, whom they thought a friend.
Their foes already had caused them trials without end.

2177 "Now God in Heaven forbid," Lord Gunther shouted,
"That your devotion to us should be thus flouted,
The trust which after all we assumed of you.
But I prefer to think that this you would never do."

2178 The brave knight cried, "I cannot help it now.
I have to fight with you because of a vow,
So on your guard, brave lords, if ever life
Means much to you. I'm held to this by Attila's wife."

2179 Gunther answered, "Your challenge comes too late,
Ruedeger, God's repayment would be great
For the loyal love you give, if in the end
It were more tempered by the action of a friend.

2180 We'd owe you thanks for what you deigned to give,
My kin and I, if you would let us live—
Your splendid gifts, when in good faith you brought
Our men to Attila's land: my lord, give that your
    thought!"

2181 Said Ruedeger, "How I wish this could be granted,
And I could give you presents, openhanded,
With such good will as I had hoped to show!
For then I should not bare myself to censure so."

2182   Gernot spoke: "Noble sir, refrain!
No host has ever thought to entertain
His guests with kindness such as you prepared
To welcome us. Reward is yours if we be spared."

2183   "Gernot, would to God," Lord Ruedeger said,
"That you were by the Rhine and I were dead,
In some degree of honor, since now by force
I fight you. Never have heroes' friends treated them worse."

2184   "For these rich gifts of yours," came his reply,
"God bless you! I regret that you must die,
And that such excellence of mind must perish.
Your weapon which you gave me, here in my hand I
        cherish.

2185   For me it never yet has failed its pledge
In all this trouble. Dead beneath its edge
Lie many knights. Sound and true, no stain—
So fine a gift I think no knight will give again.

2186   If you won't end your plan to interfere—
Kill one single friend I still have here,
And with your very sword I'll take your life!
I pity you, Ruedeger, and pity your lovely wife."

2187   "Sir Gernot, would to God we might fulfill
Here and now the tenor of your will,
And all your friends might be returned to life.
Now both must look to you, my daughter and my wife."

2188   Spoke fair Uta's child, of Burgundy,
"Why do you do this? Those who came with me
Respect you, sir. You do an evil thing—
You plan for your lovely daughter too quick a widowing.

2189   When you and all your knights take up offense
Against me here you give poor evidence
Of why, above all men, I trusted you,
And why I took your daughter's hand in marriage too."

2190   "Most noble king, remember your loyalty,"
Cried Ruedeger, "if here God set you free,
And let my poor young daughter not incur
What blame is mine. As you are good, be kind to her!"

2191   "That I should rightly do," Giselher cried.
"But any of my high kinsmen still inside—
If they should die at your hand, all ties must end,
Joining you and your daughter as kin of mine or friend."

2192   "Then God have mercy on us," the brave lord said.
They lifted up their shields, about to head
For battle with the guests in Kriemhild's hall,
When loudly down from the stairs they heard Lord
        Hagen call:

2193   "One moment more, most noble Ruedeger, stay!"
(Thus spoke Hagen.) "We have more to say,
My lords and I, from dire necessity.
What good to Attila could our wretched dying be?

2194   And I am in perilous straits," Hagen went on.
"The shield that Gotelind gave me to bear is gone,
Hacked to bits by the Huns in my very hand,
And as a friend I brought it into Attila's land.

2195   If only God in Heaven," he said, "would deign
To let me carry such a shield again
As you have now on your arm, oh Ruedeger,
In storm of battle I should need no hauberk to wear."

2196   "I'd gladly offer my shield as a favor to you.
Because of Kriemhild, that I dare not do—
But take it, Hagen, wear it at your hand,
And may you bring it back with you to Burgundy land!"

2197   When he offered him so willingly the shield,
Eyes were red with hot tears unconcealed.
This was the very last gift under the sun
That Ruedeger of Pöchlarn gave to anyone.

2198   As fierce as Hagen was, his heart as hard,
He still was moved by the gift that noble lord
Had made with the moments left to him so brief.
Many noble warriors joined with him in grief.

2199   "God in Heaven bless you, Ruedeger,
There'll never be one like you anywhere,
To give to outcast men so great a favor.
May the good Lord grant your virtues live forever!

2201* And noble Ruedeger, I'll repay that gift.
      However these knights treat you, I'll not lift
      My hand against you here in enmity,
      Even though you kill the whole of Burgundy."

2202   Courteous Ruedeger bowed, and warriors wept
      On every side, that peace could not be kept
      Among these wounded spirits—woe most dread!
      The model of chivalry would lie in Ruedeger dead.

2203   Down from the hall there came the minstrel's voice:
      "Since my comrade Hagen swears you peace,
      You have the same assurance from my hand.
      You earned it well enough when first we came to
           this land.

2204   You shall be my herald, noble margrave.
      These are the red arm-rings your lady gave,
      Telling me to wear them at the feast.
      You can see them now and be my witness at least."

2205   "Would to Heaven," Margrave Ruedeger cried,
      "The margravine might grant you more beside!
      I shall give my beloved wife your word,
      If ever I see her safe, of that much be assured."

2206   And as he promised this, he lifted shield,
      Unleashed his rage, and would not wait nor yield,
      But fell on the guests, a hero upon his foe,
      The mighty margrave striking blow on fearful blow.

2207   Folker and Hagen stood aside, these two.
      They'd given him their promise so to do,
      And still he found by the doorway men of mettle
      Great enough to cause him worry in this battle.

---

*Following C, the translation omits what is in effect an interruption of his own speech by Hagen. B's strophe 2200 reads:

    "Now this is a wretched turn," Lord Hagen spoke.
    "With all the grief of which we bear the yoke—
    God help us if we must fight with friends and kin."
    The margrave answered him, "What pain this leaves me in!"

2208   With will to slay, they let the margrave past,
Gunther and Gernot, men of heroic cast.
Giselher turned away—how sad this made him!
He hoped to live; with Ruedeger there, he must evade him.

2209   Then the margrave's men attacked their foe.
After their master, as true warriors go,
In their hands sharp-cutting swords to wield.
Helmets burst apart, and many a splendid shield.

2210   Weary men lashed out, savagely felling
The knights of Pöchlarn, deep their blows and telling,
Cutting clear through shining armor rings
To the lifeblood. Their battle deeds were glorious things.

2211   Now came all of Ruedeger's retinue,
But Folker and Hagen rushed up quickly too,
And granted no one peace, except one man.
Their hands were busy; down through helmets the red
        blood ran.

2212   Within, the many swords made awesome sound,
And many shield-bands sprang from the clasps around,
Their jewels falling, scattered, in the blood.
Warriors never fought so fiercely—nor ever would.

2213   Back and forth went Ruedeger, well comparing
On that day with any man of daring,
At his best in battle. Thus he gave
Full proof that he was a knight, worthy of praise, and brave.

2214   Here stood warrior Gunther, Gernot the knight.
They slaughtered many heroes in that fight!
Dankwart and Giselher let nothing weigh
Upon their minds, ushering men to their final day.

2215   Ruedeger proved he was strong, valor-filled,
And nobly armed. What numbers of men he killed!
A king of Burgundy saw, was moved to wrath,
And thus began the course of noble Ruedeger's
        death.

2216   Gernot summoned the bold margrave and cried,
"Great Ruedeger, you would have their life denied
To all these men of mine. My heart is sore
Beyond all measure. I can stand to see no more.

2217   Your gift may end by bringing you injury
         For all the many friends you took from me.
         Come over here, highborn and gallant man,
         I'll set upon your gift the highest price I can."

2218   Before the margrave forced his way clear through,
         Bright rings were doomed to turn a darker hue.
         They rushed upon each other, men who ventured
         All for glory, each on guard lest he be injured.

2219   Nothing withstood, so sharp was each man's sword.
         Through flint-hard helmet Ruedeger the lord
         Struck Gernot, and the blood ran down from the blow.
         This the gallant knight repaid, and was not slow.

2220   Wounded to death, he still had strength to lift
         And swing with both his hands the margrave's gift,
         Cleaving the shield to where the helm-straps lie,
         A blow from which fair Gotelind's lord was doomed to die.

2221   Never did splendid gift bring worse reward.
         Gernot and Ruedeger fell, slain each lord,
         Alike in battle, by the other's hand.
         Such damage done was more than Hagen's wrath could
                  stand.

2222   Trony cried, "We bear a heavy cross.
         In both of them we suffer such a loss,
         The end for lands and people will never be.
         But we, the outcasts, have his men as surety."

2223   "My poor brother! Death has had free rein.
         These times bring me no news but that of pain.
         Ruedeger's death is also grief to me;
         The loss is on both sides, and the terrible injury."

2224   When Giselher saw his own brother dead,
         It was for those inside a thing most dread.
         Death looked about for his retainers then,
         And not a one survived of all of Pöchlarn's men.

2225   Giselher and Gunther, Hagen too,
         Dankwart and Folker, excellent knights, walked through
         To where they found the two great heroes lying.
         And now there rose the sound of knights in sorrow
                  crying.

2226   "Death robs us cruelly," spoke young Giselher.
         "Now end your weeping, let us go where the air
         Will cool the rings of our mail; we're tired with strife.
         I doubt if God will leave us much more time for life."

2227   Some sat, and others leaned; many a thane
         With idle hands once more, for they lay slain,
         All of Ruedeger's knights. The din had turned
         To silence lasting so long Attila grew concerned.

2228   "What kind of service is this?" exclaimed his wife.
         "Not loyal or true enough to cost the life
         Of any of our foes by Ruedeger's hand!
         He's trying to get them back again to Burgundy land.

2229   We gave him all he wanted, everything.
         What good? Our knight has done us wrong, great king.
         He who should avenge us must have tried
         To sue for peace!" To this the handsome Folker replied:

2230   "That, great queen, I regret is not the case.
         Dared I cast the lie in so noble a face,
         I'd say that you had played him a fiendish ruse.
         For Ruedeger and all his men there is no truce.

2231   He did with such a will what Attila said,
         That he and his retainers lie here dead.
         Look around you, Kriemhild! Where is a friend
         To give commands to? Ruedeger served you till
              the end;

2232   And if you won't believe it, you shall be shown."
         And so to her heart's sorrow it was done.
         They carried him out, cut down, for the king to see.
         Attila's thanes had never known such misery.

2233   And when they saw the margrave borne in death—
         This frantic sorrow no man's pen or breath
         Could ever describe, this grief of women and men,
         Which in their heartfelt sadness they gave vent to then.

2234   Attila's pain was such, the great king's voice
         Thundered out, as with a lion's noise,
         In the cry of his anguished heart—joined by his wife.
         They mourned without restraint for noble Ruedeger's life.

THIRTY-EIGHTH ADVENTURE
How All of Theodorich's Knights Were Slain

2235   So loud were the cries of mourning all around,
That tower and palace echoed with the sound.
A man of Verona, Theodorich's servant, heard,
And he was quick to pass along the dreadful word.

2236   He ran and told his prince: "Hear, my chief!
With all I've lived through, this is past belief—
Such lament as just now struck my ear.
King Attila himself has come to harm, I fear.

2237   What else would plunge them so in grief and pain?
The king or Kriemhild, one of them is slain
By strangers overbold in their enmity.
Handsome knights arc weeping uncontrollably."

2238   "Beloved men," said Verona's hero son,
"Do not be hasty! Whatever they may have done,
These foreign knights, they had urgent cause indeed.
Do not begrudge them now the truce I guaranteed."

2239   Brave Wolfhart offered, "I shall be the one
To go and ask the truth of what they've done
And then to you, beloved lord, present
What I find to be the cause of this lament."

2240   Theodorich said, "If men anticipate
Hostility and someone comes to state
A question rudely, heroes may turn in fury.
Wolfhart, you arc not the one to put this query."

2241   Quickly then he bade Lord Helfrich go
And find out all that Attila's men might know—
Or the guests themselves—about these last events.
No one had seen a people whose grief was so immense.

2242   The herald came and asked, "What happened here?"
Said one among them, "All our joy and cheer
In the land of Huns is lost beyond regain.
Here, at Burgundy's hands, Ruedeger lies slain.

2243   Of those that came with him, not one is left."
Never had Helfrich felt so greatly bereft,

And never so loath to say what he had to tell.
Theodorich's herald returned, and from his eyes tears fell.

2244   "Warrior, what have you found out for us?"
Theodorich asked. "Why are you weeping thus?"
"If I mourn," replied the knight, "it is only fair.
Burgundians have slain most noble Ruedeger."

2245   "May God forbid!" the lord of Verona spoke.
"That would be awful vengeance, a mocking joke
For the devil's laughter. What has he done to owe
Such debt to them? He liked these strangers, that I
        know!"

2246   Wolfhart answered this: "Their lives should pay
If they did that. Let them get away
With such a thing, and all of us shall stand
Disgraced and shamed. We've been well served by
        Ruedeger's hand."

2247   Theodorich asked for news more certain still.
Despairingly he sat at a window sill,
Sending out Sir Hildebrand to face
The strangers there and ask them what had taken
        place.

2248   Bold in battle, Master Hildebrand,
With neither shield nor weapon in his hand,
Prepared to meet them, courteously and mild.
For this the knight was chided by his sister's child:

2249   Fierce Lord Wolfhart cried, "If you remove
Your armor to go, don't think men won't reprove.
Your trip returning you will make in disgrace.
Go there armed, and that will keep them in their place."

2250   So wise man armed at headstrong youth's behest.
Theodorich's men, before he knew it, dressed
And had their swords in hand—to his distress,
For Hildebrand would gladly have avoided this.

2251   He asked them where they headed. "We'll join you there.
Maybe then Lord Hagen will not dare
Address you with his usual scorn and jest."
Hearing what they said, the warrior acquiesced.

2252 Brave Folker saw them come, these many lords,
Theodorich's men of Verona, girt with swords,
Nobly armored, bearing shield in hand.
This he told his master, king of Burgundy land.

2253 The fiddler spoke, "Theodorich's men I see
Are coming here in open enmity:
Armed and helmeted for war they come.
I think an evil turn awaits us, far from home."

2254 Meanwhile, as he spoke, came Hildebrand;
He set his shield at his feet, there to stand,
And put his question to Gunther's retinue:
"Good lords, alas, what did Ruedeger do to you?

2255 Theodorich sent me to ask if this is true—
Whether the hand of one among you slew
The noble margrave here, as we were told—
Pain so great that we shall never be consoled!"

2256 "The word you have is true," Hagen cried.
"I'd gladly grant you (had your herald lied)
For love of Ruedeger, that he might keep
That life which now forever men and women
   weep."

2257 Hearing beyond a doubt that he was killed,
They mourned him as their true devotion willed.
Bitter tears rolled down on beard and chin
Of all Theodorich's men, for the sorrow they were in.

2258 Cried Sigestab, Duke of Verona, "Ended thus
Is all the aid and comfort given us
By Ruedeger, after the days of our pain.
The joy of men in exile lies at your hands slain."

2259 Vassal lord of Amelung, Wolfwin, said,
"And if today I saw my father dead,
I could feel no greater pain than for his life.
Alas, and who shall now console the margrave's wife?"

2260 Cried, in anger of spirit, Wolfhart the thane:
"Who now will lead our warriors on campaign,
As the margrave did so often? Woe to the day,
Most noble lord, that you were lost to us this way!"

2261   Wolfbrand and Helfrich, Helmnot, and all their kith
And kindred fell to mourning for his death.
Sobbing, Hildebrand could ask no more.
He cried, "Do now the thing my master sent me for.

2262   Warriors, bring Lord Ruedeger from the hall,
Dead, and give him to us—the final fall
Of all our joy in woe—we'll not ignore
The loyal things he did for us and many more.

2263   For we are exiled men, like Ruedeger—
Why make us wait like this? Let us bear
His corpse away, after death now giving
Homage to him that we should rather grant him living."

2264   "No service is so worthy," Gunther replied,
As friend may do for friend when he has died.
I call it constant and loyal so to do.
Well may you honor him, he was a friend to you!"

2265   "How long are we to beg?" said Wolfhart the thane.
"Since you have left our greatest solace slain—
Which sadly is no longer ours to have—
Let us take him away and find for him a grave."

2266   "No one will give him to you!" Folker cried.
"Come and get him where he lies, inside,
In the blood, with deep and deadly wounds, where he fell.
Do that if you would really serve Lord Ruedeger well."

2267   "Minstrel," valiant Wolfhart cried, "God knows
We need no provoking! You've brought us enough woes.
If I dared, in my lord's presence, you'd be inviting
Strife and trouble. But no! He said hold back from
        fighting."

2268   The fiddler answered, "He fears more than he ought to,
Who stops whatever someone tells him not to.
I can't call that heroic." Good and right,
To Hagen's thinking, were the words of his fellow knight.

2269   "Don't ask for proof of that," Lord Wolfhart cried.
"Or I'll tangle your fiddle strings so when you ride
Back to the Rhine, you'll have a tale to recite.
I can't, for my good name, endure your haughty sight."

2270   "If you untune my strings of melody,"
       The fiddler said, "your shining helm will be
       A duller shade by far for work of my hand,
       Whether or not I ride back to Burgundy land."

2271   Wolfhart was set to spring, but Hildebrand
       His uncle stopped him, seizing him by the hand.
       "You seem to lose your head, in youthful anger.
       Believe me, you would have my liege's grace no
             longer!"

2272   "Release the lion, Master, he's so grim
       And fierce!" cried Folker. "Let me get hold of him—
       Had he slain the world and all, he'd get a beating
       Such to put the tale, for him, beyond repeating."

2273   The hearts of all the men of Verona were filled
       With terrible rage. Bold Wolfhart seized his shield
       And most like a savage lion raced ahead,
       and all his friends were quick to follow where he led.

2274   As fast as he sprang to reach the building there,
       Old Hildebrand outran him to the stair—
       He'd not let Wolfhart be the first who fought!
       They found among these foreign warriors what they sought.

2275   Hildebrand fell on Hagen, clashing swords
       Resounding in the hands of both these lords,
       And one could see how they were stirred with ire.
       From their two swords there came a wind all red with fire.

2276   But they were forced apart in the battle-surge,
       As warriors of Verona felt the urge
       To deeds of strength. When Hildebrand turned back,
       Wolfhart fell on gallant Folker in fierce attack.

2277   He struck the fiddler's helm, the sword blade edge
       Cleaving its way down to the metal ridge.
       The fearless bard paid back his valor's due,
       Striking Wolfhart till the sparks of fire flew.

2278   Mighty hewers of fire from rings of chain—
       The hatred each bore the other plain!
       Verona's Wolfwin forced the two apart—
       And he could not have done it without a hero's heart.

2279 Champion Gunther welcomed with ready hand
   Lords of highest praise from Amelung land;
   And Giselher the king—where helmets shone,
   He left great numbers of them with the wet blood on.

2280 Hagen's brother was a man enraged.
   All that Dankwart had done, in battles waged
   With Attila's knights before, was but a flurry,
   Now bold Aldrian's son fought in awful fury.

2281 Ritschart and Gerbart, Helfrich and Wichart, these
   Were fighting men who never took their ease,
   Proof of which they gave to Burgundy.
   Wolfbrand strode about in battle, gloriously.

2282 Old Hildebrand fought like a man possessed.
   At the hands of Wolfhart many of the best,
   Struck dead by swords, in blood lay fallen there.
   Thus Theodorich's knights avenged Lord Ruedeger.

2283 Lord Sigestab fought, true to his valiant standard.
   His foes in battle found their helmets sundered
   By Theodorich's nephew, his sister's son.
   No greater feats of war could Sigestab have done.

2284 When Folker of savage power came to look
   Upon bold Sigestab and the bloody brook
   He hewed from hardened rings, his anger rose.
   He rushed at him, and life moved swiftly to its close

2285 For Sigestab, at the fiddler's hands, who taught him
   Such a lesson in his art as brought him
   By Folker's swordsmanship, to deathly pallor—
   But this old Hildebrand avenged, urged on by valor.

2286 "Alas for the loss of so beloved a lord,"
   He cried, "as here lies dead by Folker's sword.
   Now the fiddler shall be safe no longer."
   Dauntless Hildebrand had reached the height of
      anger.

2287 He struck the minstrel then a blow so hard
   That rim of helm and shield both flew apart,
   Scattered on every side to the walls of the room,
   And thus it was that mighty Folker met his doom.

2288   Theodorich's warriors pressed to join the fray,
Striking so that rings spun far away,
And high in the air broken sword-tips shot.
They drew from under helmets rivers flowing hot.

2289   Hagen of Trony saw Lord Folker slain.
In all that festival this was the greatest pain
He suffered for loss of fellow knight or man.
Alas, what work of vengeance Hagen now began!

2290   "Old Hildebrand shall have from this no gain.
At hands of him my aid and help lies slain,
The best companion I have ever known."
He raised his shield and, lashing out with his sword,
        strode on.

2291   Dankwart fell to Helfrich, mighty thane—
To Gunther and Giselher most grievous pain,
Seeing how in bitter throes he fell.
He died, but for his death his hands had paid them well.

2292   Meanwhile Wolfhart, striding to and fro,
Dealt King Gunther's men blow after blow,
Making his third foray through the room.
There at his hands many champions met their doom.

2293   Now Giselher addressed Lord Wolfhart so:
"Alas that I ever gained so fierce a foe!
Bold and highborn knight, turn here to me,
And I shall help to end it; this can no longer be."

2294   So Wolfhart turned to him, in the battle-tide,
Each one leaving deep wounds gaping wide.
He pushed his way to the king—so hard he sped,
The blood beneath his feet splashed above his head.

2295   With fearsome savage blows, fair Uta's child
Met the hero Wolfhart. However wild
And strong this valiant knight, he could not save
His very life. No king so young could be so brave!

2296   He struck Theodorich's vassal then, a blow
That cut through his byrnie, causing the blood to flow—
A fatal wound for Wolfhart, such a one
As no other man could strike, except this champion.

2297   When Wolfhart felt the wound he quickly slipped
His shield to the ground, and with his hand he gripped
A sharp and powerful sword. With a mighty swing
He struck Lord Giselher, piercing helm and ring.

2298   Each had brought the other bitter death.
Of all Theodorich's men, none drew breath.
Old Hildebrand had seen Lord Wolfhart fall—
It was, till his own death, his greatest pain of all.

2299   Theodorich's men were dead, Gunther's as well.
Master Hildebrand came where Wolfhart fell
And now lay deep in blood. He went to fold
His arms about him—he was an excellent man and bold.

2300   He meant to carry him out, but he seemed to weigh
Too much, he had to leave him where he lay.
Then the dying man looked up from the blood
And saw that his uncle would have helped him if he
        could.

2301   "Dear uncle," cried the doomed and wounded lord,
"You can no longer help me. Be on guard
Before Lord Hagen. This is wisdom's part.
I tell you, he bears a fierce resolve within his heart.

2302   And if my best and closest kin incline
To mourn my death, say this wish is mine:
They should not weep for me, there is no call.
In glory, at a king's own hand, in death I fall.

2303   And in this room I've so repaid my life
That tears are due from many a hero's wife.
If men should ask, let this be freely said:
At my own hand alone, a hundred men lie dead."

2304   Now Hagen thought of Folker, who was slain
By valiant Hildebrand, and cried to the thane:
"You shall pay me back my pain and sorrow.
You've here denied us joy of more than one proud hero."

2305   He struck at Hildebrand, and one could tell
The sound of Balmung, Sigfrid's blade that fell
To dauntless Hagen when he slew that knight.
But he was brave, the old man, and he fought with
        might.

2306   Theodorich's vassal swung on Trony's lord
A blow with his broad and fearsome cutting sword,
But could not wound King Gunther's man, whose blade
In turn struck through his byrnie, though it was skillfully
    made.

2307   Old Hildebrand felt the wound. In worried fear
That greater hurt at Hagen's hand was near,
He threw his shield across his back and ran
From Hagen, wounded as he was, Theodorich's man.

2308   Not one was living of all the warriors there
Except for Gunther and Hagen, this one pair.
Covered with blood, Hildebrand fled, to bring
Most painful tidings to Theodorich the king.

2309   He saw him sitting, sadly, unaware
That he had greater pain by far to bear.
When he saw Hildebrand, his byrnie red,
Moved by anxious fear, he asked the truth; he said:

2310   "Tell me, Master, why are you soaked through
With men's lifeblood? Or who did that to you?
You must have fought, it seems, with the guests inside.
What I forbid so strictly, you might well avoid!"

2311   He told his liege-lord, "Hagen did it all.
These wounds I got from him, inside the hall,
As I was trying to turn from him to go.
I fled that devil, still alive, but barely so."

2312   The lord of Verona cried, "That serves you right.
You heard me swear them friendship, knight to knight,
And you broke the peace I gave! Could I dismiss
From mind the long disgrace, you'd lose your life for
    this."

2313   "Theodorich, lord, do not be so irate!
The harm to me and my men is far too great.
We tried to carry Ruedeger away,
But royal Gunther's men were there, to answer nay."

2314   "Oh Lord, this pain! If Ruedeger has died
Then I am plunged in grief, and sorely tried,
For Gotelind is child of my father's sister.
Alas for all in Pöchlarn, orphaned and without master!"

2315   His death recalled true help in times of pain.
Bitterly he wept—the cause was plain.
"Oh, loyal help that will be mine no longer!
Oh, grief for Attila's men, which I shall never conquer.

2316   Can you tell me, Master Hildebrand,
The truth of this? Who is the knight whose hand
Has struck him down?" "Gernot did it," he said,
"Great is his strength. At Ruedeger's hand he too lies dead."

2317   He said to Hildebrand, "Tell my men to get
Their armor on, and quickly; my mind is set,
I mean to go there. Have them bring to me
My shining gear. I'll question the men of Burgundy."

2318   He answered, "Who is to join your enterprise?
All who live you see before your eyes:
I alone am left. The rest are dead."
Theodorich was stunned, as well might be, at news so dread.

2319   For never had he suffered such great pain.
Theodorich cried, "If all my men are slain,
Then I am poor, and God has forgotten me.
I once was a glorious king, in power and property."

2320   He cried again, "How can this be so,
That all my worthy knights are thus laid low
By war-weary men, themselves in a perilous state?
They would be strangers to Death, but for my own
        ill fate.

2321   Since my unlucky star must work its will—
Tell me, are any Burgundians living still?"
Answered Hildebrand, "None, God knows,
But Hagen alone, and great King Gunther, of all our foes."

2322   "Alas, dear Wolfhart, losing you, I mourn
With the best of cause, the day that I was born.
Sigestab and Wolfwin, good Wolfbrand!
Who is there to help me back to Amelung land?

2323   Valiant Helfrich—what if he is killed?
And Gerbart, Wichart? When is my mourning stilled?
This is the last of all my days of joy!
Alas that grief is not enough to make men die."

THIRTY-NINTH ADVENTURE

How Gunther and Hagen and Kriemhild Were Slain

2324   Theodorich went himself to get his gear,
     And Hildebrand helped him arm. One could hear
     The building echo with the sound of his voice,
     This mighty man in mourning raised so great a noise.

2325   But then his true heroic will returned,
     And as he armed, the warrior's temper burned.
     Taking up a sturdy shield in hand,
     He went his way, he and Master Hildebrand.

2326   "I see Theodorich coming," said Trony's knight.
     "He means to seek us out and force the fight.
     After all the pain that he has suffered.
     Today we'll see to whom the prize of war is offered!

2327   My lord Theodorich here will scarcely find
     That he's so strong of frame, so fierce of mind—
     Wanting to make us pay for the injury done him—
     That I should ever feel compelled in war to shun him."

2328   Theodorich heard him, as did Hildebrand.
     They came where they could see the champions stand
     Outside the building, leaning against the wall.
     Theodorich set his shield upon the ground, to call,

2329   In pain and sorrow: "Great King Gunther, say,
     Why you have treated me in such a way,
     A homeless man? What have I done to you?
     I stand alone, deprived of help, my comfort through!

2330   You did not think unhappy fate fulfilled
     Enough when our lord Ruedeger was killed—
     You now begrudge me all my warriors slain.
     Truly, never have I caused you lords such pain.

2331   Think of your own case, the pain you feel,
     Death of friends, and all your great travail—
     Does this not leave your hearts weighed down with care?
     Alas, how harsh to me is the death of Ruedeger!

2332   In all this life, no man was stricken worse.
     Little you thought of the hurt, mine or yours.

What joy I had lies slain by you, and the end
Will never come of my lament for kin and friend."

2333 Hagen cried, "Our guilt is not so great!
Your heroes entered this room in such a state
Of readiness and with so vast a might—
I do not think that you have heard the story right."

2334 "What else shall I believe? Hildebrand
Has told me when my lords of Amelung land
Asked that you let Ruedeger be borne
From out the hall, you offered my men nothing but scorn."

2335 The king of the Rhine replied, "This was their word:
They wanted to take him away. Not to hurt
Men of yours but Attila did I refuse—
Until Sir Wolfhart answered this with his abuse."

2336 The lord of Verona spoke, "So let it be.
Great King Gunther, now make up to me,
By your good breeding, the pain you caused, and harm,
And give atonement, sir, that I may so affirm.

2337 Give yourself to me, along with your man,
As hostages. I'll see, as best I can,
That none among the Huns shall do you ill.
All you'll find in me is loyalty and good will."

2338 "God in Heaven forbid," came Hagen's words,
"That you should have surrender of two lords
Who in good defense, and armed, oppose
Your hand and walk untrammeled here before their foes!"

2339 "You should not refuse," Theodorich cried.
"Gunther and Hagen, both of you have tried
My spirit sorely, in heart as well as mind.
Well might you make amends, and well be so inclined!

2340 I pledge to you my faith and certain hand
That I will ride with you, home to your land,
Escorting you in honor—if not so,
To die—and for your sake forgetting all my woe."

2341 "Stop asking that!" said Hagen. "It would not do
To have the story told of us that two,
Both valiant men, surrendered to your hand.
I see no one beside you but Master Hildebrand."

2342 "Hagen," cried Master Hildebrand, "God knows,
A man has offered you peace, to go as you chose—
Of which the time has come to make good use.
You may as well agree to take my master's truce."

2343 "I'd probably take truce," Lord Hagen said,
"Before, in shame and plain disgrace, I fled
A room as you did here, Sir Hildebrand.
I thought you could better face your foes and make your
  stand."

2344 Cried Hildebrand, "Why give me that reproach?
Who was it sat on his shield at Mountain Vosges
While Walter of Spain destroyed his friends and slew
So many kin? There's enough to point to, sir, in you."

2345 Theodorich spoke, "It suits a hero ill
To shriek abuse the way old women will.
I forbid you, Hildebrand, to speak again.
I am a homeless man, hard oppressed by pain."

2346 And he went on, "Hagen, let us hear
What both of you were saying as I came near
And you saw that I was armed. You professed
That singlehanded you would put me to the test."

2347 Hagen answered, "You hear no denial.
I'll trade you heavy blows in such a trial,
Unless the sword of Nibelung breaks apart.
Your wanting us as hostage brings fury to my heart."

2348 Hearing Hagen's fierceness thus revealed,
Bold Theodorich quickly snatched his shield.
Straight at him from the stairway Hagen bounded.
The blade of Nibelung fell on Theodorich—how it
  resounded!

2349 Then Theodorich knew the valiant man
Was fierce at heart indeed, and he began
To guard himself against his furious blows.
Well did he know Hagen, most glorious of foes.

2350 At Balmung, too, that vicious sword, he quailed,
But often countering skillfully, prevailed;
And Theodorich conquered Hagen. As they fought
He had opened up a wound, deep and long. He thought:

2351 "Fighting wore you out. I'd gain no shred
   Of honor here if I should leave you dead.
   Rather I shall try to capture you
   As hostage first." (A thing most dangerous to do!)

2352 He dropped his shield. Theodorich's strength was vast;
   In his arms he seized Lord Hagen fast,
   And so the gallant man was overcome.
   Noble Gunther mourned to see him thus succumb.

2353 Theodorich carried Hagen to Kriemhild's side,
   Into her hand delivering bound and tied
   The bravest knight who ever drew a sword.
   After her bitter pain, her joy was now restored.

2354 Delighted, Kriemhild bowed to him and said,
   "Good Fortune descend upon your heart and head!
   You've made up all my hurt. My gratitude
   Shall ever again reward you, unless my death preclude."

2355 Theodorich said, "Grant to him his life!
   And if you do this, oh great Attila's wife,
   The injury he brought you he'll repay,
   But you must not make him suffer for being bound this
     way."

2356 She ordered Hagen led to where he would find
   But prison comfort. There he lay confined,
   Seen by no one. Shouting, Gunther said,
   "The lord of Verona caused me this pain—where has he
     fled?"

2357 Theodorich went to Gunther—the king was a man
   Much praised for strength and valor; Gunther ran
   Out in front of the hall, waiting no longer
   The swords on both men's hands raised a fearful clangor.

2358 For all Theodorich's fame, from time long past,
   Gunther's rage and fury were so vast—
   Sworn foe of his, for the hurt he suffered under—
   That still they tell of his escape as of a wonder.

2359 Both were so great in valor and in power,
   That with the force of their blows palace and tower
   Echoed with swords on helmets hacking down.
   In royal Gunther's heart lay glory and renown.

2360   Yet Theodorich conquered him, as was before
    The lot of Hagen, causing his blood to pour
    From corselet rings, by the sharp sword in his hand.
    For his fatigue, King Gunther made a worthy stand.

2361   But now Theodorich bound him hand and foot,
    Though in such bonds no king should ever be put.
    Theodorich wondered then if he should try
    To free them both, but any who met them would surely
        die.

2362   The lord of Verona took him by the arm
    And led him to the queen. And through the harm
    That came to him, her great anxiety
    Was stilled. She cried, "Welcome, Gunther of Burgundy!"

2363   "Dear sister, before you I should bow my face
    If in your greeting there had been more grace.
    I know you, queen, to be so filled with hate,
    Your welcome to me and Hagen will be both little and
        late."

2364   Theodorich cried, "Wife of a noble king!
    Never were such heroes as I bring
    To you, milady, taken hostage yet.
    Let my good offices gain these men some benefit,

2365   So far from home." She said she would, and gladly.
    Theodorich left the heroes, weeping sadly.
    In grim and fearsome vengeance afterwards
    She took the very lives of both these excellent lords.

2366   She prisoned the two apart, to cause them pain.
    Neither would see the other one again,
    Until she brought to Hagen her brother's head—
    Kriemhild's revenge on both of them, a cause for dread.

2367   And then she went to Hagen—hostile and grim
    The tone of voice in which she spoke to him!
    "If you will give me back what you took from me,
    You may yet return alive, home to Burgundy."

2368   Fierce Hagen answered her, "You waste your breath,
    Highborn queen! I have sworn an oath
    Not to reveal the treasure, and to give
    No part away, while any of my lords shall live."

2369   "I'll bring an end to that," cried Attila's wife.
She gave the word to take her brother's life.
They struck off his head; she carried it by the hair
To show to Hagen, lord of Trony, to his despair.

2370   When, sick at heart, he saw his master's head,
Hagen the warrior, turning to Kriemhild, said,
"And so your will is done, and you have brought
An end to things, and all has turned out as I thought.

2371   Now the noble king of Burgundy's gone,
Young Giselher, and Gernot, leaving none
Who knows where the treasure is, but God and me.
Discover, fiend of evil, how secret that will be!"

2372   "You rob me foully of my due redress,"
Cried the queen, "but I shall still possess
The sword my darling Sigfrid took to wear
When I saw him last—the pain is mine, the guilt you
        bear!"

2373   She took it from the sheath—what could he do?
She wanted the warrior's life. And so she drew,
And lifting high her hands, struck off his head.
Great King Attila saw it all; and his heart bled.

2374   "God help us!" cried the king. "Here lies slain
At a woman's hands, alas, the finest thane
Who ever carried shield or went to war.
My heart is sad, for all the enmity I bore."

2375   "She dared to kill him—little good will it be!"
Old Hildebrand cried. "Whatever happens to me—
And though he left me, too, in desperate plight—
I shall avenge the death of Trony's gallant knight."

2376   In wrath he sprang at the queen and cruelly swung
His sword upon her. Kriemhild, now unstrung
By fear of Hildebrand, began to wail
And scream most terribly, but all to no avail.

2377   Now all whose fate it was to lose their life
Lay slain, and cut to bits the great king's wife.
Attila and Theodorich now began
To mourn most pitifully the death of kin and man.

2378   All their glory and splendor now lay dead,
          And people were in grief, beset with dread.
          Sorrow ended the feast of Attila the Hun—
          As ever pleasure turns to pain when all is done.

2379   I cannot say what afterwards occurred,
          Except that ladies, knights, and squires were heard
          Lamenting for the death of kin and friend.
          This is the fall of the Nibelungs, and of this tale the end.

Translated by Frank G. Ryder

Notes

These notes are arranged according to adventure. Most elements of interest in the particular adventure will be noted within the context of the longer narrative. Occasionally individual strophes or lines will receive separate consideration. Not all adventures as such will be noted, however. It is hoped that the discussions provided below will serve not only to provide basic "information," but also to offer modest interpretative suggestions that will enhance the reader's pleasure with and interest in the *Nibelungenlied*.

    1. The first strophe is taken from the C manuscript and probably was not part of the original version of the epic, but rather was added by a later redactor. Editors of the *Nibelungenlied*, however, tend to include the strophe in the editions, irrespective of the redaction they are publishing, since it provides a type of prologue to the work. (One indication that it is a more recent addition is the presence of internal rhyme, rendered also in the translation: *told/bold, life/strife*.) The first line represents an "appeal to veracity," a conventional element of heroic poetry. Compare for example the beginning of the *Older Lay of Hildebrand*: "I've heard tell." The intention of such statements is to emphasize that the poet is working within a tradition and is not inventing the story. In other words, he is telling the "truth."

    The purpose of the first adventure is to introduce one of the main characters—indeed, perhaps the most important individual—in the *Nibelungenlied*, Kriemhild. Kriemhild is described as a royal princess of great beauty, who grows up amid great power and wealth. She is of noble and high lineage, and her three brothers—Gunther, Gernot, Giselher——rule the country of Burgundy, with Gunther as king. Worms is the capital. Kriemhild's brothers are described as strong, well-descended, and, above all, generous. This attribute is especially important. For in Germanic society, generosity was the true hallmark of a leader of men, in that by being generous the ruler demonstrated that he recognized and valued the efforts of his men and rewarded them appropriately. Tacitus mentions this custom

in his *Germania* and, of course, many of the epithets in Old English literature, such as "treasure giver" and "giver of rings," reflect this practice. And
a doughty assemblage of men they are indeed! Foremost among them is
Hagen of Trony, the chief adviser to the king. Following Hagen is a list of
great heroes, presumably well-known to the listeners, who were themselves
most likely quite familiar with the matter of the *Nibelungenlied*. The purpose of this rather unadorned listing is to demonstrate that the three Burgundian kings must be great lords indeed, if they are able to attract and
retain the loyalty of so many worthy men.

Interspersed throughout this adventure, however, are ominous hints
that the tale will end tragically, i.e., ". . . in womanhood, she [Kriemhild]
cost the lives of many men" (strophe 2). This type of epic foreshadowing is
repeated throughout the *Nibelungenlied* and is a standard rhetorical device
of heroic poetry, the purpose being, among other things, to increase tension
and heighten suspense; more of this is added in the sixth strophe when we
learn that the kings die because of "two women's hate." Thus already in
the second strophe of the work we are informed not only that the *Nibelungenlied* will not have a "happy ending," but also that Kriemhild will be a
major agent of this tragedy. The sixth strophe adds the information that
another woman will be prominently involved in the catastrophe to come.

Dreams in the *Nibelungenlied* also have a very important foreshadowing function, and they invariably presage doom. Kriemhild has two, both of
which foretell the death of Sigfrid. The first one is in the first adventure,
namely her dream of the falcon and its subsequent death during the attack
by two eagles (strophes 13–14). Although her mother, Uta, correctly inter-
prets the dream and foretells that her daughter will marry the man represented by the falcon, Kriemhild will have none of that and boldly vows to
remain untouched by love. But that is not to be, and the final strophe of the
first adventure (19) makes clear again that a great tragedy will take place
and that Kriemhild will be at the center of it. But this strophe, too, like strophe 6, provides some new information. We learn for the first time, for
example, that Kriemhild's husband will be killed by her kin, and she will
take vengeance upon them. Essentially, then, strophes 2, 6, and 19 provide
all the necessary information about the calamity of the *Nibelungenlied*:
Kriemhild's kin will kill her husband; another woman is involved;
Kriemhild avenges her husband's death most terribly; and many, many
brave men die as a result.

One other clear message that runs through these strophes is that
women bring disorder into the world of men and, by so doing, can be a
threat to men. The world of the *Nibelungenlied* is essentially a male one,
and the attitude toward women that is found in the text reflects a male
point-of-view, i.e., assertive females are dangerous to male well-being while
docile women are most desirable. The depiction of and opinion about the
female characters in the work will be analyzed when encountered in the
remaining adventures.

2. The second adventure relates the upbringing of the young prince, Sigfrid, and the ceremonies attendant upon his knighting. Missing in this adventure is any reference to the heroic Sigfrid of myth: Sigfrid the dragon-slayer and possessor of the treasure of the Nibelungs. Instead we are presented with the description of a young prince who is loved and protected and appears to be in every way a product of conventional courtly society, i.e., he is trained to bear arms and he has an effect on the ladies. He is, in every respect, the male counterpart to Kriemhild.

It seems clear that the Sigfrid of myth was not of paramount interest to the *Nibelungenlied* poet. It is only in connection with the Burgundians and their adventures (the Saxon War, the courting of Brunhild, the great hunt before he is killed) that the Sigfrid of myth appears. Why that is the case is difficult to say. Certainly it is clear from a reading of the epic that the "coexistence" between the heroic and courtly is an uneasy one at best, and one that ultimately brings about a contest that both lose. Is this a depiction of the archetypical conflict between the old and the new? I suspect that in a way it is. We will see in later sections how the two value systems come into conflict and in each a different solution is proposed, only one of which receives the poet's approbation.

But now things are still serene. The long scene describing Sigfrid's knighting may be intended to be reminiscent of the *Hoffest* at Mainz (1184), where Frederick Barbarossa had his two sons knighted with great pageantry and splendor. The description of the opulence of the festival and the generosity of Sigfrid's parents serves to enhance their own nobility (see note 1).

We receive one interesting insight into Sigfrid's character in this adventure. He declines to assume rulership of Xanten because his parents were still in excellent health. Rather he wished to root out injustice in the land, a sentiment that speaks of Sigfrid's character and bodes well for a future ruler. A good king is a *just* king, and it seems that Sigfrid is on his way to attaining that goal.

3. But in the third adventure, courtly love strikes Sigfrid (strophe 47). Tales of the beautiful Burgundian princess, Kriemhild, have reached his ears and he is determined to court her. He is warned against these plans by his parents on the grounds that the Burgundians are too dangerous. But he persists in his intentions, as does Gunther in the sixth adventure in his determination to make Brunhild his queen. As hindsight has it, the warnings were justified in both instances.

It is in this adventure that we are introduced to Sigfrid the mythical hero, not by his deeds in this adventure but rather by the descriptions of past exploits through the words of Hagen, Gunther's chief adviser. Hagen relates in a few short strophes (86–100) Sigfrid's fabulous adventures in the land of the Nibelungs, his battles against the Nibelung warriors and against the dwarf Alberich, his securing of the magic cloak that made its wearer invisible, and his possession of the Nibelung treasure. Almost as an afterthought he adds that Sigfrid fought and killed a dragon and bathed in its blood with the result that he became invulnerable. Hagen's prudent advice is that Gunther should treat the young guest with honor and caution. These words of Hagen are the only indication to the listener/reader up to this point that this tale is indeed the tale of powerful Sigfrid, the owner of the Nibelungen treasure and the slayer of the dragon. Sigfrid, himself, will have few chances to show his heroic side in the epic.

Perhaps that is an explanation for Sigfrid's rather boorish behavior at Worms and his rudeness to Gunther and his followers. Ostensibly he came to Worms to court Kriemhild, something he fleetingly remembers in strophe 123. More often than not, though, he acts like a bully, challenging Gunther to battle for rulership over Burgundy, for no reason, at least for no reason that we can discern. This conduct is certainly not "heroic" in any real sense (see the *Older Lay of Hildebrand*), but perhaps it reflects an understanding of the term "heroic" around 1200. Nonetheless, the inconsistency between what Sigfrid originally intended and his subsequent actions is one of the greater paradoxes of the *Nibelungenlied*.

Another inconsistency, but one upon which we will spend no further time, is the concern of his parents that something could actually happen to Sigfrid at Worms. Surely they must have noticed that he had an invulnerable skin and so on.

It is also appropriate that this adventure begins and ends with epic foreshadowing. At the beginning we are told that there lived a maiden in Burgundy who "later [would be the] cause of his many joys and deep distress" (strophe 44). Strophe 138, the final strophe of the adventure also describes Kriemhild as ". . . the beauty who was to bring him pleasure, yes, and pain."

4. The fourth adventure has two main purposes to fulfill: (a) to tighten the bonds between Sigfrid and Gunther; (b) to provide Sigfrid an opportunity to demonstrate his heroic fighting skill at least once in the *Nibelungenlied*.

It is Hagen who suggests that Gunther tell Sigfrid about the impending attack of Liudeger and Liudegast: "Why not tell Sigfrid what has passed?" (152). Gunther does just that by telling Sigfrid, in response to the latter's remark about how somber things had become, "True friends alone can share our deep concerns" (strophe 155). Upon hearing these words, Sigfrid grows pale and flushes, a sure sign of deep emotional feelings in the *Nibelungenlied*, and reassures Gunther that if he is looking for friends, he has found one in Sigfrid! Thus begins the first real bond between Sigfrid and the Burgundians, one that may not be so lightly broken.

5. In the fifth adventure the strengthening of the bond between the Burgundians and Sigfrid continues. For finally—after all this time!—Sigfrid gets a chance to approach Kriemhild. It is Pentecost, the most joyous time in the medieval calendar. It is warm and all wear their best finery and can see and be seen. Usually Pentecost is the time of great festivals in medieval works, and here the *Nibelungenlied* is no exception. The great victory over Liudeger and Liudegast will be celebrated. But first the ladies of the court

must make their grand entrance, Sigfrid catches a glimpse of Kriemhild, and "he swiftly paled and then blushed red" (strophe 285). The alternation of pale and red provides evidence of Sigfrid's intense emotional agitation as it did in the fourth adventure when Gunther tells him that one can confide "in true friends alone."

Sigfrid is also sought out for his advice. Liudeger and Liudegast have offered the king an enormous amount of gold if Gunther will free them (strophe 314). Sigfrid finds such an offer ignoble and suggests instead that Gunther simply let his former enemies go free with their pledge not to attack again. One purpose of the scene is to demonstrate the true noble nature of Sigfrid. Possibly, too, there is an "echo" here of another, earlier work in which Gunther appears, the Latin *Waltharius* (eighth/ninth century). In the *Waltharius*, Gunther was a weak and greedy king. It must be stressed that Gunther is not portrayed as such in the *Nibelungenlied*, but consciously or unconsciously this unflattering character trait may have been hinted at by the Nibelungen poet. These "echoes" appear again and again in the epic.

6. The similarities between the third and sixth adventures cannot easily be overlooked. In both, a man proposes to go in quest of a beautiful woman. In both, the men are warned that the quest is too dangerous. We have seen in the third adventure that the immediate danger to Sigfrid was overstated. But here in the sixth adventure, the potential for harm to Gunther is quite real, for Brunhild is possessed of superhuman strength.

But the chief purpose of the sixth adventure is to cement even further the bonds between Sigfrid and Gunther. And again it is Hagen who provides the stimulus when he suggests to Gunther that the king ask Sigfrid for aid (strophe 331). The condition that Sigfrid sets, Kriemhild's hand in marriage, is accepted by Gunther. At this point the two men are as closely bound by ties of personal obligation as possible.

One more point worthy of note is that it is in this adventure that the great deception of Brunhild begins. In strophe 386 Sigfrid instructs his companions to insist that he is Gunther's vassal when confronted by Brunhild. This is quite a statement for the status-conscious Sigfrid, who, when he first arrived at Worms in his belligerent manner, scathingly shouted at Ortwin, Hagen's nephew, who wished to fight Sigfrid:

> "Not against me shall you dare to lift your hand!
> I am a mighty king, and what are you?
> A vassal! . . . "(strophe 118)

And since awareness of one's status plays a large role in the *Nibelungenlied*, Sigfrid's gesture toward Gunther will prove to be most fateful.

Brunhild, more so than Kriemhild, is never treated quite honestly by the men of the *Nibelungenlied*, and they appear to be supported in their behavior by the poet. In the first place, she is presented to us in a very negative way: "this queen is a thing of terror," Sigfrid says when he tries to dissuade Gunther from his mission. Essentially, however, she is a physically powerful woman, generally superior to the usual run of men. Thus the only way to deal with such a woman is deceitfully, not openly and honestly. The prevalent attitude toward women in the *Nibelungenlied* is that they ought to be decorous and malleable. They certainly must not be allowed to challenge men on any level. If they do, then they may be treated shamefully, as we will see.

7. The seventh adventure continues this deception of Brunhild. She recognizes Sigfrid and welcomes him (strophe 419). Sigfrid, however, stoutly maintains that he is Gunther's vassal and that he came along only because he was ordered to do so (strophes 420–22). It is, of course, a bold-faced lie that everyone recognizes as such, including the poet and his audience—everyone, I should say, *except* Brunhild. She then ignores Sigfrid and turns her full attention to Gunther. It is amusing to note the Burgundians' reaction to the preparations for the contests, from Hagen's dark muttering about the "devil's wife," again a very unflattering reference to Brunhild, to the almost audible quaking of Gunther's knees. But Sigfrid comes to the rescue with the aid of his magic cloak that renders him invisible. Thus, Gunther "wins" the contests.

One question worthy of discussion, however, is how Sigfrid and Brunhild know each other. Is this also an unconscious "echo" from Scandinavian tales about the prior betrothal of Sigfrid and Brunhild?

9. The ninth adventure serves the basic purpose of bringing Sigfrid and Kriemhild together. Again, it is Hagen who arranges this. He suggests that Sigfrid be sent as the messenger to Worms to announce the happy conclusion to the island adventure and to instruct the Burgundians to prepare to receive their new queen.

It is worthwhile to keep in mind that it has consistently been Hagen who has maneuvered Gunther and Sigfrid into ever closer bonds of friendship and alliance.

10. The tenth adventure has many points of interest, not the least of which are the court ceremonies depicted therein, e.g., the ceremony of greeting and especially the form of the marriage ceremony. Sigfrid and Kriemhild speak their vows within the circle of knights, which is an ancient Germanic legal procedure (strophes 614–16).

Most interesting, of course, is Brunhild's reaction to the marriage of Sigfrid and Kriemhild. On the one hand this could be one of those "echoes" mentioned above and represent jealousy on the part of Brunhild. On the other hand the scene might mean exactly what it says: namely that Brunhild cannot understand how a powerful king like Gunther would give his sister in marriage to someone who freely admitted that he was Gunther's vassal, i.e., probably of the rank of ministerial. Since some of the most powerful and wealthiest men in the twelfth century were ministerials, such marriages were not unusual and were generally the only salvation for many impoverished members of free nobility. Nonetheless, such *mésalliances* were considered to be socially degrading for the noble partner. Essentially, the problem is one of status, *not* wealth or actual power. One other point to consider: if this were truly a mismatch between Sigfrid and Kriemhild, not only would Kriemhild be forced to take on the unfree status of her new husband, but their children would do so as well. Further, this state of affairs would reflect very dishonorably on Gunther's entire family, including his newly won bride, herself a high noble. Thus, Brunhild's sorrow is most understandable (strophe 620 and 622).

This adventure provides another occasion in the continuing deception of Brunhild. Gunther cannot, of course, tell her the truth about Sigfrid because that would expose his dishonest behavior during the contests of strength. But Gunther underestimated the determination of Brunhild to discover the truth. As a result he spent his wedding night hanging by a nail on the wall. Gunther laments his lot to Sigfrid, and the latter agrees to subdue Brunhild. The only condition that Gunther makes is that Sigfrid may not deflower Brunhild (strophe 655). Aside from the cruel treachery toward Brunhild that this request implies, one further problem remains: as long as Brunhild is a virgin, she is invincible. This is a problem that the poet does not solve.

Sigfrid's wrestling match with Brunhild is a long drawn-out bit of misogyny that seeks its counterpart in the literature of the court. Brunhild is strong and, at first, gets the better of Sigfrid whose only thought is that should Brunhild win, how many other women might get the idea to turn against their husbands (strophe 673)! Finally, after a vicious, knock-down fight, Sigfrid strikes her so hard that "her body cracked in every bone" (strophe 677). With that the battle was over, and Brunhild became no "stronger than any woman." The question remains, however: *How* did Sigfrid win, if Brunhild was invincible while a virgin? It should mean that she lost her virginity at Sigfrid's hands, although that is not expressed. The line: "her body cracked in every bone" could have the meaning, in Middle High German, of "her hymen cracked." I believe that the *Nibelungenlied* poet meant the scene the way that he described it. But the ambiguity in the Middle High German could be yet one more example of an "echo" from another tradition. Equally ambiguous is why Sigfrid took Brunhild's ring and belt—a symbolic deflowering?

The lesson from this scene is essentially that a woman, Brunhild, who assumes a male gender role, i.e., strength, and causes distress to a male, is a danger to the world of men, and she must be controlled regardless of the duplicity and violence involved. As has already been indicated, women must adhere not only to the strictures of the female sex but also of the female gender roles assigned to them.

11. The departure of Sigfrid and Kriemhild for Xanten in the eleventh adventure is remarkable in that this scene provides further insight into the very status-conscious character of Kriemhild. Before Sigfrid and Kriemhild

leave on their journey to Sigfrid's home, the Burgundian kings state that they wish to provide their sister with a dowry and to this end are prepared to divide their kingdom with her, a proposal that she is willing to accept. This offer is peremptorily rejected by Sigfrid. Undaunted, Kriemhild then insists upon taking a personal escort of Burgundian knights with her to Xanten, and she asks Hagen and Ortwin to join her company. Hagen is angry and replies that he and his family only serve the kings of Burgundy. Indeed, the fact that Kriemhild would even attempt to take Hagen with her is but one further indication of her awareness of herself and of her status in society. It was a heedless request, for the loss of Hagen, their chief vassal and adviser, would indisputably be a sore one for the Burgundian kings. Nonetheless, the desire to take some fighting men from her homeland with her was very prudent of the new young queen, who would be moving to a strange land. Although it is not the case in the *Nibelungenlied*, the life of a young bride was not always secure, let alone happy, in her husband's homeland. Thus, it was only sensible to have several men-at-arms upon whose loyalty one could depend. This time Sigfrid wisely says nothing.

12–16. Adventures twelve through sixteen form the narrative complex dealing with the betrayal and death of Sigfrid. The immediate instigator of the tragedy is Brunhild, who cannot understand why Sigfrid, Gunther's vassal, does not appear at Worms and do service, as would be expected of vassals. In other words, Brunhild is every bit as aware of her status in society as Kriemhild and is resolved to see both Sigfrid and her sister-in-law in attendance in Worms. Since Gunther will not "command" Sigfrid to appear, Brunhild resorts to subterfuge, as the glaring discrepancy between her words and thoughts at the beginning of the twelfth adventure demonstrates. Once again, it is clearly evident that the ultimate cause of the coming catastrophe lies in the continuous deception of Brunhild by Gunther and Sigfrid.

The problematic surrounding the key concept of the entire work, loyalty, is especially prominent in these adventures. And once plans for killing Sigfrid are formulated, the emphasis placed on loyalty or lack of same is not to be overlooked. For his part, however, Sigfrid is convinced that Gunther and the Burgundians are loyal to him as a friend, an ally, and a relative. Thus he is ever ready with his service; e.g., in strophe 749 Sigfrid says to the Burgundian messengers:

> "Has someone since we parted offered ill
> To my lady's kin? Let me know! I will,
> In faith and always, help them bear the blow,
> Until their foes shall weep at the *loyalty* I show."
> [emphasis mine]

For their part, the Burgundians welcome Kriemhild and Sigfrid most warmly, and things are peaceful enough at first. Yet the thirteenth adventure is rife with foreshadowing of the disastrous events to come.

The argument of the two queens, portrayed in the fourteenth adventure, forms the "point of no return." The insults that each hurls at the other are massive: Brunhild expresses her belief that Sigfrid is a vassal of Gunther. Kriemhild reacts strongly to this assertion because of its implications about her and her status (see the notes to the tenth adventure) and responds with her own contention that she is *adelvrî* ("noble and free"), a formal, legal term used to describe the status of the original nobility, i.e., noble by dint of birth, as opposed to the ministerials, noble by virtue of service. The most serious insult, however, was Kriemhild's labeling of Brunhild as a "vassal's mistress" (strophes 839–40). What made this insult all the worse was the fact that it was uttered before others; as a result Brunhild's humiliation was *public*.

Gunther's reaction to this situation is very interesting. He asks Sigfrid to swear that he did not *boast* about having sex with Brunhild—not that he *refrained* from sexual intimacy, which was, after all, the condition that Gunther set for Sigfrid's help during the former's difficulties with Brunhild (see the tenth adventure). Again, is this a further "echo" from another tradition? Nonetheless, no oath of Sigfrid's would be sufficient to hinder the inevitable, and Hagen swears revenge on the hero for the indignities that his queen has suffered (strophe 864).

The fourteenth adventure also provides further opportunities to display the attitude that women have the tendency to throw man's orderly world into chaos. In strophe 862, for example, Sigfrid proposes the male response to the situation brought about by the quarrel between the queens:

"Women should be trained in a proper way,"
Said Sigfrid, "to curb the haughty things they say.
Warn your wife, and I will do the same.
Their immoderate conduct fills my heart with shame."

Further in strophe 866, Giselher, while exhorting the Burgundians not to follow Hagen's plans for revenge, states that "the things that women find to get upset about are a vain and petty kind." By implication, then, these "things" are not worthy of a man's attention. And even in the final strophe of the adventure (strophe 876), the poet states:

The king fell in with Hagen's evil plan.
Without a soul suspecting, they began
To shape their perfidy, these men of pride.
From two women's wrangling many heroes died!
[emphasis mine]

Thus even here while censuring Gunther and Hagen for their disloyalty toward Sigfrid, the poet assigns the ultimate blame to the two women.

Before proceeding any further, it might be useful to ask if Hagen was justified in seeking Sigfrid's death. The answer, surprising as it might seem, is, according to customary law, essentially yes. Put succinctly: As chief vassal of Gunther, it is Hagen's responsibility to protect the life and honor of his king. It must be kept in mind that the king extends beyond his own person. Thus if his warriors lose a battle, it is the king who is dishonored. Likewise, if the king's wife is dishonored, so too is the king. If these actions are allowed to go unanswered, the dishonor will adhere to the king and all his actions, so that eventually he will no longer be an effective ruler, a situation that can lead to chaos in the country. Hagen is motivated to kill Sigfrid not for personal gain, but simply and solely to avenge the *public* insult done to Brunhild by Kriemhild.

If Hagen plans to kill Sigfrid, then he also wants to succeed. As a prototype of a Germanic hero he is motivated less by the strictures of chivalry and the brave and sometimes futile noble gesture. No, Hagen is the absolute pragmatist who will do all that is necessary to accomplish his task. When it comes to the restoration or preservation of honor, the Germanic hero was *not* sentimental, e.g., the battle between father and son in the *Older Lay of Hildebrand*. With regard to Sigfrid: Hagen knew that Sigfrid was invulnerable (indeed he related this fact in the third adventure—see above). Thus he had to devise a strategy that would give him an opportunity to kill Sigfrid. This he does very cleverly by deceiving Kriemhild into betraying the one vulnerable spot on her husband's body, between his shoulder blades. And so it is that Hagen later thrusts a spear between Sigfrid's shoulders and kills the hero. By so doing Hagen has avenged the insult done to his queen, and by extension his king, and has restored the ruling credibility of Gunther. Nonetheless, the deed receives the unqualified scorn of the Nibelungen poet. Again and again he refers to the deed as an act of unparalleled treachery and to Hagen and Gunther as faithless: "The faithless man [Gunther], all in deceit, bowed low" (strophe 887); "Hagen the false and faithless man" (strophe 911); "A deed of faithlessness" (strophe 915); "Gunther and Hagen, bold, but with the face of false deceit . . ." (strophe 916); "Hagen broke faith with him [Sigfrid]—and he broke it wretchedly" (strophe 971); "faithless plotting" (strophe 988).

From the above, it is clear that the poet is not only excoriating the actions of his characters, but is also attempting to manipulate his audience to do the same. He is using this situation to drive the lesson home that no insult is sufficient cause for the taking of a life. There is no justification for revenge, he is claiming, although there is ample historical documentation from the period to indicate that revenge-taking was a very usual occurrence. Possibly, then, this is a lesson that the poet wants to impart to his listeners. Possibly he is stressing that the bonds of friendship that securely bound Gunther and Sigfrid and Hagen, by extension, have more validity in the world than the rigid strictures of the heroic ethos that demands satisfaction for every affront. Gunther stood before the choice and was on the right path when he accepted Sigfrid's offer of oath as a peaceful way to end the strife. He went wrong when he followed the advice of Hagen. As mentioned earlier within the discussion of the second adventure, we may be confronted here with the archetypal struggle between the old and the new. We will return to this suggestion in our discussion of the thirty-seventh adventure.

17–18. The seventeenth adventure is fascinating in that it contains an illustration of the medieval belief that the wounds of a murdered individual will bleed if the murderer is near. Strophes 1044 and 1045 describe the procedure as Sigfrid's wounds profusely bleed when Hagen stands at the bier. Although Hagen appears to be unmasked as the killer, apparently more "proof" was required, because Kriemhild prevents any rash act of vengeance by Sigfrid's father, Sigmund. Indeed in the eighteenth adventure Sigfrid's men say upon their departure from Worms:

> "This country yet
> May see us on the march if we should get
> *Certain proof* by whom our lord was slain."
> (1093, [emphasis mine])

Most important, of course, is that Kriemhild *knows* who killed her husband, and this knowledge determines the course of events in the second part of the *Nibelungenlied.* Also of interest in the eighteenth adventure is the refusal of Kriemhild to return to Xanten with Sigmund, because she has no kin there. This situation reflects a piece of medieval reality. It was by no means certain that a young widow would be well-treated in her former husband's lands. Attempts could be made by unscrupulous nobles to usurp power for themselves or if, as is the case with Sigfrid, their lord met his death at the hands of his wife's relatives, it was not a given that the widow's safety was guaranteed. And although it might strike one today as grotesque that Kriemhild would feel safer among those who were responsible for the murder of her husband than among his family, the truth is that her sisters in the real world probably would be.

A further interesting discrepancy in the eighteenth adventure is the self-stylization of innocence by Gernot. In strophe 1097 he states to Sigmund:

> "God in heaven knows, though Sigfrid's dead,
> I bear not even the blame of having known
> Who hated him."

Certainly a straightforward enough statement, but one strangely at variance with the description in strophe 865, where we are told that "Ortwin and Gernot joined the plotting twain [Gunther and Hagen], as they discussed how Sigfrid might be slain." We will note that Giselher and Gernot play dubious roles at best in the entire conflict between Hagen and Kriemhild, preferring "no knowledge" to actively protecting their sister and her interests. We see this attitude again on the occasion of Hagen robbing her of Sigfrid's treasure.

19. The nineteenth adventure contains the famous scene of the coming of the Nibelungen treasure to Worms, its subsequent robbery by Hagen, and its sinking in the Rhine. With the immeasurable wealth of the

Nibelungen at her disposal, Kriemhild was busy attracting foreign, i.e., non-Burgundian knights to Worms who owed their loyalty to her and not to the kings. This is the situation to which Hagen is reacting. He perceives that if this practice is left unchecked, these multitudes of strange warriors could pose a real threat to the rule of his kings. As with Sigfrid, so also here, Hagen advocates swift and decisive action: take the treasure from Kriemhild. The kings do not wish to *know* anything of this. Thus they ride off on some errand or other. When they return the treasure is gone and sunk in the Rhine. Once again, Hagen has acted to preserve the ruling viability of Gunther and by so doing has once again incurred the inextinguishable wrath of Kriemhild.

20–22. The twentieth through twenty-second adventures begin the second half of the *Nibelungenlied* and switch the scene of the action to Gran, Attila's kingdom. Attila, known as Etzel in the *Nibelungenlied*, is a kind, enlightened ruler with many positive courtly traits, completely unlike his Old Norse counterpart Atli, who was fierce and warlike but also completely heroic. In the southern (i.e., German) tales Etzel is a very generous ruler without the rigid edges of a Germanic hero. Indeed very little separates him—in attitude—from Christian courtly princes, and he is, therefore, not so much perceived as an Other (although Kriemhild does make repeated reference to the fact that the Huns are pagans). He has attracted brave warriors to his service; he is a model of tolerance (Christians and pagans enjoy respect and honor at his court: see strophe 1335); and he is sympathetic to the plight of those unjustly exiled, e.g., Theodorich (cf. the *Older Lay of Hildebrand*).

More importantly, in addition to the change of locale, we also witness a slow but sure change in the characterization of Hagen and Kriemhild. Kriemhild is depicted in an ever more negative light, both by the poet and by other characters, while Hagen gains in nobility and honor. Attention will be drawn to the character transformations when encountered in the remaining adventures.

In this second part of the epic the familiar characters appear (with the exception of Brunhild; she has played her part and now disappears), and familiar personalities from heroic legend materialize, e.g., Theoderich and Hildebrand. In addition, there is one completely new character, Ruedeger of Pöchlarn, who is not found in ancient tales and is, thus, considered to be the creation of the Nibelungen poet. Ruedeger appears to be the most modern character in the entire epic (modern in the sense of the twelfth century). He is courtly, a Christian, and a man of probity, whose word is respected and who is, himself, greatly honored. In some ways he can be viewed as a sort of antithesis to Hagen, and we will later have opportunity to view a most important interaction of the two characters. There is also a further connection between Hagen and Ruedeger: They are friends from Hagen's youth when he was a hostage of Attila's (related in the *Waltharius*).

Of interest is the fact that, once again as was the case with Sigfrid's arrival, it is Hagen who is able to identify the strangers who have appeared at Worms. From the reaction of the Burgundians it is clear that even if Ruedeger was not known by sight, he was renowned for his honorable reputation. A noteworthy confirmation of this high regard is strophe 1192 where Gunther gives Ruedeger permission to present Attila's communication without first assembling his advisers, which would have been the customary practice. The message, Attila's proposal of marriage to Kriemhild, is warmly received by all except Hagen, who correctly foretells that such a marriage will bring disaster upon the Burgundians (strophes 1210, 1212).

Of course, the most significant section of the twentieth adventure depicts the meeting between Kriemhild and Ruedeger when she finally agrees to marry Attila after extracting a fateful promise of support from the noble emissary (strophes 1255, 1258). Ruedeger's pledge of loyalty arouses the desire for revenge in Kriemhild's heart (strophe 1259), a desire that soon turns into an obsession, in spite of the fact that she had reconciled herself publicly with Gunther! But however Kriemhild may have understood Ruedeger's oath, it is clear that Ruedeger himself did not intend his pledge to include avenging the death of Sigfrid. With this scene the change in the poet's attitude toward Kriemhild begins. Up to now Kriemhild has been the beautiful and loyal wife and (later) widow. As soon as she embarks upon her plans for revenge, however, she is viewed by the poet as being as much in the wrong as were Gunther and Hagen when they plotted to kill Sigfrid. And in strophe 1281 with the last of her wealth either taken by Hagen or given away by her for the salvation of Sigfrid's soul is also the last mention of Kriemhild being "loyal":

> Stunned by the force of Hagen's works,
> She kept as an offering a thousand marks
> And spent it for her beloved husband's soul,
> Playing, to Ruedeger's mind, a loyal woman's role.

The depth of her love and loyalty to Sigfrid will from now on be matched by her commitment to revenge.

23. As the track to tragedy in the first part of the *Nibelungenlied* began with an invitation to a festival, so also does it in the second. Indeed the very setting is identical: the king and queen are in bed together, Gunther and Brunhild in the twelfth adventure and Attila and Kriemhild in the twenty-third adventure. Both women cajole their husbands into inviting supposed friends and/or relatives to a joyous festival of reunion. In both instances there is a grotesque incongruity between what each queen is saying and what she is *thinking*, i.e., really intends: Brunhild wishes to have Sigfrid and Kriemhild in attendance as a confirmation of her higher and their lower status; Kriemhild wants the Burgundians at Gran so that she can harm (at first only) Hagen:

One intention never left her mind:
She thought, "I have power of such kind,
And wealth enough, to hurt my enemies badly—
This I swear I'd do to Hagen of Trony gladly." (strophe 1396)

and

"Often my heart cries out for loyalty.
I wish I were near to those who injured me—
Vengeance would then come for my lover's life.
For that I can hardly wait." So *thought* Attila's wife.
(strophe 1397 [emphasis mine])

In both instances, however, events quickly slipped the queens' grasps and assumed a tragic dynamic of their own.

And doubtless because of Kriemhild's overt preoccupation with revenge and her setting of the unholy events into action that it is also in the twenty-third adventure that the Devil is first brought into association with Kriemhild and her deeds (strophe 1394).

24–26. The twenty-fourth through twenty-sixth adventures deal with the tendering of Attila's invitation, the opposition of Hagen to the Burgundians' to travel to Hungary, and the journey to Gran itself. Instead of heeding their chief adviser, the kings ascribe Hagen's exhortations against the journey to his (assumed) fear of personal retribution for the killing of Sigfrid, something that is, however, clearly not the case, for Hagen couches all his comments not in personal terms but in terms of the harm that could befall the kings. Indeed, Hagen is not alone in his opposition. Rumold, the master of the kitchen, speaks against the kings' leaving (strophes 1465–69), and, most dramatically, Uta, the queen mother, relates her ominous dream:

Then the noble Uta spoke these words
To all her sons: "Stay here, most excellent lords!
I had a dream last night, of things I dread
And fear to see: for all the birds in the land were dead."
(strophe 1509)

This strophe is, of course, reminiscent of Kriemhild's dream reported in the first adventure (see above), where the heroes (Sigfrid, Gunther, Hagen) are depicted as birds (falcon and eagles). The question naturally arises as to why the kings ignored all the above advice and portents. Possibly here, too, we are confronted with the conflicting ideologies of the old and the modern. The kings do not fear danger because of the reconciliation with their sister. But Hagen, the embodiment of the Germanic hero, *knows* that Kriemhild, whom he recognizes as a kindred spirit, will use every opportunity to avenge the terrible wrong done to her, regardless of the supposed peace with her brothers.

As mentioned above, the characterization of Hagen is presented in a much mellower light in the second part of the epic than in the first part, and in the twenty-fifth adventure the poet calls him a "solace" of the Burgundi-ans (strophe 1526), certainly one of the more positive designations of Hagen in the work.

The prophecy of the mermaids that no one except the king's chaplain will return alive to Burgundy confirms Hagen's worst fears (strophe 1542). It is here that Hagen demonstrates his true Germanic, heroic stature. He realizes that he can do nothing to change the Burgundians' fate, but he will do all that he can to challenge it and gain the advantage for as long as pos-sible. Thus he attempts to drown the chaplain—who cannot swim—and fails. Knowing then that the prophecy is indeed true, he destroys the boat so that no Burgundian will even contemplate running away, something that would bring great dishonor upon his lords even after their deaths.

27. The twenty-seventh adventure relates the sojourn of the Burgundi-ans at Pöchlarn. Here the poet continues the "metamorphosis" of Hagen. As mentioned earlier, it is not that Hagen "changes," but that the poet elects to stress the positive side of Hagen the Germanic hero and less that of Hagen the killer of Sigfrid. Note the special greeting given to Hagen by Ruedeger, as well as his instructions to his reluctant daughter that the fear-some-looking Hagen deserves her kiss of welcome.

It is also in this adventure that the friendship between Ruedeger and the Burgundians is deepened through the betrothal of Giselher with Ruedeger's daughter, through the gifts of Gotelind, and through the escort to Attila's court provided by Ruedeger.

28. In the twenty-eighth adventure we meet Theodorich, the exiled king of the Ostrogoths (see the Introduction to this volume). One of the most positive characters of Germanic heroic poetry, Theodorich is a model of just and ethical behavior and is regarded by all as a paragon of honor. Thus it is no small matter that Theodorich greets Hagen warmly and warns the Burgundians of Kriemhild's true intentions. The adventure proceeds with a more approving depiction of Hagen, who is remembered fondly by Attila (strophes 1752–57) as his former hostage. Kriemhild's portrayal, on the other hand, continues to become progressively negative. The highlight of this changing characterization is Theodorich's bitter denunciation of her as an "evil woman" (strophe 1748).

One other matter in this adventure that has long puzzled readers of the *Nibelungenlied* concerns Kriemhild's demand that Hagen return Sigfrid's treasure to her (strophes 1741–43). As in the first part of the tale, so also here we are confronted with a conflict inherent in the narrative itself. What we may ask, is the true reason that Kriemhild wishes revenge? Is it to avenge the death of Sigfrid, whom she still mourns, according to Theodorich? Or is it to avenge the loss of the treasure which granted her power and influence and the ability to direct events herself? Are we deal-ing with Kriemhild the haunted widow consumed by the idea of vengeance? Or are we confronted with Kriemhild the calculating, power hungry individual, of whom we got a few glimpses in the first part of the work? (see above).

29. The twenty-ninth adventure is notable for the confrontation between Hagen and Kriemhild. Kriemhild accuses Hagen, directly and for the first time, of murdering Sigfrid. Hagen acknowledges that he is the one who brought her injury and also provides his reason:

> "Why go on? We've talked enough, I'm through.
> I am Hagen still, the one who slew
> The mighty hero Sigfrid. *How he suffered*
> *for the slur on Brunhild's name that Kriemhild offered!*"
> (strophe 1790 [emphasis mine])

What grand and magnificent boldness! With this one statement Hagen makes evident for all that he killed Sigfrid *not* for any tawdry reasons like jealousy or hope for personal gain, but rather because the honor of his king and queen were at stake—in his view. With these words of defiance the poet effectively allows Hagen to dim the memory of the opprobrium attached to the deed and the perpetrators. Thus, the confession does not diminish Hagen, quite the contrary! He emerges more heroic than ever, while Kriemhild, who is still the wronged party, becomes more twisted and shrill. Both, then, follow the pattern of changing characterization laid down by the poet in the second part of the epic. Kriemhild becomes more ignoble because she is engaged in changing gender roles, i.e., she is taking the initiative and actively pursuing revenge, thereby bringing chaos into the world of men. The fact that she was indeed wronged, that her life was altered dramatically by the treacherous and self-serving actions of some of her male relatives does still not permit her to move beyond the roles traditionally assigned to women. (See discussion of tenth adventure above.)

30–36. The thirtieth through the thirty-sixth adventures deal with the events leading up to the outbreak of hostilities between the Burgundians and the Huns and the aftermath of the great conflict. As terrible and appalling as the individual episodes are, it must be kept in mind that all serve the purpose of leading into the key adventure, the thirty-seventh. By the time of the thirty-seventh adventure, the Huns have menaced the Burgundians while they slept, only to be driven off by Volker and Hagen, and have attacked Dankwart and the squires; Hagen has chopped of the head of Ortlieb, Attila's and Kriemhild's son, so that it landed in his mother's lap; the Burgundians were besieged in the great hall where they had to drink the blood of the fallen to slake their thirst and in order to survive the incineration of the hall that was ordered by Kriemhild.

The purpose of these adventures is a threefold one. In the first place, the depictions of the battle scenes and the tensions underlying them are absolutely first rate and quite exciting. Thus an entertainment objective is realized. But the scenes also have an edifying purpose, namely: how do true warriors engage in battle, how do they approach death, and how is the symbiosis between lord and vassal presented? The third purpose is perhaps the most important one, but unthinkable without the other two: everything must be prepared for the confrontation between Ruedeger and the Burgundians in the thirty-seventh adventure. All arguments, pro and con, that either side could employ must be clearly delineated *before* the encounter, for in that adventure a vital decision will have to be made.

37. The thirty-seventh adventure is, without doubt, the most important in the entire *Nibelungenlied*. For once again the conflict between the old and the new is given magnificent illustration. This time the two main protagonists are Hagen and Ruedeger, each a representative of a well-defined ethos which should make the actions of the two heroes predictable, but surprisingly each acts differently than expected. As in the episode dealing with the killing of Sigfrid, here, too, the protagonists are faced with making a choice, only one of which is acceptable in the view of the poet and, thus, ideally in our view too. Briefly recapitulating: The choice in the case of Sigfrid's death was between strict adherence to the dictates of the heroic ethos which demanded revenge on the person of Sigfrid because of Kriemhild's insult of Brunhild; and, as Gunther himself favored from the start, accepting Sigfrid's word that he is innocent in view of all the faithful service he has performed for the Burgundians. By following the first course, the poet leaves no doubt (see note 12–16 above) that the Burgundians, especially Hagen and Gunther, have manifestly made the wrong choice.

Here, too, the choice seems to be between loyalty to one's lord and obligation to a friend, that is, to someone with whom one stands in a condition of amity. Not that Hagen was Sigfrid's friend—but Gunther was. Gunther knew the right thing to do and yet allowed himself to be swayed by his vassal, Hagen, who was acting out of loyalty to Gunther as he understood it. Here, too, it is a matter of the conflict between vassal loyalty and personal bond, i.e., friendship. Ruedeger, who was the host and friend of the Burgundians, who gave his daughter in betrothal to Giselher, and who provided the Burgundians with safe conduct to Attila's court, is called upon by his liege lord Attila to avenge the wrongs done to him by the Burgundians. These wrongs included the wholesale slaughter of many of his men and, more important, the brutal murder of his only son by Hagen. Kriemhild adds her pleas and reminds Ruedeger of his promise to her years ago when he presented her with Attila's proposal of marriage. In reply, Ruedeger utters what must surely be one of the most anguished replies in heroic literature. He says:

> "That I do not deny, great king's wife.
> I swore to risk for you both honors and life,
> *But not to lose my soul—that I've never sworn.*
> I brought to your tourney here these warriors, royally born."
> (strophe 2150 [emphasis mine])

For Ruedeger, then, the decision is clearly a moral, ethical one that transcends the obligation to one's liege lord. The fact that he laments the loss of his soul should he perform his expected service for Attila and Kriemhild as well as the loss of his greatest virtues of breeding, honor, and loyalty (strophe 2153) demonstrates indisputably the moral gravity of the situation, even though there should, technically, not be any question in Ruedeger's mind. After all, if nothing else, the Burgundians did kill the young prince of the Huns. Surely that alone ought to be enough to galvanize Attila's loyal men into action, all—apparently—except Ruedeger. The latter's hesitation and his futile attempts to persuade Attila to release him from his obligations are clear signals to us that things are not as simple as they seem and that he is about to make the wrong choice. Nonetheless, the poet does not criticize him for doing so, as he did with Hagen and Gunther earlier, since Ruedeger himself is well aware of the wrongness of his decision. That is the real tragedy of Ruedeger: he knows what is right, but is not strong enough to do right when the conflict lashes at the very essence of his being as a vassal of Attila.

At first the Burgundians expect that Ruedeger will fight on their side, again an indication that the battle situation is quite different than normal, e.g., his advent is hailed by Giselher (strophes 2171–72). But soon Ruedeger tells why he has come, much to the consternation of the Burgundians. The three kings, Gunther, Gernot, and Giselher, are unable to accept Ruedeger's decision and all either censure him or swear to seek his death. Further, Giselher renounces his betrothal with Ruedeger's daughter!

It looks bleak indeed for Ruedeger as well as for the Burgundians when suddenly a loud voice calls from the crowd:

> "One moment more, most notable Ruedeger, stay!"
> (Thus spake Hagen.) "We have more to say,
> My lords and I, from dire necessity.
> What good to Attila could our wretched dying be? . . ."
> (strophe 2193)

With this strophe begins one of the most moving and important episodes of the entire epic. For in the next few strophes Hagen shows a side that, with the exception of his relationship to Folker, we have not often glimpsed in the *Nibelungenlied*: We see Hagen the *friend*. In a seemingly inconsequential statement Hagen laments the loss of the splendid shield that he received as a gift from Gotelind, Ruedeger's wife. And he makes note of the intact shield that Ruedeger is carrying. Ruedeger, in a display of unselfish generosity, gives Hagen his shield with the wish that he may return safely with it to Burgundy (strophe 2196). With this gift, Ruedeger has demonstrated once more his generosity and nobility of spirit, thereby restoring his lost honor in his eyes and those of the world. It is truly a magnificent gesture, and had the exchange ended there, our focus would remain on Ruedeger. But let us shift our gaze to Hagen, who is, after all, the agent for the restoration of Ruedeger's honor. It is Hagen who asks for the shield, although it might be expected that somewhere in all the carnage about him was also a shield that he could use! It seems that Hagen recognizes the quandary that Ruedeger is in and offers him a last chance to manifest his admirable character. Thus it is not only a noble gesture on Ruedeger's part, but also on Hagen's, who provides Ruedeger with this opportunity. With this exchange the poet allows Hagen to demonstrate his true, praiseworthy character. But the scene continues. Hagen, moved by the gift says:

> "God in Heaven bless you, Ruedeger,
> There'll never be one like you anywhere,
> To give to outcast men so great a favor
> May the good Lord grant your virtues live forever!"

and

> "And noble Ruedeger, I'll repay that gift
> *However these knights treat you, I'll not lift*
> *My hand against you here in enmity,*
> *Even though you kill the whole of Burgundy."*
> (strophes 2200–2201 [emphasis mine])

This is an incredible statement by Hagen! For here he discards his vassal loyalty to his lords and declares that even if Ruedeger *kills* his kings, he would not attempt to avenge their deaths. This is quite a change from the Hagen who killed Sigfrid in order to protect Gunther's honor. Whereas he was severely castigated for his rigorous maintenance of his vassal loyalty then, now there is not one word of reproach for his manifest disloyalty—not even from Gunther. Yet Ruedeger, who is upholding his vassal loyalty to Attila, condemns his own actions and laments the loss of his soul. It is clear that the poet is conveying a strong message with this scene: it is wrong to draw blood in revenge. Whether the queen of the land has been dreadfully insulted or whether the only child of a king has been brutally killed, neither occurrence is sufficient cause for the spilling of more blood.

Further, the themes of loyalty and friendship are amalgamated. Hagen is Ruedeger's friend and, as such, determines that his allegiance to his friend supersedes his loyalty to Gunther and the other Burgundian kings. Hagen was not in the same situation with Sigfrid, for he was not the hero's friend. On the other hand, Gunther was Sigfrid's friend and failed to honor his friendship when he allowed Hagen to kill Sigfrid, for which he, as well as his vassal, are severely criticized (see above). By putting precisely Hagen in the situation of choosing between two conflicting loyalties (although for Hagen there is no conflict; see below), the poet also leaves no doubt about where, in his view, the bond of friendship, which is the antithesis of violence and represents a state of peace and harmony, should stand in the scale of values.

39. Finally in the thirty-ninth adventure only Hagen and Gunther are left of the Burgundians, and they are taken captive by Theodorich and Hildebrand. Hildebrand's taunt of Hagen in strophe 2344 "who was it sat on his shield at Mountain Vosges while Walther of Spain destroyed his

friends and slew his kin?" refers to an episode in the *Waltharius* that does have bearing on Hagen's behavior in the *Nibelungenlied*. Hagen and Walther had been hostages at Attila's court and became fast friends. Hagen escaped and went back to serve a not very noble Gunther (see previous discussion above), and then Walther escaped with his fiancee and a great amount of Attila's gold. Gunther attacked the pair unjustly out of greed. Hagen, realizing that his king is acting unethically, refused to fight his friend Walther. He went and sat on his shield while the rest of Gunther's men were killed by Walther. Only when no one was left to protect the king did Hagen enter the fray and fight Walther. In the *Nibelungenlied* we have seen that Hagen's character has developed in this regard in that he refuses to do battle with Ruedeger under any circumstance. This is just one more indication of the mastery of the poet in using Hagen to illustrate his view of the importance of friendship and the subtle distinctions that friendship imposes on an individual's judgments.

Kriemhild confronts Hagen for the last time and again—curiously—asks him to return the treasure (see note 28 above). Hagen's response that he can say nothing while his lords live prompts Kriemhild to order the execution of her brother Gunther. Confronting Hagen with the head of his lord only serves to make him more defiant and also intensifies the negative depiction of Kriemhild, for it is now Hagen who calls her a "fiend of evil." This statement represents the complete rehabilitation of Hagen and the concomitant total malevolent transformation of Kriemhild at the hands of the poet. Because she is a woman, Kriemhild should not have pursued the path of revenge (see note 29 above). Her actions, which transgress traditionally assigned gender roles, serve to bring down upon her not only the disdain of the poet and the other characters, but also function to place her outside of society, to make her an "outlaw," so to speak (a situation that did not happen to Hagen, for example!). In fact, it is Attila, himself, who mourns the fact that Hagen was slain by a woman (strophe 2374). Thus, Kriemhild can be brutally killed by Hildebrand, without the old hero suffering any repercussions. Indeed his action is accepted by Attila and Theodorich as representing the just consequences of Kriemhild's own deeds.

THE YOUNGER LAY OF HILDEBRAND

That the story of a father and his son who faced one another in combat survived as a popular tale throughout the Middle Ages is evidenced by the large number of manuscripts from the fifteenth and early sixteenth centuries which contain the *Younger Lay of Hildebrand*. Though extant only in these later books and manuscripts, the poem was probably composed in its present form in the thirteenth century. Centuries after the composition and copying of the older *Lay*, the alliterative half-line of older Germanic literature has been replaced by the four-line stanzas of the so-called Hildebrand melody, very similar to those used by the poet of the *Nibelunglied*. The tense drama and sense of doom which dominates the older *Lay* has been replaced as well; in this ballad-like narrative potential tragedy gives way to happy reunion. The warrior ethic of the earlier work is presented in an exaggerated, almost comic fashion, typified in the heavy-handed taunts which father and son hurl at each other, and by their eagerness to do battle. Western Europe had indeed undergone a great shift in all aspects of culture in the eleventh and twelfth centuries, and the visible change in attitude towards the older, predominantly Germanic warrior ethic is no small proof of such a transformation. The circumstances surrounding the two men's duel in the older *Lay*, so heavily laden with irony, and the bitter battle itself, in which father and son are forced to take up arms against one another by their obedience to a societal ethic, have been trivialized in the younger work into a chance encounter of two characters whose motivations are lost to us, and quite possibly, to the later medieval compilers as well; more important to those who would rework this material in the later Middle Ages was the opportunity to develop the old tale into a sentimental ballad of the long-lost father who returns home to his happy son and faithful wife.

1   'Ich wil zu land ûsrîten,'   sprach sich meister Hildebrant
     'der mich die weg wîse   gen Bern wol in die lant.
     die sint mir unkunt gewesen   vil menegen lieben tag,
     in zwei und drîssig jâren   fraw Uten ich nie gesach.'

2   'Wiltu zu lant ûsrîten,'   sprach sich herzog Abelon
     'was begegnet dir ûf der heide?   ein schneller degen jung.
     was begegnet dir ûf der marke?   dîn sun her Alebrant.
     jâ rittestu selbzwelfte,   von im wurdest angerant.'

3   'Jâ rennet er mich ane   in sînem übermut,
     ich zehowe im sînen grünen schilt,   es tut im nimmer gut,
     ich zehow im sîn brinne   mit einem schirmeschlag
     und das er sîner muter   ein ganz jâr zu klagen hât.

4   'Das ensoltu niht tun,'   sprach sich von Bern her Dietrîch
     'wan der jung her Alebrant   ist mir von herzen lieb.
     du solt im fruntlîch zusprechen   wol durch den willen mîn,
     das er dich lâss rîten,   als lieb ich im mög sîn.'

5   Dô er zum rosengarten ûsreit   wol in des Berners marke,
     dô kam er in grôss arbeit   von einem helden starke;
     von einem helden junge   da wart er angerant
     'nu sag an, du vil alter,   was suchst in dînem lant?

6   Du fürest dîn harnesch lûter und clâr   reht wie du sîst
                          eins küniges kint,
     du wilt mich jungen helden   mit gesehenden ougen
                          machen blint;
     du soltest da heimen blîben   und haben gut hûsgemach
     ob einer heissen glûte.'   der alte lachet und sprach

7   'Solt ich da heimen blîben   und haben gut hûsgemach?
     mir ist bî allen mînen tagen   zu reisen ûfgesatzt,
     zu reisen und zu fechten   bis ûf mîn hinefart.
     das sag ich dir, vil junger,   darumb grawet mir mîn bart.'

8   'Dîn bart wil ich dir ûsroufen,   das sag ich dir, vil alter man,
     das dir das rosenfarbe blut über die wangen muss abgân.

dîn harnesch und dîn grüenen schilt   den must du mir hie ûfgeben,
dar zu bis mîn gefangner,   wilt du behalten dîn leben.'

9 'Mîn harnesch und mîn grüener schilt   die hânt mich dick ernert;
ich trûwe vol Crist von himel,   ich wolle mich dîn erweren.'
sie liessen von den worten,   si zugen zwei scharfe schwert.
was die zwên begerten,   des wurden si gewert.

10 Ich weiss nicht wie der junge   dem alten gap ein schlag,
das sich der alte Hildebrant   von herzen sêr erschrack.
er sprang hinder sich zu rücke   wol siben clafter wît
'nun sag, du vil junger,   den streich lert dich ein wîb.'

11 'Solt ich von wîben lernen,   das wer mir immer ein schand.
ich hân vil ritter und knechte   in mînes vaters land,
ich hân vil ritter und grâfen   an mînes vaters hof:
und was ich nicht gelernet hân,   das lern ich aber noch.'

12 Er erwischet in bi der mitte   da er am schwechsten was,
er schwang in hinder sich zu rücke   wol in das grüene gras.
'nu sag du mir, vil junger,   dîn bîchtvater wil ich wesen,
bistu ein junger Wölfinger,   von mir magst du wol genesen.

13 Der sich an alte kessel rîbet,   der enpfâhet gern ram.
als geschicht dir, vil junger,   wol von mir alten man.
dîn bîcht soltu hie ûfgeben   ûf diser heiden grün,
das sag ich dir vil eben,   du junger helde kün.'

14 'Du sagst mir vil von wolfen,   die loufen in dem holz:
ich bin ein edler degen   ûs Kriechenlanden stolz,
mîn muter heist fraw Ute,   ein gewaltige herzogîn,
so ist Hiltebrant der alte   der liebste vater mîn.'

15 'Heist dîn muter fraw Ute,   ein gewaltige herzogîn,
so bin ich Hiltebrant der alte,   der liebste vater dîn.'
er schlôss im ûf sîn guldîn helm,   er kust in an sînen munt
'nun muss es got gelobet sîn,   wir sîn noch beid gesunt.'

16 '*Ach vater, liebster vater mîn,*   *die wunden die ich dir*
                                            hân geschlagen,
    die wolt ich drîstunt lieber   *in mînem houpte tragen.*'
    '*nun schwîg, lieber sun,*   *der wunden wirt gut rât,*
    sîd das uns got al beide   *zusamen gefüget hât.*'

17 *Das weret von der nône*   *bis zu der vesperzît,*
    bis das der jung her Alebrant   *gên Bern îne reit.*
    was furt er ûf sînem helme?   *von gold ein krenzelîn.*
    was furt er an sîner sîten?   *den liebsten vater sîn.*

18 *Er furt in in sîner muter hûs,*   *er satzt in oben an den tisch.*
    das dûcht sîn muter   *gar unbillich.*
    '*ach sun, mîn liebster sun,*   *ist dir der êren nicht zu vil,*
    das du ein gefangen man   *setzest oben an den tisch?*

19 '*Nun schwîgent, liebste muter,*   *und lând euch sagen,*
    er het mich ûf der heide   *gar nâch erschlagen.*
    und hörent, liebste muter,   *kein gefangner sol er nicht sîn;*
    es ist Hiltebrant der alte,   *der liebste vater mîn.*

20 *Ach muter, liebste muter,*   *nun biet im zucht und êr.*
    [dô hub sie ûf und schenket în   *und trug ims selber her.*
    was het er in sînem munde?   *von gold ein fingerlîn.*
    das liess er in becher sinken   *der liebsten frawen sîn.]*

"I wish to ride home," Master Hildebrand declared. "Point out the roads to Verona's country for me; it's been a very long time since I was familiar with them. I haven't seen Lady Ute in thirty-two years."

"If you wish to ride home," Duke Abelon[1] answered, "think what you will encounter on the heath: a brave young warrior. Think what you will encounter in the marches: your son Lord Alebrand. He'll attack you even if you ride in a company of twelve."

"Even if he attacks me in his pride, I'll chop away his green[2] shield; it will never do him any good. I'll chop away his armor with such a blow that he'll complain about it to his mother for a whole year."

"You mustn't do that," Lord Dietrich of Verona said, "because young Lord Alebrand is a friend of mine. For my sake you should address him in a quite friendly manner, that he may let you ride on out of friendship for me."[3]

When he'd ridden out to the Rose Garden in the territory of Verona's lord,[4] he found himself in great difficulty at the hands of a strong warrior. He was attacked by a young warrior: "Now tell me, old man, what do you seek in your own country?" You wear your armor bright and shiny, just as though you were a king's son. I'm a young man with good eyesight; do you wish to make me blind? You ought to stay in your house and enjoy the comforts of home by a hot fire."

The old man laughed and answered: "Should I stay in my house and enjoy the comforts of home? It has been my lot my whole life to ride to battle, to ride and fight until the day I die.[5] I tell you, young man, my beard is turning gray from it."

"I'd like to rip your beard out, that's what I say to you, old man, so your rosy-red blood runs down over your cheeks. You'll surrender your armor and green shield to me here, and be my prisoner besides, if you want to stay alive."[6]

"It's my armor and green shield that have often kept me alive. I trust Christ in heaven that I can hold my own against you."

They left off talking and drew two sharp swords. The two were granted just what they desired. I don't know, but the young man gave the older man such a blow that old Hildebrand was truly frightened.

He jumped back a good seven arms-lengths: "Admit it now, young man; you learned that stroke from a woman."

"If I had to learn from women, I would always be disgraced. In my father's land I have many knights and squires; at my father's court I have many knights and counts.[7] And what I have not learned up to now, I'll learn later."

Hildebrand struck him in the middle where he was most vulnerable, knocking him all the way back into the green grass.

"Now tell me, young man,—I want to be your confessor[8]—if you are a young Wolfing,[9] I'll let you live. Whoever handles old kettles surely gets dirty,[10] which is what's happened to you, young man, at the hands of an old man like me. You should offer your confession here on this green heath. I tell it to you straight, bold young man."

"You tell me a lot about wolves that run in the woods. I'm a noble man, of the pride of Greece.[11] My mother's name is Lady Ute, a powerful duchess, and that means my father is old Hildebrand."

"If your mother's name is Lady Ute, a powerful duchess, then I am old Hildebrand, your father!"

He[12] clasped him by his golden helmet and kissed him on the mouth: "God be praised, we are both unharmed!"

"Father, I would rather bear three times over on my own head all the wounds that I gave you!"[13]

"There, there, my son, the wounds can be healed, now that God has brought the two of us together."

It took young Lord Alebrand from afternoon until evening to ride to Verona. What did he carry on his helmet?—A garland of gold. What did he carry at his side?—His own father![14] He carried him into his mother's house and seated him at the head of the table.

His mother thought this quite inappropriate: "My son, is that not too much hospitality for you, to seat a prisoner at the head of the table?"

"Now be still, mother, and let me tell you. He very nearly killed me on the heath. And listen, mother: this is no prisoner; it's old Hildebrand, my father! Mother, please offer him food and hospitality."

Then she got up and poured something to drink and took it to him herself. And what did he have in his mouth?—A golden ring,[15] which he dropped into his dear wife's cup.

Translated by James K. Walter

Notes

1. One would expect "Abelon" to rhyme with "jung" and so give "Abelung," a corruption of "Amelung," the name of Dietrich's clan. This man may have originally been a "Duke of the Amelungs."

2. "Green" in the sense of "undamaged."

3. This scenario differs greatly from the one found in the older *Lay of Hildebrand*. There is no return from exile with Dietrich, rather old Hildebrand decides it is time to go back home to see his wife. That he has a son is well known; this son is, in fact, a friend of Dietrich. Duke Abelon warns Hildebrand that Alebrand will attack him; exactly why there should be hostility between the two is unexplained. Alebrand is a friend of Dietrich and therefore not a warrior in a hostile army. Furthermore, there seems to be no reason for Hildebrand to be out of contact with his family; they obviously share the friendship of Dietrich. Though the older *Lay of Hildebrand* also lacks any explanation or background information, such lack does not weaken the sense of drama in the confrontation between father and son. In the younger *Lay* the lack of understanding for the characters' motives and for the situation in which they find themselves robs the work of much dramatic tension.

4. In *Laurin* Version D (Version A as well as if a common emendation is accepted), Hildebrand is described as "meister Hildebrant/von Garten ein wîser wîgant" (281–282), a warrior from Garda, an Italian town on the shores of Lake Garda, not far to the west of Verona. The Middle High German form of Garda, "Garte," can easily be confused with "garten" ("garden"), and subsequently with Princess Kriemhild's Rose Garden at Worms. Hildebrand is now in his own lands near Garda and must be recognizable as a native (by his coat of arms?) because Alebrand asks him what he seeks in his own country.

5. Hildebrand's speech here is reminiscent of the passage in the older *Lay* where he describes his perilous existence in the ranks of the spearthrowers. The younger *Lay* differs, however, in that there is no mention of going into exile with Dietrich.

6. Alebrand challenges the older man out of a desire to win his armor. See the older *Lay of Hildebrand* notes 2 and 18; the younger *Lay's* motivation may reflect a tradition concerning the cause of the duel.

7. Alebrand enjoys the benefits of a court which must belong or have belonged to Hildebrand; he was not left "without an inheritance" (older *Lay*, line 22).

8. Hildebrand offers to take up the role of priest and hear Alebrand's final confession of sin before his death.

9. The Wolfings are Hildebrand's ancestral clan. In light of the warnings he received earlier, Hildebrand surely suspects that he is fighting his son.

10. Apparently a proverb or folk saying.

11. A knight in the tradition of Alexander the Great, a popular example and ideal figure for knights of the twelfth century and later, as evidenced by the widespread and numerous versions of the *Alexanderlied*.

12. "He": Hildebrand.

13. Alebrand bears no ill will against his father, for he immediately abandons the quarrel. Apparently, he has attacked Hildebrand just as he would attack any stranger passing through the country.

14. Alebrand carries Hildebrand home on his horse as though his father were a prisoner. Unless Hildebrand's wound is more serious than the author has described, and he must be carried, Alebrand must wish to conceal his father's identity from his mother Ute. Ute does indeed assume that this man is a prisoner. In Version D of the *Lay*, the desire to conceal Hildebrand's identity is carried to the point of staging a mock combat upon arrival in Verona whereby Ute finally recognizes her husband. A tradition that Ute/Uote waited patiently and faithfully for her husband to return after so many years is reflected in two lines of Wolfram von Eschenbach's *Willehalm*: "meister Hildebrants vrou Uote/mit triuwen nie gebeite baz." (439, 16–17).

15. There are a number of endings to the poem; these lines represent the best sense of the variants. The ring which Hildebrand drops into the

cup is obviously one which Ute will easily recognize. This sentimental ending, in contrast to the stark tragedy of the older *Lay of Hildebrand* and its concept of all-powerful fate, is quite in line with the author's wish to portray a happy reconciliation for all the members of this family, and reflects an entirely different set of presuppositions and values. These happy circumstances do not shed light on the missing ending of the older *Lay*, where the characters are trapped by tragic circumstances beyond their control.

THE BATTLE OF RAVENNA

Hildebrand went into exile, abandoning his home and his son, in support of his lord Theodorich (Dietrich), and it is as a member of this king's army that he returns home. Though remaining on the sidelines in the *Lay of Hildebrand*, in the later Middle Ages Dietrich became the major figure of a large cycle of poems which are centered around his struggle for control of those Italian kingdoms which are rightfully his against his treacherous uncle Ermanrich who attempts to take control of the entire country. This struggle for control of Italy is told in two long epic poems, *Dietrich's Flight* and the *Battle of Ravenna*, the second of which is presented in this volume. These works form a core for a larger number of poetic works which deal either with Dietrich's youthful exploits as dragon-slayer and giant-killer (*Goldemar*, the *Eckenlied*, *Laurin*, *Sigenot*, the *Virginal*, and the *Wunderer*) or with the deeds of some of his vassals, with Dietrich himself being relegated to a more peripheral role (*Biterolf and Dietleib* and the *Rose Garden*). *Dietrich's Flight*, which relates the story of Dietrich's loss of Italy and subsequent refuge at the court of Attila, king of the Huns (Etzel in medieval German), was compiled around 1280 by an author known only as Heinrich der Vogler (the Fowler). The *Battle of Ravenna* is a continuation of the story begun in the *Flight*, written at about the same time, but not likely by the same author. Composed in rhyming couplets, it is the tale of Dietrich's return to Italy to defeat his uncle Ermanrich and the treasonous former vassal Witege. In the scenes of the *Battle of Ravenna*, just as in the older *Lay of Hildebrand*, a warrior code is encountered, though it is often rather baldly expressed. Nonetheless, the characters of this work (and its audience too, one assumes) consider a man to be of low repute should he avoid a fight when challenged to it; for the sake of his name as knight and for his reputation among those noble women whom, according to the dictates of courtly society in the later Middle Ages, he theoretically served, a warrior had to take up arms in such instances, and could not allow himself to be seen as a coward. But a new concern seems to be introduced here, another side to this knightly ethic, that those who take up a fight, who seek military adventure, must not do so in arrogance or false pride. Those who fail to recognize this condition meet with some sort of defeat. Etzel's sons Scharpf and Ort, along with Dietrich's younger brother Diether, are too quick to seek adventure and too eager to fight, and thus meet their death. Witege's nephew Rienold is also deeply concerned with his reputation as a knight and falls in combat against an opponent against whom he knowingly stands no chance. Witege, though unwilling to fight, must do so nonetheless, and heaps scorn on himself by killing his youthful adversaries, and then is disgraced completely by his flight from Dietrich and his less than honorable rescue. Finally, Dietrich himself experiences humiliation for his failure to make good his all too easily offered promises to Etzel and Queen Helge. Unlike the fate suffered by Hildebrand and Hadubrand in the *Lay of Hildebrand* which is, as far as we know, undeserved, defeats met by the characters in the *Battle of Ravenna* appear to result from some kind of moral failure. The later work then offers a moral judgement or at least a strong warning against overconfidence and arrogance and against overstepping one's abilities and place in knightly circles.

> *Ez het Etzel der rîche*
> *bî den selben tagen*
> *zwêne süne hêrlîche,*
> *als wir daz buoch hœren sagen.*
> *Vil liep wârn sî im beide,*
> *an in lac sîner vreuden ougenweide.*

A. SCHARPF AND ORT

(strophes 154–87)

Returning to the Huns after his campaign in Italy, Dietrich was overcome by sorrow at the loss of so many of his comrades.[1] In order to console him, Etzel and Lady Helge arranged a marriage for him to Helge's niece Herrad. After the wedding celebration Etzel and Dietrich organized a new campaign to Italy. Before the army leaves, Etzel's two sons, Scharpf and Ort, came onto the scene.

In those days, according to what we read in the book, mighty Etzel[2] had two splendid sons. They were both very dear to him, the delight of his eyes. Now we see the noble young princes, greatly troubled at heart (as we know from the story), as they came before good Lady Helge.

She approached her sons cheerfully: "God's greeting to you both, dear sons! The flowers of my eyes, my highest joy, my very springtime; how my joy abounds whenever I see you!"

She tenderly kissed the boys on the mouth.

"Have mercy, dear mother," the mighty young princes said, then Scharpf continued: "Alas, if anyone here were so kind, we would gladly ask him. We would like to accompany the lord of Verona to Italy.[3] We would very much like to see the good city of Verona by which he is named. Mother, dear lady, please ask my Lord Etzel, as I trust you will, if he would grant us permission to go on this campaign with his blessing. Our friends and relatives are traveling there; he can have them protect us on the way. The good and brave warriors will have us in their care and will not allow us to come to harm. Please bring our request to our Lord Etzel!"

Lady Helge gave the boys a sorrowful look. Gently she answered the mighty princes: "You must reconsider your request, dear sons. You should give up going on this campaign. No good will come to you from it, take my word for it. Put it out of your thoughts and give up this campaign. You think like children. There is no peace in the Italian kingdoms. I will surely regret it if I let you go there," said the true-hearted woman. "Unfortunately I must greatly fear Ermrich's treachery.[4] Please heed my advice and stay at home. No matter how eagerly the good and brave men would guard you at all times on the campaign, if it came to combat you would be forgotten and killed," she said resolutely.

"You mustn't worry about that, dear mother. We'll be safe day and night with Lord Dietrich. He'll guard us well, you can be certain of that."

At this point Etzel came in and with him (as I have learned) the lord of Verona. As you know, Etzel found his two sons together.

When the good lady looked at Etzel, and spoke sorrowfully with darkened eyes, King Etzel asked her privately: "I truly wonder, lovely lady, who has done you harm? Your tears trouble me deeply, noble queen."

"No one has harmed me. Etzel, your two sons will not listen to sound advice. Now they want to ride with the army to Italy.

That is what they intend to ask you, mighty king. Please take them to the side and deny them. I truly fear for the time when I'd never again see them unharmed."

"That will never be my will, or my advice, either to the side or in view of everyone. It will never happen by my consent."

Turning to his sons, Etzel asked: "What do you two foolish boys want? May you and I avoid such a great misfortune!"

Then young Ort said sadly: "Mighty King Etzel, we will never stay behind. Therefore let us out from under this guard. So many good warriors are going there who also want to see Verona and Italy. If you allow us to go, we promise you here and now, that when we get to Verona, we won't ride any further, if that makes you happy."

"Say what you will about it, it will never happen. No matter how you explain it to me, I will certainly not allow you to go there. Should any harm come to you there, it would be the death of me, my two sons."

The lord of Verona said, "Please place the boys in my care, since they are so eager to go on the campaign. I will never leave them unguarded. I will appoint good noble warriors to take care of them everywhere we go. This much they have to agree to," said Verona's lord, "that they not ride any further. Wherever I leave them, they'll wait for me there."

Mighty Etzel said then to Lord Dietrich, "I truly fear Ermrich's plots; if he finds out about the boys, he'll concentrate on how to lead them away and kill them."

Lord Dietrich responded immediately: "That will never be a problem for us; I will keep then under such protection that they'll be safe and in peace there."

"For God's sake, please leave them out of the campaign, Lord Dietrich. Don't put me in a difficult position," mighty King Etzel said. "If I suffer the loss of the boys, I will simply waste away."

"Nothing can harm us," said Ort. "I trust my lord that he won't leave us behind anywhere. If you refuse us this campaign, noble king, you'll never see us happy again."

Tearfully but gently Lady Helge then said to the king of the Huns: "My dear Lord Etzel, your sons have driven you this far, you may as well let them ride, since they won't listen to reason. Just send along both relatives and vassals and commit the boys to Lord Dietrich, mighty king."

"Great pain is at hand; you shall see, lady. I sigh so deeply that my eyes water over. Heartache is at hand, whatever happens," said noble Etzel.

"You will be spared that," said Ort then. "Why should you worry, noble king of the Huns? We'll certainly take care not to come into any danger from the enemy."

Bravely Lady Helge said to the lord of Verona: "So help you God, you must address yourself to that which my Lord Etzel and I ask you. To that extent I entrust my sons to you. But I will always regret this campaign to Italy. On your honor, Lord of Verona," added Lady Helge, "I hold you responsible for my glorious young sons."

"Entrust them to me," said Lord Dietrich, "and you will soon see them safely back in Hunnish realms. Have it on my good faith, you will never regret their journey."

B. THE DEATH OF SCHARPF AND ORT

(strophes 340–54; 441–63)

After arriving at Verona with his army, Dietrich entrusted Etzel's sons and his younger brother Diether to the care of old Elsan[5] and ordered him not to let the boys out of the city under any condition.

As I was told later, blameless Helge's sons took each other by the hand and went off with Diether[6] to where they found their master Elsan in order to ask him. Kneeling before him, they asked him without delay for what would afterwards be their undoing. (I know that to be true.) They kissed him on the hands. Alas! Sadly, their end was drawing near.

"Lord Master Elsan," said Ort, "we have an urgent request of you. We are in your care here; please allow us to ride about outside the city. We'll come back shortly. We would like to see the splendid plan of the city of Verona. For if it were located in Hunnish lands, what more would we need? My father Etzel would always be honored by it."

In good faith Elsan answered: "My dear lords, you best give up this request, for nothing can come of it. My honor stands as guarantee to the courageous king of Italy. You are to wait inside here; in no way will I dare let you out, in no way will I let you ride. Forget about this without getting angry. I would sooner see myself dead than should misfortune befall you."

"We certainly do not wish to ride very far," said the boys. "Elsan, dear lord, we're not entirely blind. We'll watch out for ourselves so that no harm will come to us on the way."

"Please spare me much trouble," said Lord Elsan. "You know I fear the Lord of Verona to whom I have made a promise. I could easily regret this, and my loyalty would always be suspect."

Lord Diether said: "However unwilling you might be to go against Lord Dietrich's will, I can easily reconcile matters, so that it won't lead to difficulty for you.[7] Who, do you think, would tell the lord of Verona? Let us ride now. We don't intend to fight anyone; we're not carrying any defensive gear.[8] We'll be back here quickly, believe me," said the splendid warrior.

Mighty Elsan said, "Very well, your request is granted. But I won't stay behind after you. Since you so desire to ride, I can do nothing less than ride with you on the way."

You can imagine how glad the handsome boys became. The mighty young princes hurried off joyfully to where they found the war-horses. The noble princes, determined, mounted the horses at once and hurried off out of the city. Unfortunately all three came onto the wrong road, which they began to follow. That very road then led them to their misfortune across the wide heath to Ravenna[9] on the sand, as I know the tale. May that ride be cursed! A most grievous peril befell them before Lord Elsan got himself out of the city.

In vain, Elsan looked for the boys all around the city. He was concerned, for he thought that they had gone to find the army. He rushed after them, but could not catch up to them. The boys rode all the way to Ravenna, where, on a deserted stretch of land, they encountered Witege, a former vassal of Dietrich who had gone over to the service of Ermanrich. He refused to fight at first, but was forced into action by their words. Ort, then Scharpf, quickly died at the hands of the experienced warrior. Diether was left alone to face Witege.

Diether of Italy grew deeply sorrowful. Taking his sword in hand, the courageous warrior charged, striking at Witege, who for his part fought back with ferocity. Full of anger, they yielded to the demands of combat. The swords began to ring out so loudly in the excellent noble warriors' hands that you could hear the sound a mile or more away. Grimly they landed many blows on each other. Unfortunately mighty Diether would thereafter lie dead because of it. They both grew furious and trampled out a long path on the heath. Diether was so deeply affected by his lords' deaths that blood ran from the excellent young warrior's eyes. Never would such misfortune befall him, except for when he himself would die by Witege's hand on the heath. Their swords' blows rang out fiercely; they lost their will to live. Mighty King Diether landed Witege a savage blow, wishing as he did to avenge the excellent young princes. The mood of the good and noble men turned fierce. They ran at each other, having dismounted from their horses. Their blows echoed solidly; fire glowed from their eyes.

Now hear the extraordinary things that we read in the book. I know from the story, how Diether stayed alive so long, and I wish to inform you of it. Do not allow the story to make you sad! From his youngest years, as all those who were alive then, who had seen Diether, would explain to us, there had never been another equal to him in bravery.

Diether kept leaping back and forth, all the time measuring out blows to Witege despite the latter's efforts to defend himself. But very little was accomplished by them; he was all too inferior to Witege in strength. Here I'd like to inform you how the battle between the two of them lasted until it was time for evening to fall, as is its custom. No matter how young a boy Lord Diether was, he nonetheless caused Witege some pain. I know in fact from the story, and now you may learn more, that splendid Diether dealt Witege four serious wounds. That caused Witege severe pain, and the hardy warrior threw down his shield and took his sword in both hands. They then moved toward each other, wielding their sharp swords in anger. Fiercely Witege ran at Diether, and alas, handsome Prince Diether was little match for him then. Damn those swords! He hit him in just the spot he wanted. Now hear the story, as I've learned it, and along with it the grievous hardship. Faithless Witege struck mighty young King Diether with all his strength; the sword tore through his shoulder and down through his body, no doubt a massive injury. He sliced his liver and heart in two. Alas, the great shame for which Witege became known!

The king of Italy said then, as he was dying: "Alas, brother Dietrich, I know I will never see you again!"

The worthy young king's strength ebbed away completely. He then clutched at the ground with both hands and brought them back up to his mouth right away, as for the Sacrifice of our Lord.[10] With reverence and repentance he met his end there.

Faithful Diether lay down on the grass and raised up his hands: "Lord, by Your resurrection, I ask You to have mercy on my great need, and by Your holy death, have mercy on me, a most wretched man. Now I can do no more!"

And with that the excellent and noble king died.

In the face of this great suffering, faithless Witege started to weep with all his heart.

Then he kissed all of Diether's wounds. "Even if I should heal you of all your injuries, may God condemn me to death for this.[11] Alas, now I must surely leave all these lands in flight from Dietrich."

He could take no more of this heartache, and struck at his eyes with both hands: "Alas, how unhappy the story which Verona's lord will now hear concerning me."

He went to Schemming,[12] intending to ride away. But his entire strength began to desert him, and alas, he grew sorrowful more than anything else and had to lie down there on the heath.

C. DIETRICH AND WITEGE

(strophes 886–974)

The great battle between the armies of Dietrich and Ermanrich ended after eleven days with Ermanrich's defeat and subsequent flight. It was then that Dietrich saw Elsan, who was still looking for the boys, coming to him. Helmschart, one of his men, announced that the bodies of Scharpf, Ort, and Diether had been found and led Dietrich to them.

Then the man of Verona threw himself on his lords in considerable anguish, the severity of his heartache readily apparent.

He kissed them on their wounds: "Now I have truly experienced heartache!"

He took both his hands and struck himself in the eyes: "Alas, what great misfortune! May God have mercy that my mother ever bore me! He never created any man as wretched as I. Alas, alas, that I was ever born!"

The excellent and noble warrior tore his hair out by the roots and started to weep bitterly: "May the moment and the hour be cursed, and the day as well," said Lord Dietrich, "on which my birth occurred! I regret it utterly. Who will trust me now? When my Lady Helge is told, she will never cease to remind me of my promise to her. Alas, how sorry I am! It is worse than any pain."

He kissed both lords: "I've never known such misfortune in all my days."

Then Margrave Ruedeger[13] said to the king of Italy: "It's quite likely that you will always make lament; God has demanded a high price of you. I feel deeply sorry for you; you'll never again see the land of the Huns."[14]

"Woe is me, poor Dietrich, woe, woe! If I lose the Italian kingdoms like this,[15] what good will I ever be? My heartache is relentless. May God grant that my heart quickly burst!"

He began to beat on his wounded heart: "God, by the salvation brought by Your sufferings and by the blood that ran from You, allow me, I pray, simply to die and perish utterly in cruel death!"

He started to tear at his hands and feet: "May God strike me dead, since He has no intention of honoring me, and send me to my end!"

Then he bit at his arms and hands: "I ask you, Mother and Virgin, Queen of Heaven, consider my misfortune! May there be a call to arms[16] today and every day for the sake of my life and my honor!"

He bit one of his fingers: "May God quickly bring me to shame, may misfortune be poured over me! May I never be healed, may I be denied all joy! I pray you in earnest, most holy God, I, poor Dietrich, at whose expense the devil has had his fun! Misfortune clings to me; I will never again have a cure for it as long as I live. Wherever I turn, people everywhere, far and near, will say: 'Look, there's the man who betrayed his lord!' That is what every one of them will say, no matter how innocent I may be. Alas, poor Dietrich, where will you turn now? How shall I carry on? Would to God I had died many years ago!"

Lord Dietrich took hold of the young princes who would never reach maturity, turned them both over, and looked at the frightful wounds. Then he grew more sorrowful than at first.

Please note carefully what I am about to tell you: he looked at the deep wounds, at how wide they were, and said: "I see clearly now: in short, these wounds were made by Mimming's point.[17]

That is clear to me. I trust to God, he[18] will be disgraced for it yet! Wicked villain, would to God that I had you here with me! I desire nothing more than that I should most surely avenge my heartache," said Lord Dietrich. "Now may God not let me die, for I must still defeat you!"

That of which I inform you now is the truth. As I've been told, Verona's lord was so sorrowful that blood ran from both his eyes. I deceive you not concerning the heartache of which Lord Dietrich complained to praiseworthy Margrave Ruedeger, who answered: "Most noble lord of Verona, if I could help you, I most certainly would."

The lord of Verona went over to where he found his brother. Immediately a cry went up from the warrior. Who could refrain? He broke into uncontrolled weeping. "Now my loss is multiplied and my lament increased. Alas, brother, lord, that I do not lie slain beside you! I'll bitterly complain of that to God."

His eyes were as red as fire: "Lord God, consider my great need. Do not afflict me and do not let me die until I have found revenge! I don't know what more I can say about it. I've now lost the height of my joys. Alas, what virtues you possessed, excellent young knight! How God has separated me from you! I'll suffer it the rest of my life. My joy and my delight are laid to rest in you. You were my nearest kin. Alas, what a warrior you'd have grown to be, a comfort to me," said Verona's lord.

"You were like a spring day to your people and your family, an equal balance of kindness! Ah, what virtue you practiced! Now all that has passed away, and I am completely imprisoned in heartache. You were the keeper of virtues at all times, what's more, a flowering month of May. Alas, how that is laid down to rest now! No one will see either your virtue or your honor again."

He grabbed his hair with both hands and tore it out. I've never heard of grief so acted out in all my days.

In the meantime Witege was seen riding by, racing hard over the heath.

Margrave Ruedeger interrupted: 'What are you waiting for, Lord of Verona? Do you like to watch your enemy so much? If not, hurry to your horse, excellent warrior!"

The mighty man jumped up. The fine war like Valke was ready for him to ride. He saddled up in sorrow. His misfortune began to affect him and his anger grew fierce. Then he lowered the spurs into the horse's sides. When he rode onto the heath, he saw both a good thing and a bad thing. What good thing did he see there? That is something I know about, as surely as it happened. The good thing at that time was that he saw Witege riding in front of him. Then there was the bad thing that came against him, that he'd left his two lords and his brother lying dead.

That was very difficult, and he said: "It's too bad, my heart, that you are so strong."[19]

Then Etzel's men[20] delayed no longer; together with Ruedeger, they began to race hard. Dietrich's heart was so overcome that they could not keep up with him on the heath. They were forced to drop back, I tell you truly. Lord Dietrich kept spurring on the exceptionally noble horse. Verona's noble lord wanted very much to ride up with Witege. The noble horse leapt far forward. Its spirit was willing. Sparks flew from the horseshoes, as they often do.

Then the lord of Verona complained, as this tale is known to me, and called out as loudly as he could after Witege: "Hold up, valorous man! For the sake of all ladies, let me see your courage, if you please! If you're a hero in battle, then you'll heed my request. Since you are so brave in fierce fighting, why don't you have some courage and get off your horse until I catch up to you?"

"I had best not wait," Witege thought.

Lord Dietrich called out again and again over the edge of his shield:[21] "Hold up, excellent man," the warrior cried, "for the sake of all the girls, so that I don't take my leave of you like this, without a fight. And consider this, warrior, for the sake of your virtue," said Verona's brave lord, "so that you may be known as a man who is bold to attack and fight. If you are bold, you'll wait for me."

The more he called out, the further Lord Witege rode away from him. He was very much afraid of him, as I've been told, and dared not wait.

Then Lord Dietrich called out: "Alas, Lord Witege, why don't you act like a man and consider after all how you have acted courageously before, and wait for me on the heath. Part me from this heartache which I have suffered here at your hands. I must live on in misery. You've done all that to me. Now dismount, good man, and set me free from a sorrowful spirit. This much I urge you for the sake of knighthood. For the sake of your manly strength, agree to what I now ask you, Lord Witege. I beg you not to disregard it."

By these hard words Verona's noble lord wished to make him stop, though, unfortunately, it would not turn out that way. Lord Witege was too wise for him.

Witege said quietly to Rienold:[22] "Dear nephew, please hurry away. I truly fear for you. I myself have no reason to fear, if you can get away. I'll be safe, as I figure it."

Verona's noble lord, however, kept calling: "Brave and glorious man, if you wish to be an honorable man, then dismount for me. I know perfectly well that I'll never come away alive from a fight."

Witege did not want to wait. Verona's courageous lord was sorry for that, and cried: "Alas! Alas!"

Then the excellent lord of Verona said this: "Tell me now, Lord Witege, how the boys whom you killed on the heath defended themselves. I'd really like to hear that, if you'd tell me. What had the boys whose life you took on the heath done to you? What revenge did you seek against them? Unfortunately I can't catch you as I'd like, as would be my pleasure. Hold up, good man! You'll surely defeat me; my arms and hands are as good as dead. If you don't wait, may God bring disgrace on you! May Saints Gangolf and Zeno[23] stand by you now, even though there are two of you as it is," said the valorous man. "Turn around, sir, turn around! If you kill me, you'll always have honor from it. Verona and Milan will be given to you, along with everything I have, and if you take my life, then Rome will be at your disposal," said Lord Dietrich. "So turn around, famous man, for the sake of all worthy women!"

Verona's lord continued: "I know, that you will take my life on this heath. Please part me from a great heartache."

Right then Rienold said to Witege: "Since we serve for a reward from the ladies, outstanding warrior, what will it hurt us to wait? He can never fight both of us."

Mighty Witege said to Rienold: "Just gird your horse and get away in a hurry. Let us simply not delay any longer, or we'll lose both life and honor."

Fearlessly Lord Rienold answered: "I wouldn't take the kingdoms of Italy and all the gold in Greece if it meant I were found running away. I want to wait here now."

"No, no, my dear nephew, don't do it! And take some advice; you know that good will come to you if you do. Please follow me, excellent warrior, or we'll never see each other again."

"Let it be as God wills," said Rienold the warrior. "Witege, dear friend, I must first try my hand against the Lord of Verona."

"Then may you be in God's care!" said the famous Witege.

But Rienold, Witege's sister's son, continued: "Uncle, you must consider that running away isn't respectable for anyone; please wait, famous warrior. We'll surely kill the lord of Verona."

Witege answered angrily: "You speak just like a child. Excellent warrior, you don't know the Lord of Verona's ways. Just look how he roars like a house on fire."

"That's no surprise," said Rienold. "We would kill him, all by himself as he is back there, without any harm, if you'd dare to wait. Look then, I'll fight him by myself."

"I see clearly, my dear nephew, that you wish to make a stand here. I simply must despair of you; there's nothing else left to do. If you knew lord Dietrich as I do, famous warrior, you would run from him. Rienold, good man, may you be in God's care! Even if you were my father or mother, I'd have to go on without you. I take leave of you unwillingly."

He rode off and Rienold the warrior stayed on the heath and dismounted. But then, as Lord Dietrich of Verona rode up, the worthy noble warrior immediately girded his horse and sat on it courageously. As I've learned since, the gentle warrior had left his spear, helmet, and shield on the battlefield. Famous Rienold charged, striking Verona's lord with his spear, driving it through his mailed hood. Please believe me: they quickly went for their swords. Their horses brought them together, and they struck one another with their swords so that sparks flew up from the blades. Verona's dear lord, wielding his weapon grimly with strong hands, struck Rienold through the helmet down to his teeth, so that the famous warrior dropped down from his horse with grievous injury at the great stroke. Never had such misfortune befallen him. Then, seized by extreme anger, Dietrich let his spurs down into his horse's sides and turned to ride after Witege on the heath, as his heart told him he must.

The king of Italy began to call as loudly as he could: "Hold up, Witege, and hear what I have to say. I have indeed avenged my misfortune to a small extent. If you were sorry now, you'd avenge this misdeed. Rienold lies dead at my hands on the heath. If you're a brave and famous warrior, you'll avenge him," said the Lord of Verona.

The longer this went on, the more Witege hurried. He spurred on Schemming to great effort, as I have indeed learned. Verona's courageous lord took no pleasure at the sight of that.

"Here's how I'll make you happy if you save my life: I'll give you some nice soft hay,"[24] Witege said. It took long strides as it carried him from a bitter fight.

Then the Lord of Verona complained bitterly about these things: "Alas, what an unhappy turn of events! You do me wrong, Schemming, it makes me sad at heart.[25] You carry my enemy away from me. I'll always complain of it," said the good man. He spurred Valke on so hard that it snorted blood and started to hurry faster, coming so close to mighty Witege that there was scarcely a horse's stride between them. Now I'll inform you, if you wish to hear: they both began to race.

By now Witege had come quite close to the sea, and thought: "There is nothing else left. I can't fight you; oh Lord, what will happen to me? Nor can I get away like this. Lord God, please help me get away from here."

I tell you plainly here and now, that while Witege worried for his life there on the open heath, there came a mermaid.[26] She went up to Witege, as I understand it, took the mighty man and led him away with her, together with his horse. She saved the bold man, and brought him down to the bottom of the sea with her. Now that the lord of Verona could no longer see him in front of him, he was very greatly distressed. No greater misfortune had ever befallen him in all his days. He started to ride into the sea after him.

What good is more talk? The water came up to the excellent man's saddle (I haven't lied about it) and he had to turn back. His heart pained him severely at that. The mighty king of Italy got off his horse there on the beach and let it rest, while he waited longer to see if he might spy Witege riding anywhere.

When the famous Witege reached the bottom of the sea, Lady Wachild asked him with some interest: "Now tell me, sir, I'd really like to hear: why do you flee from the lord of Verona?"

"I have not done it without cause, my lady; unfortunately, I do not have the lord of Verona's favor. I've done him great offense by killing his brother Diether on the heath."

"You've behaved in a cowardly fashion.[27] You would have surely defeated Lord Dietrich. Why did you act so, excellent man? Now you'll have to be on your guard forever."

"Then I'll ride back and go against him. I will fight him," said the courageous man.

"It's too late for that now. I'd advise against the undertaking."

"What are the reasons I would have killed him so easily? I would surely have no success!"

She answered: "I will tell you: at the time the noble metalwork of his armor was all ablaze. By now it's become hard.[28] Trust me in this, sir, your undertaking would come to naught. He would utterly defeat you. He's full of rage now; thirty of you could never withstand him."[29]

Translated by James K. Walter

Notes

1. Dietrich is the son of Dietmar, one of three sons of Dietwart (Diether and Ermanrich are the others), of the family of the Amelungs. Upon Dietwart's death, Italy was divided among the three sons. Ermanrich, ruling in Rome, attempted to wrest control of all of Italy from his brothers' sons. He attacked his nephew Dietrich, who held northern Italy. Dietrich was victorious, but had to yield his territory in order to win release of captured comrades. Through Ruedeger's intervention he was received at the court of Etzel. He later returned home with supporting troops from Etzel (the scene of the older *Lay of Hildebrand?*), was victorious, and returned to Etzel's country to celebrate. In Italy the treachery of Witege, a former vassal, forced Dietrich to undertake a second campaign. Once again victorious, Dietrich has returned another time to Etzel's court.

2. Etzel, or Attila, the ruler of the Huns (died 453). Though the Dietrich of legend takes refuge in Attila's kingdom after his exile from Italy, the historical Attila and Theodorich were not contemporaries.

3. "Italy": *gein Rœmisch lant*. Throughout the poem the Italian kingdoms of the former Western Empire are referred to simply as "Rome" or "Roman lands."

4. Ermanrich (Ermrich) is Dietrich's treacherous uncle who usurps his nephew's kingdom. The historical Ermanarich was ruler of a Gothic kingdom in present-day southern Russia. He died ca. 375, probably in a war against invading Huns.

5. In the *Rose Garden* Elsan (Ilsan) is Hildebrand's brother, and a monk.

6. Diether is Dietrich's younger brother with whom he shares rule of the Italian kingdoms.

7. Diether is, after all, Dietrich's brother.

8. The young princes must at least, however, be bearing the swords which they use in combat against Witege.

9. Ravenna, Middle High German "Raben," the site of the battle between Dietrich and Ermanrich.

10. Diether performs actions imitative of receiving the consecrated bread in the Eucharistic Rite.

11. From their first encounter, Witege had no desire to fight Diether or Etzel's sons.

12. Schemming is Witege's horse.

13. Ruedeger, Dietrich's friend, is a vassal of Etzel. His city is Pöchlarn. Mention of his ties to Dietrich is made in the *Nibelungenlied*.

14. Dietrich's mourning is caused both by the disgrace which Dietrich will suffer because of the deaths of Scharpf and Ort, and sorrow over the death of his brother Diether.

15. Dietrich has regained control of Italy only by Etzel's help, and may not be able to maintain his rule without the Huns' continued support.

16. Literally: "may *wâfen* ("to arms!") be cried."

17. Mimming is Witege's sword.

18. "He": Witege.

19 If Dietrich's heart were not so strong, it would break and Dietrich would be spared his heartache.

20. The Hunnish troops who accompanied Dietrich to Italy.

21. Here Dietrich has a shield, though later, when he fights Rienold (ll. 951–954), we are told that he has not been carrying one.

22. Rienold is Witege's nephew who has apparently been riding with him.

23. Sts. Gangolf and Zeno have ties to Verona; Zeno was a fourth-century bishop of the city.

24. Witege speaks here to Schemming, his horse.

25. Witege was formerly one of Dietrich's closest vassals, and so Dietrich knows his horse.

26. Wachild is a mythical ancestor of Witege and so takes interest in his plight.

27. Wachild chides Witege because he should have fought Dietrich for three reasons, also stated either by Dietrich and or by Rienold during the chase: (1) for the sake of knighthood and its accompanying warrior ethic; (2) a knight's reputation among the noble women whom he at least theoretically serves must be maintained; and (3) Witege has a duty to avenge Rienold's death.

28. Is this to mean that Dietrich's armor was softened by the heat given off by his body in his rage?

29. The poem ends with Dietrich giving up his watch for Witege. He goes back to the Huns, is reconciled to Etzel and Helge by the efforts of his friend Ruedeger, and does not return to Italy.

BITEROLF AND DIETLEIB

Biterolf and Dietleib, found in the *Ambraser Heldenbuch* associated with Emperor Maximilian in the early sixteenth century, was probably composed, in rhyming couplets, around 1250 by a typically unnamed author. This work and the one that follows present us with a sort of "review" of knightly heros in the framework of the medieval tournament. The larger structure of *Biterolf and Dietleib* is that of the return home of Biterolf the father to Dietleib his son, but the section presented in this volume describes a tournament joined by the army of Dietrich and his Hunnish allies and that of their Burgundian adversaries during an arranged truce in hostilities between the two forces. A good deal of insight into the structure of a medieval tournament can be gained from this poem, but much more important for its audience was the large number of famous warriors, many known from the strophes of the *Nibelungenlied*, who are described as they engage in this "knightly sport." The author centers his attentions on descriptions of these heroes' valorous acts and on the sights and sounds of the tournament, which doubtless proved entertaining to his medieval listeners and readers. We are offered a look at the chaotic jumble of men and weapons on the tournament field, but the author is also able to put certain individual contests in sharper focus as well. Despite these scenes' attraction, a strong undercurrent of negative commentary runs through the work. While all of Dietrich's men, as well as their opponents, the champions of the Burgundian kings, are very restless and impatient for action and prove quite eager to take part in this tournament, most of them will be disappointed in the outcome of the contest; in a number of places the author is quick to point out the contradiction between seemingly heroic boldness and the less glamorous results of such keenness for battle. This element of disappointment which most of the participants in the tournament will suffer receives a good deal of emphasis in the figure of Wolfhart, whose impatience leads to the organization of the tournament. Though the passage in question is in a humorous vein, Wolfhart voices most clearly the humiliation which awaits the over-zealous warrior. As in the *Battle of Ravenna*, the overly eager, immoderately bellicose warrior must reckon with a seemingly deserved setback.

(lines 8170–8224; 8501–8774; 8818–9010; 9025–9082)

> 'mir ist lange her gesaget
> daz Gunther und die sîne,
> die recken von dem Rîne,
> alle zît phlegen ritterspil
> und wie si turnieren vil,
> bêdiu ûf vlust und ouch gewin:
> dâ mite gênt ir jâr hin.'

Etzel's vassal Dietleib had been attacked by the Burgundians, and refused any attempt at reconciliation. Etzel and Dietrich raised an army to avenge the attack and march on Worms, the seat of the Burgundian kings. After a long time had passed without a battle, some of their men began to lose patience.

Then Wolfhart[1] started to complain: How long would they sit there? Whom did they plan to defeat with gentleness and nice manners?

"It would be a strange thing," bold Wolfbrant[2] added, "if a prince vacated his lands because he should hear that someone threatened him, though nothing more than that happened to him."[3]

Wolfhart replied: "I've yet to see a campaign where knights are so bored. See, we pass our days like silly women. Must it stay this way, that we have absolutely nothing to do?"

Then Ermanrich's man, Duke Berchtung,[4] said: "Many old and young men are here who would gladly see knightly sport take place on a wide field like this."

Bold Dietleib asked: "What would make this campaign more to your liking, Wolfhart?"

The courageous man answered: "I've long been told of how Gunther[5] and his men, the knights from the Rhine, practice knightly sport all the time and of how often they hold tournaments, both for loss and for gain: that is how they pass their years.[6] If our Lord of Verona wanted to do this, we would be happy to see it. I'm concerned that I've never missed a campaign in Lombardy[7] and have still never experienced this thing called a tournament," Wolfhart said, "since it is said to bring honor to a knight."

Lord Witege[8] then asked if this seemed a good plan to them; the good men agreed that it would lift their spirits.

The warrior Lord Biterolf[9] said, "I have experience in these matters; they'll not refuse us a contest. They have a lot of good knights. If we send an emissary there, you'll see how quickly you'll be granted your wish for a tournament."

Ruedeger,[10] Dietrich's faithful friend, is chosen as emissary and goes to Worms to speak to Gunther.

Then the excellent king accepted Ruedeger's offer of a truce;[11] he also offered the visitor a truce, so solidly backed up with guarantees that he agreed to the prince's offer.

The margrave said to him: "Please let me hear how the tournament will be run with regard to the truce and loss of property.[12] Tell me how you are inclined," said Lord Ruedeger.

Excellent King Sigfrid[13] answered: "We can certainly hold it with a truce and with the condition that each man, whether old or young, give a thousand marks unweighed for ransom money, with which every man may ransom himself and his armor as well."[14]

Young Nantwin[15] spoke against that immediately: "What good is a man's battle gear unless he get some use from it? I say, let everything that is brought to the field be fair game,[16] for I've set my hopes very high on Witege's helmet and on that sword that he has.[17] Should it come into my possession, no one would ever get it back from me," said the excellent duke.

Etzel's man Ruedeger scoffed and said, "You may very well be courageous; that can, however, turn out to be trouble. I wouldn't want to represent him falsely: I stand on my honor, that even if Lombardy were his, he'd give it up before he'd yield his armor and that sword of his. I'll set you straight about it: we've come across a great number of tough tournament fighters, but never in my days have I seen any one as tough, who defends himself so fiercely. Young warrior, you must not be too quick to stretch out your hand for Witege's bridle.[19] Even if only in a dream, you'd likely lose it. I'll let anyone who has seen him in battle testify that I have spoken the truth."

Then Lord Sigfrid added, however: "He may well come upon certain men where he can put his Mimming to use."

"Where shall we set the price?" asked Ruedeger.

Mighty Sigfrid said: "Let it stand at a thousand marks each."

Then the dependable man replied: "Understand, king, that we are strangers and do not have the Nibelung gold.[20] I would have lost eighty thousand in debts in half a day, if I could have what you won. I have a better idea," Ruedeger went on. "Excellent King Etzel's treasury is too far away from me, though my lord would easily ransom me and every one of his men. Let us set the tournament at everything a man has, both horse and armor, not less than three hundred marks."[21]

Then they agreed to that among themselves.

"How will you do it?" Ruedeger asked. "Tell me, excellent king, may it proceed without kippers?"[22]

"Yes, on my true honor," powerful Gunther replied, "I'm in complete agreement with that. Should any knight be touched by a kipper's hand, be he a squire or a sergeant,[23] for whom the tournament is off limits, it will cost him[24] his hand."

Thus was the truce established. Then the noble knight Gernot,[25] to whom Ruedeger had offered his truce, went with Ruedeger to the place where they were setting the boundaries, short or wide as they thought best.[26] Splendid Gernot rode there with thirty of his men. When the tournament was set to begin, he rode back to town. Then a thousand men from Worms hurried onto the field of contest. Those about to practice knightly sport had their hopes quite high.

By then Ruedeger had also come back to his men. Quickly they learned the news from him, how a truce had been called for them and for those from the town as well. Before he had asked them to keep his promise and oath, four thousand or more[27] were ready in armor.

That grieved Ruedeger, and he said: "I will never again be the friend of anyone who breaks the truce I've arranged, if they hang me by a rope.[28] Forbid your troops to do that, Lord Dietrich," the excellent warrior said, "or I'll quickly declare myself unbound by it. I warn them in good time that they may not carry out just any act of warfare against them.[29] I stand by that as I ought."

Each prince had to hear from his men as they stood before him that they would not break the oath made by the most excellent emissary Ruedeger. The sergeants were very sorry to hear about the strict prohibition; no matter what success they might have had, they would have taken their chances there.[30]

A thousand knights had now gone to their horses. Everyone took notice of them because of their bright armor. I imagine tournaments had been fought at the Rhine for many days without reaching such heights. Very many of them were killed.

Then ten beautiful banners could be seen moving in front of the men, around each of which a hundred bold armed men were easily recognized.[31] The glistening of their helmets could be seen all the way to Worms. Shortly thereafter the gates were seen standing open. By that time Lady Brünhild[32] had come out onto the battlements with her ladies, six other queens with her, the loveliest ladies. They wanted to see the contest, just as the chaste young girls wished to see the worthy tournament. After they sat down, they could bear many horns blaring loudly, holunders[33] blowing in front of the brave men, and the sound of many drums, hand-drums beating so loudly that the palace shook. By that time the people of the court had come out with Ortwin[34] to where the visitors could see them.

In Brünhild's chamber you could hear the noise made by the visitors. The many heralds could be heard in front of the host,[35] as they led the visitors there towards the castle with plumed helmets, the finest of all men. Now here rode one of the town's citizens, so well armed that no one has ever come upon a knight better equipped. He was from Burgundy and was named Ortwin. From his family he had also inherited the right to be called "of Metz." Then Dietrich's man Wolfhart turned his gaze upon him. He thought that he was Gunther or Gernot, because he wore a helmet shining red with gold. He pointed this out to his comrades there so that they turned to see what he was looking at. At the same time, Ortwin also went to meet him, since mighty Wolfhart's helmet decorations gave off a brilliant sheen.

The fine young man said: "That must be Lord Dietrich. You men, help, I want to take the first jousts here from him."

The young man had to be pleased with a tilt at a long gallop.[36] Wolfhart aimed his lance at Ortwin. Both of them showed their valorous spirits. But then Dietrich's man's fine horse stumbled beneath him, and Ortwin struck down at him from his saddle with some force. Wolfhart's shaft shattered to pieces in his hands. The warrior jumped up, and was quickly back in the saddle, though Ortwin had turned his fine horse around. Then Wolfhart, ashamed that he'd been knocked down, drew a very good sword. Ortwin's valor was put to the test against him.

The swords and shields of both men began to ring out. Then help arrived for Wolfhart from the land of Amelungs.[37] Everyone who looked on agreed that there was good riding there: shields were chopped up, all the while a good many men-in-arms had rings broken off their chain mail. From out of his troop came charging Stuotfuchs of Apulia:[38] Ramung[39] took aim at him. You could see old men and young men striking and stabbing there. Shafts broke with a loud noise everywhere in those hosts. Even if there had been no other kind of noise except that of the spearshafts, you'd still have been able to hear how the palace echoed from the melee. The lovely ladies, who had wanted to see it, were also able to take it in and hear the great noise. Ramung jumped back up. (He'd been knocked down to the grass by Stuotfuchs, who wished to lead him away captive.) Then came Iring, the fierce man from Lorraine.[40] You could see the rings on many hauberks burst from the blows the worthy man gave before he rescued Ramung. The swords rang out loudly as he attempted to escort him away. He was given protective cover within a troop and so Stuotfuchs had to let Ramung ride away.

Everywhere there was much swordplay to be seen. Still bold Ortwin would have never escaped from Wolfhart, who wanted to lead him away to his own troop, for then a troop of proud Harlungs,[41] a hundred young knights, had come to Wolfhart's aid. Who could begin to comprehend all the weapons in their hands there? Then you could see a hundred of Walther's[42] men turn to face them. By that time the knightly sport had begun to spread out to the ends of the boundaries . . .[43]

Indeed I wish to tell you, that just wherever they'd come from, twenty-banners[44] had now massed together. Helmet decorations had been completely torn off by the swords, what's more, rings had been sheared from some of their sides. You could see many shield edges chopped up there or with holes in them. From in front of the palace, before the castle at Worms, where the ladies had gone up to get a look, you could tell which of the men were fighting best. The host himself[45] sat at the fortifications (they were elevated on all sides) with a large number of other men and watched the knightly sport there. There was sword-play and fighting there—rarely did anyone ride for profit.[46]

Then famous Stuotfuchs, the Apulian, saw the chopping and sword playing there and heard the men's blades ring out loudly in their hands. (You could often make out a blood-red glow that looked like fire there.) Stuotfuchs and his comrades, intent on leading most powerful Wolfhart away from his men captive, drove the Veronans back, the sight of which did not please

Wolfhart. The splendid warrior[47] fought with such blows that his helmet and the edge of his shield gave off a reflection like fire. Wolfhart's horse could not stand up because of the force exerted by that proud man in both his arms. He struck so fiercely that both man and horse fell down to the ground. However eager the men of Verona were to help Wolfhart get away by then the mighty man of Palermo[48] had attacked him so that he was never able to find a way out from under the bitter blows. In sight of everyone, mighty Stuotfuchs pulled him onto his horse. No matter what blows anyone struck or how anyone tried, or how Wolfhart struggled, he nonetheless had to go with him. Then many bold men cried: "To arms! What a fiend!"

Hildebrand,[49] who had also ridden there to get a look, saw it quite clearly. He never regretted a tournament as much as this one, because he couldn't help him[50] then and there, and spoke of it to Dietrich. Then all together the splendid and famous men wished that things had gone on without a truce.[51] That however could not be. Palermo's lord showed off his strength, which the host was glad to see.[52] He then brought Wolfhart to him; many men were surprised that such a thing had happened.

The men of Pöchlarn[53] had also seen this. Because of it, Ruedeger's men grew so determined that they captured eight of the men from Denmark.[54] Then a good number of the men from the Sand[55] were taken captive. They had planned to pursue a reward; quite a few had no success there. Curses on you, Fate, that it ever proved to be so!

By now bold Wolfhart had been led all the way to fortifications, where the squires tried to disarm him in an unseemly fashion. He struck two of them down dead with his fist.

King Gunther responded: "What else can I say, except that they received what they justly deserved?"[56]

Then his helmet was unfastened, and the king commanded him to sit down. When they removed his sword, the Burgundians asked him to tell them what his name was.

Lying about it, the warrior answered: "I'm from Hunnish lands, and my Christian name is Gotele." He was ashamed that anyone should see him captured there.

The warrior Gernot said: "You're known to us by a different name; yes, your name is Wolfhart."

It was no use; he couldn't deny it, so bold Wolfhart declared: "I'm sorry I ever came along on the campaign to this country; no one has ever captured me before today, and so I'll always be sorry that I ever started fighting tournaments."[57]

The king and his men broke into laughter at what he said. How many wolfish[58] glances he cast when they carried the weapons near him! How often he thought of how he could get away from there!

I tell you what I've learned: many men were captured. The Huns for their part took hostage ten warriors who were from the Sand. The visitors shut them in securely. Regardless of how rarely Ruedeger and his men had taken part in tournaments there at the Rhine, they captured fifteen knights. This came from the skills they'd seen before in Arabia.[59] Walther's warriors for their part pulled seven of Ruedeger's men through the boundary. Berchtung's men then took twenty of Nantwin's men prisoner. They'd been in too much a hurry for gain. Very often it's not so close at hand, no matter what you think you have. The Saxons and Thuringians[60] knew the game well, and so captured many of the visitors and led them away.

But no matter what anyone accomplished there, Hildebrand was sorry for it. He rode to his lord, and spoke forcefully to Prince Dietrich: "Alas, dear lord. It appears we've been done great harm. The fighting has been going on since morning and none among us has seen my nephew Wolfhart. Gunther and his men will never let him go willingly."

"What of it?" Lord Dietrich responded. "They act just as I would. Had I captured a man by whom I might be harmed, I'd be loath to let him go."

Verona's lord added: "As you yourself have undoubtedly seen, this has befallen many here and will befall more until it's over."[61]

Hildebrand said: "It's my advice, however, that we still free the man; we shouldn't leave my sister's son Wolfhart behind. Of all those who are here with you, none serves you better. It would be old Hildebrand's advice that the tournament be fought without a truce.[62] So a number of men receive blows to the arms and legs tonight—no matter that old age prevents me from fighting in a tournament, I must get in there to them. I'll help my nephew get away by offering guarantees or with knightly skill.[63] If his prowess helps us tomorrow, we'll always be honored all the more."

Then he argued vehemently for his plan that they reject the truce arranged for the combatants.

Dietrich then accepted Hildebrand's advice.

Lord Dietrich then asked noble Ruedeger if that excellent man could be of assistance to them in any way, so the truces might be revoked.

He answered: "I'm ready to do whatever you command, Lord Dietrich."

They asked praiseworthy Dietleib if they could count on his support in this.[64]

"Yes," the renowned man said, "as long as I can be the cause of some harm, I don't wish to depart from here."

The margrave then rode off. He and those with him saw how the wide field was strewn with the wounded, which Hagen was glad to see.[65] The best of all men[66] rode to the host's castle where he found the king. Gunther the warrior observed him. He brought them a message there by which many would come to grief. As the king caught sight of him, he asked him to inform him as to what his business there was. Ruedeger started to laugh at brave Wolfhart where he sat with the others. He made note of it; how quickly he began to motion to King Etzel's man that he should hold back anything he might wish to say to him! [67] Ruedeger kept silent about it.

Then the excellent margrave spoke: "Lord King, the visitors in your land have sent me here. They think they have too much peace and quiet, so would like to be in the contest as well, if it can be agreed upon.[68] I've been sent here to see if you would revoke the truce for which I gave you my hand in assurance."

The famous man responded: "If that is my guests' counsel, then I'll allow it without a truce."

They asked Sigfrid and also Walther of Spain, Hildegunde's husband, and the knight[69] said immediately: "Why do you only ask me?"

Then they all said together: "Since they have no desire for a truce, we too will allow it to continue as they wish."[70]

Translated by James K. Walter

Notes

1. Wolfhart is one of Dietrich's men, and the nephew of Hildebrand; here, just as in the *Rose Garden*, he is eager for a fight. In the *Nibelungenlied,* Wolfhart and Giselher die at each other's hand.

2. Wolfbrand is another of Dietrich's men.

3. A mocking description of Dietrich's campaign against Worms.

4. Berchtung is one of Ermanrich's men. Here Ermanrich is an ally of his nephew Dietrich, and not the bitter enemy of the *Battle of Ravenna*. Witege, too, is in Dietrich's camp, and so we can place the events of this work before the treacherous acts of Ermanrich and Witege which led to the battle against Dietrich at Ravenna.

5. As in the *Nibelungenlied*, Gunther is the King of the Burgundians.

6. France and the area around the Rhine were renowned for their practice of the tournament, which later spread to areas farther east. See W. H. Jackson, "Das Turnier in der deutschen Dichtung des Mittelalters" in *Das ritterliche Turnier in Mittelalter*, No. 80, 1985, pp. 266ff.

7. Wolfhart, like Dietrich, is a native of Northern Italy, an area to which tournaments had apparently not yet spread.

8. Witege is still counted among Dietrich's men, though he will later (*Battle of Ravenna*) be known as "faithless" because of his defection to Ermanrich. See note 4 above.

9. Biterolf is the king of Toledo in Spain, Dietleib's father and also a vassal of Etzel.

10. For Margrave Ruedeger as Dietrich's faithful friend, see the *Battle of Ravenna*, note 13.

11. Truce: Middle High German "fride." First the hostilities between the Burgundians and Etzel and Dietrich must be called off, and then the tournament can proceed with constraints placed on the use of force.

12. Victors in the tournament are rewarded either in that they seize the property (weapons, armor, horse, etc.) of a captured opponent, or receive money from that opponent in return for his release from capture.

13. As in the *Nibelungenlied*, Sigfrid, king of the Netherlands, is present at the court of the Burgundian kings into whose family he has married.

14. A captured knight must pay a thousand marks in order to buy his release from captivity or to reclaim his lost possessions.

15. Nantwin is a Burgundian warrior; not the Näntwin of the *Nibelungenlied*, who is an inlaw of Etzel.

16. Nantwin does not wish the ransom money to be so high that it can be used to reclaim lost possessions.

17. "the sword that he has": the famous Mimming.

18. "him": Witege.

19. "for Witege's bridle": one means of pulling an opponent from the field of contest into captivity.

20. A reference to the rich hoard brought to the Burgundians by Sigfrid in the *Nibelungenlied*. See the Third Adventure.

21. Since Etzel's (and Dietrich's) men are so far away from home and do not have much money with them, Ruedeger argues for the ransom money to be set at the value of the equipment a knight brings with

him, provided it is not less than three hundred marks. It will be necessary to give up one's armor or weapons in order to be set free from capture.

22. **"kippers"**: Middle High German "kipper"<"kippen," "to beat, kick": These are fighters of non-knightly status (thus not on horseback) who would single out and overpower a mounted and better armed knight by force of their numbers. They will not be permitted to participate in this tournament.

23. **"Squire"** (Middle High German "kneht") and "sergeant" ("sarjant"): two ranks of kippers.

24. **"him"**: the kipper.

25. Gernot is Gunther's brother, also a king of the Burgundians.

26. To capture an opponent, a knight had to carry him over the boundary line.

27. Since only one thousand of the knights of Worms have prepared for the tournament, that must be the agreed upon number of participants in the contest. That four thousand of Dietrich's and Etzel's men are gearing up for the tournament causes Ruedeger concern that the arrangements to which he swore agreement will be violated.

28. Zink's text reads "an der wîde" ("on the willow"), but the line ought to rhyme with "fride." "Wit" (dat. sg. "wide") is a cord or rope and makes good sense here. (Compare Middle High German "bî der wide": "by hanging.") Such could be Ruedeger's fate if his side breaks the truce for which he has made guarantees.

29. **"against them"**: against the Burgundians. If Dietrich's men will not abide by the terms of the truce with the Burgundians, then Ruedeger will remove himself as a party to the agreement in order to save his honor or even his life.

30. The sergeants (kippers) are prohibited from participating in the contest. Their possible participation has swelled the number of Dietrich's men to over four thousand, well past the limit of one thousand.

31. The thousand men are organized into ten groups of a hundred knights each.

32. Brünhild is the wife of Gunther, Queen of the Burgundians.

33. A type of wind instrument.

34. Ortwin of Metz is introduced below. In the *Nibelungenlied* he is Hagen's nephew and cup bearer to the Burgundian kings.

35. The heralds ("garzûne")announce the coming of the troop as a whole, and probably each individual warrior as well. Cf. *Nibelungenlied*, 223, 1, where "garzûne" announce the Burgundian victory over the Saxons.

36. Middle High German "puneiz": the initial activity of tournament combat in which two knights on horseback ride at one another, each trying to unseat his opponent with a blow from the lance.

37. The Amelungs are Dietrich's clan.

38. Stuotfuchs is one of Gunther's men. He is from Apulia ("Püllelant") in southern Italy.

39. Ramung is one of Etzel's men, in the *Nibelungenlied* he is the Duke of Wallachia.

40. Iring is, in the *Nibelungenlied*, a warrior in Etzel's retinue who is from Denmark and not from Lorraine.

41. The Harlungs are nephews of Ermanrich; in the *Book of Verona* Ermanrich has them put to death.

42. Walther of Spain is the hero of the Latin *Waltharius*. He fights on the side of Gunther.

43. Wolfhart, now with the aid of the one hundred young Harlungs, attempts to capture Ortwin, who is helped by Walther's men. There are now so many knights involved in the tournament that the fighting has filled the playing field.

44. Ten banners from each of the two armies; all two thousand knights have been drawn into the fray.

45. The "host" is Gunther.

46. Many of the participants have been captured or have lost weapons and armor.

47. **"the splendid warrior"**: Stuotfuchs.

48. **"man of Palermo"**: Stuotfuchs.

49. Hildebrand, Dietrich's master and confidant, has been watching the tournament because he is too old to take part.

50. **"him"**: his nephew Wolfhart.

51. Dietrich's camp wishes the tournament's rules to be withdrawn, so that they may use any means necessary to rescue Wolfhart.

52. Gunther, the host, is glad to see that Stuotfuchs has captured Wolfhart.

53. Pöchlarn is the city of Margrave Ruedeger.

54. The Danes fight on Gunther's side.

55. The Sand is an area in the vicinity of Nuremberg; these are supporters of the Burgundian kings.

56. Probably some of the kippers try to strip Wolfhart of his armor. Since kippers have been previously banned from the tournament, Gunther does not defend the actions of those killed.

57. In the section of *Biterolf and Dietleib* translated here, the major characters appear to be Ruedeger, whose trustworthiness as negotiator and as vassal is upheld; Hildebrand, whose loyalty to his nephew Wolfhart is portrayed; and Wolfhart himself, who is depicted as the most eager of Dietrich's men for combat of some type. It is ironic, and the author probably means that there is a lesson to be learned here, that it is the eager Wolfhart who is captured and now, of all the characters, most clearly states his regret at having taken part in this tournament. This punishment for such over-eagerness is hinted at in other places,

compare lines 8902–8903, "They had planned to pursue a reward; quite a few had no success there," and at line 8963–8965, where the author comments that Nantwin's men have been "in too much hurry for gain. Very often it's not so close at hand."

58. Middle High German "wülvisch": a play on the name Wolfhart.

59. Arabia: "Arabî," which probably means Arab (Moorish) Spain here.

60. The Saxons and Thuringians are allied with the Burgundians here.

61. Dietrich's lack of concern over Wolfhart's capture may reflect that fact that he was initially unwilling to undertake any hostilities, the attitude that led to his men's impatience. Dietrich may well believe that Wolfhart has suffered the fate that he deserves.

62. Hildebrand wishes to allow the tournament to become a battle with no limits placed on the use of force.

63. Hildebrand will win Wolfhart's release either by guaranteeing a ransom payment or by fighting.

64. Since this campaign was undertaken to avenge the attack on Dietleib, it is only right that his support be solicited. It is no surprise that Dietleib is eager to do the Burgundians harm.

65. Hagen, a vassal of the Burgundians kings, is not one of the men riding with Ruedeger, and so mention of him at this point is unexpected. The author draws attention to him as a bloodthirsty man who enjoys seeing so many wounded men, almost a caricature of the Hagen of the *Nibelungenlied*.

66. "the best of all men": Ruedeger.

67. Wolfhart makes note of Ruedeger's laughter and motions (probably in a threatening manner) to Ruedeger, who decides to be quiet.

68. Revocation of the truce would allow any number of warriors to participate.

69. "knight": Walther.

70. The battle which ensues ends indecisively, and Biterolf and Dietleib return to Etzel's court, and are given the Steiermark, where they settle. The poem, in which Dietleib plays a much larger role than in this section, is usually thought to be of Styrian origin and so to celebrate Dietleib, an original ruler of that region of Austria.

THE ROSE GARDEN

The *Rose Garden* offers us, also within the framework of the medieval tournament, a line-up of the heroes of Germanic epic poetry. This evidently popular work, found as it is in such a large number of manuscripts from the fourteenth to the early sixteenth century, is extant in several widely divergent versions. Version A presented here probably stems from about 1300, and was composed in the "Hildebrand melody" used in the *Younger Lay of Hildebrand*. A theme of the other Dietrich-works can also be traced out here: defeat and disgrace come to the boasting, seemingly invincible warrior Sigfrid, and to his haughty fiancee Princess Kriemhild. Potentially of greater interest to the modern reader of the *Rose Garden* is the conflict faced by Dietrich, who seeks to avoid combat against his opponent, Sigfrid, whom he knows to be more than a match for him, and thus exercise some of the restraint which the overly confident Sigfrid lacks. Any serious consideration, however, of how a knight in such a circumstance might refuse combat while retaining his good reputation among other knights and with the ladies of the court, is soon cast aside as the poet takes up depiction of the desperate and somewhat comic attempts by Hildebrand and Wolfhart to persuade Dietrich to fight Sigfrid with calls to knighthood which ring hollow and seem exaggerated, and then describes the humorous "fight" between Dietrich and Hildebrand. That once Dietrich is won over by their taunting, Hildebrand and Wolfhart must employ a trick to help their lord overcome his disadvantage against Sigfrid as well as the humorous depiction of Sigfrid's defeat and humiliation show that the author's interests lie far afield from Dietrich's dilemma; the easy humor and sentimentality found throughout the *Battle of Ravenna, Biterolf and Dietlieb* and the younger *Lay of Hildebrand*, thus come to the forefront in the *Rose Garden* as well.

The Rose Garden • 333

Sîvrit von Niderlande   reit ûf den grüenen plân:
'wâ ist nu der mîne,   der mich sol bestân?
vürhtet er sich sô sêre   oder trûwet er niht genesen?
jâ solten wir von rehte   die êrsten sîn gewesen.
Man seit uns, er wære küene,   der vürste hochgeborn:
daz er so zage wære,   daz hête ich wol versworn.
warzuo sûmet er sich sô lange?   er hât niht recken sin.
swie ich ez kan gevüegen,   er kumet es niemer hin.'

THE BATTLE BETWEEN DIETRICH AND SIGFRID

(lines 322–370)

Kriemhild, Princess of Burgundy, has a wonderful Rose Garden in Worms, which is guarded by twelve champions. She challenges Dietrich of Verona and eleven of his men to combat against Sigfrid (to whom she is engaged to be married) and eleven Burgundian champions.1 Dietrich's men win ten of the first eleven combats (one ends in a draw), and now it is Dietrich's turn to go against Sigfrid.

Sigfrid of the Netherlands rode onto the green field: "And where is the opponent who is supposed to come against me? Is he so afraid or does he think he'll not come away alive? By rights we should have been the first ones. We are told how brave the high-born prince is; I would have sworn it impossible that he be so cowardly. Why does he delay so long? He does not have a fighter's spirit. However I can help it, he will never get away."

Then Master Hildebrand said: "Do you hear that, Lord? The man with skin like horn[2] scorns and despises you utterly. Noblest prince of Verona, think of beautiful women and risk your life fighting Sigfrid. The arrogant man scorns you in earnest and you have never caused him injury in your life. Let him be paid back for speaking ill of you in his pride, most good and noble prince."

Then Verona's lord said: "If you served me loyally, you would not advise me to fight Sigfrid here. You only know to advise me to go to battle, morning and evening; you and Wolfhart[3] do that all day long. If your advice leads to my death, you'll be of no account in the sight of princes. You know my brother[4] won't let you at any inheritance from me. If I'm killed here in this garden, you'll mourn me bitterly after my death."

Then old Hildebrand said: "You malign us in this matter.[5] We always counsel you to the worthiest deeds, by which your honor may increase and spread about."

"If I should go against Sigfrid, it would cost me my life," replied the Lord of Verona. "Listen, wise man and warrior, on a rock once he killed a fierce dragon that no kings could defeat. In his lifetime he has killed many knights. There are three other things about him which I shall tell you: he carries a very good sword which he found on the rock; it proves hard helmets to be false and is called Balmung. The second concerns a shirt of chain mail: you must know that it was made by worthy Eckerich, master craftsman of all mail shirts. He raised him from childhood in the smithy; that is why the hero has not been disappointed by the chain mail. He[6] constructed it well with hard work according to the best craftsmanship. He knew well that he would come to have great strength.[7] Much gold and many gems are found on it. No sword was ever good enough to prevail against it. I shall name the third thing for you: he has skin like horn and can stand up to any warrior without worry. I would be a foolish man to fight him. Do not advise me to do it, if you wish to be my friend."

"Alas, my misfortune!" said Master Hildebrand, "Must you and all knights be forever shamed? I must make complaint to God that I didn't know this when we were back home.[8] Must all knights now have occasion to make sport of you?"

Lord Dietrich of Verona answered somewhat angrily: "So you wish to see me fight Sigfrid? If he hadn't skin like horn, I would have gone up against him from the first, even if he were the basest of all knights."

Old Hildebrand responded quite angrily himself: "No one is in the garden but Sigfrid of the Netherlands. Every one of our men has defeated every one of his.[9] He waits for us in the garden, whenever you wish to go against him."

"You wish to see me lose life by going against the horn-skinned man in the garden. No matter how you advise me to do it, it means nothing to me. I'll not go against Sigfrid of the Netherlands."

He said: "Dear lord, please come with me, to see if I can find a solution agreeable to both sides, as to how we may retain our honor before Queen Kriemhild if neither one of you on either side fights."[10]

He led him away from his retainers into a hollow, and said, "Lord of Verona, are you injured? So tell me, dear lord, why do you act as though you are by not going against your opponent in the garden?"

"You have scolded me much too long," said Lord Dietrich. "I would have gone against him from the first, if he were my equal.

If he were of flesh and bone, I would have gladly gone against him, even if he'd put on four shirts of mail, one atop the other."

"Indeed," Master Hildebrand agreed, "you should be given this much credit: you'll dare risk your life against fierce dragons. There in a forest you were once full of courage.[11] It is in front of ladies where you ought to pursue a reward that you won't fight. If you don't go against him soon, I'll give you an injury."

"How will you go about that?"

"Let me show you."

Old Lord Hildebrand had lifted up his fist. Then the old man punched the prince in the mouth, hitting him so hard that he fell to the ground. Lord Dietrich was enraged, and Hildebrand paid for it. He[12] took his sword in hand by the pommel, and struck viciously at his vassal.

He said: "Because of your taunting, you will be the one who is injured! You'll never punch me in the mouth again!"

He started to give him blows with the flat of his sword, from which Hildebrand very nearly lost his life.

Wolfhart caught sight of this and called out to his lord: "What are you doing, lord of Verona? Are you beating your vassal? You don't have the courage to compete for a reward in front of the ladies. You're a brave man only where no one can see it.[13] Whoever takes you for a knight is mistaken and truly tells a lie. You will fight against your own men, who are bound in duty toward you, but you won't go against Sigfrid of the Netherlands."

Then the lord of Verona said: "Enough talk! Never in my life have I acted so cowardly. Just bring me Valke, my good horse. I'll go up against him, even if he's made of nothing but steel."

Then the furious Wolfhart said: "I like what you say. You speak as a man should speak."

He led his horse to him there on the green field. Then Verona's praiseworthy lord leapt into the saddle and rode at once into the garden. Toward him, very boldly, came Sigfrid of the Netherlands on a good horse, which, as we hear tell of it, had carried him to high honors in bitter fighting.

"Where have you been so long?" the horn-skinned man asked.

"Believe me, I still come too early for you. Now strap on your helmet, you will surely regret it.[14] May you be confounded on account of your arrogance."

Bold Sigfrid answered, "Most noble lord of Verona, I've wanted to hear this more than anything all year."

Both strong men pulled down their viziers; they charged at each other fiercely, driving their horses at one another. These galloped as though they were flying. Their spears shattered, filling the air with splinters. When they dismounted, a very great battle ensued in the rose garden.[15] They lunged at each other there on the field, drawing from their sides two shiny pale blades. crouching behind their shields they began to fight so hard that sweat poured out through their chain mail. The two bold men battled mightily. You could see the rings from their shirts of mail flying about on the field.[16]

No matter where they leapt the grass would be bloodstained there. They struck one another with great fearful blows, so that it ceased to be entertaining for the two men's retinues. Because of the blows of their swords and the clanging of their helmets, no one could hear anywhere in the garden.

Sigfrid of the Netherlands was a mighty man. Angrily he charged Lord Dietrich, striking him a wound in his steel helmet, so that blood spurted from him.

"How does my lord fight?" Hildebrand asked quietly.

"Unfortunately he's fighting poorly," Wolfhart said back. "He has a deep wound in his steel helmet and is covered all over with his own blood."

"He's still not angry enough," is what Lord Hildebrand said. "Say, bold warrior, call out into the garden and tell him that I am dead and they want to bury me. Then the lord will start to mourn very much."

Wolfhart called out into the garden, so that they could hear through their helmets: "Woe is me my misfortune; how great and mighty it is! Hildebrand is dead; we have to bury him! If I lose my lord, how I will mourn over the misfortune!"

"If Hildebrand is dead," Lord Dietrich said, "then truly his equal will never be found. Now be on guard, bold Sigfrid, you have need of it! I'm ashamed of how I have fought up till now. Because of you I have lost a man whom I could not surpass as long as I live. Now defend yourself with vigor, you are in much need of it. No one will pull us apart unless one of us is dead."

Bold Sigfrid responded: "You know how to make threats. No matter how you fight me, it will be a game for me. The one who suffers for it on his head is the one who will take the loss."[17]

Then they ran at each other grimly. Lord Dietrich of Verona became furious. You could see a flame coming out of his mouth as fire does from a stove.[18] Sigfrid grew so warm that his sweat poured through his chain mail. Fierce anger came over Lord Dietrich of Verona and he struck Sigfrid through the armor and horn-skin, so that his red blood poured out all over the grass. As bold as he had been, now Lord Sigfrid had to run away. Lord Dietrich chased him about with mighty blows until he fell down into the queen's lap. She threw an apron over the bold man, thus sparing Lord Sigfrid's body and life.

The queen said: "If you wish to be an honorable man, you will permit me to save this knight."

The lord of Verona answered: "Your request means nothing to me. Whatever you ask of me now, I will not do it. I'll bring hardship to all you knights and ladies. You'll all die at my hands as payment for Hildebrand's death!"

As we hear tell of it, Lord Dietrich would have killed everybody in the garden in his anger.

Old Hildebrand acted honorably and leapt into the garden and called out to his lord: "No, no, dear lord, forgo your great anger. You won the victory, and so I was born all over again."

As noble Lord Dietrich looked at Hildebrand, the praiseworthy prince's mood grew calm. Then Verona's lord said: "Most noble queen, give up all claims to victory, and I will gladly forgo my anger here and now."

And so the queen struck herself in the mouth with her fist,[19] and said: "You are an honorable man; no one your equal is to be found anywhere."

She placed a rose garland on the lord of Verona; an embrace and a kiss awaited him as well.[20]

Translated by James K. Walter

Notes

1. This emphasis on Kriemhild as an instigator of combat and bloodshed has parallels to her character in the second part of the *Nibelungenlied*.

2. Sigfrid (as Dietrich explains to Hildebrand later) has skin as hard as horn, which is supposed to make him invulnerable to weapons. In the Third Adventure of the *Nibelungenlied* we learn that Sigfrid's impenetrable skin is a result of his bath in the blood of the dragon he has slain.

3. Wolfhart, Hildebrand's nephew, is one of Dietrich's men. He is an important figure in *Biterolf and Dietlieb*, where is he also characterized by his keenness for fighting.

4. **"my brother"**: Diether, killed by Witege in the *Battle of Ravenna*.

5. A line is missing from the manuscript here.

6. Eckerich made the shirt of chain mail.

7. "He (Eckerich) knew well, that he (Sigfrid) would come to have great strength."

8. If Hildebrand had known that Dietrich would not fight Sigfrid, he would have advised against accepting Kriemhild's challenge. He urges Dietrich to fight for reasons similar to those used by Dietrich against Witege in the *Battle of Ravenna*: knighthood demands it, and one's reputation with noble women must be upheld.

9. Actually Dietrich's man Dietleib fought the Burgundian champion Walther of Spain to a draw.

10. Hildebrand will try to negotiate a settlement of the challenge by which Dietrich can avoid the fight, yet not lose face.

11. According to the Old Norse *Thidrekssaga,* Dietrich slew the giant Ecke in a forest.

12. **"He"**: Dietrich.

13. Both Wolfhart and Hildebrand have accused Dietrich of being courageous only when no one is there to see it. Just as no one else was present in the forest when Dietrich killed Ecke, so no one can see him beating Hildebrand. These taunts finally goad Dietrich into action against Sigfrid.

14. Some manuscripts include the lines "You and the queen [Kriemhild] know plenty of clever tricks. By my honor I will not endure them any longer."

15. Their combat follows the typical tournament procedure: first a mounted charge (tilt) with lances in an attempt to unseat one's opponent, then combat with swords on foot.

16. A line is missing from the manuscript here.

17. Sigfrid refers to the head wound which he has given Dietrich.

18. Dietrich is frequently connected with flame in this manner. In the *Heldenbuch* (appendix) it is told how the demon [*sic*] Mohammed was present at the conception of Dietrich and promised his mother that in times of anger, Dietrich would spit fire.

19. Kriemhild answers Dietrich's demand with this sign. She thereby acknowledges that Dietrich and his champions are victorious in the contest she has arranged.

20. The same prize has been awarded to the other victorious knights in Dietrich's retinue. In this version of the *Rose Garden*, Ilsan (Elsan in the *Battle of Ravenna*), a monk, and the brother of Hildebrand, comes on the scene and challenges fifty-two rose garlands and fifty-two kisses from Kriemhild. His beard is so scratchy, however, that her face bleeds from all the kisses she must give him. After this humiliation Kriemhild gives up her garden.